The
Canadian
Writer's
Workplace

The Canadian Writer's Workplace

Building Writing Skills

John Roberts
Sandra Scarry
John Scarry

Holt, Rinehart and Winston of Canada, Limited
Toronto

Acknowledgements

Pp. 3 and 16: from *Compact Dictionary of Canadian English,* copyright © 1976, Holt, Rinehart and Winston of Canada, Limited; reprinted with permission. **P. 7:** from "How the Law of Rasberry Jam Applies to Culture," by Mavor Moore; copyright © 1976, Mavor Moore; reprinted with permission. **Pp. 8, 9, 10, 11-12, 15, 16, 19, 282:** dictionary entries © 1981 by Houghton Mifflin Company; adapted and reprinted by permission from *The American Heritage Dictionary of the English Language.* **P. 110:** from *My Remarkable Uncle,* by Stephen Leacock; copyright © 1942, Dodd, Mead and Company. **P. 279:** from "Gender Apartheid," by Emil Sher; reprinted by permission of the author. **Pp. 326-330:** adaptation of the essay "Performing on the Piano," by Erica Lane; used with permission of the author. **Pp. 333-335:** "My Financial Career," from *The Leacock Roundabout,* by Stephen Leacock; copyright © 1946 by Dodd, Mead and Company. **Pp. 342-344:** "Klondike Baked Beans," by Pierre Berton; from *Pierre and Janet Berton's Canadian Food Guide;* copyright © 1966, McClelland and Stewart; reprinted with permission. **Pp. 350-351:** Peter Gzowski; from *The Morningside Papers;* copyright © 1985, McClelland and Stewart; reprinted with permission. **Pp. 357-358:** "There is No Excuse for Physical Abuse," by Emil Sher; from *The Globe and Mail,* September 27, 1988; copyright © 1988, Emil Sher; reprinted with permission.

Canadian Cataloguing in Publication Data

Roberts, John A., 1944 –
   The Canadian writer's workplace

Canadian ed.
ISBN 0-03-922761-8

1. English language—Rhetoric—Problems, exercises, etc. 2. English language—Grammar—1950–   —Problems, exercises, etc. I. Scarry, Sandra, 1946– II. Scarry, John. III. Title.

PE1413.R62 1990   808'.042   C89-090573-8

Publisher: David Dimmell
Acquisitions Editor: Heather McWhinney
Developmental Editor: Graeme Whitley
Publishing Services Manager: Karen Eakin
Copy Editor: Judith Turnbull
Cover Design: Michael Landgraff
Typesetting and Assembly: Lithocomp Phototype Limited
Printing and Binding: Webcom Limited

Printed in Canada

1 2 3 4 5   94 93 92 91 90

For Our Students

An incidental likeness exists between food and words; or, rather, cooks and essayists: it is possible but unnecessary to possess natural talent. Cooking or writing well can be learned by reading manuals and studying the work of experts. Almost anyone, with practice, can become proficient and may, indeed, achieve a literary feast.

Kathleen Darlington,
Concordia University*

* From "How to Write an Essay," submitted for the HBJ-Holt College Essay Contest, 1989.

Preface

The Canadian Writer's Workplace is a complete composition program. It is intended for students who need to build their writing skills in order to produce college-level work. The book gives the basic writing student the ability to write with control, a crucial skill that is needed not only in English courses but also in virtually every other course taken in college. *The Canadian Writer's Workplace* can help students get the most out of all their college courses.

The book contains a number of important features that are designed to help both teacher and student in the basic skills classroom.

Completeness

The book begins with a fresh look at *the word*, proceeds to a detailed study of *sentences*, helps students practise solid *paragraph development*, and then shows them how to develop the *complete college essay*. At each step along the way, numerous practice exercises and writing assignments confirm what is being learned.

At the end of Part I ("The Word"), a diagnostic test is provided for the material contained in the Appendices (pp. 387–428); this material includes work on parts of speech, spelling, capitalization, the apostrophe, and irregular verbs. The rationale for placement of the diagnostic test at this early point in the book is that each student should master this material before going on to Part II. All students should take the test so that the instructor will know what percentage of a class will need to do the work in the Appendices.

Flexibility

The format of *The Canadian Writer's Workplace* allows an instructor to work on different exercises with an entire class or allows individual students (or groups) to work with a tutor in a lab situation. The answers to most of the exercises and practices are included at the end of the book; remaining answers are to be found in the instructor's manual. As a result, students can do many of the exercises on their own, checking their answers as they work. The book is also flexible in that certain sections may be skipped if the material is not needed for a particular class—or a class might begin with a later section, the earlier chapters being used for review.

A major feature of the book is the fact that Part III, "Mastering the Paragraph," can be a useful point of departure for a writing class. Using this section as a starting point, an instructor can work backward to concentrate on the sentence if the needs of a class lie in that direction, or ahead to the essay work in Part IV if the students' abilities are strong enough.

Stimulating Content

The exercises in the book present material that deals with current events or subjects that are of contemporary interest. Not only are many of the exercises based on material from such fields as history and science, but the model paragraphs and essays in Parts III and IV are taken from a wide range of novels, essays, short stories, and books of nonfiction, many of them by world-famous writers. Also included as models and for analysis are selections of student writing taken from essays submitted to the HBJ-Holt College Essay Contest.

Self-Guidance

Parts I and II of *The Canadian Writer's Workplace* contain pre-tests to determine how much students know about using the dictionary and about specific areas of grammar. Part III provides step-by-step guidance in the careful construction of well-developed paragraphs. This is the foundation for Part IV, in which the student composes longer, more challenging pieces of college writing; Part IV concludes with a special emphasis on structuring an argument and producing essays under pressure in class. All of these writing activities are designed in such a way that the more advanced student can do them almost independently, while the student who needs more direction can work closely with the instructor on assignments of appropriate difficulty.

The Canadian Writer's Workplace is a flexible tool for the basic writing classroom, one that works *for* the instructor and *with* the student. It strengthens grammar skills and places special emphasis on strong paragraph writing, which is the basic building block of the complete essay. It also enables the student to understand and construct the complete college essay, often the goal of the English instructor at this level. The student who carefully uses this book, and works consistently with his or her instructor throughout the semester, should be able to look forward with confidence to success in college.

An instructor's manual is available for use with the book. It contains answers to at least one exercise from each group of exercises so that instructors may use these particular exercises for testing, if desired. In addition, the manual supplies answers for the pre-tests and post-tests in the book. The instructor's manual also contains the post-tests for Parts I and II, a diagnostic test for the Appendices, hints for teaching basic writing students (including the use of groups in the classroom), and specific suggestions for activities that work in the basic writing classroom.

The Canadian Writer's Workplace contains a number of unique features that will afford the college student in Canada an insight into various aspects of Canadian culture. In addition to works by internationally known authors, this book features short stories, essays, and novels by Canadian authors covering such topics as Canadian English, painting, geography, and history, among others. *The Canadian Writer's Workplace* is intended to be, then, more than a writing and composition book—it is a tool to explore Canadian culture as well.

Of particular interest are the selections from student essays in Chapters 19 and 26. The selections reproduced in these chapters are taken from essays submitted by students in Canadian colleges and universities for the HBJ-Holt College Essay Contest. Students using *The Canadian Writer's Workplace* are given an opportunity to analyze material written by their peers, and it is hoped that these selections will inspire students to submit essays of their own work to future HBJ-Holt essay contests.

J.R./S.S./J.S.

Publisher's Note to Instructors and Students

This textbook is a key component of your course. If you are the instructor of this course, you undoubtedly considered a number of texts carefully before choosing this as the one that will work best for your students and you. The authors and publishers of this book spent considerable time and money to ensure its high quality, and we appreciate your recognition of this effort and accomplishment.

If you are a student, we are confident that this text will help you to meet the objectives of your course. You will also find it helpful after the course is finished, as a valuable addition to your personal library. So hold on to it.

As well, please don't forget that photocopying copyright work means the authors lose royalties that are rightfully theirs. This loss will discourage them from writing another edition of this text or other books, because doing so will simply not be worth their time and effort. If this happens, we all lose — students, instructors, authors, and publishers.

And since we want to hear what you think about this book, please be sure to send us the stamped reply card at the end of the text. This will help us to continue publishing high-quality books for your courses.

Contents

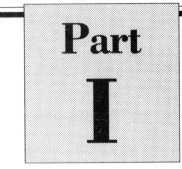

Part I

Building Your Word Power

How Much Do You Already Know?

The following test will check the skills you already have in working with words. Below are 50 test questions covering material from Part I.

Understanding Your Basic Sourcebook: The Dictionary

The dictionary provides you with a wealth of information. How much of this information do you already know?

Below is a dictionary entry. List at least five different kinds of information this dictionary entry gives you.

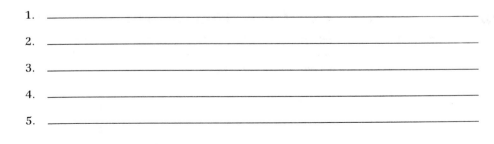

Ca·na·di·an·ism (kə nā′ dē ən iz′ əm) *n.* 1. a word, phrase, or expression peculiar to or originating in Canadian English or French: *The Mounties always get their man.* 2. a trait or custom characteristic of Canada or Canadians. 3. devotion to Canada, its laws, traditions, etc. 4. the condition of being Canadian.

1. _____

2. _____

3. _____

4. _____

5. _____

To make full use of the dictionary, you need to understand the significance of commonly used abbreviations, terms, or concepts.

6. What does the abbreviation *sing.* mean?   _____

7. What does the abbreviation *adv.* mean?   _____

8. Why would a word such as *rock* be given more than one entry in the dictionary?   _____

9. What do these abbreviations mean when they are found in a dictionary entry?
   Brit.   pl.   masc.   _____

10. Why are Canadian writers, such as Laurence and Haliburton, sometimes quoted in dictionary entries?   _____

In college writing and other formal writing, the appropriate level of language is an important part of the writing process. Read each of the following sentences, and choose the most appropriate word or phrase for college writing.

11. _____   The local officials could often be seen (nosing around, snooping around, searching) for evidence by the empty warehouse.

12. _____   The entire day, filled with anxiety and pain, had been (a nightmare, the pits, a bummer).

13. _____   The detective agreed to let her assistant choose the (dining environment, joint, restaurant) for the meeting.

14. _____   The plan was to have two police officers waiting in the (john, bathroom, comfort station) in case there was trouble.

15. _____   These men would wait until the (guys, fellows, menfolk) finished their conversation.

Dictionaries put labels on certain words to help us understand how to use them. Match each of the following underlined words with one of the following labels: nonstandard, informal, slang, vulgar, obsolete, archaic, regional, or foreign.

16. There <u>ain't</u> many dinners like the one I went to last night.   _____

17. The chef served the dinner guests a tasty <u>mousse</u>.   _____

18. *Gad,* the government is going to sell Air Canada!   _____

19. She decided to order a *grinder* for lunch.   _____

20. Everyone thought the host was a <u>ham</u>.   _____

Distinguishing between Words That Are Often Confused

In each of the following sentences, pick the word that correctly completes the meaning of the sentence.

21. _____   The sunbather (laid, layed, lay, lyed) on the beach until sunset.

22. _____   The children wore very creative (customs, costumes) to the Halloween party.

23. _____   Keep your (receipt, recipe) in case you must return the jacket.

24. _____   Everyone knew the story of (they're, their, there) private lives.

25. _____   He walked (passed, past) me without speaking.

26. _____   What is the (principal, principle) reason for this change in staff?

27. _____   The building was constructed on a historical (sight, site, cite).

28. _____   You won't be sorry if you do a (thorough, through, though) job.

29. _____   I (can not, canot, cannot) finish my breakfast.

30. _____   Have you (access, excess) to a good library?

31. _____   Every (vane, vain, vein) stood out on his head.

32. _____   The college student was injured in the poorly planned initiation (right, rite, write).

33. _____   I (use, used) to work at that store.

34. _____   My favourite (desert, dessert) is homemade pumpkin pie.

35. _____   I need someone to (consul, council, counsel) me on what courses to take next semester.

In the following paragraph, fifteen words are underlined. If you think the correct word has been used, mark the word with a C. If the word is incorrect, write the correct word on the line provided.

   <u>Whose</u> going to help me out of this mess? The bank in town <u>aloud</u> me to borrow ten thousand dollars to buy a new car. Meanwhile, I neglected to calculate the <u>effect</u> this would have on my monthly budget, since I already had borrowed a large sum of money on my credit cards. I currently work <u>forty</u> hours a week. I don't see how I could work any longer <u>then</u> that. Nothing can <u>altar</u> the fact that I haven't enough income to pay all my bills. <u>It's</u> difficult to figure out what I should do. I must not <u>set</u> back and think the problem will go away, or else I might <u>lose</u> the car. Of <u>coarse</u>, I won't buy any new <u>clothes</u> this season. I won't be able to go out to <u>diner</u> even once. I need a nice <u>quite</u> rest home where I can let someone else <u>advice</u> me about my <u>personnel</u> finances.

36. whose   _____

37. aloud   _____

38. effect   _____

39. forty   _____

40. then   _____

41. altar   _____

42. it's   _____

43. set   _____

44. lose   _____

45. coarse   _____

46. clothes   _____

47. diner   _____

48. quite   _____

49. advice   _____

50. personnel   _____

Score _____

Understanding Your Basic Sourcebook: The Dictionary

In recent weeks, I have received a number of letters asking me to define culture . . . . What does Prime Minister Brian Mulroney mean when he talks about our "cultural identity"? Is there some other kind? What does Joe Clark, our Minister for External Affairs, mean when he tells a U.S. audience that "What is entertainment for you is culture for us"?

Actor, playwright, professor, and columnist Mavor Moore asked these questions in a column dedicated to defining Canada's culture that was published in the *Globe and Mail*. An accomplished Canadian writer, Moore realized that the Canadian cultural identity is not an easy thing to define, so he turned to the dictionary.

The dictionaries are more bewildering than precise concerning a definition of "culture." We learn that culture can signify everything from refinement of the mind to manure, from good manners to a colony of viruses, from a particular school of art to boundaries on a map.

When Mavor Moore turned to the dictionary for help, he was making a wise decision. The dictionary is one of the greatest resources you have for building your word power. In school and at work, everyone should have a good hardcover or paperback dictionary that contains full definitions of many thousands of words. This should be one of the first books that students buy when they enter college. Riffle through the book to get the feel of it; there's a lot of valuable information there.

One of your most important goals in studying words in college is to write effective college essays. The building blocks you will need for your compositions and term papers are appropriate words, strong sentences, and well-developed paragraphs. As you observe the power of individual words in sentences and paragraphs that you read, and as you use a wide variety of words in your own writing, that first "bewildering" foray into the dictionary quickly evolves into an understanding of the value of the book and the right variety of word usage that you can incorporate into your own work. Consider Moore once again:

So I prefer to keep the word "culture" in its valuable common sense (because there really is no other word) of collective preparation for, and maintenance of, human development.

Mavor Moore consulted the dictionary and found that he could in fact define the word he was attempting to place in a Canadian context.

By mastering words in the dictionary, you will realize that your dictionary is an important tool for your college work. The dictionary will increase your sense of security when using the language: you can communicate with other people without fear or hesitation; you can write letters that you know will carry your ideas in a clear, expressive way; you can construct oral presentations in the classroom that will have maximum effect on your listeners; and you can construct essays and other college-level assignments and know that they are logical and persuasive.

The starting point for Mavor Moore was to consult the dictionary for a definition of the word. In this book, your starting point will also be the word. In Part I you will develop your word power, beginning with an understanding of how the dictionary can be an important key to unlocking the power of language.

One Word, Many Meanings

When you read a word that is unfamiliar, you first try to figure out the meaning by studying the context in which the word is found. If you still do not understand it, you should look up the word in the dictionary to find out the possible meanings. Finally, you decide which meaning fits the word you are reading or that you are considering for your own writing. As you have seen, Mavor Moore had a number of contexts for the word "culture." Understanding words in their context helps make you a more perceptive reader; knowing how to create the right context in your own compositions helps make you a more effective writer.

It was suggested that you "riffle" through the dictionary when you first get it. If the word *riffle* is unfamiliar to you, you might look more closely at the context of the word in order to arrive at its meaning. Would a person who examines a book for the first time go through that book page by page? Probably not, and when you first riffle through your dictionary, you'll likely just be having a quick look at the type of material contained in the book.

If you were not sure that you had figured out the meaning of the word from the context, you would look up the word in the dictionary. Here is the dictionary entry for the word *riffle:*

> **rif·fle** (rĭf′əl) *n.* 1. A rocky shoal or sandbar lying just below the surface of a waterway. 2. A stretch of choppy water caused by such a shoal or sandbar; a rapid. 3. *Mining.* a. The sectional stone or wood bottom lining of a sluice, arranged to trap mineral particles, as of gold. b. A groove or block in such a lining. 4. The act of shuffling cards. —*v.* **riffled, -fling, -fles.** —*tr.* 1. To shuffle (playing cards) by holding part of a deck in each hand and raising up the edges before releasing them to fall alternately in one stack. 2. To thumb through (the pages of a book, for example). —*intr.* 1. To shuffle cards. 2. To become choppy, as water. [Perhaps blend of *ruffle* (disturb) and *ripple.*]

Which meaning in this dictionary entry fits the meaning of *riffle* as we are using it in this section?

Exercise 1   Using the Dictionary to Find the Correct Meaning of a Word

Each of the ten sentences below contains the word *table*. In each sentence, find the correct definition for the meaning of the word *table* by referring to the dictionary entry that is provided for you. Write the definition under each sentence.

ta·ble (tā′ bəl) *n. Abbr.* **tab.** 1. An article of furniture supported by one or more vertical legs and having a flat horizontal surface on which objects can be placed. 2. The objects laid out for a meal upon a table. 3. The food and drink served at meals; fare. 4. The company of people assembled around a table, as for a meal. 5. *Often plural.* A gaming table as for faro, roulette, or dice. 6. a. Either of the leaves of a backgammon board. b. *Plural. Obsolete.* The game of backgammon. 7. A plateau or tableland. 8. a. A flat facet cut across the top of a precious stone. b. A stone cut in this fashion. 9. *Music.* The front part of a stringed instrument, the **belly** *(see).* 10. *Architecture.* a. A raised or sunken rectangular panel on a wall. b. A raised horizontal surface or continuous band on an exterior wall; stringcourse. 11. *Geology.* A horizontal rock stratum. 12. In palmistry, a part of the palm framed by four lines. 13. An orderly written, typed, or printed display of data, especially a rectangular array exhibiting one or more characteristics of designated entities or categories. 14. An abbreviated list, as of contents; a synopsis. 15. A slab or tablet, as of stone, bearing an inscription or device. 16. *Plural.* A system of laws or decrees; a code: *the tables of Moses.* **—on the table.** Postponed or put aside for consideration at a later date. **—turn the tables.** To reverse a situation and gain the upper hand. —*tr. v.* **tabled, -bling, -bles.** 1. To put or place on a table. 2. To postpone consideration of (a piece of legislation, for example); shelve. 3. *Rare.* To enter in a list or table; tabulate. [Middle English, tablet, board, table, from Old French, from Latin *tabula,* board, list.]

1. The <u>table</u> of contents will give you some idea of what the book is about.

   _____

2. The <u>table</u> of the guitar was cracked.

   _____

3. They rode their horses across the <u>table</u> and up into the highlands.

   _____

4. Guests can always be sure of a delicious <u>table</u> when they are invited to one of Rosemarie's parties.

   _____

5. They <u>tabled</u> the tax reform bill.

   _____

6. The geologist took samples from the <u>table</u> of rock.

   _____

7. One of the legs on the <u>table</u> needs to be glued.

   _____

8. The <u>tables</u> were turned when the party in power lost the election.

   _____

9. On what page of the chemistry textbook will I find the <u>table</u> of the elements?

_____

10. A list of the king's victories was inscribed on a <u>table</u> that was placed on the wall of the temple.

_____

Exercise 2   Using the Dictionary to Find the Correct Meaning of a Word

Each of the ten sentences below contains the word *base*. In each sentence, find the correct definition for the meaning of the word *base* by referring to the dictionary entry that is provided for you. Write the definition under each sentence.

base (bās) *n. Abbr.* **b., B.** 1. The lowest or supporting part or layer; foundation; bottom. 2. The fundamental principle or underlying concept of a system or theory. 3. The fundamental ingredient from which a mixture is prepared; chief constituent: *a paint with an oil base.* 4. The fact, observation, or premise from which a measurement or reasoning process is begun. 5. *Sports.* A goal, starting point, or safety area; specifically, one of the four corners of a baseball infield marked by a bag or plate. 6. A centre of organization, supply, or activity; headquarters. 7. *Military.* a. A fortified centre of operations. b. A supply centre for a large force. 8. *Architecture.* The lowest part of a structure, considered as a separate architectural unit: *The base of a column.* 9. *Heraldry.* The lower part of a shield. l0. *Linguistics.* A morpheme or morphemes regarded as a form to which affixes or other bases may be added. For example, in the words *filled* and *refill, fill* is the base. 11. *Mathematics.* a. The side or face of a geometric figure to which an altitude is or is thought to be drawn. b. The number that is raised to various powers to generate the principal counting units of a number system. c. The number raised to the logarithm of a designated number in order to produce that designated number. 12. A line used as a reference for measurement or computations. 13. *Chemistry.* a. Any of a large class of compounds, including the hydroxides and oxides of metals, having a bitter taste, a slippery solution, the ability to turn litmus blue, and the ability to react with acids to form salts. b. A molecular or ionic substance capable of combining with a proton to form a new substance. c. A substance that provides a pair of electrons for a covalent bond with an acid.

1. The politician told the crowd that they were the <u>base</u> of his support.

_____

2. The umpire shouted that the player was out at first <u>base</u>.

_____

3. I prefer makeup that has a water <u>base</u> rather than an oil base.

_____

4. Belief in human progress was the <u>base</u> of all her way of thinking.

_____

5. The <u>base</u> of the statue was made of solid marble.

_____

6. A <u>base</u> will turn litmus paper blue.

_____

7. The army returned, tired and dirty, to its <u>base</u>.

_____

8. When you take away the prefix or the suffix of a word, you are left with the part of the word called the <u>base</u>.

_____

9. The team was glad to be playing its championship game at its home <u>base</u>.

_____

10. The formula for figuring out the area of a rectangle is to multiply the <u>base</u> by the height.

_____

Exercise 3   Using the Dictionary to Find the Correct Meaning of a Word

Each of the ten sentences below contains the word _hand_. In each sentence, find the correct definition for the meaning of the word _hand_ by referring to the dictionary entry that is provided for you. Write the definition under each sentence.

hand (hănd) _n. Abbr._ **hd.** 1. The terminal part of the human arm below the wrist, consisting of the palm, four fingers, and an opposable thumb, used for grasping and holding. 2. A homologous or similar part in other animals. 3. A unit of length used especially to specify the height of a horse, about ten centimetres. 4. Something suggesting the shape or function of the human hand. 5. a. Any of the rotating pointers used as indexes on the face of a mechanical clock. b. A pointer on any of various similar instruments, such as on gauges or meters; a needle. 6. A printer's mark, **index** _(see)_. 7. Lateral direction indicated according to the way in which one is facing: _at my right hand._ 8. A style or individual sample of writing; handwriting; penmanship. 9. A round of applause to signify approval; a clapping. 10. Physical assistance; a help: _Give me a hand with these trunks._ 11. _Card games._ a. The cards held by a given player at any time: _a winning hand._ b. The number of cards dealt each player; a deal. c. A player or participant: _a fourth hand for bridge._ d. A portion or section of a game during which all the cards dealt out are played: _a hand of poker._ 12. A person who performs manual labour: _a factory hand._ 13. A person who is part of a group or crew. 14. Any participant in an activity. 15. A person regarded in terms of a specialized skill or trait. 16. The immediacy of a source of information; degree of reliability: _at first hand._ 17. a. _Usually plural._ Possession, ownership, or keeping: _The books should be in her hands by noon._ b. _Often plural._ Power; jurisdiction;

care: *in good hands*. c. Doing or involvement; participation: *"The hand of Alexander Mackenzie was evident in the early success of the North West Company."* d. An influence or effect; a share: *your professor's hand in your decision*. 18. Permission or a promise, especially: a. A pledge to wed. b. A business agreement sealed by a clasp or handshake; word: *You have my hand on that*. 19. Evidence of craftsmanship or artistic skill. 20. A manner or way of performing something; emphasis; an approach: *a light hand with makeup*.

1. He moved the <u>hands</u> of the clock back to midnight.

   _____

2. Since 1981, a woman in Quebec who has given her hand in marriage legally retains her maiden name.

   _____

3. You are in good <u>hands</u> at this hotel.

   _____

4. Give our performer another <u>hand</u> for her marvellous concert tonight.

   _____

5. The document will be in your <u>hands</u> before morning.

   _____

6. Let's deal one more <u>hand</u> before we quit.

   _____

7. I could see the fine <u>hand</u> of the jeweller when I examined the necklace.

   _____

8. The farm <u>hand</u> had become a member of the family.

   _____

9. I noticed his <u>hand</u> was nearly illegible.

   _____

10. At your right <u>hand</u> are all the reference shelves.

   _____

Shades of Meaning: Denotation/Connotation

Writing is a constant search to find the right word to express your thoughts and feelings as accurately as possible. For instance, if you were describing a young person under five years of age, you might choose one of these words:

> imp
> toddler
> preschooler
> child
> brat
> tot
> youngster

Some words are neutral. That is, they have no associations besides the strict dictionary meaning. Which word in the above list is strictly neutral? If you chose *child*, you were correct. This strict dictionary meaning of a word is called the **denotation** of that word.

In writing, you do not always want to choose a strictly neutral word. When you want to be very precise, or when you want to give a flavour to your writing, you will choose a word that has further meanings associated with it. These meanings, which some words have apart from their strict definition, are called the **connotations** of a word.

For instance, if you had a job writing a brochure for a nursery school, you would probably use the word *preschooler.* If you were talking about a child who has just learned to walk, you might use the word *toddler,* which carries the association of a child toddling along. What word might a parent use to describe a child who is constantly getting into trouble? What word might a disgusted child use to describe a younger brother or sister who has just coloured all over a favourite book?

The more experienced writer can find words that have the appropriate connotations. A good point to keep in mind is that the connotations of a word are not always the same for each person. Politicians know that if they want to get votes in a conservative area, they should not refer to their views as *liberal.* The strict dictionary meaning of *liberal* is "favouring nonrevolutionary progress or reform," certainly an idea that most people would support. However, when most people hear the words *liberal* or *conservative,* they bring to the words many political biases and experiences from their past: their parents' attitudes, the political and social history of the area in which they live, and many other factors that may correctly or incorrectly colour their understanding of these words.

Choosing words with the right connotations is a powerful skill for your writing, one that will help your reader better understand the ideas you want to communicate. As your vocabulary grows, the challenge of writing will become easier because you will begin to discover all the shades of meanings that words can have.

Exercise 1   Working with Denotation

In each group of words below, circle the word that is the most neutral. Use your dictionary if you need to look up a word that might carry a specialized meaning.

1. a. slender   b. emaciated   c. lean   d. skinny   e. thin
2. a. cheap   b. inexpensive   c. underpriced   d. chintzy
3. a. active   b. frantic   c. energetic   d. hyperactive
4. a. unique   b. unusual   c. strange   d. remarkable
5. a. possessions   b. things   c. stuff   d. junk
6. a. zealous   b. committed   c. fanatical   d. devoted
7. a. enthralled   b. fascinated   c. enticed   d. interested   e. enchanted
   f. captivated   g. mesmerized   h. charmed
8. a. taste   b. devour   c. nibble   d. eat   e. gorge   f. gnaw   g. munch
9. a. clever   b. smart   c. cunning   d. shrewd
10. a. plump   b. flabby   c. dumpy   d. overweight   e. chubby   f. fat

Exercise 2   Working with Connotation

In each example below, a "neutral" word and its strict dictionary meaning are given along with several synonyms. Look up each synonym in the dictionary to find out the special association or additional meaning of the word.

1. **partner:** a person associated with another or others in some activity of common interest

    colleague   _____

    confederate _____

    ally   _____

    accomplice   _____

    associate   _____

2. **pity:** sorrow or grief aroused by the misfortune of another

    compassion   _____

    commiseration _____

    sympathy   _____

    condolence   _____

    empathy   _____

3. **burn:** to destroy with fire

    scorch   _____

    singe   _____

    sear   _____

    char   _____

    parch   _____

4. **sad:** low in spirit

    melancholy   _____

    downhearted _____

    sorrowful   _____

    doleful   _____

    desolate   _____

Exercise 3   Working with Connotation

In this exercise, you have the opportunity to think of words that are richer in associations than the neutral words that are underlined in the sentences below. Write your own word choice in the space to the right. Discuss with others in your class the associations you make with the words you have chosen.

1. I live in a <u>house</u> at the edge of town.   _____

2. I <u>walk</u> home from work every night.   _____

3. Usually the same <u>person</u> is always walking be-
    hind me.   _____

4. She is always carrying a lot of <u>stuff</u>.   _____

5. She looks as if she is very <u>old</u>.   _____

6. She has <u>marks</u> all over her face. _____

7. Sometimes I try to <u>talk</u> to her. _____

8. She has such an <u>unusual</u> look in her eyes. _____

9. Sometimes I can hear her <u>talking</u> to herself. _____

10. At night when I am <u>sitting</u> in my favourite arm-chair, I often think of her and wish she could tell me the story of her life. _____

Words with Special Limitations

The dictionary uses several key terms to label a word that is limited in its use. Students often use some of these words incorrectly in formal writing. Such errors can be avoided by looking up any suspected word in the dictionary. The dictionary will tell you whether or not the word is appropriate. Here are the most frequently used labels.

NONSTANDARD: This label refers to any word or expression that is not generally accepted as educated speech or writing. For example:

> **ain't** (ānt). *Nonstandard.* Contraction of *am not.* Also extended in use to mean *are not, is not, has not,* and *have not.*

INFORMAL: This label describes the language people generally use in conversation. Although this kind of English is more relaxed than written English, it is perfectly acceptable in everyday speech. For example:

> **hon·ey** (hŭn'ē) *n., pl.* **-eys** 1. A sweet, yellowish or brownish, viscid fluid produced by various bees from the nectar of flowers and used as food. 2. A similar substance made by certain other insects. 3. A sweet substance, such as the nectar of flowers. 4. Sweetness. 5. *Informal.* Sweet one; dear. Used as a term of endearment. 6. *Slang.* Something remarkably fine. Often used with *of a.* —*tr. v.* **honeyed** or **-ied, -eying, eys.** 1. To sweeten with or as if with honey. 2. To cajole with sweet talk. —*adj.* Of or resembling honey. [Middle English *hony,* Old English *hunig.* . . .]

SLANG: This label refers to the way a particular group of people uses special words or phrases, often with the intention of keeping the meaning to themselves. A characteristic of a slang word or expression is that it is often used only for a limited period of time and then is forgotten. For example:

> **fat·head** (făt' hĕd') *n. Slang.* A stupid person; a dolt.

VULGAR: This label describes words that are not acceptable in writing or conversation because of a strong social taboo against their use. For example:

> **crap** (krăp) *n.* 1. A losing throw of the dice in the game of **craps** *(see).* 2. *Vulgar.* Excrement. 3. *Vulgar slang.* Nonsense. 4. *Vulgar slang.* Something worthless. —*intr. v.* **crapped, crapping, craps.** *Vulgar.* To defecate. —**crap out.** 1. To make a losing throw in the game of craps. 2. *Slang.* To fail. ["Throw of dice," back-formation from *craps.* In other senses, Middle

English *crappe*, residual rubbish, chaff, from Middle Dutch *crappe*, probably from *crappen*, to tear off.]
—**crap'py** *adj.*

OBSOLETE: The term *obsolete* indicates that at least one meaning of a word was commonly used at one time in the past, but that meaning is no longer used. For example:

> **dame** (dām) *n.* 1. A title formerly given to a woman in authority or to the mistress of a household. Now only used in expressions such as *Dame Fortune.* 2. A married woman; matron. 3. *Slang.* A woman; female. 4. *British.* a. *Archaic.* The legal title of the wife or widow of a knight or baronet. b. A title of a woman, equivalent to that of a knight. 5. *Obsolete.* A schoolmistress. [Middle English, from Old French, from Latin *domina*, feminine of *dominus*, master, lord.]

ARCHAIC: Archaic language refers to old-fashioned words that were commonly used a long time ago, but now are no longer used at all. For example:

> **foot·pad** (foŏt' păd') *n. Archaic.* A highwayman or street robber who goes about on foot. [*Foot* + earlier *pad*, path, probably from Middle Dutch *path*. . . .]

REGIONAL: Regional words and expressions are often used in a particular section of the country, but they are almost unknown outside of that area. For example:

> **jin·ker** (jin'kər) *n. Cdn.* In Newfoundland, an imaginary creature or person who is supposed to bring bad luck; a gremlin or jinx.

BRITISH: This label is for words that are commonly used in England and other countries where English is spoken, but are not used in the same way in Canada. For example:

> **guy** (gī) *n.* 1. *Informal.* A man; fellow. 2. *British.* One who is odd or grotesque in appearance or dress. 3. An effigy of Guy Fawkes, formerly paraded through the streets of English towns and burned on Guy Fawkes day. . . .

FOREIGN: This label is for words, and sometimes phrases, that have been borrowed from another language and used directly as English vocabulary. For example:

> **tou·ché** (too shā') *interj.* Used to express concession to an opponent for a point well made, as in an argument. [French, *touched*, indicating that one has been touched by the opponent's foil in fencing.]

Exercise 1   Recognizing Words with Special Limitations

Each of the following sentences contains words that are inappropriate for formal writing. The dictionary labels such words as "informal" or "slang." Rewrite each sentence, changing every inappropriate word or expression to an acceptable word choice.

1. My old man gave me enough dough last night to take a chick to the flicks.

    _____

2. The fuzz finally caught the junkie and stuck the dude in the cooler.

    _____

3. The sucker was conned by the guy he met in the street.

    _____

4. That kid has flunked every lousy French test because she always goofs off in class.

    _____

5. My older brother is swell, but my younger brother is a real creep; he's always bugging me.

    _____

6. Since I'm broke, my buddy will bring the grub.

    _____

7. I'll sack out for a while in this dump if it's okay with you.

    _____

8. I don't have the guts to level with my prof.

    _____

9. Her bum leg is driving her crazy.

    _____

10. Frank's ghetto blaster is awesome.

    _____

    _____

Exercise 2 Recognizing Words with Special Limitations

Each of the following sentences contains an italicized word that is an example of either _informal usage_ or _slang._ Using your dictionary, look up each of the italicized words and write a more formal word choice in the space provided.

1. He worked with her for years, but he could never _cotton_ to her way of doing things.   _____

2. Many years after they dated, he told her he still had a *crush* on her. _____

3. As I was taking the exam, I became *rattled* by the sirens that went off every ten minutes. _____

4. We told our teacher that we really could not *dig* Shakespeare. _____

5. He wore a *classy* suit to the first dance of the school year. _____

6. The producers had high hopes for the movie, but all of the critics said it was a real *turkey*. _____

7. When the police arrested the gang, each member had some *hardware* that the police immediately confiscated. _____

8. They went to a *super* party last weekend. _____

9. After he answered the sergeant, all the other soldiers said it was a *gutsy* reply. _____

10. As she passed the scene of the accident, she heard one driver call the other a *jerk*. _____

Exercise 3   Recognizing Words with Special Limitations

Each of the following sentences contains an italicized word. In the space after each sentence, choose whether the word should be labelled *nonstandard*, *informal*, *slang*, *vulgar*, *obsolete*, *archaic*, *regional*, or *foreign*. Use the dictionary to find the answers.

1. Don't give me any *lip*. _____

2. The dealer told us that if we really wanted the car, it was going to cost us a few more *grand*. _____

3. I'm not sure if it's *gonna* rain tomorrow or not. _____

4. When he broke four plates in a row, I called him a *klutz*. _____

5. The *seigneurs* of New France often controlled great amounts of territory. _____

6. When they went on a picnic, they usually chose one of the *bluffs* on the prairies. _____

7. When the child sneezed, the teacher said, "*Gesundheit!*" _____

8. She *sure* was lucky to find that job. _____

9. On her grandparents' wedding night, the entire village turned out for the *shivaree*. _____

10. He decided not to buy the suit because he thought the style was too *passé*. _____

The Dictionary as a Working Tool

You have already studied some very important aspects of dictionary information. You have learned that a word can have many meanings, and you have seen how a word can have different shades of meaning, depending on how it is used in a particular context. In addition, you have seen that the use of a word may be limited to informal conversation, or it may be used only in certain regions of the country.

However, a dictionary entry can tell you even more about a word. Study the following entry for the word *gentle*.

Information Contained in Dictionary Entry for "gentle"

1. The spelling of the word, divided into syllables (capitalization and different spellings given here when necessary).
2. Pronunciation
3. Part of speech
4. The comparative and superlative forms of the word
5. First meaning
6. An example, illustrating the first meaning
7. Second, third, fourth, fifth, and sixth meanings, with examples as needed
8. Seventh meaning, identified as "archaic"
9. Two noun meanings
10. Transitive verb (a verb that takes a direct object). The entry gives the past tense, the present participle, and the third person singular of the present tense of the verb
11. The three meanings of the verb, including an obsolete meaning
12. The origin of the word, traced through more than one language
13. Additional forms of the word

Exercise 1   Understanding Dictionary Entries

Use your dictionary to answer each of the following questions.

1. What is the meaning of the word *catholic?*   _____

2. What would you be if you were *on the pogey?*   _____

3. What is a synonym for *transient?*   _____

4. What is a *steelhead?*   _____
5. What are all the possible parts of speech for the word *home?*   _____
6. What label does the dictionary give for the word *betwixt?*   _____
7. How do you divide the word *tenacious* into syllables?   _____

8. How do you pronounce the word *niche*? _____

9. What part of speech is the word *sometimes*? _____

10. What is a *Sam Browne*? _____

Exercise 2 Understanding Dictionary Entries

Use your dictionary to answer each of the following questions.

1. What is *pemmican*? _____

2. What is a second way to spell the word *theatre*? _____

3. What are four synonyms for the verb *contract*? _____

4. What is a *composite school*? _____

5. How do you pronounce the word *receipt*? _____

6. What is a second way to spell the word *council- lor*? _____

7. What is the slang meaning of *pen*? _____

8. What are the *dog days*? _____

9. How do you divide the word *magisterial* into syllables? _____

10. What are all the possible parts of speech for the word *solo*? _____

Exercise 3 Understanding Dictionary Entries

Use your dictionary to answer each of the following questions.

1. What are the possible parts of speech for the word *hustle*? _____

2. What is a second way to spell the word *judge- ment*? _____

3. Divide the word *crescendo* into syllables. _____

4. What does the word *malemute* describe? _____

5. What is another name for a *whisky-jack*? _____

6. What is the archaic meaning for the word *cutpurse*? _____

7. What is a second spelling for the word *colour*? _____

8. What is the meaning of *hoi polloi*? _____

9. What are five synonyms for the word *sloppy*? _____

10. How do you pronounce the word *solder*? _____

Distinguishing between Words That Are Often Confused

Words That Sound Alike: Group I

Practise inserting the correct word into each of the practice sentences. Mark the sets that give you trouble so you can return for further study.

it's   contraction of "it is"
its   possessive

1. _____ obvious that the car has lost _____ muffler.

2. The dog has no licence, so _____ possible _____ owner doesn't care about the dog very much.

they're   contraction of "they are"
their   possessive
there   at that place

3. When _____ in school, _____ parents work in the restaurant _____ on the corner.

4. Now that _____ living in the country, _____ expenses are not so great, so they might stay _____.

who's   contraction of "who is"
whose   possessive

5. _____ car is double-parked outside, and _____ going to move it?

6. _____ the pitcher at the game today, and _____ glove will he use?

you're   contraction of "you are"
your   possessive

7. When _____ a father, _____ free time is never guaranteed.

8. Please give me _____ paper when _____ finished writing.

allowed *(verb)*   permitted
aloud *(adv.)*   out loud

9. The sign told us we were not _____ to read _____ in the library.

10. She called _____ to him, and then she was _____ to go on the boat to speak with him.

altar *(noun)*   an elevated place or table for religious rites
alter *(verb)*   to change or adjust

11. The museum announced that it would not _____ the artist's famous painting of the Roman _____.

12. The architect decided to _____ her ideas of where the _____ should be placed.

aural *(adj.)*   having to do with the ear or hearing
oral *(adj.)*   having to do with the mouth or speech

13. The doctor's _____ report on my _____ examination was encouraging.

14. The _____ medicine I took helped my _____ condition clear up, and now I can hear much better.

brake *(verb)*   to stop
       (noun)   a device used for slowing or stopping
break *(verb)*   to smash, crack, or come apart

15. Because I had a good emergency _____ on my car, I was able to stop without _____ even a headlight.

16. When he had to _____ suddenly, he was grateful that his _____ was in good condition.

capital *(adj.)*   chief; major; fatal
        (noun)   leading city; money
capitol *(noun)*   a building in which a U.S. state legislature assembles

17. The senators met in Athens, the _____ of Greece, to discuss the question of _____ punishment.

18. If I could raise some _____, I would be able to make some _____ changes in my home.

19. On a class trip to Montana, we visited the state _____ where we

saw the members of the legislature meet in the _____ building

itself.

chord *(noun)*   three or more tones sounded together; harmony
cord *(noun)*   a small rope of twisted strands; any ropelike structure; a unit of
cut fuel wood

20. The lumberman would be cutting no more _____ of wood; his

spinal _____ was badly injured in a car accident.

21. She couldn't play the _____ on the electric guitar because some-

one had unplugged the _____.

close *(verb)*   to shut
clothes *(noun)*   garments
cloth *(noun)*   fabric; a piece of material

22. Please don't _____ the closet door; I want to put away these

_____ and this piece of striped _____.

23. I hurried to bring several metres of wool _____to the tailor to

make some new winter _____ for me; I knew he would

_____ at five o'clock.

coarse *(adj.)*   rough; not fine; common or of inferior quality
course *(noun)*   direction or path of something moving; part of a meal; a school
subject

24. I would have enjoyed the _____, but some of the students told

_____ jokes during every class.

25. The captain was a very _____ man, but he could keep a ship on

_____.

complement *(noun)*   something that completes or makes up a whole
       (verb)   to complete
compliment *(noun)*   an expression of praise
        (verb)   to give praise

26. She always wears clothes that _____ each other, but she never

expects a _____.

27. I gave the artist a _____ when I told him that the colours in his

painting _____ each other.

fair *(adj.)*   unbiased; light colour; free of clouds;
       promising; lovely
    (noun)   an exhibition; regional event; market
fare *(noun)*   a charge for transportation

28. It was such a _____ day that he decided to save the bus

_____ and walk.

29. I never thought it was _____ that Dad wouldn't let me go to the

    county _____.

flour *(noun)*   the powder produced by grinding a grain
flower *(noun)*   a blossom of a plant
    (verb)   to blossom

30. The child dropped the fresh _____ into his mother's bowl of

    _____.

31. After you put the _____ in a vase, sift the _____ for the
    cake.

for *(prep.)*   directed to; in the amount of; on behalf of; to the extent of
four *(noun, adj.)*   number

● **forty**: Notice that this number is spelled differently from *four, fourteen,* or
  twenty-four.

fore *(noun, adj.)*   situated near the front

32. My uncle has _____ telephone books on his desk, one

    _____ every town in which he has lived.

33. The passenger walked to the _____ of the ship _____
    a better view of the coastline.

forth *(adv.)*   onward in time, place, or order
fourth *(noun, adj.)*   number

34. He was the _____ one to walk _____ that morning.

35. She paced back and _____ in her _____ floor office.

forward *(verb)*   to send on to another address
    (adj.)   bold; progressive
    (adv.)   moving toward the front
foreword *(noun)*   introduction at the beginning of a book; preface

36. The editor thought that the _____ to the book was too

    _____.

37. Since the publisher had moved, I decided to _____ the manu-

    script and send the _____ later.

grate *(verb)*   to shred; to annoy or irritate
    (noun)   a metal grill
● **grateful** *(adj.)*   appreciative
great *(adj.)*   large; significant; excellent; powerful; skilful; first-rate

38. After I _____ the onions for dinner, I place them on the

    _____ to get warm.

39. I am _____ that the landlord placed a _____ over the
    window for safety.

40. The _____ athlete was _____ for all the mail from her
    fans.

knew *(verb)*   past tense of *know*
new *(adj.)*   not old

41.   Dan _____ yesterday morning that the car would need a

_____ battery.

42.   By the time she _____ that they had moved to a _____
town, it was too late to help them.

know *(verb)*   to understand
no *(adv.)*   a negative response
   (adj.)   not any; not one

43.   They _____ there is _____ way to cross these mountains in the winter.

44.   I am _____ artist, but I _____ what I like.

Exercise 1   Words That Sound Alike

Choose the correct word, and write it in the space at the right.

1.   Members of my family enjoy telling their dreams
(allowed, aloud) at the breakfast table.   _____
2.   (It's, Its) not easy to know the meaning of our
dreams.   _____
3.   (You're, Your) dreams may be interpreted differently depending on who does the interpreting.   _____
4.   (They're, Their, There) is no firm agreement
about what all the various parts of a dream
mean.   _____
5.   (Who's, Whose) to say that if I dream about eating a sundae, it means that I'm frustrated?   _____
6.   People often dream they are falling (foreword,
forward).   _____
7.   Does what we dream (altar, alter) the way we
live in our waking hours?   _____
8.   In one dream, my old boyfriend was paying me
a (complement, compliment).   _____
9.   In another dream, I was so rich I had enough
(capital, capitol) to buy four race horses.   _____
10. Of (coarse, course), before I had time to race
them, I woke up.   _____

Exercise 2   Words That Sound Alike

Choose the correct word, and write it in the space at the right.

1.   The driver claimed her (brakes, breaks) had
failed.   _____

2.   The bus (fare, fair) has been increased again.   _____

3.   He walked (foreword, forward).   _____

4.   He paced back and (forth, fourth).   _____
5.   After I (grate, great) the carrots, I will peel the
potatoes.   _____
6.   I do not (know, no) the answers to the accounting problem.   _____

7. I need whole wheat (flour, flower) to make this bread.

_____

8. We always invite several guests (for, four) Thanksgiving dinner.

_____

9. Stuffed trout is my favourite main (coarse, course).

_____

10. (They're, Their, There) going to renovate the old village museum.

_____

Exercise 3   Words That Sound Alike

Edit the following paragraph for errors in word confusions. Circle each error and write each word correctly on the lines below the paragraph.

Jean-Baptiste Cadot was a grate, if unknown, French-Canadian fur trader and interpreter in eighteenth-century Canada. The French wanted to expand there fur-trading interests westward from the Grate Lakes, and they needed someone who's stature among the native people would make the job of obtaining furs easier. Cadot's sense of the inflections of the Ojibway language, and his way of complementing the native people for their trapping exploits, led him to be named a chef among a local band near what is now Sault Ste. Marie. His fare treatment of the natives also gained their respect. In the coarse of his life on the upper lakes, wearing native-style close and travelling back and fourth many times between native camps and fur-trading posts, Cadot came to no the native people's way of life with a knew understanding that led to his assumption of a major role in the Indian wars of the 1760s and the early success of the North West Company.

_____   _____

_____   _____

_____   _____

_____   _____

_____   _____

_____

Words That Sound Alike: Group II

Here is a second set of words often confused because they sound alike. Find out how well you know these words by inserting the correct word into each of the practice sentences.

pain _(noun)_   suffering
pane _(noun)_   a panel of glass

1. When the child's arm went through the window _____, the

    _____ was not so bad as the sight of the blood.

2. The young father considered it a _____ to spend Saturday re-

    placing the cracked window _____ on the sunporch.

passed *(verb)* the past tense of *to pass*—to move ahead
past *(noun)* time before the present
  (prep.) beyond
  (adj.) no longer current

3. I have spent the _____ few days wondering if I _____ the exam.

4. She walked _____ the old house thinking about her _____.

patience *(noun)* calm endurance; tolerant understanding
patients *(noun)* persons under medical treatment

5. The young doctor has not learned to have _____ with her _____.

6. All of the _____ in this understaffed hospital need a good deal of _____.

peace *(noun)* absence of war, calm
piece *(noun)* a portion, a part

7. Each person in the writing group wrote a _____ of the article on world _____.

8. We will have _____ at home only if everyone does a _____ of the housework.

plain *(adj.)* simple; ordinary; unattractive; clear
  (noun) a flat, treeless land region
plane *(noun)* an aircraft; a flat, level surface; a carpenter's tool for levelling wood; a level of development

9. The _____ flew directly over the _____.

10. Although the man's features were very _____, his mind was on a higher _____ than the mind of his supervisor.

presence *(noun)* the state of being present; a person's manner
presents *(noun)* gifts
  (verb) (third person singular) to introduce; to give a gift

11. The children claimed they felt Santa's _____ as they looked for their _____.

12. Each year the mayor always _____ an award as well as several lovely _____ to outstanding members of the community.

principal *(adj.)* most important; chief; main
  (noun) the head of a school; a sum of money
principle *(noun)* rule or standard

13. The _____ lost his job because he would not compromise his _____.

14. The _____ reason she had to see the bank clerk was to have the terms of the loan explained to her, including the _____ and interest.

rain *(noun, verb)*   water falling to earth in drops
reign *(noun, verb)*   a period of rule for a king or queen
rein *(noun)*   a strap attached to a bridle, used to control a horse

15. The museum had on display a horse's bridle and _____ that dated from the _____ of Henry the Eighth.

16. When it started to _____, he pulled the _____ tighter to control the horse.

raise *(verb)*   to move upward; to awaken; to increase; to collect
    (noun)   an increase in salary
rays *(noun)*   thin lines or beams of radiation
raze *(verb)*   to tear down or demolish

17. They are going to _____ that old building if the town cannot _____ enough money to save it.

18. When he met his boss, he _____ the question of a _____ for the new year.

19. Before the last _____ of the sun had disappeared behind the hills, the woman who had run the farm and _____ five children by herself had died.

sight *(noun)*   the ability to see; a view
site *(noun)*   the plot of land where something is located; the place for an event
cite *(verb)*   to quote as an authority or example

20. You do not have to _____ statistics to convince us of the importance of caring for our sense of _____.

21. They tried to convince her that the _____ was a good one for a house, and they even began to _____ all kinds of evidence to prove their point.

stair *(noun)*   one of a flight of steps
stare *(noun, verb)*   a fixed gaze; to look at insistently

22. Please don't _____ at the old woman who is sleeping on the _____.

23. She stood on the top _____ giving him a long, hard _____.

stake *(noun)*   a post sharpened at one end to drive into the ground; a financial share
    (verb)   to attach or support; to set limits with a stake
steak *(noun)*   a slice of meat, usually beef

24. She drove the last _____ into the ground, then built a fire and cooked a _____.

25. If you catch the vampire, feed him raw _____ and then drive a _____ into his heart.

26. The young man _____ out a claim for a _____ in the company.

stationary *(adj.)*   standing still
stationery *(noun)*   writing paper and envelopes

27. He bought the _____ from a clerk who said nothing and remained _____ all the time behind the counter.

28. The bus remained _____ for a few moments, so I quickly wrote a few sentences on my flowered _____.

to *(prep.)*   in a direction toward
to *(+ verb)*   the infinitive form of a verb
too *(adv.)*   also; excessively; very
two *(noun)*   number

29. It is _____ bad that the _____ of you cannot agree on anything.

30. I want _____ go _____ the movies, and I hope you do _____.

vain *(adj.)*   conceited; unsuccessful
vane *(noun)*   a plate of wood or metal, often in the shape of a rooster, that pivots to indicate the direction of the wind; the weblike part of a feather
vein *(noun)*   a blood vessel; the branching framework of a leaf; an occurrence of an ore; a strip of colour; a streak; a transient attitude

31. I saw a beautiful antique weather _____ from an old barn at an auction, and I made a _____ attempt to get it.

32. I could tell the old miner was _____ when he bragged endlessly about striking a rich _____ of silver.

33. It was a good thing the patient was not _____ because during the stress test every _____ stood out on his head.

waist *(noun)*   the middle portion of a body, garment, or object
waste *(verb)*   to use thoughtlessly or carelessly
   (noun)   objects discarded as useless

34. The inexperienced seamstress _____ a metre of material trying to cut out the pattern of a gown for her client with the large _____.

35. It is a _____ of time trying to get him to admit the size of his _____.

wait *(verb)*   to remain inactive
weight *(noun)*   the measure of the heaviness of an object

36. When you are _____ for something important, time can seem

like a heavy _____.

37. I decided to _____ and see if the nurse would record my

_____.

weather *(noun)*   atmospheric conditions
whether *(conj.)* if it is the case that

38. _____ or not you choose Quebec City for your vacation, there is

no argument that the _____ there is pleasant in the summer.

39. We always listen to the _____ report _____ it's right or
wrong.

ware *(noun)*   an article of commerce
wear *(verb)*   to have on
where *(adv.)* at or in what place

40. The peddler always _____ a tweed jacket as he sells his

_____ on the street.

41. The salesclerk was helpful after I explained _____ I intended to

_____ the strange combination of clothes.

whole *(adj.)* complete
hole *(noun)*   an opening

42. I am telling you the _____ story about the _____ in
our new carpet.

43. The _____ problem about that dress was that moths had eaten

a _____ in it.

wood *(noun)*   the tough substance made from trees
would *(verb)* past tense of *will*

44. He _____ make the cabinets of solid _____ if he could
afford it.

45. Helen said she _____ come if I _____ promise to be
there.

write *(verb)* to form letters and words; to compose
right *(adj.)* conforming to justice, law, or morality; correct; toward a conser-
                    vative political point of view
         (noun)   that which is just, morally good, legal, or proper; a direction; a
                    political group whose policies are conservative
         (adv.)   directly; well; completely; immediately
rite *(noun)*   a traditional, solemn, and often religious ceremony

46. Every Canadian has the _____ to participate in the religious _____ of his or her own choosing.

47. You are probably _____ Robertson Davies will continue to _____ novels.

48. Be sure to _____ this down: make a _____ turn at the first three lights and then a left at the next stop sign; we'll be _____ there as soon as we can.

yoke *(noun)*   a harness fastening two or more animals together; a form of bondage

yolk *(noun)*   the yellow of an egg

49. _____ are used to make many sauces.

50. They struggled under the _____ of slavery.

51. He unfastened the _____ from the oxen.

Exercise 1   Words That Sound Alike

Choose the correct word, and write it in the space at the right.

1. The Hurons at one time occupied almost the (whole, hole) of what is now Simcoe County in central Ontario.   _____

2. They were efficient farmers, but relied on hunting (to, too, two).   _____

3. Their (reign, rain) extended over five tribes that came together from various parts of Ontario to form the Huron confederacy.   _____

4. Even though the (weather, whether) was inhospitable during the winter, the Hurons stored food and were comfortable in their longhouses.   _____

5. Their (principal, principle) crops were corn, beans, and squash.   _____

6. At the time of the Hurons' first contacts with the French, some of their village (cites, sights, sites) were populated by up to 3500 people.   _____

7. Their population was (raised, razed) by a smallpox epidemic in 1639.   _____

8. The Huron villages were visited by Récollet and Jesuit missionaries, whose (rights, rites, writes) convinced some Hurons to convert to Christianity.   _____

9. We (know, no) that the Hurons became important suppliers of furs to the French.   _____

10. Even though they wanted (piece, peace), the Hurons were defeated and dispersed by the Iroquois in 1649.   _____

Exercise 2   Words That Sound Alike

Choose the correct word, and write it in the space at the right. Then, on the lines provided, write a sentence using each of the words you did not choose.

1. The emperor's (rain, reign, rein) was filled with wars and revolution.   _____

_____

_____

2. We climbed to a higher point of the mountain
to get a (cite, sight, site) of the valley.   _____

_____

_____

3. I brought the meat back to the butcher because
the (wait, weight) marked on the package was
wrong.   _____

_____

_____

4. The (principal, principle) crop of Canada is
wheat.   _____

_____

_____

5. Even after the floats passed by, the children
continued to (stair, stare) down the street.   _____

_____

_____

6. The (pain, pane) was broken, and shattered
glass lay on the floor.   _____

_____

_____

7. Nutritionists feel that we should not eat too
much (stake, steak) or other red meat.   _____

_____

_____

8. Since she loved to read books on history, she
knew a great deal about the (passed, past).   _____

_____

_____

9. A (stationary, stationery) car was hit by a speed-
ing motorcycle.   _____

_____

_____

10. The pizzeria sells pizza by the (peace, piece).   _____

_____

_____

Exercise 3   **Words That Sound Alike**

Edit the following paragraph for errors in word confusions. Circle the errors and write the correct word on the lines below the paragraph.

> The magazine article sited three reasons why retired persons should consider moving to Florida. Its a serious decision for senior citizens because they don't want to waist there limited amount of time, money, or energy. The first advantage is the mild climate. Older people lose patients with the cold and dark winter whether in Canada. The days are to short, and they wish for the feeling of the warm raze of the sun. The yolk of shovelling snow and feeling chilled or isolated in the home makes winter a dreaded period to be endured. Another reason for moving to Florida is that the cost of homes and other basic needs tends to be cheaper. Senior citizens are jumping on planes from all over Canada and going to Florida to have a look at what their missing.

_____   _____

_____   _____

_____   _____

_____   _____

_____   _____

Words That Sound or Look Almost Alike

Some words are often confused with other words that sound or look almost the same. Learning to spell these words correctly involves a careful study of pronunciations along with meanings.

After studying each set for the spelling, pronunciation, and meaning, fill in the blanks with the correct word.

	Pronunciation	*Meaning*
accept	*a* as in *pat*	to receive; to admit; to regard as true or right
except	the first *e* as in *pet*	other than; but; only

1. I will buy all of the shirts _____ the blue one.

    The judge refused to _____ the evidence the lawyer presented.

    Please _____ my apologies for the delay.

access	*a* as in *pat*	a means of approaching; the right to enter or make use of
excess	the first *e* as in *pet*	a quantity or amount beyond what is required

2. The secretary denied us _____ to her files.

My father had to pay an additional $25 for his _____ baggage on the plane.

We heard that _____ to the valley would be difficult.

| advice | Pronounce -ice like the word ice. | noun: opinion as to what should be done about a problem |
| advise | Pronounce -ise like the word eyes. | verb: to suggest; to counsel |

3. I wish I had someone to _____ me.

The officer will _____ you of your rights.

She always gives her daughter good _____.

| affect | a as in about | verb: to influence |
| effect | the first e as the i in pit | noun: result verb: to bring about a result |

4. This medicine has several adverse side _____.

The new tax law will _____ the middle class.

The _____ of the tornado near Edmonton were disastrous.

| allusion | a as in about | an indirect reference |
| illusion | the first i as in pit | a mistaken concept or belief |

5. A fast elevator can give the _____ that one is not moving at all.
When the magician seemed to make his assistant hang in midair, everybody clapped at the _____.
I could tell the student was knowledgeable because of all her _____ to Atwood's novels.

| breath | ea as the e in pet | noun: the air that is inhaled or exhaled in breathing |
| breathe | the ea as the e in be | verb: to inhale and exhale air |

6. Mouthwash promises to give you a fresh _____.

The skier could see his _____ in the chilly winter air.

She told me to _____ deeply.

| clothes | o as the oe in toe | garments; wearing apparel |
| cloths | o as the aw in paw | pieces of fabric |

7. I will need three clean _____ to wash the windows.

Take warm _____ when you go camping next week.

When the family went away, they covered their furniture with large

_____.

conscience	kŏn' shəns (2 syllables)	*noun:* recognition of right and wrong
conscientious	kŏn shē en' shəs (4 syllables)	*adj.:* careful; thorough
conscious	kŏn' shəs (2 syllables)	*adj.:* awake; aware of one's own existence

8. The thief gave himself up to the police because his _____
    was bothering him.

    She was not _____ when the ambulance came to take
    her to the hospital.

    She had done nothing wrong, so she was able to give her testimony in

    court with a clear _____.

    When the company hired a night watchman, they needed someone who

    was very _____.

| costume | *o* as in *pot, u* as the *oo* in *boot* | a special style of dress for a particular occasion |
| custom | *u* as in *cut, o* as in *gallop* | a common tradition |

9. It's the _____ every Halloween for children to wear

    _____.

    Before you visit a foreign country, you should become familiar with its

    _____ so that you won't unknowingly offend anyone.

council		*noun:* a group that governs
counsel	*ou* as in *out*	*verb:* to give advice
		noun: a lawyer; advice
consul	*o* as in *pot*	*noun:* a governmental official in the foreign service

10. The doctor gave the patient good _____.

    I wrote to the Canadian _____ to inquire about my
    visa.

    Your faculty adviser will _____ you about what
    courses you should take.

    The _____ met to discuss the new laws.

| desert | di zurt' *i* as in *pit* | *verb:* to abandon |
| | dez'ert the first *e* as in *pet* | *noun:* barren land |

dessert	di zurt' *i* as in *pit*	*noun:* last part of a meal, often a sweet

11. The teenagers _____ the old car on the side of the road.

    She dreamed of a cruise to a _____ island.

    We made a chocolate layer cake for _____ .

    The camel is an animal suited to the _____ .

diner	*i* as the *ie* in *pie*	a person eating dinner; a restaurant with a long counter and booths
dinner	*i* as in *pit*	chief meal of the day

12. We went to the _____ for an inexpensive meal.

    All I want for _____ is a salad.

    The _____ asked the waitress for another cup of coffee.

emigrate emigrant	} *e* as in *pet*	to go out of a country someone who leaves a country to settle in another country
immigrate immigrant	} the first *i* as in *pit*	to come into a country someone who enters a country to settle there

13. My parents _____ from Greece.

    They _____ to Canada in 1948.

    Irish _____ have been arriving in Canada since the seventeenth century.

farther	*a* as in *father*	greater physical or measurable distance
further	*u* as in *urge*	greater mental distance; more distant in time or degree; additional

14. I walked one kilometre _____ .

    She advised us to think _____ about the problem.

    Let's not travel any _____ tonight.

local	lo' kəl *a* as in *about*	*adj.:* relating or peculiar to a place
locale	lo kal' *a* as in *pat*	*noun:* a place, scene, or setting, as of a novel

15. While I am in the _____ , I will visit my cousin.

    Is there any interesting _____ news today?

The _____ is a small town in southern Saskatchewan.

moral	mor' al Pronounce the *a* as in *about;* the accent is on the first syllable.	*adj.:* a sense of right and wrong *noun:* the lesson of a story, fable, or event
morale	mo ral' Pronounce the *a* as in *pat;* the accent is on the second syllable.	the attitude or spirit of a person or group of people

16. Mr. Jefferson felt a _____ obligation toward his neighbours.

    The _____ of the prisoners is very low.

    The _____ of the story is "Look before you leap."

personal	per' son al Accent is on the first syllable.	*adj.:* pertaining to a particular person
personnel	per son nel' Accent is on the third syllable.	*noun:* the people employed by an organization; an administrative division of an organization concerned with the employees

17. She went to the _____ office to discuss her problem. Chico wouldn't tell us what his problem was; he said it was

    _____.

    Most of the _____ at this company are well trained.

precede	Pronounce the first *e* as the *i* in *pit.*	to come before
proceed	Pronounce the *o* as the *oe* in *toe.*	to continue

18. When Stuart changed schools, his reputation _____ him.

    You may now _____ through the intersection.

    The chef will describe how you should _____ with the pastry.

quiet	qui' et *i* as the *ie* in *pie, e* as in *pet*	silence
quit	*i* as in *pit*	to give up; to stop
quite	*i* as the *ie* in *pie;* the *e* is silent	somewhat; completely; truly

19. That woman is _____ a dancer!

    Be _____ while she is performing.

    She says she will _____ soon if she cannot find a job.

| receipt | Pronounce the first *e* as the *i* in *pit*, *ei* as in the *e* in *be*; the *p* is silent. | a bill marked as paid; the act of receiving something |
| recipe | Pronounce the first *e* as in *pet*, the *i* like the *a* in *about*, the final *e* as in *be*. | a formula for preparing a mixture, especially in cooking |

20. Please give me your special _____ for boiled dumplings.

    I cannot return the dress because I lost the _____.

    Keep your _____ for tax purposes.

| special | spe cial | *adj.*: exceptional; distinctive |
| especially | Notice the extra syllable at the beginning. | *adv.*: particularly |

21. He made several _____ trips to visit his father when he was in the hospital.

    The father was _____ happy to see his son.

    Now that he was so sick, they seemed to get along _____ well.

| than | a as in *pat* | *conj.*: used to make a comparison |
| then | e as in *pet* | *adv.*: at that time; in that case |

22. First he came home late; _____ he blamed me for the cold food.

    This cake is sweeter _____ the one my mother makes.

    I would rather try and fail _____ never try at all.

thorough	the first *o* as the *u* in *urge*, *ou* as the *oe* in *toe*	finished; fully done
though	*ou* as the *oe* in *toe*	however; despite the fact
thought	*ou* as the *aw* in *paw*	past tense of *to think*
through	*ou* as the *oo* in *boot*	preposition used to indicate entrance at one side and exit from the other

threw	sounds like *through*	past tense of *to throw*

- *Thru* is only an informal spelling for the word *through*.

23. He was deep in _____ when the doorbell rang.

    When she walked _____ the door, he didn't recognize

    her even _____ he had known her all his life.

    Then she _____ him a set of keys and said, "You've

    made such a _____ mess of everything. I'm

    _____!"

Exercise 1 Working with Words That Sound or Look Almost Alike

Complete each of the following sentences by choosing the correct word.

1. She told the manager she would like very much to work in the

   _____ office of the company.
   (personal, personnel)

2. He told the police that his _____ mind could not re-
   (conscious, conscience, conscientious)
   call what happened.

3. Northern Africa is becoming a vast _____.
   (desert, dessert)

4. The apartment was dangerous to live in because there was no

   _____ to a fire escape.
   (access, excess)

5. I met her after work at the _____, where we both
   (diner, dinner)
   joked with the owner and the waiters.

6. We decided it was not a good _____ for a store.
   (local, locale)

7. The snow is so deep I cannot walk any _____.
   (further, farther)

8. The magician gave the _____ of starting a fire on stage.
   (allusion, illusion)

9. The machine isn't working well even _____ it's new.
   (thorough, though, thought, through)

10. My father wears that clown _____ every Halloween.
    (custom, costume)

Exercise 2 Working with Words That Sound or Look Almost Alike

Complete each of the following sentences by choosing the correct word.

1. It is _____ a place to take a vacation!
   (quiet, quite)

2. His case was so complicated that he knew he needed a lawyer's

   _____.

   (council, counsel, consul)

3. A weekend vacation is better _____ none at all.

   (than, then)

4. Please _____ my apologies for all the damage done to

   (accept, except)

   your car.

5. They had to _____ from their native country in order

   (emigrate, immigrate)

   to find work.

6. The captain tried to improve the _____ of his crew by

   (moral, morale)

   showing them a movie.

7. If you are going to wash the car, take several of the clean

   _____ from the bag under the sink.

   (cloths, clothes)

8. As she wandered in the desert, she had the _____ that

   (illusion, allusion)

   there was a city in front of her.

9. One _____ of the strike was an increase in the work-

   (affect, effect)

   ers' salaries.

10. Do not speak about the matter any _____.

    (further, farther)

Exercise 3 Writing Sentences Using Words That Sound or Look Almost Alike

Write your own sentences using the following words.

1. special

   _____

   especially

   _____

2. breath

   _____

   breathe

   _____

3. precede

   _____

   proceed

   _____

4. receipt

   _____

   recipe

   _____

5. advice

_____

advise

_____

Words That Sound or Look Almost Alike: *sit/set; rise/raise; lie/lay*

These six verbs are among the most troublesome verbs in English because each verb is similar in sound, spelling, and meaning to another verb. Since they are all irregular verbs, students must be careful to learn to spell the principal parts correctly. The key to learning how to use the verbs *sit*, *rise*, and *lie* is to remember that these are actions the subject can do without any help; no other person or thing has to be included in the sentence. When you use the verbs *set*, *raise*, and *lay* in a sentence, the actions of these verbs are done to other persons or objects; these persons or things have to be included directly in the sentence. For example, when you use the verb *to sit*, all you need is a subject and a form of the verb:

I sit.

However, when you use the verb *to set*, you need a subject, a form of the verb, and an object. For example:

I set the glass on the table.

The subject *I* and the verb *set* are followed by the object *glass*, which is what the subject set on the table.

sit: to take a sitting position *never* takes an object	**set:** to place something into position *always* takes an object

Present:	I *sit*.	I *set the glass* down.
Present participle:	I *am sitting*.	I *am setting the glass* down.
Past:	I *sat*.	I *set the glass* down.
Past participle:	I *have sat*.	I *have set the glass* down.

Fill in each of the following blanks with the correct form of the verb *sit* or *set*. Check your answers in the Answer Key.

1. I _____ the table today.

   I have _____ the suitcases in your room.

   I am _____ in my favourite rocking chair.

   She likes me to _____ by her bed and read to her in the evening.

rise: to stand up; to move upward *never* takes an object	**raise:** to make something move up or grow *always* takes an object

Present:	I *rise*.	I *raise the flag*.
Present participle:	The sun *is rising*.	I *am raising the flag*.
Past:	He *rose* at eight o'clock.	I *raised the flag*.
Past participle:	I *have risen* early today.	I *have raised the flag*.

Fill in each of the following blanks with the correct form of the verb *rise* or *raise*. Check your answers in the Answer Key.

2.   Last spring the manufacturer _____ the prices.

Yesterday the prices of the magazines _____ by a dime.

When I entered the room, the woman _____ to greet me.

The woman _____ her head when I entered the room.

The verbs *lie* and *lay* are easily confused because two of their principal parts have the same spelling. It takes concentration to learn to use these two verbs correctly.

lie: to recline
  never takes an object

lay: to put
  always takes an object

Present:	I *lie* down.	I *lay the pen* down.
Present participle:	I *am lying* down.	I *am laying the pen* down.
Past:	Yesterday I *lay* down.	I *laid the pen* down.
Past participle:	I *have lain* down.	I *have laid the pen* down.

- The verb *lie* can also be a regular verb meaning "to tell an untruth." The principal parts of this verb are *lie, lying, lied, has lied.*

Fill in each of the following blanks with the correct form of the verb *lie* or *lay*. Check your answers in the Answer Key.

3.   I usually _____ down in the afternoon.

The auto mechanic is _____ under the car.

I can't remember where I _____ my keys.

The child has _____ in the crib all afternoon.

This young man always _____ the carpet in our house.

The witness _____ under oath when she was questioned.

Her coat _____ on the floor until I noticed it.

Exercise 1   Understanding *sit/set; rise/raise; lie/lay*

Fill in the blanks with the correct form of the verbs.

1.   The cat has _____ in the sun all day.
     (lie, lay)

2.   If you feel sick, _____ down on that bed.
     (lie, lay)

3.   The elevator always _____ quickly to the tenth floor.
     (rise, raise)

4.   The boss _____ her salary twice this year.
    (rise, raise)

5.   The parents _____ down the law when their son came
    (lie, lay)
home late.

6. The carpenters _____ the roof when they remodelled
   (rise, raise)
   the house.

7. The dog _____ up every night and begs for food.
   (sit, set)

8. Last week I _____ in front of my television set nearly
   (sit, set)
   every night.

9. I always watch the waiter _____ on a stool after his
   (sit, set)
   shift is done.

10. We have _____ a plate of cookies and milk out for
    (sit, set)
    Santa Claus every year since the children were born.

Exercise 2 Understanding *sit/set; rise/raise; lie/lay*

Fill in the blanks with the correct form of the verbs.

1. New apartment buildings are _____ in the city.
   (rise, raise)

2. When the baby-sitter arrived, the child's toys were

   _____ scattered all over the house.
   (lie, lay)

3. The moon has _____ behind the clouds all week.
   (lie, lay)

4. _____ those apples on the table, please.
   (Sit, Set)

5. My mother has _____ four children.
   (rise, raise)

6. The kitten _____ in the basket for three weeks.
   (lie, lay)

7. He _____ the cup to his mouth and drank.
   (rise, raise)

8. I will _____ and knead the bread dough.
   (sit, set)

9. A snowstorm is _____ in the north.
   (rise, raise)

10. I _____ the bricks by the driveway yesterday.
    (lie, lay)

Exercise 3 Understanding *sit/set; rise/raise; lie/lay*

Fill in the blanks with the correct form of the verbs.

1. This year the price of food has _____ dramatically.
   (rise, raise)

2. Robert had _____ unconscious for several minutes be-
      (lie, lay)

   fore the ambulance arrived.

3. Let's _____ here awhile and rest.
      (sit, set)

4. She came right home and _____ down.
      (lie, lay)

5. Please _____ the windows for some fresh air.
      (rise, raise)

6. I _____ my feet on Canadian soil in 1983.
      (sit, set)

7. I had _____ at my favourite table.
      (sit, set)

8. The waiter, as usual, had _____ a reserved sign on the
      (lie, lay)

   table to save it for me.

9. The aroma of fresh bread _____ up from the table.
      (rise, raise)

10. I would probably have to _____ down after this
      (lie, lay)

   meal.

Exercise 4   Understanding *sit/set; rise/raise; lie/lay*

Construct your own sentences using the following words correctly.

1. lie (to recline)

   _____

2. laying

   _____

3. set

   _____

4. rose

   _____

5. lain

   _____

6. lying

   _____

7. raised

   _____

8. laid

   _____

9. lay (to put)

   _____

10. risen

   _____

Words That Sound or Look Almost Alike: *choose/chose; lose/loose; lead/led; die/dye*

These verbs are often misspelled because there is confusion about how to spell the vowel sounds of the verbs. Study the spelling of the principal parts below.

Present	*Present Participle*	*Past*	*Past Participle*
choose	choosing	chose	has chosen
lose	losing	lost	has lost
lead	leading	led	has led
die	dying	died	has died

- *Loose* is an adjective meaning "not tightly fitted." Remember, it rhymes with *goose*.
- *Lead* can also be a noun meaning a bluish white metal. Remember, it rhymes with *head*.
- *Dye* is another verb meaning "to colour." Its principal parts are *dye, dyeing, dyed, has dyed*.

1. Fill in the blanks with the correct form of the verb *choose*.

   Yesterday I _____ Maggie for my lab partner.

   Today I _____ Jeff.

   He always _____ his friends for his partners.

2. Fill in the blanks with the correct form of the verb *lose*.

   Our team _____ the game Sunday.

   We always _____ when we play that team.

   Whenever she plays chess with her sister, she _____ .

3. Fill in the blanks with the correct form of the verb *lead*.

   Yesterday I _____ the students in singing our class song.

   Tomorrow I will _____ the students again.

   Have you ever _____ a group in singing?

4. Fill in the blanks with the correct form of the verb *die*.

   The sound of the train whistle is slowly _____ away.

   The deer have _____ from lack of food.

   Her hope _____ when she saw the empty mailbox.

Words That Sound or Look Almost Alike: *use/used; suppose/ supposed*

To use means *to bring or put into service; to make use of.*

> *Present:* I usually *use* my brother's bike to get to school.
> *Past:* Yesterday I *used* my father's car.

Used to means *to have as a custom* or *regular practice* in the past.

I *used to* take the bus downtown, but now I get a ride with my neighbour.

A form of *to be* + *used to* means *to be familiar with* or *accustomed to*.

I am not *used to* walking to school.

To suppose means *to guess*.

Present: I *suppose* he is trying.
Past: I *supposed* he was trying.

A form of *to be* + *supposed to* means *ought to* or *should*.

Waiters *are supposed to* be courteous.

Many people have difficulty knowing when to choose *used* and *supposed* in their writing because in speaking, the final *d* is often not clearly heard.

Incorrect: I am *suppose to* be in school today.
Correct: I am *supposed to* be in school today.

Fill in the blanks with the correct form of the verb *use* or *suppose*.

use or *used to*

I always _____ a pen in English class now.

I always _____ to write with a pencil.

Were they _____ to studying several hours a day?

suppose or *supposed to*

I am _____ to help my sister today.

I _____ I will have to help my sister tomorrow.

I was _____ to help her yesterday.

Exercise 1   Using *choose, lose, lead, die, use,* and *suppose*

Fill in the blanks with the correct form of the verb.

1. I am _____ what courses to study next semester.
          (choose)

2. Last semester my friend _____ me to believe I would
                                    (lead)
    love astronomy.

3. He forgot to tell me I was _____ to have a good math
                                        (suppose)
    background.

4. Next semester I will be sure to _____ from the fresh-
                                            (choose)
    man-level courses.

5. I hope I won't _____ my scholarship.
                        (lose, loose)

6. My father _____ last year, so I need financial support.
                    (die)

7. I am _____ to working hard.
              (use)

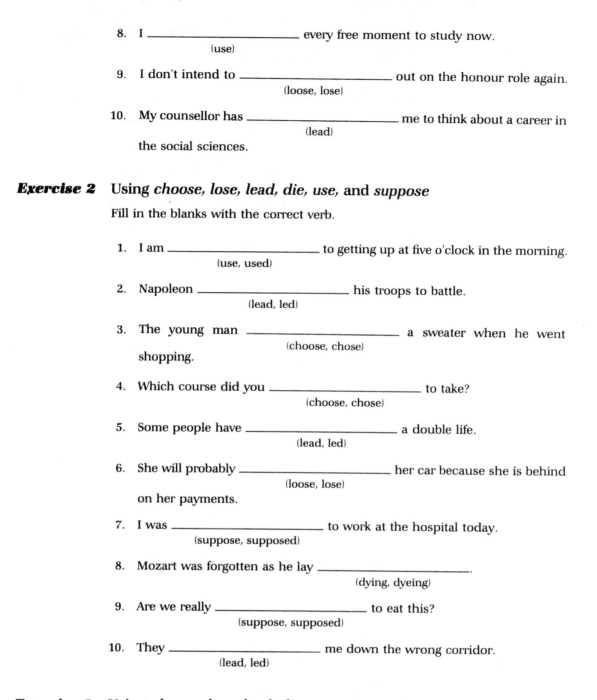

8. I _____ every free moment to study now.
    (use)

9. I don't intend to _____ out on the honour role again.
    (loose, lose)

10. My counsellor has _____ me to think about a career in
    (lead)
    the social sciences.

Exercise 2   Using *choose, lose, lead, die, use,* and *suppose*

Fill in the blanks with the correct verb.

1. I am _____ to getting up at five o'clock in the morning.
    (use, used)

2. Napoleon _____ his troops to battle.
    (lead, led)

3. The young man _____ a sweater when he went
    (choose, chose)
    shopping.

4. Which course did you _____ to take?
    (choose, chose)

5. Some people have _____ a double life.
    (lead, led)

6. She will probably _____ her car because she is behind
    (loose, lose)
    on her payments.

7. I was _____ to work at the hospital today.
    (suppose, supposed)

8. Mozart was forgotten as he lay _____.
    (dying, dyeing)

9. Are we really _____ to eat this?
    (suppose, supposed)

10. They _____ me down the wrong corridor.
    (lead, led)

Exercise 3   Using *choose, lose, lead, die, use,* and *suppose*

Ten words in the following paragraph are underlined. If the word is used correctly, mark the answer blank with a C. If the word is used incorrectly, write
the correct word choice.

Tomorrow we (1) chose partners for tennis. I hope I won't (2) loose
every game this summer. Jennifer and Corey always (3) lead no matter
whom they play. Jason's enthusiasm for the game seems to be (4) dieing.
Like me, he also (5) loses every game he plays. He and I should (6) chose
a sport we are better suited for. We both (7) use to do much more
swimming in the summer. I (8) suppose we stopped because the pool
fees doubled in price. Now we (9) use the tennis courts behind the

elementary school for free. The town is (10) <u>suppose</u> to charge a fee, but nobody ever enforces the ruling.

1. _____   6. _____

2. _____   7. _____

3. _____   8. _____

4. _____   9. _____

5. _____   10. _____

How Much Have You Learned?

Name _____

Date _____

1. _____
2. _____
3. _____
4. _____
5. _____
6. _____
7. _____
8. _____
9. _____
10. _____
11. _____
12. _____
13. _____
14. _____
15. _____
16. _____
17. _____
18. _____
19. _____
20. _____
21. _____
22. _____
23. _____
24. _____
25. _____

26. _____
27. _____
28. _____
29. _____
30. _____
31. _____
32. _____
33. _____
34. _____
35. _____
36. _____
37. _____
38. _____
39. _____
40. _____
41. _____
42. _____
43. _____
44. _____
45. _____
46. _____
47. _____
48. _____
49. _____
50. _____

How Much Do You Already Know?

The Appendices cover several other problems with words that you may or may not need to study. Your instructor may at this point give you a test to find out what areas of the Appendices you should study. Before going on to Part II, you will need to practise those areas in which you are weak.

1. _____	18. _____	35. _____
2. _____	19. _____	36. _____
3. _____	20. _____	37. _____
4. _____	21. _____	38. _____
5. _____	22. _____	39. _____
6. _____	23. _____	40. _____
7. _____	24. _____	41. _____
8. _____	25. _____	42. _____
9. _____	26. _____	43. _____
10. _____	27. _____	44. _____
11. _____	28. _____	45. _____
12. _____	29. _____	46. _____
13. _____	30. _____	47. _____
14. _____	31. _____	48. _____
15. _____	32. _____	49. _____
16. _____	33. _____	50. _____
17. _____	34. _____	

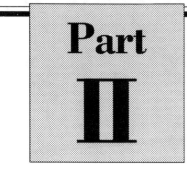

Part II

Developing the Complete Sentence

How Much Do You Already Know?

The following test will check what you already know about effective English sentences. Below are test questions from each chapter in Part II. Follow the directions under each heading.

Finding Subjects and Verbs in Simple Sentences

In each of the following sentences, find the subject and verb. Write your answers in the spaces provided.

Subject	*Verb*	
_____	_____	1. Nearly 65 000 couples end their marriages every year in Canada.
_____	_____	2. In this country, the average length of a marriage is just over twelve years.
_____	_____	3. Many studies have been done on the reasons for the breakup of marriages.
_____	_____	4. There has not been so much attention given to successful marriages.
_____	_____	5. A positive attitude toward the partner appears to be the most important quality in a successful marriage.

The Fragment

Some of the examples below are complete sentences; some are fragments (only parts of sentences). Write *C* if the example is a complete sentence. Write *F* if the example is a fragment.

_____   6.   Chocolate was discovered in the New World.

_____   7.   By explorers such as Columbus and Cortés.

_____   8.   The natives drinking a beverage never seen before by the Europeans.

_____   9.   Spanish conquerors added cane sugar to the drink.

_____   10.   To make it more pleasant for European tastes.

Combining Sentences Using Subordination and Co-ordination

Each of the following pairs of sentences could be combined into a single sentence. Among the four choices given, place an *X* in front of the example that is correct.

11.   Chocolate became a popular drink throughout Europe.
      It was thought to be good for your health.

_____   a.   Chocolate became a popular drink throughout Europe, it was thought to be good for your health.

____✓____   b.   Chocolate became a popular drink throughout Europe because it was thought to be good for your health.

_____   c.   Chocolate became a popular drink throughout Europe, but it was thought to be good for your health.

_____   d.   Chocolate became a popular drink throughout Europe and good for your health.

12.   A method was found in Switzerland in 1875 to make solid milk chocolate.
      Modern chocolate candy was born.

_____   a.   A method was found in Switzerland in 1875 to make solid milk chocolate then modern chocolate candy was born.

_____   b.   A method was found in Switzerland in 1875 to make solid milk chocolate; and modern chocolate candy was born.

_____   c.   A method was found in Switzerland in 1875 to make solid milk chocolate therefore modern chocolate candy was born.

____✓____   d.   When a method was found in Switzerland in 1875 to make solid milk chocolate, modern chocolate candy was born.

13.   Most people think chocolate causes tooth decay.
      Some researchers claim chocolate has an ingredient that actually helps prevent cavities.

____✓____   a.   Most people think chocolate causes tooth decay; however, some researchers claim chocolate has an ingredient that actually prevents cavities.

_____   b.   Since most people think chocolate causes tooth decay, some researchers claim chocolate has an ingredient that actually prevents cavities.

_____   c.   Most people think chocolate causes tooth decay, and some researchers claim chocolate has an ingredient that actually prevents cavities.

_____   d.   Most people think chocolate causes tooth decay, some researchers claim chocolate has an ingredient that actually prevents cavities.

Give two ways of combining the following two sentences into one sentence.

Living near a candy store is no advantage.
I have gained three kilograms and lost sixteen dollars this month.

14.   _____

_____

_____

15.   _____

_____

_____

The Run-on

Some of the examples below are complete sentences; some are run-ons (sentences incorrectly joined together). Write *C* if the example is a complete sentence. Write *R* if the example is a run-on.

_____   16.   Strong competition exists among chocolate companies, each carefully guards its own recipes.

_____   17.   In 1980, newspapers all over the world carried the story of the great chocolate recipe robbery it sounded like a spy movie.

_____   18.   A young worker for a Swiss chocolate company needed money to buy an automobile so he tried to sell the secret company recipes to Saudi Arabia, Russia, and China.

_____   19.   The worker thought the recipes were safely hidden in a locker in a train station, but the Swiss police caught him and recovered the recipes.

_____   20.   The company decided not to press charges the worker was given a suspended sentence.

Punctuation: Commas

In each of the following sentences, place commas wherever they are needed.

21.   White-collar criminals dishonest company executives are being exposed in growing numbers.

22. White-collar criminals are found in industrial plants government offices and banks.

23. For example manufacturers have been caught cheating the government and well-known banks have been caught laundering money.

24. In the past white-collar criminals have not been prosecuted very vigorously by the law.

25. However some executives are now being given jail sentences for their white-collar crimes.

26. The small fines and short prison terms are rarely effective.

27. If the management of the company is unethical that attitude filters down to other workers in the company.

28. Both judges and laymen are uncertain whether those who have been convicted for acts against consumers employees rivals or the environment are truly criminals.

29. Breaking computer codes and copying private information or records is an example of modern white-collar crime.

30. When more corporations emphasize the importance of ethical conduct the public will regain the trust that has been lost by business government and all institutions.

Other Marks of Punctuation

In each of the following sentences, place marks of punctuation wherever they are needed. Choose from the list of punctuation marks below.

semicolon   ;
colon   :
dash   —
parentheses   ( )
quotation marks   " "

31. Last Sunday our local newspaper carried an article entitled Why References Aren't Available on Request.

32. Employers even my own boss are increasingly afraid to give out frank and detailed references because of the growing trend among individuals and companies to sue one another over real or imagined wrongs.

33. The key word, say attorneys, is safer.

34. The less information an employer gives, the safer he is the less subjective that information is, the greater his safety.

35. There are three main grounds on which lawsuits over letters of reference have been filed libel, discrimination, and negligence.

Making Agreement within the Sentence

On the line before each sentence, write the correct form of the verb.

_____   36. The history of trading in spices (goes, go) back thousands of years.

_____ 37. Some writers from ancient Rome (has, have) recorded cinnamon being brought to Italy from Africa in the first century A.D.

_____ 38. In the year 1252, the famous traveller Marco Polo reported that pepper and ginger (was, were) being imported to China from India.

_____ 39. Each group of explorers that went to Asia (was, were) astonished at the number of unusual spices to be found there.

_____ 40. Not only pepper but also cloves (was, were) among the spices that offered great wealth to those who could supply European and North American markets.

Parallel Structure

Each of the following sentences needs parallel structure. Underline the word, phrase, or clause that is incorrect, and write the correct form on the line provided.

_____ 41. Agents generally agree that most fashion models should be tall, young, and with a slender body type.

_____ 42. Having an elaborate portfolio, owning a fashionable wardrobe, or to have connections with the right people are not necessary in modelling, despite what people think.

_____ 43. With good planning and lucky, the successful model can enjoy a career of ten to twelve years.

More Practice with Fragments and Run-ons

Revise the following sentences so that they are acceptable.

44. Because of the severity of the snowstorm and the fact that my brother was ill.

_____

_____

_____

_____

45. We tried to take him to the hospital on our neighbour's toboggan and being in the middle of the night with the wind howling and no cars or other vehicles getting up or down our wretched mountain.

_____

_____

_____

_____

Editing Sentences for Errors

Each of the following sentences contains a sentence error. Revise the sentence so that it is complete and correct.

46.   These sort of tests are very helpful because you realize what you need to learn.

_____

_____

47.   No one wants to spend their time working on things they already know.

_____

_____

48.   It said it was going to rain today.

_____

49.   Please bring me the following items from the store, paper towels, a roll of film, a litre of milk, and a loaf of rye bread.

_____

_____

_____

50.   The assignment for Monday is long however I know I'll enjoy the reading because the topic interests me.

_____

_____

_____

Score _____

3 Finding Subjects and Verbs in Simple Sentences

Why Should We Use Complete Sentences When We Write?

If you walk up to a friend at noon and say, "Lunch?" you are expressing an idea by using a shortened form of a complete thought: you are asking your friend to join you for lunch. Even though we do not always use complete sentences in daily conversation, we usually have complete thoughts in mind. We say and hear words and phrases such as "Lunch?" every day, and these words and phrases seem to be complete thoughts because both the speaker and the listener supply the missing words in their own minds. When your friend hears you say the word "Lunch?" he or she is able to quickly understand the meaning: "Would you like to join me for lunch?"

You are free to use language in this way when you speak, but you must use a different approach in your college writing. In writing down your thoughts, you cannot assume that another person will finish your thoughts for you. Each of your written thoughts must be a complete expression of what is in your mind.

The purpose of writing is to communicate something of value to a reader. Once you understand how the parts of a complete sentence work, you will be able to focus as much attention on *what* you are saying as you devote to *how* you are saying it. Once you understand how the parts of a complete sentence work, you can take control of the sentence. You will have the power to make words work for you.

What Is a Complete Sentence?

A complete sentence must contain a subject and a verb, as well as express a complete thought.

How Do You Find the Subject of a Sentence?

To find the subject of any sentence, ask yourself this question: Who or what is the sentence about? When you have answered this question, you have found the subject of the sentence.

Practice   Examine each of the following sentences and ask yourself who or what each sentence is about. Draw a line under the subject in each sentence.

1. Niki Turner ran.
2. The young girl ran.
3. She ran.
4. The streetlights glowed.
5. They illuminated the village.
6. A thought suddenly struck her.
7. Her brother and his wife would be astonished.

Now that you have worked with these seven sentences, study the following explanations, which will give you a more thorough understanding of subjects in sentences. As you study these explanations, pay special attention to the following terms: proper and common nouns, concrete and abstract nouns, adjective, pronoun, direct object, and compound subject.

1. *Niki Turner* ran.

   Who is this sentence about? The sentence is about "Niki Turner." Words such as *Niki, Alan Paton,* and *South Africa* are called proper nouns. *Proper nouns* name particular persons, places, or things. Notice that proper nouns are always capitalized.

2. The young *girl* ran.

   Who or what is the sentence about? The sentence is about a "girl." It is a *common noun.* Most nouns are common nouns. Common nouns are not capitalized.

   • Words like *the* and *young* can be put in front of nouns to describe them further. These words are called *adjectives.* (The words *the* and *a* are also known as *articles.*)

3. *She* ran.

   Who or what is the sentence about? The sentence is about "she." Words such as *she, he, it, we, I, you,* and *they* are called *pronouns.* Pronouns can be used in the place of nouns.

4. The *streetlights* glowed.

   Who or what is the sentence about? The sentence is about "streetlights." Subjects are often things rather than people. These "things" can be proper nouns or common nouns.

5. *They* illuminated the village.

   Who or what is the sentence about? The sentence is about "they." The pronoun *they* refers to a noun already mentioned. In this case the noun already mentioned is the word *streetlights* in the sentence above.

   Nouns and pronouns can be subjects of sentences, but they can also have other functions in a sentence. Do not confuse the subject noun or pronoun with other nouns or pronouns in a sentence. Remember that subjects are usually found in the early part of the sentence, before the verb. In this case the word *village* is a noun, but it is not the subject of the sentence. The noun *village* has a different function in the sentence. (It is called the *direct object* of the verb.) A noun that is the direct object in a sentence cannot be the subject.

6. A *thought* suddenly struck her.

Who or what is the sentence about? The sentence is about "thought." The noun *thought* is an abstract noun. It cannot be seen or touched. *Abstract nouns* can be concepts, ideas, or qualities. Nouns like *truth, justice,* and *health* are other examples of abstract nouns. The opposite of an abstract noun is a *concrete noun* like *girl, streetlights,* or *village.* These concrete nouns can be seen and touched.

7. Her *brother* and his *wife* would be astonished.

Who or what is the sentence about? The subject of this sentence has two nouns: *brother* and *wife.* This is called a compound subject. A *compound subject* is made up of two or more nouns joined together by *and, or, either/ or,* or *neither/nor.*

> *Examples:*   Her brother or his wife will come.
>
> Either her brother or his wife will come.

Guide to Finding the Subject of a Sentence

Definition: The subject of a sentence is who or what the sentence is about.
How to find the subject: Ask yourself, "Who or what is this sentence about?"

- Subjects usually come early in the sentence.
- Subjects can be modified by adjectives.
- Subjects can be compound.

Look for these two kinds of words as your subjects:

1. **Nouns:** the names of persons, places, or things

Common	or	Proper	Concrete	or	Abstract
aunt		Aunt Mary	face		loneliness
country		Nigeria	people		patriotism
watch		Timex	jewellery		time

2. **Pronouns:** take the place of nouns

Personal	Indefinite		Relative	Demonstrative
I	one		who	this
you	each		that	that
he, she, it	some, someone, somebody, something,		what	these
we	any, anyone, anybody, anything			those
they	nobody, nothing			
	everyone, everybody, everything,			
	all			
	many			
	several			

Exercise 1   Finding the Subject of a Sentence

Underline the subject in each of the following sentences.

1. The train stopped.
2. Steven Laye had arrived!

3.   He was afraid.
4.   Everything looked so strange.
5.   The fearful man held his bag tightly.
6.   The tunnel led up to the street.
7.   Buses and cars choked the avenues.
8.   People rushed everywhere.
9.   The noise made his head ache.
10.   Loneliness filled his heart.

Exercise 2   Finding the Subject of a Sentence

Underline the subject in each of the following sentences.

1.   The road twisted and turned.
2.   A young boy hurried along briskly.
3.   He carried an important message.
4.   A red-winged blackbird flew overhead.
5.   Dark clouds and a sudden wind encouraged him to hurry faster.
6.   His family would be elated.
7.   Someone was working in the yard.
8.   His father called out his name.
9.   The old man tore open the envelope.
10.   The message was brief.

Exercise 3   Finding the Subject of a Sentence

Underline the subject in each of the following sentences.

1.   The race to the South Pole was won by Roald Amundsen.
2.   Some were not so lucky to return alive from the race.
3.   Adventure and suffering fill the pages of Antarctica's history.
4.   It is being developed largely by the efforts of science rather than by the needs of politics or religion.
5.   A great percentage of Antarctica is covered in ice with an average thickness of 1.6 kilometres.
6.   Sixteen nations have laid claims to the mineral resources there.
7.   International co-operation among scientists in Antarctica is common.
8.   One project is to better understand glacial history.
9.   The fate of Antarctica's ice sheet may be linked to the "greenhouse effect."
10.   According to this theory, many cities around the world would be flooded in the event of any significant melting of Antarctica's ice.

How Do You Find the Subject in Sentences with Prepositional Phrases?

The sentences you worked with in Exercises 1 and 2 were short and basic. If we wrote only such sentences, our writing would sound choppy. Complex ideas would be difficult to express. One way to expand the simple sentence is to add prepositional phrases.

Example: He put his suitcase on the seat.

On is a preposition.
Seat is a noun used as the object of the preposition.
On the seat is the prepositional phrase.

A *prepositional phrase* is a group of words containing a preposition and an object of the preposition with its modifiers. Prepositional phrases contain nouns, but these nouns are *never* the subject of the sentence.

In sentences with prepositional phrases, the subject may be difficult to spot. Consider the following sentence:

In the young man's apartment, books covered the walls.

Who or what is the sentence about?

To avoid making the mistake of thinking that a noun in the prepositional phrase could be the subject, it is a good practice to cross out the prepositional phrase. In the sentence above, what is the prepositional phrase?

~~In the young man's apartment~~, books covered the walls.

With the prepositional phrase crossed out, it now becomes clear that the subject of the sentence is the noun *books*.

- When you are looking for the subject of a sentence, do not look for it within the prepositional phrase.

You can easily recognize a prepositional phrase because it always begins with a preposition. Study the following list so that you will be able to quickly recognize all of the common prepositions.

List of Common Prepositions

about	between	on
above	by	over
across	during	to, toward
after	for	through
among	from	under
around	in, into	up, upon
at	like	with
before	near	
beside	of	

Exercise 1   **Finding Subjects in Sentences with Prepositional Phrases**

Below are ten common prepositions. Use each preposition to write a prepositional phrase. Then write a sentence containing that prepositional phrase. Two examples are done for you.

- Notice that when a prepositional phrase begins a sentence, a comma usually follows that prepositional phrase. (Sometimes, if the prepositional phrase is short, the comma is omitted.)

Preposition	*Prepositional Phrase*	*Sentence*
before	before breakfast	My cousin called before breakfast.
between	between the two barns	Between the two barns, the old Buick lay rusting.
1. in	_____	_____
		_____
		_____

2.   with   _____   _____
                                       _____

3.   of   _____   _____
                                       _____

4.   from   _____   _____
                                       _____

5.   during   _____   _____
                                       _____

6.   by   _____   _____
                                       _____

7.   for   _____   _____
                                       _____

8.   through   _____   _____
                                       _____

9.   on   _____   _____
                                       _____

10.   beside   _____   _____
                                       _____

Exercise 2   Finding Subjects in Sentences with Prepositional Phrases

Remember that you will never find the subject of a sentence within a prepositional phrase. In each of the following sentences, cross out any prepositional phrases. Then underline the subject of each sentence. An example is done for you.

In the house of the old woman, a <u>letter</u> was found.

1.   A child arrived at the house beside the church.
2.   She knocked timidly on the door.

3. From his table, the Reverend Steven Laye looked across the room.

4. The girl had brought a letter from Johannesburg.

5. In the hope of getting some food, she waited by the side of the table.

6. The letter in her hand was dirty, especially around the stamp.

7. It had obviously been handled by many people.

8. The pastor feared the contents of the letter.

9. In Johannesburg lived several members of his family.

10. All of these close relatives seemed like phantoms to him.

Exercise 3   **Finding Subjects in Sentences with Prepositional Phrases**

Each of the following sentences contains at least one prepositional phrase. Cross out any prepositional phrases, and then underline the subject in each sentence.

1. The disappearance of sons and daughters from the lives of their parents can be devastating.

2. In their late teens and early twenties, young people often move away from home.

3. For many of them, a city offers jobs and excitement.

4. With little money and almost no experience, these young people can encounter difficulties of all kinds.

5. The fun of being independent can quickly turn into a nightmare.

6. On the other hand, young adults living with their parents often feel cheated.

7. They have no life of their own.

8. These young adults are frequently treated like children.

9. During this time, parents can be too critical.

10. From the parents' point of view, one mistake made at this time can ruin their child's life.

What Are the Other Problems in Finding Subjects?

A. Sentences with a Change in the Normal Subject Position

Some sentences begin with words that indicate that a question is being asked. Such words as *why, where, how,* and *when* give the reader the signal that a question will follow. Such opening words are not the subject. The subject will be found later on in the sentence. The following sentences begin with question words:

> Why is *he* going away?

> How did *he* find his sister in the city?

Notice that in each sentence the subject is not found in the opening part of the sentence.

B. Using *there*

The word *there* can never be the subject of a sentence.

> There is a new teacher in the department.

Who or what is this sentence about? This sentence is about a teacher. *Teacher* is the subject of the sentence.

C. Commands

Sometimes a sentence contains a verb that gives an order:

> Go to Johannesburg.

> Help your sister.

In these sentences the subject *you* is not written, but it is understood. This is the only case where the subject of a sentence may be left out when you write a sentence.

D. Sentences That Contain Appositive Phrases

An appositive phrase is a group of words in a sentence that gives us extra information about a noun in the sentence. For example:

> Stephen Laye, the aging minister, sat at his desk.

In this sentence, the words *the aging minister* make up the appositive phrase because they give you extra information about Stephen Laye. Notice that commas separate the appositive phrase from the rest of the sentence. If you leave out the appositive phrase when you read this sentence, the thought will still be complete:

> Stephen Laye sat at his desk.

Now the subject is clear: *Stephen Laye*.

- When you are looking for the subject of a sentence, you will not find it within an appositive phrase.

Exercise 1   **Finding Hidden Subjects**

Each of the following sentences contains an example of a special problem in finding the subject of a sentence. First, cross out any prepositional phrases or appositive phrases. Then underline the subject of each sentence.

1. Look at a map of South America.
2. Where is the ancient city of Chan Chan?
3. Here on the coastal desert of northern Peru stand the remains of this city of the kings.
4. Chan Chan, once the fabulously wealthy centre of the Chimor, is situated in one of the driest, bleakest regions in the world.
5. It was the largest pre-Columbian city in South America.
6. In the ruins of this city, scientists have found fragments to piece together the mystery of the past.
7. How could this civilization have survived this hostile environment and become so advanced?
8. There the people had engineered an astonishing irrigation system.
9. Unfortunately for the Chimor, Incas captured the city in the late fifteenth century and carried away much of its wealth.
10. Later, the Spanish armies brought disease and destruction to this desert people.

Exercise 2   **Finding Hidden Subjects**

Each of the following sentences contains an example of a special problem in finding the subject of a sentence. First, cross out any prepositional phrases or appositive phrases. Then underline the subject of each sentence.

1. How can you tell a stranger from a native?
2. There are sometimes unmistakable signs.
3. However, be careful not to assume too much.
4. A middle-aged man with three cameras around his neck and a family following behind him is nearly always a tourist.
5. People who stop and ask directions are obviously not familiar with the area.
6. On the other hand, a strange hairdo or an exotic outfit may just be the sign of a creative individual.
7. In Canada, even a foreign language is not always the sign of a stranger.
8. Lester B. Pearson Airport, Canada's busiest terminal, is a good place for people watching!
9. Where else can you see strangers from all over the world?
10. On your next trip, try to separate the strangers from the natives.

How Do You Find the Verb of a Sentence?

Every sentence must have a verb. The verb has two important jobs: to show what the subject is doing, and to tell the time of that action. If a word does not perform both of these jobs, it is not the verb of the sentence.

There are three kinds of verbs to recognize:

> action verbs
> linking verbs
> helping verbs

A. Action Verbs

Action verbs tell us what the subject is doing:

> Her eyelids (closed.)

> She (dreams) of a long journey.

In addition to telling us what the subject does, the action verb tells us *when* the subject does the action. For example, in the first sentence above, the verb *closed* is in the past tense, while in the second sentence, the verb *dreams* is in the present tense.

- A good test to make sure a word really is a verb is to try to put the word into different tenses:

> *Past:*   Her eyelids closed.

> *Present:*   Her eyelids close.

> *Future:*   Her eyelids will close.

Exercise 1   Finding Action Verbs

Each of the following sentences contains an action verb. Find the action verb by first underlining the subject of the sentence and then circling the verb (the word that tells what the subject is doing). Note also the time of the action (past, present, or future).

1. A woman told her dream to several research scientists.
2. In the dream, she lay in bed alone.

3. Confusion and noise filled the room.

4. Suddenly, a middle-aged woman entered and gave her a key.

5. Later, a man came and led her upstairs to an unknown room.

6. Scientists asked several therapists to interpret this dream.

7. Each one proposed a different meaning.

8. According to one therapist, the woman suffered from being entirely passive.

9. According to another, this dream showed the woman's erotic impulses toward her own therapist!

10. The third therapist predicted a creative future for the young woman on the basis of this dream.

B. Linking Verbs

A linking verb is a verb that joins the subject of a sentence to one or more words that describe or identify the subject. For example:

The child is a constant dreamer.

She seems distracted.

We feel sympathetic.

In each of these examples, the verb links the subject to a word that identifies or describes the subject. In the first example, the verb *is* links *child* with *dreamer.* The verb *seems* links the pronoun *she* with *distracted.* Finally, in the third example, the verb *feel* links the pronoun *we* with *sympathetic.*

Common Linking Verbs

act	feel
appear	grow
be (am, is, are,	look
was, were, have been)	seem
become	taste

Exercise 2   Finding Linking Verbs

Each of the following sentences contains a linking verb. Find the linking verb by first underlining the subject of the sentence. Then draw an arrow to the word or words that identify or describe the subject. Finally, circle the linking verb. An example is done for you.

Dreams are very important to the **native peoples of Canada.**

1. My dream last night was wonderful.

2. I had become middle-aged.

3. In a sunlit kitchen with a book in hand, I appeared relaxed and happy.

4. The house was empty and quiet.

5. In the morning light, the kitchen felt cozy.

6. The brewing coffee smelled delicious.

7. The bacon never tasted better.

8. I looked peaceful.

9. I seemed to have grown calmer.

10. I felt satisfied with life.

C. Helping Verbs

Some verbs can be used to help the main verb express a special time or meaning.

He is sleeping.	Time—right now
He might sleep.	Time—maybe now or in the future
He should sleep.	Time—ought to, now or in the future
He could have been sleeping	Time—maybe in the past

List of the Helping Verbs

be ⎫
have ⎬ These three verbs can be helping verbs, or they can be used by
do ⎭   themselves.

I have read the book.

I have the answer.

can, could ⎫
may, might, must ⎬ These verbs are usually used only as helping verbs.
shall, should ⎪
will, would ⎭

- Watch out for adverbs that may come in between the helping verb and the main verb.

    Dreams (can) often (frighten) young children.

- The word *often* is an adverb coming between the verb phrase *can frighten*. Adverbs are words that can modify verbs, adjectives, or other adverbs.

Exercise 3   Finding Helping Verbs

Each of the following sentences contains a helping verb in addition to the main verb. In each sentence, first underline the subject. Then circle the entire verb phrase. An example is done for you.

In some writing classes, students (must keep) a diary of their work.

1. There could be several advantages in keeping a diary.

2. In a journal, a person can safely express true feelings without fear of criticism by family or friends.

3. Well-kept diaries have helped to give people insight into the motivations for their actions and have also been a help in dealing with change.

4. Diaries do improve a person's powers of observation: to look inwardly at one's own feelings as well as to look outwardly at actual happenings.

5. You will be able to capture your memories before they fade.

6. Important, too, would be the development of a writing style and the improvement of language skills.

7. A journal might awaken your imagination.

8. It may unexpectedly bring pleasure and satisfaction.

9. Keener observations will add to the joys of life.

10. You should seriously consider the purchase of one of those lovely fabric-bound notebooks.

Chapter Review Exercises

Exercise 1 Finding Subjects and Verbs in Simple Sentences

In each of the following sentences, cross out any prepositional phrases or appositive phrases. Then underline the subject and circle the complete verb.

1. Mother and Dad always blame me for any trouble with my sister.
2. My sister, the most popular girl in her class, is two years older than I.
3. Yesterday, for instance, she was trying on her new graduation dress.
4. Helpfully, I took out her new shoes and purse for her.
5. Margaret instantly became furious with me.
6. Then mother walked into the room with a necklace for Margaret.
7. Margaret's new shoes and purse were immediately put back in the closet.
8. Why couldn't they have understood?
9. I was only sharing Margaret's excitement about her new clothes.
10. Far from their assumptions, my intentions had been the best.

Exercise 2 Finding Subjects and Verbs in Simple Sentences

In each of the following sentences, cross out any prepositional phrases or appositive phrases. Then underline the subject and circle the complete verb.

1. There are several kinds of journals.
2. Which is the right one for you?
3. Your personality and interests will determine your choice.
4. Some people do not write an entry in their journal every day.
5. A growing number of people are keeping dream journals.
6. In these journals, the writer makes his or her entry first thing in the morning.
7. Otherwise, the dream might be forgotten.
8. Busy people often need to keep an activity-oriented diary.
9. Another kind of journal, the writer's journal, could benefit every college student.
10. In such a notebook, one would save for future use any interesting phrases, overheard conversations, or quotes from books and magazines.

Exercise 3   **Finding Subjects and Verbs in Simple Sentences**

In each of the following sentences, cross out any prepositional phrases or appositive phrases. Then underline the subject and circle the complete verb.

1. Go West!
2. Western Australia, one of the remaining great boom areas of the world, comprises one-third of the Australian continent.
3. Why did people by the tens of thousands go to western Australia in the late 1800s?
4. In 1894 Leslie Robert Menzies jumped off his camel and landed in a pile of gold nuggets.
5. In less than two hours, this man gathered over a million dollars in gold.
6. He eventually took six tonnes of gold to the bank by wheelbarrow!
7. Kalgoorlie and Boulder, the two boom towns that grew up there, boast of the richest golden mile in the world.
8. With all the gold seekers, this surface gold did not last very long.
9. Now the only bands of rich ore lie more than 1200 metres down under the ground.
10. There are many ghost towns with their empty iron houses and run-down chicken coops.

A First Look
at Correcting
the Fragment

Once you have learned that a sentence must have a subject and a verb, and that a sentence must also express a complete thought, you are on your way to correcting one of the most frequent errors in student writing—the fragment. Although many of our daily conversations are informal and sometimes contain fragments, standard writing is always more formal and requires complete sentences.

The fragment is a major problem for many student writers. In the writer's mind, a thought may be clear; however, on paper the idea may turn out to be incomplete, missing a subject or a verb. In this section, you will improve your ability to spot incomplete sentences or fragments, and you will learn how to correct them. This practice will prepare you to avoid such fragments in your own writing. Here, for example, is a typical conversation between two people at lunchtime. It is composed entirely of fragments, but the two people speaking have no trouble understanding each other.

RON: Had any lunch?
JAN: A sandwich.
RON: What kind?
JAN: Ham and Swiss on rye.

If we rewrote this brief conversation using complete sentences, it would look something like this:

RON: Did you have any lunch yet?
JAN: Yes, I had a sandwich.
RON: What kind of sandwich did you have?
JAN: I had a ham and Swiss sandwich on rye bread.

In the first conversation, misunderstanding is unlikely, since the two speakers stand face to face, see each other's gestures, and hear the intonations of each other's voice in order to help figure out the meaning. These short phrases may be enough for communication, since the speakers are using more than just words to convey their thoughts. They understand each other because each one can complete the thoughts that are in the other one's mind.

In writing, however, readers cannot be present at the scene to observe the situation for themselves. They cannot be expected to read the author's mind. Only the words grouped into sentences and the sentences grouped into paragraphs provide the clues to the meaning. Since writing often involves thoughts that are abstract and even complex, fragments cause great difficulty and sometimes total confusion for the reader.

Practice Putting a Conversation into Complete Sentences

The following conversation is one that a couple of students might have at the start of their English class. Rewrite the conversation in complete thoughts or standard sentences. Remember the definition of a sentence:

- A complete sentence has a subject and a verb and expresses a complete thought.

JOHN: Early again.
ELAINE: Want to get a front-row seat.
JOHN: Your homework done?
ELAINE: Nearly.
JOHN: Think he'll give a quiz today?
ELAINE: Hope not.
JOHN: Looks like rain today.
ELAINE: Better not; haven't got a bag for these new books.
JOHN: Going to the game Saturday?
ELAINE: Probably.

1. _____

2. _____

3. _____

4. _____

5. _____

6. _____

7. _____

8. _____

9. _____

10. _____

Remember, when you write in complete sentences, this writing may be somewhat different from the way you would express the same idea in everyday conversation with a friend.

Although you will occasionally spot incomplete sentences in professional writing, you may be sure the writer is using these fragments intentionally. In such cases, the fragment may capture the way a person thinks or speaks, or it may create a special effect. A student developing his or her writing skills should be sure to use only standard sentence form so that thoughts will be communicated effectively. Nearly all the writing you will do in your life—letters to friends, business correspondence, papers in school, or reports in your job—will demand standard sentence form. Fragments will be looked upon as a sign of ignorance rather than creative style!

What Is a Fragment?

A **fragment** is a piece of a sentence that lacks one of the following:

1. the subject
2. the verb
3. both the subject and the verb
4. a complete thought (even though it contains the subject and verb)

Exercise 1 Recognizing Fragments

Each of the following groups of words is a fragment. In the blank to the right of each fragment, identify what part of the sentence is missing:

a. subject
b. verb
c. both subject and verb
d. a complete thought (even though it contains the subject and verb)

An example has been done for you.

Fragment	*Missing Part*
on the very first day of spring	c. both subject and verb

1. will be walking to work _____

2. large square bricks worn smooth _____

3. within walking distance of the factory _____

4. the couple to pay the rent _____

5. a pipe from some scrap heap _____

6. could look up and down the street _____
7. one of our neighbours, the gray-haired cigar maker _____

8. on a hook, he put _____

9. was kept under my mother's bed _____

10. home workshops around our neighbourhood _____

Exercise 2 Recognizing Fragments

Each of the following groups of words is a fragment. In the blank to the right of each fragment, identify what part of the sentence is missing:

a. subject
b. verb
c. both subject and verb
d. a complete thought (even though it contains the subject and verb)

Fragment	*Missing Part*
1. returned to the river	_____
2. a bird in the forest	_____
3. between the island and the mainland	_____
4. the hawk in a soaring motion	_____
5. the gold- and green-coloured fish on the beach	_____
6. to outwit a stronger enemy	_____
7. the fishing boats on the lake	_____
8. dropped like a stone into the water	_____
9. carried the fish to a tree	_____
10. the silence of the forest	_____

Exercise 3   Recognizing Fragments

Each of the following groups of words is a fragment. In the blank to the right of each fragment, identify what part of the sentence is missing:

a. subject
b. verb
c. both subject and verb
d. a complete thought (even though it contains the subject and verb)

Fragment	*Missing Part*
1. to sketch a picture	_____
2. the mountains and the rivers	_____
3. sitting on a small chair under a tree, a brush in his hand	_____
4. the purple morning sun	_____
5. the tremendous beauty of the valley	_____
6. the mountains in the distance	_____
7. feels close to nature and tries to capture it	_____
8. surrounding the artist and giving him advice	_____
9. too many people too close	_____
10. gathers his equipment and leaves	_____

For additional practice, go back and construct correct sentences from the fragments of these three exercises.

Don't Confuse Phrases with Sentences

Fragments are usually made up of phrases. These phrases are often mistaken for sentences because they are words that go together as a group. However, they do not fit the definition of a sentence.

What Is a Phrase?

A **phrase** is a group of words that go together but that lack one or more of the elements necessary to be classified as a sentence.

How Many Kinds of Phrases Are There?

In English there are six phrases you should learn to recognize. Some of them you have already studied in previous chapters.

1. **Noun phrase:** a noun plus its modifiers

    large square bricks

2. **Prepositional phrase:** a preposition plus its object and modifiers

    around our neighbourhood

3. **Verb phrase:** the main verb plus its helping verbs

    should have been walking

    The three remaining phrases are formed from verbs and are often mistaken for verbs.

4. **Participial phrase:** the present form of a verb ending in *-ing* and any other words necessary to complete the phrase

    running home

    looking very unhappy

    or

    the past form of a verb, usually ending in *-ed*, and any other words necessary to complete the phrase

    organized poorly

    treated lovingly

Participial phrases function as adjectives in a sentence. Study how the above examples could be made into complete sentences.

a. The present participle

Running home, the worker lost her wallet.

   Running is the participle.
   Running home is the participial phrase.
   The phrase *Running home* is used as an adjective to modify the noun *worker*.

Looking very unhappy, the worker searched everywhere.

   Looking is the participle.
   Looking very unhappy is the participial phrase.
   The phrase *Looking very unhappy* is used as an adjective to modify the noun *worker*.

b. The past participle

Organized poorly, the strike was not a success.

   Organized is the participle.
   Organized poorly is the participial phrase.

The phrase *Organized poorly* is used as an adjective to modify the noun *strike*.

Treated lovingly, most children are eager to learn.

Treated is the participle.
Treated lovingly is the participial phrase
The phrase *Treated lovingly* is used as an adjective to modify the noun *children*.

- Students often make the mistake of confusing a participle with a verb. When a participle is used as a verb, there *must* be a helping verb with it.

  Incorrect: I running in the marathon
  Correct: I *am running* in the marathon.

5. **Gerund phrase:** the present form of the verb ending in *-ing*, and any other words necessary to complete the phrase
The gerund phrase functions as a noun.

Running in a marathon is strenuous exercise.

Running is the gerund.
Running in a marathon is the gerund phrase.
The phrase *Running in a marathon* is used as a noun and as the subject of the sentence.

6. **Infinitive phrase:** *to* plus the verb and any other words necessary to complete the phrase

to pay the rent

to walk downtown

to have a good job

Exercise 1   Identifying Phrases

Identify each of the underlined phrases in the following sentences.

1. Visiting Montreal is a thrill for most Canadians.   _____

2. Many people love to see the French culture.   _____

3. Museums, restaurants, shopping, and the varied night life offer endless possibilities for the tourist.   _____

4. Riding the subways, tourists experience one of the cleanest underground transit systems in North America.   _____

5. My brother Don rode the subway under the St. Lawrence River.   _____

6. Coming from the country, he enjoyed the continental atmosphere of Quebec's largest city.   _____

7. Finding a parking lot may have been his most frustrating experience.   _____

8. In addition to the culture, Montreal boasts several professional sports teams.   _____

9. The Canadiens and the Expos have been drawing thousands of fans.   _____

10. Montreal's continual fascination is the rich mix of cultures and lifestyles from all over the world.   _____

Exercise 2 **Identifying Phrases**

Identify each of the underlined phrases in the following sentences.

1. In Canada, crime seems <u>to</u> <u>be increasing</u> <u>at an alarming rate.</u>

2. Stories about <u>many major crimes</u> <u>can be seen</u> almost daily <u>in the newspapers.</u>

3. <u>Avoiding</u> the issue will not solve the problem.

4. Citizens <u>should be concerned</u> and <u>try to make their views known</u> <u>to their elected officials.</u>

1. _____
2. _____
3. _____
4. _____
5. _____
6. _____
7. _____
8. _____
9. _____
10. _____

Exercise 3 **Identifying Phrases**

Identify each of the underlined phrases.

1. <u>Walking near the farm,</u> I could see the growing coffee plants. _____
2. It is a very difficult job <u>to supervise a farm.</u> _____
3. Growing any kind <u>of crop</u> is a time-consuming procedure. _____
4. <u>Helped constantly,</u> crops will tend to do well. _____
5. <u>Appearing very tiny,</u> the coffee plants needed more moisture. _____
6. The plants <u>should have been watered</u> last week. _____
7. I walked through different parts <u>of the plantation</u> to see what other problems I <u>could identify.</u> _____
8. <u>Around the edge of the farm,</u> I could see evidence of insect damage to the plants. _____
9. <u>Looking very brown,</u> the leaves showed signs of invasion by different insects. _____
10. <u>Organized properly,</u> this farm could be a source of both profit and pride. _____

Exercise 1 **Using the Participial Phrase as an Adjective**

Each of the words underlined below is a present participle. Use each word, along with the phrase provided, to compose a sentence in which the phrase will function as an adjective. Such a phrase is called a participial phrase. An example has been done for you.

Covering the steps, the ice was treacherous.

- Notice that the noun phrase *the ice* immediately follows the participle.
- Notice that a comma occurs after the introductory participial phrase.

1. Building a house _____

_____

2. Crying over the broken vase _____

_____

3. Hastily writing the letter _____

_____

4. Travelling in Mexico _____

_____

5. Knowing the truth _____

_____

6. Turning into the driveway _____

_____

7. Lacking the courage to tell the truth _____

_____

8. Climbing the steep trail _____

_____

9. Selling the car _____

_____

10. Quitting my job _____

_____

Exercise 2   Using the Participle in a Verb Phrase

The words below are the same present participles as in Exercise 1. Use them now as part of a verb phrase in a sentence. An example has been done for you.

Present participle: covering
Sentence: Ice is covering the steps.

1. building _____

2. crying _____

3. writing _____

4. travelling _____

5. knowing _____

6. turning _____

7. lacking _____

8. climbing _____

9. selling _____

10. quitting _____

Exercise 3 Using the Present Participle Correctly

Below are ten present participles. For each participle, write two sentences. In the first sentence, use the participle as an adjective. In the second sentence, use the participle as part of a verb phrase. An example has been done for you.

Participle: moving
Used as an adjective: Moving from St. John's, I found Moose Jaw very different.
Used in a verb phrase: I am moving from St. John's to Moose Jaw.

1. sitting on the balcony

   a. _____

   b. _____

2. hanging on a nail

   a. _____

   b. _____

3. walking to work

   a. _____

   b. _____

4. working in a factory

   a. _____

   b. _____

5. taking the bus

   a. _____

   b. _____

6. cleaning the apartment

   a. _____

   b. _____

7. cutting tobacco leaves

   a. _____

   b. _____

8. keeping a box under the bed

    a. _____

    b. _____

9. buying bread from the neighbourhood bakery

    a. _____

    b. _____

10. sitting at a low table by the window

    a. _____

    b. _____

How Do You Make a Complete Sentence from a Fragment That Contains a Participle?

Fragment: he talking in his sleep

1. Add a helping verb to the participle:

    He is talking in his sleep.

2. Change the participle to a different form of the verb:

    He talks in his sleep.

3. Use the participle as an adjective, being sure to provide a subject and verb for the sentence:

    Talking in his sleep, he muttered something about his boss.

Exercise 1   Correcting the Fragment That Contains a Participle

Make three complete sentences from each of the following fragments. Use the following example as your model.

Fragment: using the back stairway

    a. He is using the back stairway.
    b. He uses the back stairway.
    c. Using the back stairway, he got away without being seen.

1. the rooming houses often catching fire

    a. _____

    b. _____

    c. _____

2. the tenants moving out of the house

    a. _____

    b. _____

    c. _____

3. howling in the night

a. _____

b. _____

c. _____

4. warning people not to panic

a. _____

b. _____

c. _____

5. the fire department doing its best

a. _____

b. _____

c. _____

Exercise 2   **Correcting the Fragment That Contains a Participle**

Make three complete sentences from each of the following fragments. Use the following example as your model.

Fragment: using the back stairway

    a.   He is using the back stairway.
    b.   He uses the back stairway.
    c.   Using the back stairway, he got away without being seen.

1. I walking through the deserted rooming houses

a. _____

b. _____

c. _____

2. poking around in piles of junk

a. _____

b. _____

c. _____

3. the brick walls falling into fragments

a. _____

b. _____

c. _____

4. children playing in the deserted buildings

a. _____

b. _____

c. _____

5. the city forcing hundreds of families to move out

    a. _____

    b. _____

    c. _____

Exercise 3   Correcting the Fragment That Contains a Participle

Make three complete sentences from each of the following fragments. Use the following example as your model.

> *Fragment:*   using the back stairway
>
> a.   He is using the back stairway.
> b.   He uses the back stairway.
> c.   Using the back stairway, he got away without being seen.

1. preparing to take a driving test

    a. _____

    b. _____

    c. _____

2. the papers sitting on the front seat

    a. _____

    b. _____

    c. _____

3. the inspectors waiting to see how well you drive

    a. _____

    b. _____

    c. _____

4. trying not to hit the curb

    a. _____

    b. _____

    c. _____

5. tensely waiting for the results

    a. _____

    b. _____

    c. _____

Exercise 1   Correcting Fragments

Rewrite each fragment so that it is a complete sentence.

1. early morning a time of peace in my neighbourhood

    _____

2.   the gray mist covering up all but the faint outlines of nearby houses

_____

_____

3.   the shapes of cars in the streets and driveways

_____

4.   to sit and look out the window

_____

5.   holding a steaming cup of coffee

_____

6.   the only sound the rumbling of a truck

_____

7.   passing on the highway a kilometre away

_____

8.   children all in their beds

_____

9.   no barks of dogs

_____

10.   in this soft, silent dreamworld

_____

Exercise 2   Correcting Fragments

Each of the following groups of words is a phrase. First, name each phrase. Second, make each phrase into a complete sentence.

1.   hanging in clusters over the doorways

Name of phrase: _____

Sentence: _____

_____

2.   from other parts of the city

Name of phrase: _____

Sentence: _____

_____

3.   to earn a living

Name of phrase: _____

Sentence: _____

_____

4.   for children of my age and younger

Name of phrase: _____

Sentence: _____

_____

5. making candy of various kinds

   Name of phrase: _____

   Sentence: _____

   _____

6. to sit outside on hot nights

   Name of phrase: _____

   Sentence: _____

   _____

7. at the bottom of the hill

   Name of phrase: _____

   Sentence: _____

   _____

8. shaping the dough into donkeys and clowns

   Name of phrase: _____

   Sentence: _____

   _____

9. into the oven on a wooden spatula with a long handle for a quick baking

   Name of phrase: _____

   Sentence: _____

   _____

10. walking up and down the block

    Name of phrase: _____

    Sentence: _____

    _____

Exercise 3 Correcting Fragments

Each of the following groups of words is a phrase. First, name each phrase. Second, make each phrase into a complete sentence.

1. for people of this generation

   Name of phrase: _____

   Sentence: _____

   _____

2. to watch boxing

   Name of phrase: _____

   Sentence: _____

   _____

3. in the ring

   Name of phrase: _____

Sentence: _____

_____

4. hitting each other

Name of phrase: _____

Sentence: _____

_____

5. at each sound of the bell

Name of phrase: _____

Sentence: _____

_____

6. supported by the ropes

Name of phrase: _____

Sentence: _____

_____

7. to conduct the fight by the rules

Name of phrase: _____

Sentence: _____

_____

8. the screaming fans

Name of phrase: _____

Sentence: _____

_____

9. by the second round

Name of phrase: _____

Sentence: _____

_____

10. knocked unconscious

Name of phrase: _____

Sentence: _____

_____

Chapter Review Exercises

Exercise 1   Recognizing the Fragment

The following material is taken from *St. Urbain Street Then and Now* by Mordecai Richler. The paragraph is written incorrectly with fragments. Read the paragraph. Then write *complete* after each example that is a complete sentence. Write *fragment* after each example that is a phrase or piece of a sentence. Keep in mind that a sentence must have a subject and verb as well as express a complete thought.

> Bad news. They're closing Baron Byng High School. Our Baron Byng. I speak of a legendary Montreal school. Founded in 1921. That resembles nothing so much as a Victorian workhouse. Architecturally, the loss will be minimal. (The building's a blight.) But emotionally. Ah, that's something else.

1. Bad news.   _____

2. They're closing Baron Byng High School.   _____

3. Our Baron Byng.   _____

4. I speak of a legendary Montreal school.   _____

5. Founded in 1921.   _____

6. That resembles nothing so much as a Victorian workhouse.   _____

7. Architecturally, the loss will be minimal.   _____

8. (The building's a blight.)   _____

9. But emotionally.   _____

10. Ah, that's something else.   _____

Exercise 2   Recognizing the Fragment

The paragraph below contains fragments. Read the paragraph. Then write *complete* after each example that is a complete sentence. Write *fragment* after each example that is a phrase or piece of a sentence. Keep in mind that a sentence must have a subject and verb as well as express a complete thought.

> That afternoon the street was full of children. Taking a shower in the rain. Soaping themselves and rushing out into the storm. To wash off the suds. In a few minutes, it was all over. Including the rubdown. The younger children took their showers naked. Teetering on the tips of their toes and squealing to one another. The stately coconut palm in one corner of the patio. Thrashed its branches high over the dripping children bouncing on the cobblestones.

1. That afternoon the street was full of children.   _____

2. Taking a shower in the rain.   _____
3. Soaping themselves and rushing out into the storm.   _____

4. To wash off the suds.   _____

5. In a few minutes, it was all over.   _____

6. Including the rubdown.   _____

7. The younger children took their showers naked.   _____
8. Teetering on the tips of their toes and squealing to one another.   _____

9. The stately coconut palm in one corner of the patio.   _____

10. Thrashed its branches high over the dripping
     children bouncing on the cobblestones.   _____

Exercise 3   Correcting the Fragment

Rewrite the paragraph of Exercise 2 on page 87. Correct the fragments in one of
the following three ways:

a. Join the phrase to the sentence preceding it.
b. Join the phrase to the sentence that follows it.
c. Add a subject and/or verb so that the sentence is complete.

_____

_____

_____

_____

_____

_____

_____

_____

_____

_____

_____

Exercise 4   Correcting the Fragment

Each of the following passages contains a fragment. Underline the fragment, and
on the lines beneath each passage, rewrite the passage so that it is composed
of complete sentences.

1. The moon rose high in the sky. All of us worked quickly to pitch the tent.
    Then making a fire.

    Revised passage: _____

    _____

    _____

2. Raising the drinking age to 21 saves the lives of all drivers. The drinkers and
    nondrinkers. Every province should raise the drinking age to 21.

    Revised passage: _____

    _____

    _____

    _____

3. Companies do a lot of research before they name a new product. Based on the results of a market research team. The company makes its final selection.

    Revised passage: _____

    _____

    _____

    _____

4. The day of my eighteenth birthday, the reservations made at a fine restaurant. My father came home early from work.

    Revised passage: _____

    _____

    _____

    _____

5. Francie loved to see her mother grind the coffee. Her mother would sit in the kitchen with the coffee mill clutched between her knees. Grinding away with a furious turn of her left wrist. The room filled up with the rich odour of freshly ground coffee.

    Revised passage: _____

    _____

    _____

    _____

Combining Sentences Using Co-ordination

So far you have worked only with the simple sentence. If you go back and read a group of these sentences, such as on pages 61 and 62, you will see that writing only simple sentences would result in a choppy style. Also, you would have trouble trying to express more complicated ideas.

You will therefore want to learn how to combine sentences. You can do this by using particular marks of punctuation and special connecting words called conjunctions. The two major ways of joining sentences together are called co-ordination and subordination.

What Is Co-ordination?

You can use **co-ordination** whenever you have two sentences that are related and that contain ideas of equal importance. There are three ways to combine such sentences. All three ways result in a new kind of sentence called a **compound sentence.** Before you study these three methods, however, it is important to understand the term independent clause. The **independent clause** is a group of words that could be a simple sentence. In a compound sentence we could say we are combining simple sentences, or we could say we are combining independent clauses. Don't let the term confuse you. *Independent* means that the words could stand alone as a sentence, and *clause* means that there is a subject and a verb. *IC* will mean "independent clause" in the work that follows.

Use a Comma Plus a Co-ordinating Conjunction

The first way to combine independent clauses is to use a comma plus a co-ordinating conjunction.

IC	*, and*	*IC*
He spoke forcefully	, and	I felt compelled to listen.

Connectors: Co-ordinating Conjunctions

and	***Used in Pairs***
but	either . . . or
or, nor	neither . . . nor
for (meaning ''because'')	not only . . . but also
yet	
so	

Practice   In each of the following compound sentences, draw a single line under the subject and draw two lines under the verb for each independent clause. Then circle both the co-ordinating conjunction and the comma. The following example has been done for you.

The speaker rose to his feet, and the room became quiet.

1. The audience was packed, for this was a man with an international reputation.
2. He could have told about all his successes, but instead he spoke about his disappointments.
3. His words were electric, so the crowd was attentive.
4. I should have brought a tape recorder, or at least I should have taken notes.

Did you find a subject and verb for both independent clauses in each sentence?

Exercise 1   Combining Sentences Using Co-ordinating Conjunctions

Each of the following examples contains two simple sentences. In each case, join the sentences to form a new compound sentence. Use a comma and one of the seven co-ordinating conjunctions. Be sure the conjunction you choose makes sense in the sentence. For example:

Two simple sentences: Many farmers are desperate. They are going bankrupt.

Compound sentence: Many farmers are desperate, **for** they are going bankrupt.

1. The farmers in Canada want to work.
    They are experiencing severe financial difficulty.

    _____

    _____

2. Some people are losing their farms.
    The banks are refusing to make further loans.

    _____

    _____

3. The government programs have not been effective.
    The public cannot do anything.

(Use *nor*. You will have to change the word order in the second sentence.)

_____

_____

4. The farmers feel neglected.
    They are protesting to the government.

    _____

    _____

5. Some people think the farmers are to blame.
    They went too heavily into debt in recent years.

    _____

    _____

6. There is an increased need for farm products.
    The government pays farmers not to grow food.

    _____

    _____

7. The government has co-operated with farmers for years.
    The farmers are in more difficulty today than ever before.

    _____

    _____

8. Angry farmers watch their land and machinery being sold at auction.
    They can do nothing about it.

    _____

    _____

9. Everyone needs what the farmers produce.
    We should be concerned about their problems.

    _____

    _____

10. In the future, fewer people will become farmers.
    The problem is likely to become increasingly serious.

    _____

    _____

Exercise 2   Combining Sentences Using Co-ordinating Conjunctions

Each of the following examples contains two simple sentences. In each case, join the sentences to form a new compound sentence. Use a comma and one of the seven co-ordinating conjunctions. Be sure the conjunction you choose makes sense in the sentence.

1. Many people call a doctor for minor health problems.
    Many of these problems could be handled at home.

    _____

    _____

2. The first rule is not to panic.
    The second rule is to call the doctor if the problem seems serious.

    _____

    _____

3. Many folk remedies began as folklore.
    Many of these have been found to have a basis in science.

    _____

    _____

4. For many home remedies, you need only an ordinary ability.
    You can use common items around the house.

    _____

    _____

5. You can stop a migraine headache by breathing into a paper bag.
    The increased carbon dioxide will lessen the attack.

    _____

    _____

6. You can sprinkle sugar on a burned tongue.
    You can put a swollen foot in cold water to deaden pain.

    _____

    _____

7. Drinking a cup of strong coffee helps clear up congestion.
    Eating aged Cheddar cheese will have the same effect.

    _____

    _____

8. Hiccups are very annoying.
    You can try drinking quick sips of water to get rid of them.

    _____

    _____

9. A nosebleed may look very frightening.
    You can stop it by simply squeezing your nostrils together with enough
    pressure to stop the bleeding.

    _____

    _____

10. Doctors' offices are crowded with patients.
    Some of them could be home reading a magazine.

    _____

    _____

Use a Semicolon, an Adverbial Conjunction, and a Comma

A second way to combine independent clauses is to form the compound sentence by using a semicolon, an adverbial conjunction, and a comma.

IC	; *therefore,*	IC
I had worked hard	; therefore,	I expected results.

Another set of conjunctions that have meanings similar to the common co-ordinating conjunctions are called **adverbial conjunctions** (or conjunctive adverbs). These connecting words will give the compound sentence you write more emphasis. They may also sound slightly more formal to you than the shorter conjunctions *and* and *but*. The punctuation for these connectors is somewhat more complex.

Connectors: Frequently Used Adverbial Conjunctions

Addition (**and**)
furthermore
moreover

Result (**so**)
consequently
therefore

Contrast (**but**)
however
nevertheless

Alternative (**or**)
otherwise

Practice In each of the following compound sentences, draw a single line under the subject and draw two lines under the verb for both independent clauses. Then circle the semicolon, adverbial conjunction, and comma. For example:

The jet was the fastest way to get there; moreover, it was the most comfortable.

1. The restaurant is always too crowded on Saturdays; nevertheless, it serves the best food in town.
2. The land was not for sale; however, the house could be rented.
3. The lawsuit cost the company several million dollars; consequently, the company went out of business a short time later.
4. The doctor told him to lose weight; furthermore, she insisted he also stop smoking.

Exercise 1 Combining Sentences Using Adverbial Conjunctions

Combine each pair of sentences below to make a compound sentence. Use a semicolon, an adverbial conjunction, and a comma. Be sure the conjunction you choose makes sense in the sentence. For example:

Two simple sentences: Our family would like to purchase a computer. We must wait until prices come down further.

Compound sentence: Our family would like to purchase a computer; however, we must wait until prices come down further.

1. Most people prefer to write with a pen or pencil.
   The computer is quickly becoming another favourite writing tool.

   _____

   _____

2. Computers provide a powerful way to create and store pieces of writing. They will become even more important in the future.

_____

_____

3. Some people do not like the idea of using electronics to create words. They should realize that the modern typewriter is also an electronic tool.

_____

_____

4. Computers have already revolutionized today's offices. No modern business can afford to be without them.

_____

_____

5. Many schools are using computers in the classroom. These same schools are helping students prepare for their working careers.

_____

_____

6. The prices of many computers are coming down these days. More and more people see that owning a computer is a real possibility.

_____

_____

7. Some children know more about computers than many adults. Some children are teaching the adults how to operate computers.

_____

_____

8. Professional writers have become enthusiastic about the use of computers. There are still some writers who will use only a ballpoint pen.

_____

_____

9. The electronic revolution has just begun. It is our responsibility to keep up with that revolution.

_____

_____

10. We have many technological aids to writing. Let us not forget that the source for all our ideas is the human brain.

_____

_____

_____

Exercise 2 Combining Sentences Using Adverbial Conjunctions

Combine each pair of sentences below to make a compound sentence. Use a semicolon, an adverbial conjunction, and a comma. Be sure the conjunction you choose makes sense in the sentence. For example:

Two simple sentences: Our family would like to purchase a computer.
We must wait until prices come down further.

Compound sentence: Our family would like to purchase a computer; however, we must wait until prices come down further.

1. She doesn't like her job anymore.
   She cannot find another job that pays as well.

   _____

   _____

2. The office is clean and spacious.
   The people with whom she works are very kind.

   _____

   _____

3. The work is very repetitious and boring.
   She finds herself looking at her watch twenty times a day.

   _____

   _____

4. Her best qualities are carefulness and industriousness.
   Her problem is that she wants to have some excitement and challenge.

   _____

   _____

5. She long ago learned everything about the job.
   She now has no sense of growth or personal satisfaction.

   _____

   _____

6. Even doctors sometimes grow tired of their jobs.
   They have invested too much time and energy to change careers.

   _____

   _____

7. One solution could be the establishment of regular retraining programs.
   It seems a shame for a person with years of experience in one field to leave it all behind for something new.

   _____

   _____

8. Society would lose the benefit of their expertise.
   Individuals would lose the chance to be at the top of their fields.

   _____

   _____

9. Some large companies move employees around every few years.
   Workers seem energized by new surroundings and people.

   _____

   _____

10.   Every ten years we should all switch jobs.
      We would be happier and more productive.

_____

_____

Use a Semicolon

The third way to combine two independent clauses is to use a semicolon.

IC	;	*IC*
He arrived at ten	;	he left at midnight.

This third method of combining sentences is used less often. No connecting word is used. The semicolon takes the place of the conjunction.

Two independent clauses: I used to watch the Toronto Blue Jays play baseball at Exhibition Stadium. Tonight I'm going to see them play in the SkyDome.

Compound sentence: I used to watch the Toronto Blue Jays play baseball at Exhibition Stadium; tonight I'm going to watch them play in the SkyDome.

The semicolon was used in this example to show that the content of both sentences is closely related and therefore belongs together in one sentence.

When sentences are combined by using a semicolon, the grammatical structure of each sentence is often similar:

The women pitched the tents; the men cooked the dinner.

Exercise 1   Combining Sentences Using the Semicolon

For each of the independent clauses below, add your own independent clause that is a related idea with a similar grammatical structure. Join the two clauses with a semicolon. An example has been done for you.

Independent clause: He wrote the speech.
Compound sentence: He wrote the speech; she gave it.

1.   The apartment was light and airy.

_____

_____

2.   Shoppers were pushing grocery carts down the aisles.

_____

_____

3.   I plan to learn two foreign languages.

_____

_____

4. I tried to explain.

_____

_____

5. Many teenagers spend hours listening to rock music.

_____

_____

Exercise 2   **Combining Sentences Using the Semicolon**

Below are five independent clauses. Combine each one with an independent clause of your own to make a compound sentence. Connect the two clauses with a semicolon. Be sure to construct independent clauses that are related in their grammatical structure as well as in their ideas. An example has been done for you.

Independent clause: The guests are putting on their coats.
Compound sentence: The guests are putting on their coats; the cab is at the door.

1. The pickup truck was filled with old furniture.

_____

_____

2. Children played in the streets.

_____

_____

3. We expected them to understand.

_____

_____

4. The older men wore ties.

_____

_____

5. She hoped her boyfriend would soon call.

_____

_____

Chapter Review Exercises

Exercise 1   **Combining Sentences Using Co-ordination**

Combine each pair of sentences below to make a compound sentence. Choose from the three methods you have studied in this chapter. If you choose a conjunction, be sure that it makes sense in the sentence.

1. For many people, mathematics is a necessary evil.
   To a few, mathematics provides a lifetime of challenge and fun.

   _____

   _____

2. Most Canadians have studied math only to Grade 12.
   This limits their ability to understand new scientific developments.

   _____

   _____

3. Their knowledge extends to little more than basic arithmetic.
   People in the seventeenth century knew as much about math as most Canadians today.

   _____

   _____

4. Few Canadians study math at the university level.
   Many promising mathematics graduates move to the United States.

   _____

   _____

5. Math can be very satisfying.
   Unlike in the humanities, there is usually only one correct answer.

   _____

   _____

6. Some people can have a special talent for math.
   These same people can be very ordinary in language skills.

   _____

   _____

7. Physics demands math skill.
   Engineering also involves a great deal of mathematical ability.

   _____

   _____

8. Many schools form math teams to compete in area contests.
   Other schools encourage interest in math with math clubs.

   _____

   _____

9. Some schools suffer from a lack of good science and math teachers.
   These people have found better-paying jobs in industry.

   _____

   _____

10. Our future may depend on finding and adequately paying good teachers.
    Canadian students may continue to trail behind those of many other countries in math and science ability.

    _____

    _____

Exercise 2 **Combining Sentences Using Co-ordination**

Combine each pair of sentences below to make a compound sentence. Choose from the three methods you have studied in this chapter. If you choose a conjunction, be sure that it makes sense in the sentence.

1. The large rain forests of Africa and South America are in danger.
   They can never be replaced.

   _____

   _____

2. The varieties of insects and animals in the rain forest are countless.
   Their destruction means the loss of the world's greatest biological laboratory.

   _____

   _____

3. Many countries are cutting down their rain forests every year.
   The world's natural resources are steadily decreasing.

   _____

   _____

4. Scientists are concerned about the loss of animal and plant species in the rain forest.
   They are trying to slow down this destruction.

   _____

   _____

5. The governments of the world should be concerned about the loss of the rain forests.
   They are not actively trying to stop the developers.

   _____

   _____

6. The rain forests could be a valuable source of medical knowledge.
   The forests are also an invaluable source of timber and other products.

   _____

   _____

7. Most people in our country have never seen a rain forest.
   They find it difficult to imagine how beautiful it is.

   _____

   _____

8. Rain forests appear to be fertile.
   They actually have very poor soil for growing crops.

   _____

   _____

9. Many animals of the rain forest have not yet been studied by scientists.
   Many plants may still hold the secret to medical cures.

   _____

   _____

10. Some countries pride themselves on the cutting down of their rain forests. Most scientists are deeply disturbed by this monumental destruction of nature.

_____

_____

Exercise 3   Combining Sentences Using Co-ordination

Below are five simple sentences. Using each sentence as an independent clause, construct a compound sentence. Use each of the three possible methods at least once.

1. The beach was crowded.

_____

_____

2. The first apartment had no bedroom.

_____

_____

3. January had been bitterly cold.

_____

_____

4. The young model wore dark glasses to hide her identity.

_____

_____

5. The community waited for news.

_____

_____

6 Combining Sentences Using Subordination

When you use co-ordination to combine sentences, the ideas in both the resulting clauses are given equal weight. However, ideas are not always equally important. Subordination is the method used to combine sentences whose ideas are not equally important. Subordination allows you to show which idea is the main idea.

The sentence that results when two sentences are combined using subordination is called a **complex sentence**. We identify the two or more ideas that are contained within this complex sentence by calling them **clauses**. The main idea clause is called the **independent clause**. It could stand alone as a simple sentence. The less important idea is called the **dependent clause** because even though this clause has a subject and a verb, it is dependent on the rest of the sentence for its meaning. Consider the following clauses:

> *Independent clause:* That girl will leave soon.
> *Dependent clause:* If that girl will leave soon . . .

Notice that both clauses in the examples above have a subject and a verb. (The subject is *girl* and the verb phrase is *will leave.)* The difference is that the dependent clause has an additional word. *If* is a special kind of connecting word that makes the clause "dependent" on an additional idea. A dependent clause does not make sense by itself. The thought is not complete. Below is the same dependent clause with an independent clause added to it.

> If that girl will leave soon, I can finish my homework.

Now the thought is complete.

In your work with sentences, you will want to be comfortable writing sentences with dependent clauses. For this you will need to practise using two kinds of "connecting" words: subordinating conjunctions and relative pronouns.

Using a Subordinating Conjunction to Create a Complex Sentence

Following is a list of subordinating conjunctions. These connecting words signal the beginning of a dependent clause. Be sure to learn them carefully. It is a good idea to memorize them.

Connectors: Common Subordinating Conjunctions

after	even though	unless
although	how	until
as, as if, as though	if, even if	when, whenever
because	provided that	where, wherever
before	since	while

You have two choices of how to write the complex sentence. You can begin with the dependent clause, or you can begin with the independent clause.

First way:

DC	,	IC

Example:

If Barbara leaves	,	we can finish our homework.

Second way:

IC	DC

Example:

We can finish our homework	if Barbara leaves.

- The comma is used when you begin a sentence with a dependent clause. Your ear will help you remember this rule because when a sentence begins with a dependent clause, you can hear a pause at the end of that dependent clause. This is where the comma belongs.

- When a sentence begins with the independent clause, a comma is used if the independent clause can stand alone and the dependent clause just provides more information.

    I like cereal, although I dislike porridge.

- A comma is omitted if the dependent clause is essential to the main idea of the sentence.

    Marie will attend if her friend is invited.

- If a dependent clause beginning with *while, since, as,* or *when* limits the time of action of the main verb, a comma is omitted.

    His parents haven't been the same since he left home.

- If a dependent clause beginning with *while, since,* or *as* describes a cause or condition, a comma is used.

    His parents haven't been the same, since he left home.

Practice   Below are three pairs of sentences. Combine each pair by using a subordinating conjunction. Write the sentence two different ways. First, begin the sentence with the dependent clause and use a comma. Second, begin the sentence with the independent clause and use a comma if necessary, according to the rules outlined above.

1. (Use *since.*) The librarian took constant coffee breaks.
   The boss fired him.

   a. _____

   _____

   b. _____

   _____

2. (Use *after.*) He won the wrestling match.
   He went out to celebrate.

   a. _____

   _____

   b. _____

   _____

3. (Use *when.*) Donna returned from Europe this spring.
   The family was excited.

   a. _____

   _____

   b. _____

   _____

Exercise 1   Recognizing Dependent and Independent Clauses

In the blank to the side of each group of words, write the letters *IC* if the group is an independent clause (a complete thought) or *DC* if the group of words is a dependent clause (not a complete thought even though it contains a subject and a verb).

_____   1. while the photographer was getting ready

_____   2. before the show began

_____   3. I seldom go to the movies by myself

_____   4. even if it rains

_____   5. the Trivial Pursuit game lasted five hours

_____   6. whenever I see you

_____   7. since I did not take the medicine

_____   8. I spent the day in bed

_____   9. when I was sitting on the crosstown bus

_____   10. until the day he died

Exercise 2   Recognizing Dependent and Independent Clauses

In the blank to the side of each group of words, write the letters *IC* if the group is an independent clause (a complete thought) or *DC* if the group of words is a dependent clause (not a complete thought even though it contains a subject and a verb).

_____	1.	when his back was turned
_____	2.	he stared at his watch angrily
_____	3.	even though I offered to walk with him
_____	4.	this was a new development
_____	5.	I was so astonished
_____	6.	unless I acted at once
_____	7.	after my brother arrived
_____	8.	I had to be very quiet
_____	9.	sometimes I pinched him
_____	10.	as he lay sleeping

Exercise 3 Recognizing Dependent and Independent Clauses

In the blank to the side of each group of words, write the letters *IC* if the group is an independent clause (a complete thought) or *DC* if the group of words is a dependent clause (not a complete thought even though it contains a subject and a verb).

_____	1.	Margaret Atwood is a Canadian author
_____	2.	she was born in Ottawa in 1939
_____	3.	because she has received many honours for her writing
_____	4.	she won the Molson Prize in 1981
_____	5.	after she won the Governor General's Award
_____	6.	she was a finalist in 1986 for the Booker Prize
_____	7.	since it is one of the world's most important literary awards
_____	8.	Atwood writes both poetry and prose
_____	9.	when she wrote *The Handmaid's Tale, Cat's Eye,* and *Surfacing*
_____	10.	it is considered her best-known novel

Exercise 1 Using Subordinating Conjunctions

Use each of the following subordinating conjunctions to compose a complex sentence. An example has been done for you.

> *Subordinating conjunction:* after
> *Complex:* After the game was over, we all went out for pizza.

Remember that a complex sentence has one independent clause and at least one dependent clause. Every clause must have a subject and a verb. Check your sentences by underlining the subject and verb in each clause.

- Can you explain why the following sentence is not a complex sentence?

  After the game, we all went out for pizza.

After the game is a prepositional phrase. *After,* in this case, is a preposition. It is not used as a subordinating conjunction to combine clauses.

1. as if

    _____

    _____

2. before

    _____

    _____

3. until

    _____

    _____

4. how

    _____

    _____

5. because (Begin with the independent clause. Traditional English grammar frowns on beginning a sentence with *because.* Ask your instructor for his or her opinion.)

    _____

    _____

Exercise 2   Combining Sentences Using Subordination

Combine each pair of sentences using subordination. Look back at the list of subordinating conjunctions if you need to.

1. He was eating breakfast.
    The results of the election came over the radio.

    _____

    _____

2. The town council voted against the plan.
    They believed the project was too expensive.

    _____

    _____

3. I will see Shirley Carr tonight.
    She is speaking at the university this evening.

    _____

    _____

4. The worker hoped for a promotion.
    Not one person in the department was promoted last year.

    _____

    _____

5. The worker hoped for a promotion.
    He made sure all his work was done accurately and on time.

    _____

    _____

Using a Relative Pronoun to Create a Complex Sentence

Common Relative Pronouns

who
whose
whom
which
that

First sentence: That girl is responsible for this mess.
Second sentence: She has been here for the weekend.

Combine by using the relative pronoun *who*.

That girl *who has been here for the weekend* is responsible for this mess.

Practice 1   Below are three pairs of sentences. Combine each pair of sentences into one complex sentence by using a relative pronoun. Do not use commas.

1.   The chemistry lab is two hours long.
     I attend that chemistry lab.

     Combined: _____

     _____

2.   The student assistant is very knowledgeable.
     The student assistant is always willing to help us.

     Combined: _____

     _____

3.   The equipment was purchased last year.
     The equipment will make possible some important new research.

     Combined: _____

     _____

The most difficult problem with using clauses beginning with relative pronouns is knowing how to punctuate them. Study the difference between the next two examples.

The man *who is wearing the white shirt* is my father.

The dependent clause beginning with *who* is needed to identify the subject. No punctuation is used.
NOTE: The pronoun *that* is usually in this category.

Al, *who was wearing a flannel shirt*, arrived late to the wedding.

The dependent clause beginning with *who* is not essential to the main idea of the sentence. If this clause were left out, the sentence would still make sense. Since this clause interrupts the main idea, it is surrounded by commas.
NOTE: The pronoun *which* is usually in this category.

Practice 2   Choose whether or not to insert commas in the following sentences.

1.   Canada's first census which was taken in 1667 showed 3215 nonnative inhabitants in 668 families.

2. Most of these people were French Canadians who lived near the St. Lawrence River.

3. By the time of Confederation the population of the country had risen to 3463000 which was an increase of 1077 percent over 200 years.

4. If the population which is about 26000000 persons in Canada now increases by a similar percentage we'll have a population of 280200000 by the year 2167.

5. Where do you think we will put everyone who will live in Canada then?

Exercise 1 **Combining Sentences with a Subordinating Conjunction or a Relative Pronoun**

Combine each of the following pairs of sentences using either a subordinating conjunction or a relative pronoun. Be sure the word you choose makes sense in the sentence.

1. People have been fascinated for centuries by the problem of stuttering. Modern science is only beginning to understand some of the underlying causes of the problem.

   _____

   _____

2. For some people stuttering disappears by itself. Other people continue into adulthood as stutterers.

   _____

   _____

3. Stutterers usually keep their affliction. They seek professional help.

   _____

   _____

4. Many stutterers lose their impediment when they sing or whisper. Under stress the impediment becomes worse.

   _____

   _____

5. Stutterers become unable to speak when they appear in public or when they find themselves on the phone. They try to avoid such situations.

   _____

   _____

6. You see a stutterer chanting the school cheer with everyone else. That same person is usually tongue-tied when called on by a teacher.

   _____

   _____

7. It is true that there is some psychological basis for stuttering. It is true that psychologists have not been able to solve the problem.

   _____

   _____

8. All kinds of scientists have looked at the problem from all different angles.
   There is no single answer to stuttering.

   _____

   _____

9. Stuttering runs in a family.
   A child's chances of becoming a stutterer increase.

   _____

   _____

10. You hear someone say he or she knows the causes of stuttering.
    You know that person cannot be speaking scientifically.

    _____

    _____

Exercise 2   **Combining Sentences with a Subordinating Conjunction or a Relative Pronoun**

Combine each of the following pairs of sentences using either a subordinating conjunction or a relative pronoun.

1. I live alone with two dogs.
   They sleep on the braided rug in my bedroom.

   _____

   _____

2. The police stood by the door.
   They blocked our entrance.

   _____

   _____

3. She wore high heels.
   They made marks in the wooden floor.

   _____

   _____

4. My aunt is a tyrant.
   Her name is Isabel.

   _____

   _____

5. Her outfit was classy.
   Her hair was dirty and unattractive.

   _____

   _____

6. The interviewer did not smile.
   He discovered we had a friend in common.

   _____

   _____

7. I had a test the next day.
   I stayed up to watch a Mary Pickford movie.

   _____

   _____

8. The skater fell and broke his arm.
   He was trying to skate backward.

   _____

   _____

9. For a moment her face glowed with pleasure.
   Her face was usually serious.

   _____

   _____

10. I was thinking.
    The toast burned.

    _____

    _____

Exercise 3 **Combining Sentences Using Co-ordination and Subordination**

To finish this section, we'll look at a selection from Stephen Leacock, a famous
Canadian humorist who wrote a series of essays in a book titled *My Remarkable
Uncle*. Below are some simple sentences made from parts of Leacock's
paragraphs. Look over the sentences, and then rewrite the paragraph combining
sentences wherever you think it would improve the meaning and style. The
Answer Key will give you a version, although there is certainly more than one
way to revise it. Don't be afraid to change the wording slightly to accommodate
the changes you want to make.

Just what is a "sport"? I am not saying "sportsman." Everyone
knows what he is. Every now and then, he simply has to get out and kill
something. Not that he's cruel. He wouldn't hurt a fly. It's not big enough.
He has the instinct from way back in the centuries. He's got to get out on
the water or in the bush and kill something. Or rather, not so much that
he wants to kill it. He wants to crawl around after it. He wants to crawl
under brush and stoop under branches. He wants to pretend that he's a
bushman of 10 000 years ago. He wants to kill this thing and eat it. He
won't eat it, really. He'll give it away. He'll give it to his wife to clean. Then
he'll forget about it. In my part of the country, all the "keen sportsmen"
go out after partridges. I live in Simcoe County. They go out every
autumn. There hasn't been a partridge seen for nearly twenty years. You
don't really need them for partridge shooting. You need old clothes and a
flask of whisky. A sportsman who's a real sport is satisfied with that.

_____

_____

_____

_____

A First Look at Correcting the Run-on

A teenager came home from school with a long face.

DAUGHTER: I had a terrible day.

MOTHER: What happened?

DAUGHTER: Well, to start with my hair looked terrible <u>and then</u> the science teacher called on me to give my oral report <u>and</u> I was counting on having another day at least to get ready for it <u>and</u> when I got to English class I realized I had left my purse in science class <u>and</u> I didn't have time to go back and get it <u>and</u> to top it off Mrs. Edmunds gave us a surprise quiz on our reading assignment.

MOTHER: <u>And</u> I thought my day was bad!

This is probably typical of many conversations you have had at one time or another. In telling about a series of events, we sometimes join the events together as if they were one long thought. A problem arises when you want to write down these events in acceptable writing form. Writing ideas down as if they are all one thought without any punctuation to help the reader is not acceptable. Such a sentence as the one above is called a run-on. You cannot combine independent clauses without some kind of punctuation.

The Different Kinds of Run-on Sentences

1. *The fused run-on:* two or more independent clauses that run together without any punctuation

    I met Diana again we were happy to see each other.

2. *The comma splice:* two or more independent clauses that run together with only a comma

    I met Diana again, we were happy to see each other.

3. *The* and *run-on:* two or more independent clauses that run together with a coordinating conjunction but no punctuation

    I met Diana again and we were happy to see each other.

Guide for Correcting Run-ons

1. Make two simple sentences with end punctuation:

   I met Diana again. We were happy to see each other.

2. Make a compound sentence using one of the three methods of co-ordination:

   I met Diana again, and we were happy to see each other.
   I met Diana again; furthermore, we were happy to see each other.
   I met Diana again; we were happy to see each other.

3. Make a complex sentence using subordination:

   When I met Diana again, we were happy to see each other.
   We were happy to see each other when I met Diana again.

Exercise 1 Recognizing and Correcting Run-ons

The following story is written as one sentence. Rewrite the story, making sure to correct the run-on sentences. Put a period at the end of each complete thought. You may have to omit some of the words that loosely connect the ideas together, or you may want to use co-ordination and subordination. Remember to make each new sentence begin with a capital letter.

Well, to start with my hair looked terrible and then the science teacher called on me to give my oral report and I was counting on having another day at least to get ready for it and when I got to the English class I realized I had left my purse in science class and I did not have time to go back and get it and to top it off, Mrs. Edmunds gave us a surprise quiz on our reading assignment.

_____

_____

_____

_____

_____

_____

_____

_____

_____

_____

_____

_____

Exercise 2 Recognizing and Correcting Run-ons

The following story is written as one sentence. Rewrite the story, making sure to correct the run-on sentences. Put a period at the end of each complete thought. You may have to omit some of the words that loosely connect the ideas together, or you may want to use co-ordination and subordination. Remember to make each new sentence begin with a capital letter.

My best friend is accident-prone if you knew her you'd know that she's always limping, having to write with her left hand, or wearing a bandage on her head or ankle, last week for example she was walking down the street minding her own business when a shingle from someone's roof hit her on the head and she had to go to the emergency ward for stitches, then this week one of her fingers is purple because someone slammed the car door on her hand sometimes I think it might be better if I didn't spend too much time with her you know her bad luck might be catching!

_____

_____

_____

_____

_____

_____

_____

_____

_____

_____

_____

_____

Exercise 3   Recognizing and Correcting Run-ons

The following story is written as one sentence. Rewrite the story, making sure to correct all run-on sentences. Put a period at the end of each complete thought. You may have to omit some of the words that loosely connect the ideas together, or you may want to use co-ordination and subordination. Remember to make each new sentence begin with a capital letter.

One morning, not too early, I will rise and slip downstairs to brew the coffee and no baby will wake me up and no alarm clock will rattle my nerves and the weather will be so warm that I will not have to put on my coat and hat to go out for the paper there will be no rush I will go to the refrigerator and take out eggs and sausage the bathroom will be free so I will be able to take a shower with no one knocking on the door and I will not have to run up and down the stairs first looking for someone's shoes and then for someone's car keys I will leisurely fix my hair and pick out a lovely suit to wear the phone might ring and it will be a friend who would like to have lunch and share the afternoon with me money will be no problem maybe we'll see a movie or drive to the nearby city to visit a museum and the countryside will be beautiful and unspoiled my life will seem fresh and promising.

_____

_____

_____

_____

_____

_____

_____

_____

_____

_____

_____

_____

_____

Exercise 1   **Revising Run-ons**

Each of the following examples is a run-on. Supply four possible ways to revise each run-on. Use the guide on page 113 if you need help.

1. Intelligence tests for children are not always useful they are a basic tool for measurement in most schools.

   Two simple sentences:

   _____

   _____

   Two kinds of compound sentence:

   a. _____

   _____

   b. _____

   _____

   Complex sentence:

   _____

   _____

2. Many people are opposed to gambling in all its forms they will not even buy a lottery ticket.

   Two simple sentences:

   _____

   _____

   Two kinds of compound sentence:

   a. _____

   _____

b. _____

_____

Complex sentence:

_____

_____

3. Public transportation is the major problem facing many of our cities little is being done to change the situation.

Two simple sentences:

_____

_____

Two kinds of compound sentence:

a. _____

_____

b. _____

_____

Complex sentence:

_____

_____

4. Travel is a great luxury one needs time and money.

Two simple sentences:

_____

_____

Two kinds of compound sentence:

a. _____

_____

b. _____

_____

Complex sentence:

_____

_____

5. The need for proper diet is important in any health program all the junk food on the grocery shelves makes it hard to be consistent.

Two simple sentences:

_____

_____

Two kinds of compound sentence:

a. _____

_____

b. _____

_____

Complex sentence:

_____

_____

Exercise 2 Revising Run-ons

Each of the following examples is a run-on. Supply four possible ways to revise each run-on. Use the guide on page 113 if you need help.

1. The airline has begun its new route to the islands everyone is looking forward to flying there.

   Two simple sentences:

   _____

   _____

   Two kinds of compound sentence:

   a. _____

   _____

   b. _____

   _____

   Complex sentence:

   _____

   _____

2. The movie begins at nine o'clock let's have dinner before the show.

   Two simple sentences:

   _____

   _____

   Two kinds of compound sentence:

   a. _____

   _____

   b. _____

   _____

   Complex sentence:

   _____

   _____

3. The studio audience screamed at the contestant they wanted her to try for the big prize.

   Two simple sentences:

   _____

   _____

   Two kinds of compound sentence:

   a. _____

   _____

   b. _____

   _____

   Complex sentence:

   _____

   _____

4. The baby covered his eyes he thought he could disappear that way.

   Two simple sentences:

   _____

   _____

   Two kinds of compound sentence:

   a. _____

   _____

   b. _____

   _____

   Complex sentence:

   _____

   _____

5. The waitress smiled she told us the specials of the day.

   Two simple sentences:

   _____

   _____

   Two kinds of compound sentence:

   a. _____

   _____

   b. _____

   _____

Complex sentence:

_____

_____

Exercise 3   Revising Run-ons

Each of the following examples is a run-on. Supply four possible ways to revise each run-on. Use the guide on page 113 if you need help.

1. The people stood on the street waiting for the bank to open it was their last chance to cash a cheque before Monday.

    Two simple sentences:

    _____

    _____

    Two kinds of compound sentence:

    a. _____

      _____

    b. _____

      _____

    Complex sentence:

    _____

    _____

2. We started our trip at noon it was pouring.

    Two simple sentences:

    _____

    _____

    Two kinds of compound sentence:

    a. _____

      _____

    b. _____

      _____

    Complex sentence:

    _____

    _____

3. Learning a skill on the job is very satisfying a work situation can be just as valuable as a classroom for learning practical skills.

    Two simple sentences:

    _____

    _____

Two kinds of compound sentence:

a. _____

_____

b. _____

_____

Complex sentence:

_____

_____

4. In 1918, women in Canada finally won the right to vote in federal elections now the struggle for equal rights is found in other areas besides politics.

Two simple sentences:

_____

_____

Two kinds of compound sentence:

a. _____

_____

b. _____

_____

Complex sentence:

_____

_____

5. Mrs. Brighton takes in student lodgers every year she likes to have people in the house.

Two simple sentences:

_____

_____

Two kinds of compound sentence:

a. _____

_____

b. _____

_____

Complex sentence:

_____

_____

8 Punctuating Sentences Correctly

The Eight Basic Uses of the Comma

Many students feel very uncertain about when to use the comma. The starting point is to concentrate on a few basic rules. These rules will cover most of your needs.

The tendency now in English is to use fewer commas than in the past. There is no one perfect complete set of rules on which everyone agrees. However, if you learn these basic eight, your common sense will help you figure out what to do in other cases. Remember that a comma usually signifies a pause in a sentence. As you read a sentence out loud, listen to where you pause within the sentence. Where you pause is often your clue that a comma is needed. Notice that in each of the examples for the following eight uses, you can pause where the comma is placed.

I.   Use a comma to separate items in a series.

I was angry, fretful, and impatient.

I was dreaming of running in the race, finishing among the top ten, and collapsing happily on the ground.

- A series means more than two items.
- Some writers omit the comma before the *and* that introduces the last item.

I was angry, fretful and impatient.

- When an address or date occurs in a sentence, each part is treated like an item in a series. A comma follows each item even if there are only two items:

I lived at 14 Tartan Avenue, Halifax, Nova Scotia, for many years.

I was born on October 15, 1954, in the middle of Hurricane Hazel.

121

- A group of adjectives may not be regarded as a series if some of the words "go together." You can test by putting *and* between each item. If it doesn't work, then don't use commas.

    I carried my *old, dark green* coat.

    I took the *four black spotted* puppies home.

    I rode in his *new red sports* car.

Practice 1   In each of the following sentences, insert commas wherever they are needed.

1. Problems with the water supply of the United States Europe Canada and other parts of the world are growing.
2. Water is colourless tasteless odourless and free of calories.
3. You will use on an average day 90 litres of water for flushing 120 litres for bathing and washing clothes and 95 litres for other uses.
4. It took 450 litres of water to create the eggs you ate for breakfast 13 250 litres for the steak you might eat for dinner and over 200 000 litres to produce the steel used to make your car.
5. By 1970 the English-Wabigoon river system that runs through Grassy Narrows Ontario had become polluted with mercury.

II. **Use a comma along with a co-ordinating conjunction to combine two simple sentences (also called independent clauses) into a single compound sentence. (See Chapter 5 on co-ordination.)**

    The house was on fire, but I was determined not to leave my place of safety.

    Be careful that you use the comma with the conjunction only when you are combining sentences. If you are combining only words or phrases, no comma is used.

    I was safe but not happy.

    My mother and father were searching for me.

    I was neither in class nor at work.

Practice 2   In each of the following sentences, insert commas wherever they are needed.

1. The most overused bodies of water are our rivers but they continue to serve us daily.
2. Canadian cities developed understandably next to rivers and industries followed soon after to the same locations.
3. The people of the industrial age can try to clean the water they use or they can watch pollution take over.
4. The Great Lakes are showing signs of renewal yet the struggle against pollution there must continue.
5. Most people have not been educated about the dangerous state of our water supply nor are all our members of Parliament fully aware of the problem.

III. **Use a comma to follow introductory words, expressions, phrases, or clauses.**

    A. Introductory words (such as *yes, no, oh, well*)

    Oh, I never thought he would do it.

B. Introductory expressions (transitions such as *as a matter of fact, finally, secondly, furthermore, consequently*)

Therefore, I will give you a second chance.

C. Introductory phrases

Long prepositional phrase: In the beginning of the course, I thought I would never be able to do the work.
Participial phrase: Walking on tiptoe, the young mother quietly peeked into the nursery.
Infinitive phrase: To be quite honest, I don't believe he's feeling well.

D. Introductory dependent clauses beginning with a subordinating conjunction (see Chapter 6)

When the food arrived, we all grabbed for it.

Practice 3   In each of the following sentences, insert commas wherever they are needed.

1. To many people from Canada the plans to supply more water to the United States seem unnecessary.
2. However people in the Western United States know that they have no future without a good water supply.
3. In 1935 the federal government initiated irrigation schemes on the Canadian prairies.
4. Of the total 1.4 percent of Canadian farmland was irrigated by 1981.
5. Learning from the past modern farmers are trying to co-operate with nature.

IV. **Use commas surrounding a word, phrase, or clause when the word or group of words interrupts the main idea.**

A. Interrupting word

We will, however, take an X ray.

B. Interrupting phrase

Prepositional phrase: I wanted, of course, to stay.
Appositive phrase: Ann, the girl with the red hair, has a wonderful sense of humour.

C. Interrupting clause

He won't, I think, try that again.

Ann, who has red hair, has a wonderful sense of humour.

• Sometimes the same word can function differently.

She came to the dance; however, she didn't stay long.

In this sentence, *however* is used to combine independent clauses.

She did, however, have a good time.

In this sentence, *however* interrupts the main idea.

• Sometimes the same clause can be used differently.

Ann, who has red hair, has a wonderful sense of humour.

In this sentence, *who has red hair* interrupts the main idea of the sentence and so commas are used.

That girl who has red hair is my sister Ann.

The clause *who has red hair* is part of the identity of "that girl." This clause does not interrupt the main idea but is necessary to and part of the main idea. Therefore, no commas are used.

Practice 4   In each of the following sentences, insert commas wherever they are needed.

1. Natural disasters I believe have not been historically significant.
2. They have however significantly affected the lives of many Canadians.
3. Canada's worst coal mine disaster at Hillcrest, Alberta occurred in 1914.
4. In Springhill, Nova Scotia furthermore 424 persons were killed in the mines between 1881 and 1969.
5. Avalanches, storms, and floods which are natural disasters have also made their marks on the face of our country.

V.   Use a comma around nouns in direct address.

> I thought, Maria, that I saw your picture in the paper.

Practice 5   In each of the following sentences, insert commas wherever they are needed.

1. Dear your tea is ready now.
2. I wonder Jason if the game has been cancelled.
3. Dad could I borrow five dollars?
4. I insist sir on speaking with the manager.
5. Margaret is that you?

VI.   Use a comma in numbers of one thousand or larger.

> 1,999
> 1,999,999,999

Practice 6   In each of the following numbers, insert commas wherever they are needed.

1. 4876454
2. 87602
3. 156439600
4. 187000
5. 10000000000000

- In the metric system of measurement, *spaces* — not commas — are used in numbers of one thousand or larger. (However, numbers of four digits need not be separated.) This practice is becoming more widespread in Canada.
  4000   *or*   4 000
  38 622

VII.   Use a comma to set off exact words spoken in dialogue.

> "Let them," she said, "eat cake."

- The comma as well as the period is always placed inside the quotation marks.

Practice 7   In each of the following sentences, insert commas wherever they are necessary.

1. "I won't" he insisted "be a part of your scheme."
2. He mumbled "I won't incriminate myself."
3. "I was told" the defendant explained "to answer every question."
4. "This court" the judge announced "will be adjourned."
5. "The jury" said Al Tarvin of the press "was hand-picked."

VIII.   Use a comma where it is necessary to prevent a misunderstanding.

Before eating, the cat prowled through the barn.

Practice 8   In each of the following sentences, insert commas wherever they are needed.

1. Kicking the child was carried off to bed.
2. To John Ben Wicks is the funniest cartoonist.
3. When you can come and visit us.
4. Whoever that is is going to be surprised.
5. Skin cancer seldom kills doctors say.

Exercise 1   Using the Comma Correctly

In each of the following sentences, insert commas wherever they are needed.

1. The penguins that live in an area of South Africa near the coast are an endangered species.
2. One breeding ground for these penguins tiny Dassen Island is northwest of Cape Town.
3. Today fewer than 60 000 penguins can be found breeding on this island.
4. At one time seabirds that stole the penguins' eggs were the only threat to the funny-looking birds.
5. Human egg collectors not to mention animals that simply take the eggs have constantly reduced the penguin population.
6. However the worst threat to the penguins is oil pollution.
7. If a passing tanker spills oil many penguins can die.
8. In 1971 an oil tanker the *Wafra* spilled thousands of litres of oil off the coast of southern Africa.
9. Every time there is an oil spill near this area the number of healthy penguins declines.
10. The ideal situation of course is to make the oil tankers take a completely different route.

Exercise 2   Using the Comma Correctly

In each of the following sentences, insert commas wherever they are needed.

1. The Commonwealth Games were first held in Hamilton Ontario in 1930.
2. The first games known as the British Empire Games attracted 400 competitors from eleven countries.
3. By 1978 during the Commonwealth Games in Edmonton nearly 1500 athletes from 41 countries competed.
4. Canada has been a leading supporter of these games which are held every four years.
5. Memorable performances feats by both Canadian and non-Canadian athletes have become a benchmark of the games.
6. In 1958 at Cardiff Wales ten world records were broken.
7. The "Miracle Mile" occurred in 1954 at Vancouver when Roger Bannister of Great Britain defeated John Landy of Australia.
8. Elaine Tanner furthermore was the Games' outstanding swimmer in 1966.

9. In Edmonton Canadian athletes won 45 gold 31 silver and 33 bronze medals in 1978.

10. Next to the Olympics the Commonwealth Games are one of the world's best international competitions.

Exercise 3 Using the Comma Correctly

In each of the following examples, insert commas wherever they are needed.

1. The Hope Diamond is one of the most famous if not the most famous gem in the world.

2. Mined in India the diamond reached Europe in 1668 along with the story that there was a curse on the stone.

3. The curse or so the legend goes is that bad fortune followed the diamond because it had been stolen from a temple in India.

4. The curse may be true since nearly all of its owners including Marie Antoinette of France a French actress who was shot to death and an American woman whose children were killed in accidents have met with tragedy.

5. Well if we cannot share in the history of the Hope Diamond we can see it in the Smithsonian Institution in Washington D.C.

6. Other gems not as famous have served people throughout history as payments for ransom as bribes and as lavish wedding presents.

7. One of the most famous mines in South America is in Colombia where an emerald mine started in 1537 is still being worked today.

8. Some gems are difficult to find but as the earth's crust changes rough stones may find their way into streams rivers and other bodies of water where they may be found.

9. In several parts of the world notably Africa and South America the greatest number of diamonds emeralds amethyst topaz and other precious and semiprecious stones are to be found.

10. We could travel to these places if we had the time the money and the interest but we can see the most famous not to mention the most infamous stones in the Smithsonian in Washington D.C.

Other Marks of Punctuation

Quotation Marks

Use quotation marks as follows.

A. For a direct quotation:

"Please," I begged, "don't go away."

Not for an indirect quotation:

I begged her not to go away.

B. For material copied word for word from a source:

According to Statistics Canada, "Families or individuals spending 58.5% or more of their pre-tax income on food, clothing, and shelter are in financial difficulty."

C. For titles of shorter works such as short stories, one-act plays, poems, articles in magazines and newspapers, songs, essays, and chapters of books:

"A Modest Proposal," an essay by Jonathan Swift, is a masterpiece of satire.

"The Woodcutter's Third Son," a short story by Hugh Hood, deals with both sacred scripture and mystical folklore.

• Titles of longer works such as novels, full-length plays, and names of magazines or newspapers are underlined when typed or handwritten. In a printed book, these titles appear in italics: for example, *Maclean's* magazine and *Country Living*.

D. For words used in a special way:

"Duckie" is a term of affection used by the British, the way we would use the word "honey."

Practice 1   In each of the following sentences, insert quotation marks wherever they are needed.

1. The Hot House is one of the short stories contained in Rosemary Sullivan's anthology *More Stories by Canadian Women*.
2. Nellie McClung said I'll never believe I'm dead until I see it in the papers.
3. The prime minister told his caucus that they would have to settle the problem in the next few days.
4. Punk is a particular form of rock music.
5. She read the article Whiz Kids in *The Review*.

The Semicolon

Use the semicolon as follows.

A. To join two independent clauses whose ideas and sentence structure are related:

He decided to consult the map; she decided to ask the next pedestrian she saw.

B. To combine two sentences using an adverbial conjunction:

He decided to consult the map; however, she decided to ask the next pedestrian she saw.

C. To separate items in a series when the items themselves contain commas:

I had lunch with Linda, my best friend; Mrs. Zhangi, my English teacher; and Jan, my sister-in-law.

Notice in the last example that if only commas had been used, the reader might think six people had gone to lunch.

Practice 2   In each of the following sentences, insert a semicolon wherever needed.

1. One of the best ways to remember a vacation is to take numerous photos one of the best ways to recall the contents of a book is to take notes.
2. The problem of street crime must be solved otherwise the number of vigilantes will increase.
3. The committee was made up of Kevin Corey, a writer Anita Lightburn, a professor and T. P. O'Connor, a politician.

4. The bank president was very cordial however he would not approve the loan.

5. Robots are being used in the factories of Japan eventually they will be common in this country as well.

The Colon

Use the colon as follows.

A. After a *complete* sentence when the material that follows is a list, an illustration, or an explanation:
   1. A list:

   Please order the following items: five dozen pencils, twenty rulers, and five rolls of tape.

Notice that no colon is used when there is not a complete sentence before the colon.

   The courses I am taking this semester are Freshman Composition, Introduction to Psychology, Art Appreciation, and Survey of Canadian Literature.

   2. An explanation or illustration:

   She was an exceptional child: at seven she was performing on the concert stage.

B. For the salutation of a business letter:

   To whom it may concern:

   Dear Madam President:

C. In telling time:

   We will eat at 5:15.

D. Between the title and subtitle of a book:

   Plain English Please: A Rhetoric

Practice 3 In each of the following sentences, insert colons where they are needed.

1. Three Canadian-born comedians have become well known in the United States John Candy, Dan Aykroyd, and Catherine O'Hara.
2. The official has one major flaw in his personality greed.
3. The restaurant has lovely homemade desserts such as German chocolate layer cake and baked Alaska.
4. The college offers four courses in English literature Romantic Poetry, Shakespeare's Plays, The British Short Story, and The Modern Novel.
5. Arriving at 615 in the morning, Marlene brought me a sausage and cheese pizza, soda, and a litre of ice cream.

The Dash and Parentheses

The comma, dash, and parentheses can all be used to show an interruption of the main idea. The particular form you choose depends on the degree of interruption.

Use the dash for a less formal and more emphatic interruption of the main idea.

He came—I thought—by car.

She arrived—and I know this for a fact—in a pink Cadillac.

Use the parentheses to insert extra information that some of your readers might want to know but that is not at all essential for the main idea. Such information is not emphasized.

Gabrielle Roy (1909–83) wrote *The Tin Flute*.

Plea bargaining (see page 28) was developed to speed court verdicts.

Practice 4   Insert dashes or parentheses wherever needed.

1. Herbert Simon is and I don't think this is an exaggeration a genius.
2. George Eliot her real name was Mary Ann Evans wrote *Silas Marner*.
3. You should in fact I insist see a doctor.
4. Unemployment brings with it a number of other problems see the study by Brody, 1982.
5. Mass media television, radio, movies, magazines, and newspapers are able to transmit information over a wide range and to a large number of people.

Exercise 1   Marks of Punctuation

In each of the following sentences, insert marks of punctuation wherever they are needed.

1. To measure crime, sociologists have used three different techniques official statistics, victimization surveys, and self-report studies.
2. David is one of the best-loved poems of Earle Birney.
3. The lake this summer has one major disadvantage for swimmers seaweed.
4. Farley Mowat has written numerous books for adults however, he also writes very popular books for children.
5. Tuberculosis also known as consumption has been nearly eliminated by medical science.
6. The Victorian Period 1837–1901 saw a rapid expansion in industry.
7. He promised me I know he promised that he would come to my graduation.
8. Do you know what the expression déjà vu means?
9. She wanted to go to the movies he decided to stay home and see an old film on his new video cassette recorder.
10. She has the qualifications needed for the job a teaching degree, a pleasant personality, two years' experience, and a love of children.

Exercise 2   Marks of Punctuation

In each of the following sentences, insert marks of punctuation wherever they are needed.

1. Many young people have two feelings about science and technology awe and fear.
2. Mr. Doyle the realtor Mrs. White the bank officer and Scott Castle the lawyer are the three people to help work out the real estate transaction.
3. The book was entitled English Literature The Victorian Age.

4. I decided to walk to school, she said, because the bus fare has been raised again.

5. She brought a bathing suit, towel, sunglasses, and several books to the beach.

6. The conference I believe it is scheduled for sometime in January will focus on the development of a new curriculum.

7. The song Don't Forget Me comes from Glass Tiger's album The Thin Red Line.

8. The complex lab experiment has these two major problems too many difficult calculations and too many variables.

9. The mutt that is to say my dog is smarter than he looks.

10. Violent crime cannot be reduced unless the society supports efforts such as strengthening the family structure, educating the young, and recruiting top-notch police.

Exercise 3   Marks of Punctuation

In each of the following sentences, supply marks of punctuation wherever they are needed.

1. Justa Juxta a painting by Gordon Rayner is one of the artist's abstract studies.

2. Remember the doctor told the patient the next time I see you I want to see an improvement in your condition.

3. The student's short story Ten Steps to Nowhere appeared in a collection entitled The Best of Student Writing.

4. The report stated specifically that the company must if it wanted to grow sell off at least 10 percent of its property.

5. The foreign countries she has visited are Mexico Israel and Morocco.

6. My father enjoyed spending money my mother was frugal.

7. These students made the high honour roll David Hyatt, Julie Carlson, and Erica Lane.

8. The scientist showed the class a glass of H_2O water and asked them to identify the liquid.

9. He said that he would give us an extension on our term papers.

10. The work was tedious nevertheless the goal of finding the solution kept him motivated.

9 Making Sentence Parts Work Together

Making Agreement within the Sentence

In order for your sentences to be logical, all parts of the sentence must agree. A verb must agree in number with its subject; a pronoun must agree with the noun to which it refers; and verb tenses and persons must be consistent.

Since most students frequently have problems with agreement in their writing, you should work through this chapter carefully so that you will be able to look for these trouble spots in your own writing.

Subject-Verb Agreement

A verb must agree with its subject in **number**.

he		I	
she		you	
it	sleeps	we	sleep
any singular noun		they	
		plural noun	

Example: The baby *sleeps*.   *Example:* The babies *sleep*.

- Remember that a verb that goes with a singular noun or pronoun (except *I* or *you*) needs an *s*.

Practice   Underline the correct verb in the following sentences.

1. The dog (bark, barks).
2. It (wake, wakes) up the neighbourhood.
3. The neighbours (become, becomes) very angry.
4. People (deserve, deserves) a quiet Sunday morning.
5. I (throws, throw) an old shoe at the dog.

131

Special Problems in Making Verbs Agree with Their Subjects

1. The subject is not always the noun closest to the verb. Remember, do not look for the subject within a prepositional phrase.

   The hairline *cracks* ~~in the engine~~ *present* a serious threat to the passengers' lives.

2. These indefinite pronouns take a singular verb:

   > ***Indefinite Pronouns***
   > one, nobody, nothing, none
   > anyone, anybody, anything
   > everyone, everybody, everything
   > someone, somebody, something
   > either, neither
   > each, another

   For example:

   Neither of my parents *is* able to attend the ceremony.

   - *None* takes a plural verb if its meaning is *no person or things.*

     None of the lakes *are* polluted.

     None takes a singular verb if its meaning is *no amount* or *not one.*

     None of the ice *has* melted.
     None (not one) of the runners *has* scored.

   - The indefinite pronoun *both* takes a plural verb.

     Both of my parents *are* able to attend the ceremony.

3. When a pair of conjunctions is used, the verb agrees with the subject closer to the verb.

   > ***Pairs of Conjunctions***
   > neither . . . nor
   > either . . . or
   > not only . . . but also

   For example:

   Neither the textbook nor my lecture *notes explain* the meaning of the term "tidal wave."

   Textbook and *notes* together make up the compound subject. Since *notes* is closer to the verb, the verb agrees with *notes*.

4. In some sentences, the subject can come after the verb. In these cases, be sure that the verb agrees with the subject.

   Here *is* the *surprise* I promised you.

   Who *were* the *people* with you last night?

5. A group noun in Canadian English usually takes a singular verb if the group acts as a unit. (The test is to substitute the word *it* in place of the group noun.)

   The town *council is planning* a Canada Day celebration.

   In this sentence, the council is acting as a unit. "It" is planning a celebration. Therefore, the verb is singular.

   A group noun takes a plural verb if the members of the group act as individuals. (The test is to substitute the word *they* for the group noun and see if it sounds right.)

The town *council are preparing* their speeches for this event.

In this sentence, the council members are individually preparing speeches. *They* substitutes for the group noun in this sentence. Since the individuals are acting separately, the verb is plural.

Common Group Nouns

audience	family
class	group
committee	jury
council	number
crowd	team

6. The verbs *do* and *be* are often troublesome. Remember that standard English uses *s* for the third person singular.

The Verb to do

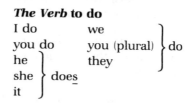

- In some parts of our country, it is common to hear people say, "He *don't* have the proper tools with him." This is not standard English.

The Verb to be (Past Tense)

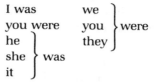

Practice   Underline the verb that agrees with the subject.

1. He (doesn't, don't) study in the library anymore.
2. We (was, were) hoping to find him there.
3. The library (doesn't, don't) close until eleven o'clock.
4. (Was, Were) you late tonight?
5. Ann (doesn't, don't) care if you stay until closing time.

Exercise 1   Making the Subject and Verb Agree

In the blanks next to each sentence, write the subject of the sentence and the correct form of the verb. An example has been done for you.

	Subject	Verb
The eleven proposals for the development of a new building at Laurier Circle (has, have) been submitted to the city.	proposals	have
1. The price of airline tickets to England (has, have) remained fairly reasonable.		
2. His decision (requires, require) a lot of thought.		
3. She (doesn't, don't) know the answers to any of the test questions.		

4. Either the elevator operator or the security guard (see, sees) every visitor. _____ _____

5. The committee (agree, agrees) to the fund-raising projects for this year. _____ _____

6. Potato chips and soda (makes up, make up) most of her diet. _____ _____

7. One of the people in the audience (is, are) my brother. _____ _____

8. There (was, were) two raccoons sleeping in the barn last night. _____ _____

9. Posted on the bulletin board (was, were) the assignments for the week. _____ _____

10. Everyone (takes, take) the test on Monday. _____ _____

Exercise 2 **Making the Subject and Verb Agree**

In the blanks next to each sentence, write the subject of the sentence and the correct form of the verb.

Subject   *Verb*

1. Included in the price of the trip (was, were) five nights in a lovely hotel and all meals. _____ _____

2. Nobody in the family (knows, know) how to swim. _____ _____

3. Jerry and Craig (works, work) well together. _____ _____

4. The number of essay questions on the apprenticeship exam (seems, seem) to be increasing. _____ _____

5. Where (is, are) the wrapping paper for these packages? _____ _____

6. In the entire building there (is, are) only two windows. _____ _____

7. Either the fruit pie or that chocolate cake (looks, look) like the best choice for your picnic. _____ _____

8. Performing in public (makes, make) me nervous. _____ _____

9. One of my most favourite shows (is, are) *Chasing Rainbows.* _____ _____

10. The book for the report (doesn't, don't) have to be from the reading list. _____ _____

Exercise 3   **Making the Subject and Verb Agree**

Using your own words and ideas, complete each of the following sentences. Be sure that the verb in each sentence agrees with the subject of each sentence. Use the verbs in the present tense.

1.   Our team _____

2.   The box of chocolates _____

3.   Both of my sisters _____

4.   The effects of his pay cuts over the last year _____

     _____

5.   Where is _____

6.   Not only the teacher but also the students _____

     _____

7.   The jury _____

8.   Each of the contestants _____

9.   Do you think there is _____

10.   The table of contents in that book _____

Pronoun-Antecedent Agreement

1.   A pronoun must agree in number (singular or plural) with any other word to which it refers. The following sentence contains a pronoun-antecedent disagreement in number:

     Everyone worked on *their* final draft.

     The problem in this sentence is that "everyone" is a singular word, but "their" is a plural pronoun. You may have often heard people use the plural pronoun "their" to refer to a singular subject. In fact, the above sentence may sound correct, but it is still a mistake in formal writing. Here are two approaches a writer might take to correct this sentence:

     Everyone worked on *his* final draft.

     Although you may encounter this approach in current writing, it is unpopular because it is widely considered a sexist construction.

     Everyone worked on *his/her* final draft.

     This form is technically correct, but if it is used several times, it sounds awkward and repetitious.

     The best solution is to revise such a construction so that the antecedent is plural:

     All the students worked on *their* final drafts.

•   Another problem with pronoun-antecedent agreement in number occurs when a demonstrative pronoun *(this, that, these, those)* is used with a noun. That pronoun must agree with the noun it modifies:

     singular: this kind, that type

Incorrect: *These kind* of shoes hurt my feet.
Correct: *This kind* of shoe hurts my feet.

Plural: these kinds, those types

Incorrect: Those type of cars always need oil.
Correct: Those types of cars always need oil.

2. Pronouns must also agree with their antecedents in **person.** The following sentence contains a pronoun-antecedent disagreement in person:

> When mountain climbing, *one* must maintain *your* concentration at all times.

When you construct a piece of writing, you choose a "person" to whom you direct your words. (In this book, the authors chose the word "you.") Some teachers ask students not to choose the first person ("I") because they believe such writing sounds too personal. Other teachers warn students not to use "you" because it is too casual. Whatever guidelines your teacher gives you, the important point is to be consistent in person.

Here are the correct possibilities for the above sentence:

> When mountain climbing, *one* must maintain *one's* concentration at all times.

> When mountain climbing, *you* must maintain *your* concentration at all times.

> When mountain climbing, *I* must maintain *my* concentration at all times.

> When mountain climbing, *we* must maintain *our* concentration at all times.

3. The antecedent of a pronoun should not be missing or ambiguous.

Missing antecedent: In Victoria *they* have many beautifully developed retirement areas.

Who are "they?" The reader cannot tell. We say the antecedent is missing from the sentence. Revise the sentence to correct the problem.

Revised: Victoria has many beautifully developed retirement areas.

Ambiguous antecedent: Margaret told Melissa that *she* needed to earn $1000 during the summer.

Who is "she?" The pronoun "she" could refer to Margaret or Melissa. Revise the sentence so that there is no question in the reader's mind who should earn the money.

Revised: Margaret said that Melissa needed to earn $1000 during the summer.

Exercise 1   Making Pronouns and Antecedents Agree

Each of the following sentences contains errors with pronouns. Revise each sentence so that pronouns agree with their antecedents and so that there are no missing or ambiguous antecedents.

1. His father mailed him his high school yearbook.

2. No one wants their income reduced.

_____

3. When a company fails to update its equipment, they often pay a price in the long run.

_____

_____

4. The woman today has many more options open to them than ever before.

_____

5. Everybody knows their own strengths best.

_____

6. Each of the workers anticipates their summer vacation.

_____

7. If the campers want to eat quickly, each one should help themselves.

_____

8. These sort of bathing suits look ridiculous on me.

_____

9. On the application, it says you must pay a registration fee of $35.

_____

_____

10. The doctor said that those type of diseases are rare here.

_____

_____

Exercise 2 Making Pronouns and Antecedents Agree

Each of the following sentences may contain an error with pronouns. Revise each sentence so that pronouns agree with their antecedents and so that there are no missing or ambiguous antecedents. If a sentence is correct, mark a *C* on the line provided.

1. The teacher suggested to the parent that he might have been too busy to have noticed the child's unhappiness.

_____

_____

2. The county submitted their proposal for the bridge repairs.

_____

3. We all rushed away from all the trees to our cars because you had to wait for the thunderstorm to stop.

_____

_____

4. A young person does not receive enough advice on how they should choose their career.

_____

_____

5. These type of watches are very popular.

   _____

6. People were taken forcibly from our homes.

   _____

7. No one brought their books today.

   _____

8. The college is holding its homecoming weekend on October 5.

   _____

9. They call it the "Trillium" province.

   _____

10. Anyone who fails the final will be unlikely to get his or her diploma.

   _____

Parallel Structure: Making a Series of Words, Phrases, or Clauses Balance within the Sentence

Which one of the following sentences achieves a better sense of balance?

> His favourite hobbies are playing the trumpet, listening to jazz, and to go to concerts.

> His favourite hobbies are playing the trumpet, listening to jazz, and going to concerts.

If you selected the second sentence, you would have made the better choice. The second sentence uses parallel structure to balance the three phrases in the series (playing, listening, and going). By matching each of the items in the series with the same -*ing* structure, the sentence becomes easier to understand and more pleasant to read. You can make words, phrases, and even sentences in a series parallel:

1. Words in a series should be the same parts of speech.

   Incorrect: The town was small, quiet, and the atmosphere was peaceful.
   (The series is composed of two adjectives and one clause.)
   Correct: The town was small, quiet, and peaceful.
   (*Small, quiet,* and *peaceful* are adjectives.)

2. Phrases in a series should be the same kind of phrase (infinitive phrases, prepositional phrases, verb phrases, noun phrases, participial phrases).

   Incorrect: Her lost assignment is in her closet, on the floor, and the clothes are hiding it.
   (two prepositional phrases and one clause)
   Correct: Her lost assignment is in her closet, on the floor, and under a pile of clothes.
   (three prepositional phrases beginning with *in, on,* and *under*)

3. Clauses in a series should be parallel.

   Incorrect: One clerk polished the antique spoons; they were placed into the display case by the other clerk.
   Correct: One clerk polished the antique spoons; the other clerk placed them in the display case.

Practice   Each of the following sentences has an underlined word, phrase, or clause that is not parallel. Make the underlined section parallel.

1. My favourite armchair is lumpy, worn out, and <u>has dirt spots everywhere</u>.

    _____

2. She enjoys reading novels, studying the flute, and <u>also sews her own clothes</u>.

    _____

3. He admires teachers who make the classroom an exciting place and <u>willingly explaining material more than once</u>.

    _____

Exercise 1   Revising Sentences for Parallel Structure

Each of the following sentences needs parallel structure. Underline the word, phrase, or clause that is not parallel and revise it so that its structure will balance with the other items in the pair or series. An example has been done for you.

> *Incorrect:*   The best leather comes from Italy, from Spain, and <u>is imported from Brazil</u>.
>
> *Correct:*   The best leather comes from Italy, from Spain, and <u>from Brazil</u>.

1. Winter in Edmonton is very windy and has many bitterly cold days.

    _____

2. I would prefer to fix an old car than watching television.

    _____

3. George is a helpful neighbour, a loyal friend, and dedicated to his children.

    _____

4. The apartment is crowded and without light.

    _____

5. The dancer is slender and moves gracefully.

    _____

6. The nursery was cheerful and had a lot of sun.

    _____

7. My friend loves to play chess, to read science fiction, and working out at the gym.

    _____

    _____

8. For homework today I must read a chapter in history, do five exercises for Spanish class, and working on my term paper for political science.

    _____

    _____

9. The painting reveals the artist's talent and it is imaginative.

    _____

    _____

10. The cars race down the track, turn the corner at great speed, and then they are turning into the home stretch.

_____

_____

Exercise 2   **Revising Sentences for Parallel Structure**

Each of the following sentences needs parallel structure. Underline the word, phrase, or clause that is not parallel and revise it so that its structure will balance with the other items in the pair or series.

1. The dog had to choose between jumping over the fence or he could have dug a hole underneath it.

_____

_____

2. She disliked going to the beach, hiking in the woods, and she didn't care for picnics, either.

_____

_____

3. As I looked down the city street, I could see the soft lights from restaurant windows, I could hear the mellow sounds of a night club band, and carefree moods of people walking by.

_____

_____

4. The singers have been on several road tours, have recorded for two record companies, and they would also like to make a movie someday.

_____

_____

5. They would rather order a pizza than eating their sister's cooking.

_____

_____

6. I explained to the teacher that my car had broken down, my books had been stolen, and I left my assignment pad at home.

_____

_____

7. That night the prisoner was sick, discouraged, and she was filled with loneliness.

_____

_____

8. As the truck rumbled through the street, it suddenly lurched out of control, smashed into a parked car, and then the truck hit the storefront of my uncle's hardware store.

_____

_____

9.   The teacher is patient, intelligent, and demands a lot.

   _____

   _____

10.   He was determined to pass the math course, not only to get his three credits but also for a sense of achievement.

   _____

   _____

Exercise 3   **Revising Sentences for Parallel Structure**

Each of the following sentences needs parallel structure. Underline the word, phrase, or clause that is not parallel and revise it so that its structure will balance with the other items in the pair or series.

1.   The first-grade teacher told us that our child was unruly, mischievous, and talked too much.

   _____

   _____

2.   The dog's size, its colouring, and whenever it barked reminded me of a wolf.

   _____

   _____

3.   Carol is not only very talented, but she is also acting kindly to everyone.

   _____

   _____

4.   He dried the dishes; putting them away was the job of his wife.

   _____

   _____

5.   Jordan would rather travel and see the world than staying home and reading about other places.

   _____

   _____

6.   For weeks he tried to decide if he should major in chemistry, continue with accounting, or to take off a year.

   _____

   _____

7.   Her depression was a result of the loss of her job, the breakdown of her marriage, and a teenage daughter who was a problem.

   _____

   _____

8.   She must either cut back on her expenses, or selling her car.

   _____

   _____

9. His office is without windows, on the fourth floor, and you have to go down a dark hallway to get there.

    _____

    _____

10. He went through four years of university, one year of graduate school, and he has spent one year teaching seventh-grade science.

    _____

    _____

Misplaced and Dangling Modifiers

Modifiers are words or groups of words that function as adjectives or adverbs. Single-word adjectives usually precede the words they modify, while adjective phrases or clauses usually follow the words they modify. If the modifier is put in the wrong place, or if the modifier appears to modify the wrong word or none at all, the sentence will be confusing or even humorous.

Misplaced modifier:	The salesperson sold the used car to the customer *that needed extensive body work.*
	Did the *customer* need *body work?*
Revised:	The salesperson sold the used car *that needed extensive body work* to the customer.
Dangling modifier:	*Working on the car's engine*, the dog barked all afternoon.
	Who worked on the engine? Was it the dog?
Revised:	*While working on the car's engine*, I heard the dog barking all afternoon.
	(By changing the subject to *I*, the modifying phrase *While working on the car's engine* now modifies a logical subject.)

Exercise 1   Revising Misplaced or Dangling Modifiers

Revise each sentence so there is no dangling modifier.

1. Victor fed the dog wearing his tuxedo.

    _____

    _____

2. Visiting the Stanley Park aquarium, the dolphins entertained us.

    _____

    _____

3. Hoping to see the news, the television set was turned on and all ready by seven o'clock.

    _____

    _____

4. A woodpecker was found in Cuba that had been considered extinct.

_____

_____

5. After running over the hill, the farm was visible in the valley below.

_____

_____

6. The truck caused a traffic jam, which was broken down on the highway, for kilometres.

_____

_____

7. Hanging from the ceiling in my bedroom, I saw three spiders.

_____

_____

8. After wiping my glasses, the redbird flew away.

_____

9. Howling without a stop, I listened to the neighbour's dog all evening.

_____

_____

10. After painting my room all afternoon, my cat demanded her dinner.

_____

_____

_____

Exercise 2   Revising Misplaced or Dangling Modifiers

Revise each sentence so there is no dangling modifier.

1. Leaping upstream, we fished most of the day for salmon.

_____

_____

2. At the age of ten, my family took a trip to Fredericton, N.B.

_____

_____

3. Skimming every chapter, my biology textbook suddenly made more sense.

_____

_____

4. Running up the stairs, the train left for Montreal.

_____

_____

5. Working extra hours last week, my salary increased dramatically.

_____

_____

6. We watched a movie in the theatre for which we had paid five dollars.

   _____

   _____

7. Dressed in a Dracula costume, I thought my son looked perfect for Halloween.

   _____

   _____

8. Last week while shopping, my friend's purse was stolen.

   _____

   _____

9. While eating lunch outdoors, our picnic table collapsed.

   _____

   _____

10. Our car is in the parking lot with two bags of groceries unlocked.

    _____

    _____

10 Solving More Problems with Verbs

It is not surprising, since every sentence must have a verb, that many of the errors in student writing have something to do with verbs. You have already studied verbs that are often confused (Chapter 2), irregular verbs (Appendix E), verbs used to make participial and gerund phrases (Chapter 4), and subject-verb agreement (Chapter 9). In addition to these four major concerns, you should also avoid the following frequent student errors.

Unnecessary Shifts in Verb Tense

Do not shift verb tenses as you write unless you intend to change the time of the action.

> *Shifted tense:* The customer *asked* the pharmacist for the prescription, but the pharmacist *tells* the customer that the ingredients *will have* to be ordered.
>
> *Revised:* The customer *asked* the pharmacist for the prescription, but the pharmacist *told* the customer that the ingredients *would have* to be ordered.

Exercise 1 Correcting Unnecessary Shifts in Verb Tense

Each sentence below has an unnecessary shift in verb tense. Revise each sentence so that the tense remains consistent.

1. After I complete that writing course, I took the required history course.

_____

_____

2. In the beginning of the movie, the action was slow; by the end, I am sitting on the edge of my seat.

    _____

    _____

3. The textbook gives the rules for writing a bibliography, but it didn't explain how to do footnotes.

    _____

    _____

4. While working on her report in the library, my best friend lost her note cards and comes to me for help.

    _____

    _____

5. The encyclopedia gave several pages of information about astronomy, but it doesn't give anything about "black holes."

    _____

    _____

6. The invitation requested that Juan be at the ceremony and that he will attend the banquet as well.

    _____

    _____

7. This is an exciting book, but it had too many characters.

    _____

    _____

8. The member of Parliament was doing just fine until along comes a younger and more energetic politician with firm support from the middle class.

    _____

    _____

9. At the end of *Gulliver's Travels*, the main character rejects the company of people; he preferred the company of horses.

    _____

    _____

10. My sister arrives, late as usual, and complained that her dinner was cold.

    _____

    _____

Exercise 2   Correcting Unnecessary Shifts in Verb Tense

The following paragraph contains unnecessary shifts in verb tense. Change each incorrect verb to its proper form.

Doctor Norman Bethune grows up in Gravenhurst, Ontario. He was educated in Toronto and serves as a stretcher bearer in World War I. He contracted tuberculosis and thereafter was devoting himself to helping other victims of the disease when he practises surgery in Montreal. He also invents or redesigned twelve medical and surgical instruments. Bethune travelled to Russia in 1935, joined the Communist party, and goes to Spain in 1936, where he organized the first mobile blood transfusion service during the Spanish Civil War. After returning to Canada, he shortly left for overseas again, this time to China, where he helped the Chinese Communists in their fight against Japan. "Spain and China," he writes, "are part of the same battle." While there, he contracted an infection and died. Mao's essay "In Memory of Norman Bethune," prescribed reading during China's Cultural Revolution, urges all Communists to follow Bethune's example of selfless dedication to others. Bethune is the best-known Canadian to the Chinese, and many Chinese visit his Canadian birthplace.

Exercise 3 Correcting Unnecessary Shifts in Verb Tense

The following paragraph contains unnecessary shifts in verb tense. Change each incorrect verb to its proper form.

Charles Dickens was a nineteenth-century author whose work is well known today. One of the reasons Dickens remained so popular is that so many of his stories are available not only as books but also as movies, plays, and television productions. We all knew from our childhood the famous story of Uncle Scrooge and Tiny Tim. Often we saw a television version of *A Christmas Carol* at holiday time. If we have never read the story of Oliver Twist in book form, we might see the musical *Oliver!* Also, there was a movie version of *Great Expectations*. Many students still studied *A Tale of Two Cities* in high school. No matter how many adaptations of Dickens's books we see, people seem to agree that there was no substitute for the books themselves. At first, the vocabulary seemed hard to understand, but if we concentrate on the story and read a chapter or two every day, we will find ourselves not only comprehending these wonderful stories but loving the richness of Dickens's use of language.

Sequence of Tenses

The term *sequence of tenses* refers to the proper use of verb tenses in complex sentences (sentences that have an independent clause and a dependent clause). The guide on page 148 shows the relationship between the verb in the independent clause (IC) and the verb in the dependent clause (DC).

Independent Clause	Dependent Clause	Time of the DC in Relation to the IC

If the tense of the independent clause is in the **present** (he *knows*), here are the possibilities for the dependent clause.

He knows	that she *is* right.	at the same time
	that she *was* right.	earlier
	that she *will be* right.	later

If the tense of the independent clause is in the **past** (he *knew*), here are the possibilities for the dependent clause.

He knew	that she *was* right.	same time
	that she *had been* right.	earlier
	that she *would be* right.	later

If the independent clause is in the future (he *will tell*), here are the possibilities for the dependent clause.

He will tell us	if she *goes*.	same time
	if she *has gone*.	earlier
	if she *will go*.	later

Exercise 1   Using the Correct Sequence of Tenses

In each of the following sentences, choose the correct verb tense for the verb in the dependent clause. Use the guide above if you need help.

1. The program <u>will only continue</u> after the coughing and fidgeting

   _____.
            (to stop)

2. Since he was poor and unappreciated by the music world when he died in 1791, Mozart <u>did not realize</u> the importance that his music

   _____ in the twentieth century.
            (to have)

3. Dad <u>will tell</u> us tonight if he _____ a new car next
                                              (to buy)

   month.

4. Albert Einstein <u>failed</u> the entrance exam at the Swiss Federal Institute of

   Technology because he _____ a very disciplined stu-
                              (to be) + never

   dent.

5. Einstein only <u>studied</u> subjects that he _____.
                                                      (to like)

6. Cancer researchers <u>think</u> it's likely that a cure for most cancers

   _____ found.
        (to be) + soon

7. We <u>know</u> that science _____ now close to finding a
                                      (to be)

   cure for leukemia.

8. The interviewer <u>felt</u> that the young woman _____
                                                            (to know)

   more than she was telling him.

9. The doctor went into the operating room. She <u>hoped</u> that the operation

_____ out all right.

(to turn)

10. The doctor came out of the operating room. She <u>said</u> that the operation

_____ well.

(to go)

Passive versus Active Verbs

Avoid using the passive voice when the active voice would be more direct, economical, or forceful.

Passive sentence: Many sights were seen by the tour group today.
Active sentence: The tour group saw many sights today.

Practice Change the following sentences from passive to active.

1. The wrong number was dialled by the child by mistake.

_____

2. The sweater was knitted very carefully by my grandmother.

_____

3. The attendance has been taken by the assistant at the beginning of class.

_____

4. The facts of the case were not known by the public.

_____

5. Those purple platform shoes were worn by somebody.

_____

The passive voice can be used effectively when the actor is not known, or when the receiver of the action is more important than the actor. History books often use the passive voice.

Active: The ambulance took the prime minister to the hospital.
Passive: The prime minister was taken to the hospital.

Active: The Canadian Corps fought at the Battle of Vimy Ridge in 1917.
Passive: The Battle of Vimy Ridge was fought in 1917.

The Subjunctive

Recognize the three circumstances in which the verb does not agree with the subject.

1. Unreal conditions using *if* or *wish*

<u>If he were</u> my teacher, I would be pleased.

<u>I wish he were</u> my teacher.

2. Clauses starting with *that* after verbs such as *ask, request, demand, suggest, order, insist,* or *command*

I demand <u>that she work harder</u>.

Sullivan insisted <u>that Jones report on Tuesday</u>.

3. Clauses starting with *that* after adjectives expressing urgency, as in *it is necessary*, *it is imperative*, *it is urgent*, *it is important*, and *it is essential*

It is necessary <u>that she wear</u> a net covering her hair.

It is essential <u>that John understand</u> the concept.

Other Problems with Verbs

Do not use more than one **modal auxiliary** *(will, would, shall, should, may, might, must, can, could, ought)* with the main verb.

Incorrect: Matt shouldn't ought to sell his car.
Correct: Matt ought not to sell his car.

or

Matt shouldn't sell his car.

Do not use *should of, would of,* or *could of* to mean *should have, would have,* or *could have*

Incorrect: Elana would of helped you if she could of.
Correct: Elana would have helped you if she could have.

Exercise 1   Solving Problems with Verbs

Revise each of the following sentences to avoid problems with verbs.

1. He hadn't ought to drive so fast.

   _____

2. It is essential that Krista goes to class tonight.

   _____

3. I wish I was a senior.

   _____

4. She sung for a huge crowd Saturday night.

   _____

5. I was shook up by the accident.

   _____

6. The books were studied by the students.

   _____

7. My father ask me last night to help him build a deck.

   _____

8. I should of kept the promise I made.

   _____

9. I insist she keeps her records on her side of the room.

   _____

10. The ship sunk off the coast of Sable Island.

   _____

Exercise 2 **Solving Problems with Verbs**

Some of the verbs in the following paragraph are incorrect. Find the errors and correct them.

When the day arrived, my mother was jubilant. We drive to the synagogue. My aunt Sophie and her daughters comes with us. Once in the temple, the women were not allowed to sit with the men. They had to go upstairs to their assigned places. I was ask to keep my hat on and was given a shawl to wear that I seen before. I was suppose to watch for the rabbi to call me. My turn finally came. I was lead to a table in the front. There I read from the Bible in Hebrew. I knew I could of read louder, but I was nervous. My mother had said that if I was good, she would be especially proud of me, so I done my best. Afterward, I was took by my mother and other relatives to a fine kosher restaurant where we celebrated. I receive a fine gold watch.

Exercise 3 **Solving Problems with Verbs**

Some of the verbs in the following paragraph are incorrect. Find the errors and correct them.

I knowed I was in big trouble in chemistry when I took a look at the midterm exam. My semester should of been a lot better. The first day I had my new textbook, I lay it on the back shelf of a taxi and forgot it when I got out. Then I catched a cold and miss the next two classes. When I finally start off for class, I missed the bus and walked into the classroom half an hour late. The teacher scowls at me and ask to speak to me after class. I use to always sit in the front row so I could see the board and hear the lectures, but now that I am late I have to take a seat in the last row. I wish I was able to start this class over again the right way. No one had ought to have such an unlucky start in any class.

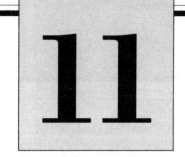

11

More Practice with Fragments and Run-ons

By now, you have learned to recognize the basic fragment or run-on error in your writing. You have worked with revising fairly uncomplicated sentences so that they are correct.

This chapter presents sentences that are more complicated. Even though a sentence may have more than one dependent clause and several phrases, you must always remember that the sentence must have an independent clause with a subject and verb. For example:

> When my family finally went on a vacation which was to take us across Canada by train, we never guessed that my three younger brothers would come down with the chicken pox on the second day.

Cross out all dependent clauses and phrases. Can you find the independent clause? What is the subject? What is the verb? *We never guessed* is the independent clause. All other parts of the sentence are dependent clauses that include many prepositional phrases.

The following exercises require mastery of all the skills you have learned through the earlier chapters on the sentence. You must now revise more complicated sentences to rid them of fragments and run-ons.

Exercise 1   Correcting More Complicated Fragments and Run-ons

Read each example below. If you think the example is a complete sentence, place a C beside the number of the sentence. If you think the example is not correct, revise it so that the sentence is complete. Use the methods you have studied for co-ordination and subordination.

1. Toronto and Montreal, two of the largest cities in Canada, but they have very different cultures.

   _____

   _____

   _____

2. While Toronto, then known as York, was being laid out in the late 1700s, Montreal had a population of over 5000 it was a major fur-trading centre.

    _____

    _____

    _____

3. Now in the twentieth century, Toronto the dominant urban centre, Montreal's population has been relatively stagnant.

    _____

    _____

    _____

4. The time of greatest growth for both cities began with the twentieth century.

    _____

    _____

    _____

5. Toronto, the capital of a rapidly industrializing province, Montreal, a regional metropolis with Old World charm.

    _____

    _____

    _____

6. After Paris, Montreal is the largest French-speaking city in the world Toronto's main language is English many Asian and European languages spoken.

    _____

    _____

    _____

7. Montreal is a key seaport on eastern North America also a rail centre.

    _____

    _____

    _____

8. The average citizen of Toronto is reasonably well-to-do the cost of living there has skyrocketed over the past few years.

    _____

    _____

    _____

9. Visitors to Toronto often comment on the safety and cleanliness of the city there are few other North American cities with such civic pride.

    _____

    _____

    _____

10. Although Toronto may be more expensive than Montreal and Montreal may lack a strong economic base among the two most accommodating cities in Canada.

_____

_____

_____

Exercise 2   **Correcting More Complicated Fragments and Run-ons**

Read each example below. If you think the example is a complete sentence, place a *C* beside the number of the sentence. If you think the example is not correct, revise it so that the sentence is complete. Use the methods you have studied for co-ordination and subordination.

1. Dinner in India is an experience that Western people find very strange things we take for granted are not always available there.

_____

_____

2. Whenever you eat an Indian meal you are not given anything to drink it is not considered appropriate to drink a beverage with a meal.

_____

_____

3. Indian food is eaten with the right hand, you pick up a piece of bread or some rice and scoop up some food.

_____

_____

4. However, when water for rinsing the fingers is given to you at the end of the meal.

_____

_____

5. Because Indian food is so spicy and there are so many different pickles and relishes that are served with nearly every meal.

_____

_____

6. Indians serve plain yogurt with their meals in order to comfort the mouth after spicy foods have been eaten.

_____

7. The habit of chewing betel leaves and betel nuts aiding digestion and sweeten the breath.

8. Breakfast in India, unlike breakfast in Canada.

9. For breakfast, people in India eat dishes of rice and lentils in addition a special lentil soup is part of their first meal of the day.

10. Canadian tourists often trying different kinds of food but always knowing that the best meal of all is a good juicy burger, all dressed.

Exercise 3   Correcting More Complicated Fragments and Run-ons

Read each example below. If you think the example is a complete sentence, place a C beside the number of the sentence. If you think the example is not correct, revise it so that the sentence is complete. Use the methods you have studied for co-ordination and subordination.

1. Because Canada has a wide variety of distinctive and beautiful national historic parks and sites.

2. The flowers that are in full bloom every spring in Grand Pré, site of an early Acadian settlement.

3. At Grand Pré, the Acadians were expelled by the British this event was made famous in the poem "Evangeline."

_____

_____

4. Some people think that the Plains of Abraham is the cradle of Canadian history.

_____

_____

5. Generals Wolfe and Montcalm who decided the fate of Canada during the battle here in 1759.

_____

_____

6. Queenston Heights the location of the decisive battle during the War of 1812.

_____

_____

7. Since everyone on a weekend trip tries to climb Brock's Monument, named after the general who fell during the battle.

_____

_____

8. You can take a tour of Rocky Mountain House in Alberta it was the site of fur-trading posts dating from 1799.

_____

_____

9. Chilkoot Trail in northwestern British Columbia the travel route during the Klondike gold rush.

_____

_____

10. Or, farther north at Dawson City, Yukon, is the actual site of the gold rush that made many fortunes.

_____

_____

_____

Exercise 4 **Correcting More Complicated Fragments and Run-ons**

Read each example below. If you think the example is a complete sentence, place a *C* beside the number of the sentence. If you think the example is not correct, revise it so that the sentence is complete. Use the methods you have studied for co-ordination and subordination.

1. In 1990 hundreds of people waiting for organ transplants.

   _____

   _____

   _____

2. All the people who need transplants are desperate they only have a certain time left to live.

   _____

   _____

   _____

3. In recent years, close to 1000 people who have needed transplants.

   _____

   _____

   _____

4. In spite of the appeals for organ transplants, very few people donate their organs.

   _____

   _____

   _____

5. Every province in need of organ donors some provinces more than others.

   _____

   _____

   _____

6. Since organs are in so much demand, all over the world and for large sums of money.

   _____

   _____

   _____

7. A group that has special problems are those who need kidney transplants who are afraid that if other treatment fails they will have no hope.

   _____

   _____

   _____

8. In 1989 when it was discovered that some people were selling their kidneys to wealthy people in need of them.

    _____

    _____

    _____

9. A whole new area of medical, legal, and ethical problems.

    _____

    _____

    _____

10. Need in the future closer government regulation of organ sales, transplants, and research.

    _____

    _____

    _____

Part II Review: Editing Sentences for Errors

In the following exercises, you will find all types of sentence problems that you have studied in Part II. If you think an example is correct, mark it with a C. If you think there is an error, correct the error so that the sentence is correct.

Major Sentence Errors
Fragments
Run-ons
Incorrect punctuation
Sentence parts that do not work together

Exercise 1   Editing Sentences for Errors

The following examples contain sentence errors studied in Part II. If you think an example is a complete and correct sentence, mark it with a C. If the example has an error, correct it. An example has been done for you.

Incorrect: A group of Gypsies who now live in Ireland.
Correct: A group of Gypsies now live in Ireland.

   or

   A group of Gypsies, who now live in Ireland, make their living by repairing pots and pans.

1. Gypsies now living in many countries of the world.

    _____

    _____

2. The international community of scientists agree that these Gypsies originally came from India thousands of years ago.

    _____

    _____

3. After the original Gypsies left India they went to Persia there they divided into groups.

   _____

4. One branch of Gypsies went west to Europe the other group decided to go east.

   _____

5. In the Middle Ages (476–1453), some Gypsies lived in a fertile area of Greece called Little Egypt.

   _____

6. Gypsies often found it hard to gain acceptance in many countries because of their wandering lifestyle.

   _____

7. Although the Gypsies needed the protection of the pope in Rome.

   _____

8. In the year 1418 when large bands of Gypsies passed through Hungary and Germany where the emperor offered them his protection.

   _____

   _____

9. Between the fifteenth and eighteenth centuries, every country of Europe had Gypsies however not every one of those countries enjoyed having them as guests.

   _____

   _____

10. Today Gypsy families may be found from Canada to Chile living much as his ancestors did thousands of years ago.

    _____

    _____

    _____

Exercise 2   Editing Sentences for Errors

The following examples contain sentence errors studied in Part II. If you think an example is a complete and correct sentence, mark it with a C. If the example has an error, correct it. An example has been done for you.

Incorrect: The Supreme Court of Canada the highest court for all legal

> issues of federal and provincial jurisdiction was created in
> 1949.
>
> *Correct:*   The Supreme Court of Canada, the highest court for all legal
> issues of federal and provincial jurisdiction, was created in
> 1949.

1. Before that time all appeals were addressed to a high court in the United
    Kingdom.

    _____

    _____

2. A chief justice heads the Supreme Court there are also eight junior justices.

    _____

    _____

3. Since at least three of the judges must be appointed from Quebec.

    _____

    _____

4. Three other judges are traditionally appointed from Ontario as well one is
    from the Maritimes and two from western Canada.

    _____

    _____

5. The Supreme Court is also a general court of appeal for criminal cases.

    _____

    _____

6. If a guilty verdict has been reached in a first-degree murder trial in a lower
    court. The Supreme Court automatically reviews the case.

    _____

    _____

7. Bertha Wilson the first woman to sit on the Supreme Court was appointed
    in 1982.

    _____

    _____

8. The Court must try to reflect the dominant characteristics of Canadian
    society such as regionalism dualism and multiculturalism.

    _____

    _____

9. A Supreme Court decision is difficult to alter in fact it takes a constitutional
    amendment approved by Parliament and seven provinces.

    _____

    _____

10. The Supreme Court is now more important than ever the interpretation of the Constitution with its Charter of Rights and Freedoms.

_____

_____

Exercise 3 Editing Sentences for Errors

The following examples contain sentence errors studied in Part II. If you think an example is correct, mark it with a C. If the example has an error, correct it. An example has been done for you.

> *Incorrect:* Science fiction writers have created magic rays that can destroy entire cities, but in recent years a magic ray in the form of laser beams have become scientific fact.
>
> *Correct:* Science fiction writers have created magic rays that can destroy entire cities, but in recent years a magic ray in the form of laser beams has become scientific fact.

1. The laser beam a miracle of modern science already has many practical uses in today's world.

_____

_____

2. Laser beams are narrow, highly concentrated beams of light that burns brighter than the light of the sun.

_____

_____

3. Scientists have found many possible military uses for the laser, but they are hoping it can be converted into constructive channels.

_____

_____

4. John Polanyi, Canadian winner of the Nobel Prize, conducted early experiments on the use of lasers.

_____

_____

5. The possibility of making a laser was first described in 1958 and two years later in California the first laser beam was created.

_____

_____

6.   Since they are so precise, laser beams are used in medicine to help make a specific diagnosis and to perform operations such as repairing delicate retinas and the removal of cancerous tumours.

_____

_____

_____

7.   In the area of communication, laser beams with the ability to carry thousands of telephone conversations at once, or transmit all of the information in a twenty-volume encyclopedia in a fraction of a second.

_____

_____

_____

8.   Lasers are also used to help in the building of bridges and tunnels, it helps make sure that both ends meet properly.

_____

_____

9.   The word laser comes from the words "light amplification by stimulated emission of radiation."

_____

_____

10.   The future uses of the laser seems endless, and it is up to us whether we want to use this invention for war or for peaceful purposes.

_____

_____

Exercise 4   Editing Sentences for Errors

The following examples contain sentence errors studied in Part II. If you think the example is a complete and correct sentence, mark it with a C. If the example has an error, correct it. An example has been done for you.

Incorrect: Most of us buy our food in stores, people in more than one part of the world still hunt for their food.

Correct: While most of us buy our food in stores, people in more than one part of the world still hunt for their food.

1.   For the Inuit, hunting for whales are important in the economy of the people.

_____

_____

2.   Among the Inuit, a good hunter one of the most respected members of the community.

_____

_____

3. In the spring, the Inuit who know that the whaling season is about to begin set up camps to prepare for the hunt.

_____

_____

4. The arrival of some Inuit from faraway places just to be present at the hunt.

_____

_____

5. Children are excused from school for as long as six weeks they help with the work of the camp.

_____

_____

6. While the men go out in their boats, the women and children stay in camp cooking meals and to take care of the dog teams.

_____

_____

7. Sometimes a period of several days go by with no success for the boat crews.

_____

_____

8. Eventually, the people in the camps hear the shouts of the boat crews a whale has been caught.

_____

_____

9. Inuit use every part of the captured whales the blubber is used for fuel, the meat is eaten, and the internal organs are fed to the dogs.

_____

_____

10. Because the Inuit are careful hunters and only kill what they use.

_____

_____

Exercise 5   Editing Sentences for Errors

The following examples contain sentence errors studied in Part II. If you think an example is a complete and correct sentence, mark it with a _C_. If the example has an error, correct it. An example has been done for you.

Incorrect: Although there are many tricks that we would like to teach our pets.

Correct: Although there are many tricks that we would like to teach our pets, few of us have the time and patience required for a training program.

1. Porpoises and their close relatives dolphins are amazing animals.

_____

2. Among their many tricks they can play baseball and basketball jump through hoops ring bells and raise flags.

_____

3. Porpoises are able to use a kind of radar to find objects it cannot see.

_____

4. The wonderful ability of porpoises to imitate human speech.

_____

5. A dolphin and a porpoise often the same thing to many people.

_____

6. Trained porpoises now do tricks for thousands of people, they are in zoos and marinelands across Canada.

_____

7. Porpoises like to swim beside moving boats because they are attracted to the sounds the boats make and because they like to ride in the waves made by the boat.

_____

_____

8. The first step in training a porpoise is observing their natural behaviour.

_____

9. Porpoises have always been helpful and friendly toward humans indeed stories of their good relationships with people go back thousands of years.

_____

10. If you throw a ball to a porpoise, it will probably throw it back to you.

_____

_____

How Much Have You Learned?

Name _____

Date _____

1. _____
2. _____
3. _____
4. _____
5. _____
6. _____
7. _____
8. _____
9. _____
10. _____
11. _____
12. _____
13. _____
14. _____
15. _____
16. _____
17. _____
18. _____
19. _____
20. _____
21. _____
22. _____
23. _____
24. _____
25. _____

26. _____
27. _____
28. _____
29. _____
30. _____
31. _____
32. _____
33. _____
34. _____
35. _____
36. _____
37. _____
38. _____
39. _____
40. _____
41. _____
42. _____
43. _____
44. _____
45. _____
46. _____
47. _____
48. _____
49. _____
50. _____

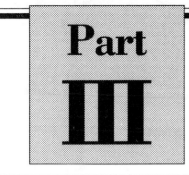

Part III

Mastering the Paragraph

Working with the Topic Sentence

What Is a Paragraph?

A **paragraph** is a group of sentences written to develop one main idea. A paragraph may stand by itself as a complete piece of writing, or it may be a section of a longer piece of writing, such as an essay.

How Long Should a Paragraph Be?

There is no single rule to tell you how long a paragraph should be, but if a paragraph is too short, the reader will feel that basic information is missing. If the paragraph is too long, the reader will be bored or confused. An effective paragraph is always long enough to develop the main idea that is being presented. A healthy paragraph usually consists of at least six sentences and no more than ten or twelve sentences. You have undoubtedly read paragraphs in newspapers that are only one sentence long, but for fully developed college writing one sentence is usually not an acceptable paragraph.

What Does a Paragraph Look Like?

Some students come to college not accustomed to using standard paragraph form. Study the following paragraph to observe standard form. Margins, indentation, and complete sentences are the essential parts of paragraph form.
This paragraph is from the novel *Obasan* by Joy Kogawa.

First word indented.   The old house is indeed old, as she is also old. Every home-made piece of furniture, each pot holder and paper doily is a link in her life line. She has preserved in shelves, in cupboards, under beds — a box of

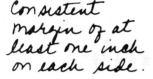
Consistent margin of at least one inch on each side.

marbles, half-filled colouring books, a red, white and blue rubber ball. The items are endless. Every short stub pencil, every cornflakes box stuffed with paper bags and old letters is of her ordering. They rest in the corners like parts of her body, hair cells, skin tissues, tiny specks of memory. This house is now her blood and bones.

Blank space after the final word.

Exercise 1   **Standard Paragraph Form**

Write the following six sentences in standard paragraph form. As you write, use margins, indentation, and complete sentences. Each sentence must begin with a capital letter and end with a period, question mark, or exclamation point.

1. In the large basement of the school, 30 families huddled in little groups of four or five.
2. Volunteer workers were busy carrying in boxes of clothing and blankets.
3. Two Red Cross women stood at a long table sorting through boxes to find sweaters and blankets for the shivering flood victims.
4. One heavyset man in a red woollen hunting jacket stirred a huge pot of soup.
5. Men and women with tired faces sipped their steaming coffee and wondered if they would ever see their homes again.
6. Outside the downpour continued.

Exercise 2   **Standard Paragraph Form**

Write the following seven sentences in standard paragraph form. As you write, use margins, indentation, and complete sentences. Each sentence must begin with a capital letter and end with a period, question mark, or exclamation point.

1. Friday afternoon I was desperate to get my English homework finished before I left the campus.
2. The assignment was due on Monday, but I really wanted my weekend free.
3. As I sat at the table in the library, I could see dictionaries and other reference books on the nearby shelves.
4. I felt in a good mood because I knew that if I had to find some information for my assignment, it would be available to me.
5. The only worry I had was whether or not I would be interrupted by my friends who might stop by, wanting to chat.

6. Luckily I worked along with no interruptions and was able to finish my work by five o'clock.

7. My weekend was saved!

_____

_____

_____

_____

_____

_____

_____

_____

_____

_____

_____

_____

_____

What Is a Topic Sentence?

A **topic sentence** is the sentence in a paragraph that states the main idea of that paragraph. It is the most general sentence of the paragraph. All the other sentences of the paragraph serve to explain, describe, extend, or support this main-idea sentence.

Most paragraphs you read will begin with the topic sentence. However, some topic sentences come in the middle of the paragraph; others come at the end. Some paragraphs have no stated topic sentence at all; in those cases, the main idea is implied. College students are usually advised to use topic sentences in all college work in order to be certain that the writing has a focus and develops a single idea at a time. Whether you are taking an essay exam in a history course, doing a research paper for a sociology course, or writing an essay in a freshman composition course, thoughtful use of the topic sentence will always bring better results. Good topic sentences help both the writer and the reader to think clearly about the main points.

Below are two paragraphs. Each paragraph makes a separate point, which is stated in its topic sentence. In both of these paragraphs, the topic sentence happens to be first. Read the paragraphs and notice how the topic sentence is the most general sentence; it is the main idea of each paragraph. The other sentences explain, describe, extend, or support the topic sentence.

Model Paragraph 1

"Turn down the volume and turn down the danger." That's the theme of a campaign by the Canadian Hearing Society, warning that walk-around stereos can be harmful to your health. The nonprofit group, which has distributed thousands of fact sheets to high school students, hopes to make them aware that permanent hearing loss can result from prolonged exposure to any intense noice — whether pleasant or unpleasant.

Model Paragraph 2

The power of a sound wave is measured in units called decibels. Normal conversations are about 60 decibels. Very busy traffic has been clocked at 80 decibels. A garbage truck operates at 100 decibels, a power saw at 110 decibels. The sound level at rock concerts can go as loud as 120 decibels. Research from industry indicates that prolonged exposure to sound over 85 decibels can cause permanent hearing loss.

Exercise 1   Finding the Topic Sentence of a Paragraph

Each of the following five paragraphs contains a topic sentence that states the main idea of the paragraph. Find which sentence best states the main idea and underline it. The topic sentence will not always be the first sentence of the paragraph.

1.   Mountains of Pampers are thrown into garbage cans every day. Tons of yogurt containers, soda cans, and other plastic items are discarded without so much as a stomp to flatten them out. If the old Chevy is not worth fixing, tow it off to sit with thousands of others on acres of fenced-in junkyards. Radios, televisions, and toasters get the same treatment because it is easier and often less expensive to buy a new product than to fix the old one. Who wants a comfortable old sweater if a new one can be bought on sale? No thought is given that the new one will soon look like the old one after two or three washings. We are the great "Let's junk it" society!

2.   The airshaft was a horrible invention. Even with the windows tightly sealed, it served as a sounding box and you could hear everybody's business. Rats scurried around the bottom. There was always the danger of fire. A match absently tossed into the airshaft by a drunk under the impression that he was throwing it into the yard or street would set the house afire in a moment. There were vile things cluttering up the bottom. Since this bottom couldn't be reached (the windows being too small to admit the passage of a body), it served as a fearful repository for things that people wanted to put out of their lives. Rusted razor blades and bloody cloths were the most innocent items.

3.   Anything can happen at a county agricultural fair. It is the perfect human occasion, the harvest of the fields and of the emotions. To the fair come the man and his cow, the boy and his girl, the wife and her green tomato pickle, each anticipating victory and the excitement of being separated from his or her money by familiar devices. It is at a fair that man can be drunk forever on liquor, love, or fights; at a fair that your front pocket can

be picked by a trotting horse looking for sugar, and your hind pocket by a thief looking for a fortune.

4.   This was one of the worst situations I had ever been in. There was a tube in my nose that went all the way to the pit of my stomach. I was being fed intravenously, and there was a drain in my side. Everybody came to visit me, mainly out of curiosity. The girls were all anxious to know where I had gotten shot. They had heard all kinds of tales about where the bullet struck. The bolder ones wouldn't even bother to ask: they just snatched the cover off me and looked for themselves. In a few days, the word got around that I was in one piece.

5.   On hot summer days, the only room of the house that was cool was the sunporch. My mother brought all her books and papers and stacked them up on the card table. There she would sit for hours at a stretch with one hand on her forehead trying to concentrate. Baby Kathleen would often sit in her playpen beside her, throwing all her toys out of the pen or screeching with such a piercing high pitch that someone would have to come and rescue Mum by giving the baby a cracker. Father would frequently bring in cups of tea for everyone and make Mother laugh with his Irish sense of humour. It was there I would love to curl up on the wicker sofa (which was too short for my long legs even at twelve) and read one of the 40 or 50 books I had bought for ten cents each at a local book fair. The sounds of neighbourhood activities — muted voices, a back door slamming, a dog barking — all these were a background that was friendly yet distant. During those summer days, the sunporch was the centre of our lives.

Exercise 2   Finding the Topic Sentence of a Paragraph

Each of the following five paragraphs contains a sentence that states the main idea of the paragraph. Find which sentence best states the main idea and then underline it. In these paragraphs, the topic sentence will not always be the first sentence.

1.   Last evening at a party, a complete stranger asked me, "Are you a Libra?" Astrology is enjoying increasing popularity all across Canada. My wife hurries every morning to read her horoscope in the paper. At the local stores, cards, books, T-shirts, and other useless astrological products bring fat profits to those who have manufactured them. Even some public officials, like the British royal family, are known to consider the "science" of astrology before scheduling an important event.

2.   The Canadian game of hockey was born during long northern winters uncluttered by things to do. It grew up on ponds and rivers, in big open spaces, unorganized, often solitary, only occasionally moving into arenas for practices or games. In recent generations, that has changed. Canadians have moved from farms and towns to cities and suburbs; they've discovered skis, snowmobiles, and southern vacations; they've civilized winter and brought it indoors. A game we once played on rivers and ponds,

later on streets and driveways and in backyards, we now play in arenas, in full team uniforms, with coaches and referees, or to an ever-increasing extent, we don't play at all.

3. When you remember something, your brain uses more than one method to store the information. You have short-term memory, which helps you recall recent events; you have long-term memory, which brings back items that are further in the past; and you have deep retrieval, which gives you access to long-buried information that is sometimes difficult to recall. Whether these processes are chemical or electrical, we do not yet know, and much research remains to be done before we can say with any certainty. The brain is one of the most remarkable organs, a part of the body that we have only begun to investigate. It will be years before we even begin to understand all its complex processes.

4. Some of the homes were small with whitewashed walls and thatched roofs. We were eager to see how they were furnished. The living rooms were simple, often with only a plain wooden table and some chairs. The tiny bedrooms usually had room for only a single bed and a small table. Occasionally, a bedroom would be large enough to also have a stove made of richly decorated tiles. Visiting these houses was an experience that would always stay in our memory. All of the windows held boxes for flowers so that even in the dark of winter there was the promise of a blaze of colours in the spring.

5. Advertisements that claim you can lose two kilograms overnight are not to be trusted. Nor are claims that your luck will change if you send money to a certain post office box in a distant province. You should also avoid chain letters you receive in the mail that promise you large amounts of money if you will co-operate and keep the chain going. Many people are suspicious of the well-publicized million-dollar giveaway promotions that seem to offer enormous cash prizes, even if they do not try the company's product. We should always be suspicious of offers that promise us something for little or no effort or money.

Exercise 3   Finding the Topic Sentence of a Paragraph

The topic sentence is missing in each of the following five paragraphs. Read each paragraph carefully and select the best topic sentence from the four possible answers that follow each paragraph.

1. Topic sentence: _____

_____

The men own little more than spears and boomerangs. The women have containers made of wood or bark. They grind their grass seeds with a stone and have no more than a simple stick to dig up tubers and small creatures. These people have never learned to weave cloth for clothes, to make pottery for cooking, or to use animals to help carry their belongings.

a. Aborigine women have very few tools with which to work.
b. The poorest people in the world.

    c. The Aborigines of Australia have very few material possessions.

    d. Aborigines can survive in the deserts of central Australia where no other people can live unless they bring their own food with them.

2.   Topic sentence: _____

_____

Actually, this idea is far from the truth. The Aborigines have been able to survive for centuries in the harsh environment of the desert because their minds are highly trained in the knowledge of food sources. Since they have no means of storing food, their entire attention must be directed toward the daily search for food. From the youngest child to the oldest member of the tribe, food gathering is the top priority. The Aborigines possess a profound understanding of the life around them.

    a. In the earliest years, children are taught when foods ripen, where foods are to be found, when animals hibernate and reproduce, and where water is likely to be found.

    b. The Aborigines' in-depth knowledge of the environment around them.

    c. The interior of Australia is arid and inhospitable to human beings.

    d. Many observers have mistakenly thought that the Aborigines, with so few tools, must have a lower intelligence than other races.

3.   Topic sentence: _____

_____

To catch the larger creatures—kangaroos, wallabies, and emus—the men often have to make long journeys in the cold of winter or the blazing heat of summer. The women, laden with the children and the camp gear, travel in a more or less straight line from one stopping place to the next, gathering vegetable foods, fruits, and small creatures on the way. The men often return empty-handed at the end of the day, for the desert animals are wary and difficult to capture, but the women always bring in some food. Sometimes it is not much, nor particularly tasty, but it is usually enough to keep the family going until the hunters are more successful.

    a. The Aborigines are very industrious, working the entire day.

    b. The labour of food gathering is fairly equally divided between the men and the women.

    c. Aboriginal men face the difficult task of finding food for their families.

    d. Food gathering among the Aborigines.

4.   Topic sentence: _____

_____

A full knowledge of the secret and ceremonial life of the tribe is possessed only by these elders. It is they who maintain the ancient laws, agree on the punishment of law-breakers, and decide when the rituals, on which the social and philosophical life of the tribe depends, will be performed. It is not, therefore, the task of a professional or priestly class to preserve the traditional myths and their associated rituals, but of a number of groups of fully initiated men, each group being responsible for memorizing myths, songs, and rites belonging to their family territories, and for passing them on, unaltered, to the succeeding generation.

    a. The government of these people is in the hands of the well-informed old men, not the physically active youths.

    b. Passing on traditions to the next generation of Aborigines.

    c. Aboriginal myths and rituals must be memorized, since there is no written language.

d. The Aboriginal government is successful in getting its people to live together in harmony.

5. Topic sentence: _____

_____

Greek tales tell of how the gods and demigods of Olympia created the volcanoes, mountains, and coastline of the Mediterranean. Sagas from Scandinavia record how gods made the universe. Myths of the Australian Aborigines tell what life was like when the world was young. They refer to this time as the "Dreamtime." Dreamtime heroes created everything in the Aborigines' daily life. Besides explaining the origin of the world about them, these myths from ancient civilizations governed the life of the people with a rich philosophy and stimulated the cultural development.

a. The myths of ancient Greece are similar to other ancient myths.
b. The myths of the Australian Aborigines are comparable to those of other ancient civilizations.
c. The myths of Greece have influenced the literature, drama, and art of the Western world for over 2000 years.
d. The myths of ancient times are accepted as absolute truth and an answer to all the questions of living.

How Can You Tell a Topic Sentence from a Title?

The topic sentence works like a title by announcing to the reader what the paragraph is about. However, keep in mind that the title of an essay or book is usually a single word or short phrase, whereas the topic sentence of a paragraph must *always* be a complete sentence.

Title: Backpacking in the mountains
Topic sentence: Backpacking in the mountains last year was an exciting experience.

Title: The stress of college registration
Topic sentence: College registration can be stressful.

Exercise 1   Distinguishing a Topic Sentence from a Title

Each of the following ten examples is either a title or a topic sentence. In each of the spaces provided, identify the example by writing *T* or *TS*.

_____   1.   The benefits of a college education

_____   2.   The outstanding achievements of swimmer Vicki Keith

_____   3.   The Mulroney administration faced major economic problems

_____   4.   The basis of the French-English conflict

_____   5.   The Japanese diet is perhaps the healthiest diet in the world

_____   6.   The astounding beauty of the Rocky Mountains at dusk

_____   7.   The finest sports car on the market

_____   8.   Fast-food restaurants are popular with families having small children

_____ 9. The expense of maintaining a car

_____ 10. Maintaining a car is expensive

Exercise 2   Distinguishing a Topic Sentence from a Title

Each of the following ten examples is either a title or a topic sentence. In each of the spaces provided, identify the example by writing *T* or *TS*.

_____ 1. Dreams can be frightening

_____ 2. The advantages of getting a job after high school

_____ 3. *The Weekend Man*, Richard B. Wright's first novel, is one of the most evocative and compelling novels of the 1970s.

_____ 4. The home of my dreams

_____ 5. Walking on the beach at sunset calms me down after a stressful day at work

_____ 6. Making your own clothes requires great patience as well as skill

_____ 7. Selecting the right camera for an amateur

_____ 8. Finding the right place to study was my most difficult problem at college

_____ 9. The worst bargain of my life

_____ 10. The old car I bought from my friend's father turned out to be a real bargain

Exercise 3   Distinguishing a Topic Sentence from a Title

Each of the following ten examples is either a title or a topic sentence. In each of the spaces provided, identify the example by writing *T* or *TS*.

_____ 1. How to make friends at college and still have time to study

_____ 2. As the computer becomes a common working tool, typing will be an even more important skill to learn than it has been before

_____ 3. The disadvantages of living alone

_____ 4. The fight to keep our neighbourhood park

_____ 5. The peacefulness of a solitary weekend at the beach

_____ 6. Our investigation into the mysterious death of Walter D.

_____ 7. The flea market looked promising

_____ 8. The two main reasons why divorce is common

_____ 9. The single life did not turn out to be as glamorous as I had hoped

_____ 10. The increasing popularity of board games

What Are the Two Parts of a Topic Sentence?

Every topic sentence has a topic and a controlling idea. The **topic** is what the paragraph is about. The **controlling idea** is the attitude the writer has about the topic.

How Do You Find the Topic in a Topic Sentence?

To find the topic in a topic sentence, ask yourself this question: What is the topic the writer is going to discuss? Below are two topic sentences. The topic for the first topic sentence is underlined. Underline the topic in the second example.

Backpacking in the mountains last year was an exciting experience.

College registration can be stressful.

Exercise 1 Finding the Topic in the Topic Sentence

Find the topic in each of the following topic sentences. For each example, ask yourself this question: What is the topic the writer is going to discuss? Then underline the topic.

1. Remodelling an old house can be frustrating.
2. College work demands more independence than high school work.
3. A well-made suit has three easily identified characteristics.
4. Growing up near a museum had a profound influence on my life.
5. My favourite room in the house would seem ugly to most people.
6. A student who goes to school full time and also works part time has to make careful use of every hour.
7. One of the disadvantages of skiing is the expense.
8. Spanking is the least successful way to discipline a child.
9. An attractive wardrobe does not have to be expensive.
10. Of all the years in college, the freshman year is usually the most demanding.

Exercise 2 Finding the Topic in the Topic Sentence

Find the topic in each of the following topic sentences. For each example, ask yourself this question: What is the topic the writer is going to discuss? Then underline the topic.

1. To my surprise, the basement had now been converted into a small studio apartment.
2. Of all the prime ministers, Pierre Trudeau probably enjoyed the greatest popularity.
3. Scientists cannot yet explain how an identical twin often has an uncanny knowledge of what the other twin is doing or feeling.
4. If you don't have a car in Canada, you have undoubtedly discovered that rail transportation is in a state of decay.
5. When we met for dinner that night, I was shocked at the change that had come over my friend.
6. According to the report, current tax laws greatly benefit those who own real estate.

7. *Reader's Digest,* the Canadian English edition, is the leading paid-circulation magazine in the country.

8. As we rode into town, the streets seemed unusually empty.

9. Canadian Tire offers its employees many long-term benefits.

10. Many people claim that clipping coupons can save them as much as 30 percent of their food bill.

Exercise 3   **Finding the Topic in the Topic Sentence**

Find the topic in each of the following topic sentences. For each example, ask yourself this question: What is the topic the writer is going to discuss? Then underline the topic.

1. Taking care of a house can easily be a full-time job.

2. Many of the daytime television shows are wasting people's time.

3. One of the undisputed goals in teaching is to be able to offer individualized instruction.

4. Whether it's a car, a house, or a college, bigger isn't always better.

5. Violence on television is disturbing to most child psychologists.

6. In today's economy, carrying at least one credit card is probably advisable.

7. Much highway advertising is not only ugly but also distracting for the driver.

8. Choosing a lifelong career involves a complicated process of making many decisions.

9. In recent years, we have seen a dramatic revival of interest in quilting.

10. The grading system of the university is quite different from that of the community college in my home town.

How Do You Find the Controlling Idea of a Topic Sentence?

Every topic sentence contains not only the topic but also a controlling idea. This controlling idea tells us the attitude the writer has taken toward the topic. For example, in the topic sentence "Backpacking in the mountains last year was an exciting experience," the topic is "backpacking" and the controlling idea is that this backpacking trip was "exciting." Another person on the same trip might have had another attitude toward the trip. This person might have found the trip exhausting or boring. A single topic can therefore have any number of possibilities for development, since the writer can choose from a limitless number of controlling ideas, depending on his or her attitude.

When you look for the controlling idea in a topic sentence, ask yourself this question: What is the writer's attitude toward the topic?

In each of the following examples, the topic is underlined and the controlling idea is circled.

Holt Renfrew is my (favourite) store in town.

Holt Renfrew is (too expensive) for my budget.

Exercise 1   **Finding the Controlling Idea**

Below are ten topic sentences. For each sentence, underline the topic and circle the controlling idea.

1. Vigorous exercise is a good way to reduce the effect of stress on the body.

2. St. John's and Corner Brook differ in four major ways.

3. Television violence causes aggressive behaviour in children.
4. Athletic scholarships available to women are increasing.
5. Caffeine has several adverse effects on the body.
6. Madame Benoit, a famous gourmet cook, had an amusing personality.
7. Training a parakeet to talk takes great patience.
8. Baby-sitting for a family with four preschool children was the most difficult job I've ever had.
9. The hours between five and seven in the morning are my most productive.
10. The foggy night was spooky.

Exercise 2 Finding the Controlling Idea

Below are ten topic sentences. For each sentence, underline the topic and circle the controlling idea.

1. Piano lessons turned out to be a disaster.
2. The training of Japanese police is quite different from Canadian police training.
3. An Olympic champion has five distinctive characteristics.
4. The candidate's unethical financial dealings will have a negative impact in this campaign.
5. A bicycle ride along the coast is a breathtaking trip.
6. The grocery store is another place where people waste a significant amount of money every week.
7. Being an only child is not as bad as people think.
8. Rewarding children with candy or desserts is an unfortunate habit of many parents.
9. A childhood hobby often develops into a promising career.
10. The writing of a dictionary is an incredible process.

Exercise 3 Finding the Controlling Idea

Below are ten topic sentences. For each sentence, underline the topic and circle the controlling idea.

1. Learning to type takes more practice than talent.
2. Shakespeare's plays are difficult for today's students because English has undergone many changes since the sixteenth century.
3. Markham, Ontario, is one of the cities in southern Ontario that has experienced significant population growth.
4. Half a dozen new magazines totally devoted to health are enjoying popularity with the public.
5. The importance of good preschool programs for children has been sadly underestimated.
6. The disposal of toxic wastes has caused problems for many manufacturers.
7. Censorship of school textbooks is a controversial issue in some towns.
8. How to make salt water drinkable by an inexpensive method has been a difficult problem for decades.

9. Developing colour film is more complicated than developing black and white.

10. The cloudberry is one of the rare berries of the world.

Choosing Your Own Controlling Idea

Teachers often assign one general topic on which all students must write. Likewise, when writing contests are announced, the topic is generally the same for all contestants. Since very few people have exactly the same view or attitude toward a topic, it is likely that no two papers would have the same controlling idea. There could be as many controlling ideas as there are people to write them. The secret of writing a good topic sentence is to find the controlling idea that is right for you.

Exercise 1   **Choosing Controlling Ideas for Topic Sentences**

Below are two topics. For each topic, think of three different possible controlling ideas, and then write a different topic sentence for each of these controlling ideas. An example is done for you.

Topic: My mother
Three possible controlling ideas:
1. Unusual childhood
2. Silent woman
3. Definite ideas about alcohol

Three different topic sentences:
1. My mother had a most unusual childhood.
2. My mother is a very silent woman.
3. My mother has definite ideas about alcohol.

1. **Topic:** My father

   First controlling idea: _____

   First topic sentence: _____

   _____

   Second controlling idea: _____

   Second topic sentence: _____

   _____

   Third controlling idea: _____

   Third topic sentence: _____

   _____

2. **Topic:** The Northwest Territories

   First controlling idea: _____

   First topic sentence: _____

   _____

Second controlling idea: _____

Second topic sentence: _____

_____

Third controlling idea: _____

Third topic sentence: _____

_____

Exercise 2   **Choosing Controlling Ideas for Topic Sentences**

Below are two topics. For each topic, think of three different possible controlling ideas, and then write a different topic sentence for each of these controlling ideas. An example is done for you.

Topic: My mother
Three possible controlling ideas:
1. Unusual childhood
2. Silent woman
3. Definite ideas about alcohol

Three different topic sentences:
1. My mother had a most unusual childhood.
2. My mother is a very silent woman.
3. My mother has definite ideas about alcohol.

1. **Topic:** Thanksgiving

    First controlling idea: _____

    First topic sentence: _____

    _____

    Second controlling idea: _____

    Second topic sentence: _____

    _____

    Third controlling idea: _____

    Third topic sentence: _____

    _____

2. **Topic:** Working in a nursing home

    First controlling idea: _____

    First topic sentence: _____

    _____

    Second controlling idea: _____

    Second topic sentence: _____

    _____

Third controlling idea: _____

Third topic sentence: _____

_____

Exercise 3   **Choosing Controlling Ideas for Topic Sentences**

Below are two topics. For each topic, think of three different possible controlling ideas, and then write a different topic sentence for each of these controlling ideas. An example is done for you.

Topic: My mother
Three possible controlling ideas:
1. Unusual childhood
2. Silent woman
3. Definite ideas about alcohol

Three different topic sentences:
1. My mother had a most unusual childhood.
2. My mother is a very silent woman.
3. My mother has definite ideas about alcohol.

1. **Topic:** Miss Canada

   First controlling idea: _____

   First topic sentence: _____

   _____

   Second controlling idea: _____

   Second topic sentence: _____

   _____

   Third controlling idea: _____

   Third topic sentence: _____

   _____

2. **Topic:** Junk food

   First controlling idea: _____

   First topic sentence: _____

   _____

   Second controlling idea: _____

   Second topic sentence: _____

   _____

   Third controlling idea: _____

   Third topic sentence: _____

   _____

Exercise 1   Further Practice Writing the Topic Sentence

Develop each of the following topics into a topic sentence. In each case, the controlling idea is missing. First, decide on an attitude you might take toward the topic. Then use the attitude you have chosen to write your topic sentence. When you are finished, underline your topic and circle your controlling idea. Be sure your topic sentence is a complete sentence and not a fragment. An example has been done for you.

> _Topic:_   My brother's car accident
> _Controlling idea:_   Tragic results
> _Topic sentence:_   My brother's car accident had tragic results for the entire family.

1. **Topic:** Teaching a child good manners

    Controlling idea: _____

    Topic sentence: _____

    _____

2. **Topic:** Two years in the armed forces

    Controlling idea: _____

    Topic sentence: _____

    _____

3. **Topic:** Making new friends

    Controlling idea: _____

    Topic sentence: _____

    _____

4. **Topic:** The old woman

    Controlling idea: _____

    Topic sentence: _____

    _____

5. **Topic:** Going on a diet

    Controlling idea: _____

    Topic sentence: _____

    _____

Exercise 2   Further Practice Writing the Topic Sentence

Develop each of the following topics into a topic sentence. In each case, the controlling idea is missing. First, decide on an attitude you might take toward the topic. Then use the attitude you have chosen to write your topic sentence. When you are finished, underline your topic and circle your controlling idea. Be sure your topic sentence is a complete sentence and not a fragment.

1. **Topic:** Compact cars

    Controlling idea: _____

Topic sentence: _____

_____

2. **Topic:** Vegetarians

Controlling idea: _____

Topic sentence: _____

_____

3. **Topic:** My home town

Controlling idea: _____

Topic sentence: _____

_____

4. **Topic:** Writing essays

Controlling idea: _____

Topic sentence: _____

_____

5. **Topic:** Subways

Controlling idea: _____

Topic sentence: _____

_____

Exercise 3 Further Practice Writing the Topic Sentence

Develop each of the following topics into a topic sentence. In each case, the controlling idea is missing. First, decide on an attitude you might take toward the topic. Then use the attitude you have chosen to write your topic sentence. When you are finished, underline your topic and circle your controlling idea. Be sure your topic sentence is a complete sentence and not a fragment.

1. **Topic:** Computer programming

Controlling idea: _____

Topic sentence: _____

_____

2. **Topic:** Jewellery fashions

Controlling idea: _____

Topic sentence: _____

_____

3. **Topic:** Zoos

Controlling idea: _____

Topic sentence: _____

_____

4. **Topic:** Motorcycles

    Controlling idea: _____

    Topic sentence: _____

    _____

5. **Topic:** Homework

    Controlling idea: _____

    Topic sentence: _____

    _____

Working with Supporting Details

What Is a Supporting Detail?

A **supporting detail** is a piece of evidence used by the writer to make the controlling idea of the topic sentence convincing to the reader.

Once you have constructed your topic sentence with its topic and controlling idea, you are ready to move on to supporting your statement with details. These details will convince your readers that what you are claiming in the topic sentence is believable or reasonable.

As you choose these supporting details, realize that the readers do not necessarily have to agree with your point of view. However, your supporting details must be good enough so that your readers will at least respect your attitude. Your goal is to educate your readers. Try to make them experts on the subject you are writing about. The quality and number of your supporting details will determine how well you do this. If you have enough details, and if your details are specific enough, your readers will feel they have learned something new about the subject. This is always a satisfying experience.

It is also true that specific details tend to stay in readers' minds much better than general ideas. The fact that over 25000 males died of cancer in Canada in 1985 is much more effective and memorable than a statement saying only that cancer killed many people.

Finally, specific details make a piece of writing more fun to read. When the reader has concrete objects, particular people, or recognizable places to hang on to, the contents of the writing become a pleasure to read.

The following paragraph, taken from an essay about the richness of North American native peoples' languages, contains a topic sentence with several good supporting details.

> Unlike solid rock, languages are remarkably adaptable, easily borrowing or coining new words as circumstances change. The horse, unknown when the Spanish landed, soon took on a central role among the

tribes, and words for the horse and its many uses were introduced. One device was to borrow some form of the Spanish word *caballo*. Another was to invent a descriptive term. Native people of eastern New York State used a word meaning "one rides its back"; in the western part, the word for horse means "it hauls out logs." Presumably these were the first uses of horses seen in the two areas. Among the Kwakiutl of British Columbia, a steamboat was "fire on its back moving in the water." To the Tsimshian of the same area, the word for rice was "looking like maggots."

Notice that the topic sentence gives us the topic (language) and the writer's attitude toward the topic (remarkably adaptable). Each of the sentences that follow this topic sentence is a supporting detail that convinces us that the controlling idea is a reasonable attitude. The writer provides more than one example and chooses these examples from more than one group of native people. This wide range makes the topic sentence convincing and, of course, more interesting.

Practice Using the lines given, copy the exact topic sentence for the paragraph above. Then, in your own words, give each of the details for each of the supporting sentences. Be prepared to discuss how each of the supporting sentences supports or explains the controlling idea contained in the topic sentence.

Topic sentence: _____

_____

_____

First supporting detail: _____

_____

_____

Second supporting detail: _____

_____

_____

Third supporting detail: _____

_____

_____

Fourth supporting detail: _____

_____

_____

Fifth supporting detail: _____

_____

_____

_____

Exercise 1   Finding the Topic Sentence and Supporting Details

For each of the two paragraphs below, divide the sentences into topic sentence and supporting details.

1. As the grayest, quietest, most culturally introverted major city in a gray, quiet, culturally introverted country, Ottawa is not a place where one expects to find architecture on the fringe. But when the Canadian Museum of Civilization officially opened last week just across the river in the city of Hull, it took its place as one of the largest museums in the world and certainly one of the more curious — a wildly eccentric, million-square-foot [93 000 m²] limestone pile of curves and ellipses, Antoni Gaudi crossed with late Frank Lloyd Wright, baroque quirkiness run amuck. Architect Douglas Cardinal's museum is more a fascinating curiosity than a masterwork. But its flamboyance and seductive, Disneyesque natural history exhibits — life-size Indian homes downstairs, replica townscapes from the past 500 years upstairs — will surely make it the capital's biggest tourist attraction, if not Canada's.

From Kirk Andersen,
"A Grand Folly in Ottawa,"
Time

Topic sentence: _____

_____

First supporting detail: _____

_____

Second supporting detail: _____

_____

Third supporting detail: _____

_____

2. I cannot teach anyone to write fiction. What I can do is to smooth the road for those who show natural talent as storytellers. But if you have your heart set on writing fiction, consider the following: you must have the ability to write complete sentences in clear, straightforward standard English; you need the imagination to create stories; passion, to love the characters you write about; and you have to have stamina, to stick with it even when you don't feel like it.

Adapted from W. P. Kinsella,
"How to Write Fiction,"
Globe and Mail

Topic sentence: _____

_____

First supporting detail: _____

_____

Second supporting detail: _____

_____

Third supporting detail: _____

_____

Fourth supporting detail: _____

_____

_____

Fifth supporting detail: _____

_____

_____

Exercise 2 **Finding the Topic Sentence and Supporting Details**

For each of the two paragraphs below, divide the sentences into topic sentence and supporting details.

1. Norman Dyer hurried down Sherbrooke Street, collar turned against the snow. "Superb!" he muttered, passing a basement gallery next to a French bookstore. Bleached and tanned women in furs dashed from hotel lobbies into waiting cabs. Even the neon clutter of the side streets and the honks of slithering taxis seemed remote tonight through the peaceful snow. *Superb*, he thought again, waiting for a light and backing from a slushy curb: a word reserved for wines, cigars, and delicate sauces; he was feeling superb this evening. After eighteen months in Montreal, he still found himself freshly impressed by everything he saw.

    From Clark Blaise,
    A Class of New Canadians

Topic sentence: _____

_____

First supporting detail: _____

_____

Second supporting detail: _____

_____

Third supporting detail: _____

_____

Fourth supporting detail: _____

_____

Fifth supporting detail: _____

_____

2. "We're very insecure in this place, you know." Alistair Rangoolam crossed his fat legs and smiled beatifically, his plump cheeks, gouged by bad childhood acne, quivering at the effect his words had had. "You fly down here, you see a beautiful island, sun, coconut trees, beaches. But I live here and I see a different reality, I see the university students parading Marx and Castro on the campus, I see more policemen with guns, I see people rioting downtown, I see my friends running away to Vancouver

and Miami. So you can see, we are very insecure down here. That's why I want you to put the money your company owes me in my Toronto bank account. It is my own private insurance. The bank will notify me the money has been deposited and the government here won't notice a thing.''

From Neil Bissoondath,
Insecurity

Topic sentence: _____

_____

First supporting detail: _____

_____

Second supporting detail: _____

_____

Third supporting detail: _____

_____

_____

Exercise 3 Finding the Topic Sentence and Supporting Details

For each of the two paragraphs below, divide the sentences into topic sentence and supporting details.

1. Occasionally I astonish friends and frighten strangers by telling them that there are valid arguments in favour of the principle of the divine right of kings. I like to think that I'd have supported Charles I against Parliament, and James II against the Whig aristocracy; and I believe I understand why Yukio Mishima, a Japanese writer who recently committed ritual suicide, could argue that his emperor was divine.

From Alden Nowlan,
''In Defence of the Divine Right of Kings''

Topic sentence: _____

_____

First supporting detail: _____

_____

Second supporting detail: _____

_____

Third supporting detail: _____

_____

_____

2.   Then my father and I walked gradually down a long, shabby sort of street, with Silverwoods Ice Cream signs standing on the sidewalk, outside tiny, lighted stores. This is in Tuppertown, an old town on Lake Huron, an old grain port. The street is shaded, in some places, by maple trees whose roots have cracked and heaved the sidewalk and spread out like crocodiles into the bare yards. People are sitting out, men in shirtsleeves and undershirts and women in aprons — not people we know but if anyone looks ready to nod and say, "Warm night," my father will nod too and say something the same. Children are still playing. I don't know them either because my mother keeps my brother and me in our own yard, saying he is too young to leave it and I have to mind him. I am not so sad to watch their evening games because the gardens themselves are ragged, dissolving. Children, of their own will, draw apart, separate into islands of two or one under the heavy trees, occupying themselves in such solitary ways as I do all day, planting pebbles in the dirt or writing in it with a stick.

From Alice Munro,
"Walker and Brothers Cowboy"

Topic sentence: _____

_____

First supporting detail: _____

_____

Second supporting detail: _____

_____

Third supporting detail: _____

_____

Fourth supporting detail: _____

_____

Fifth supporting detail: _____

_____

Sixth supporting detail: _____

_____

Avoid Restating the Topic Sentence

One of your most important jobs as you write a paragraph is recognizing the difference between a genuine supporting detail and a simple restatement of the topic sentence. The following is a poor paragraph with all its sentences merely restating the topic sentence.

My grandmother's photograph dates from a period when she and her family came to live in St. Petersburg. I like to look at the photograph and wonder about how life was in those days. From the clothes that my grandmother is wearing in the old photograph, it looks as if she is ready for a formal occasion. It is difficult to tell, though, because the picture is old and faded. I don't think she enjoyed formal occasions.

By contrast, this paragraph, from Michael Ignatieff's *The Russian Album*, has good supporting details:

> In the family album there is a photograph of my grandmother, Natasha Ignatieff, that dates from the period when she and her family came to live in St. Petersburg in the dark and cluttered apartment two blocks from the Neva river. She is dressed for a formal winter evening, a fox fur draped over her shoulders. Brussels lace on the bodice of her velvet gown, her hair swept back in a tight chignon, and a twelve-strand pearl choker around her stiffly upright neck. She is thin and pale, the cheekbones of her long angular face taking the light, the eyes deep-set and dark. Her expression is guarded, and she seems at odds with the occasion. She was a private soul: in the public glare, she shrank back. She hated Petersburg society: paying courtesy calls on the wives of Paul's superiors, making curtsies and small talk and all the while feeling she was up on a high wire one step from a fall.

Exercise 1 Distinguishing a Supporting Detail from a Restatement of the Main Idea

Each of the following topic sentences is followed by four additional sentences. Three of these additional sentences contain acceptable supporting details, but one of the sentences is simply a restatement of the topic sentence. In the space provided, identify each sentence as *SD* for *supporting detail* or *R* for *restatement*.

1. I am surprised at myself when I think how neat I used to be before I started school full time.

    _____ a. In my closet, I had my clothes arranged in matching outfits with shoes, hats, and even jewellery to go with them.

    _____ b. I always used to take great pride in having all my things in order.

    _____ c. If I opened my desk drawer, compartments of paper clips, erasers, staples, pens, pencils, stamps, and rulers greeted me without one lost penny or safety pin thrown in out of place.

    _____ d. On top of my chest of drawers sat a comb and brush, two oval frames with pictures of my best friends, and that was all.

2. Iceland has a very barren landscape.

    _____ a. One-tenth of the island is covered by ice.

    _____ b. Not one forest with magnificent trees is to be found.

    _____ c. Nature has not been kind to the people of Iceland.

    _____ d. Three-fourths of the island is uninhabitable.

3. Until recently, books have been the most important method of preserving knowledge.

    _____ a. Without books, much of the knowledge of past centuries would have been lost.

    _____ b. Leonardo da Vinci kept notebooks of his amazing inventions and discoveries.

    _____ c. During the Middle Ages, monks spent their entire lives copying books by hand.

_____ d. The National Library of Canada in Ottawa obtains a copy of many books published in Canada.

4. Most people no longer wonder whether cigarette smoking is bad for their health.

_____ a. Following the evidence from over 30 000 studies, a federal law requires that cigarette manufacturers place a health warning to all smokers on their packages.

_____ b. Studies have shown that smoking presently causes nearly 80 percent of lung cancer deaths in this country.

_____ c. Few authorities today have any doubts about the connection between cigarette smoking and poor health.

_____ d. We know that 30 percent of the deaths from coronary heart disease can be attributed to smoking.

5. When the Mexican earthquake struck in 1985, scientists and city planners learned a great deal about the kinds of buildings that can survive an earthquake.

_____ a. Buildings that had foundations resting on giant rollers suffered very little damage.

_____ b. Buildings that were made only of adobe material simply fell apart when the earthquake struck.

_____ c. Many of the modern buildings were designed to vibrate when earthquakes occur, so these received the least amount of shock.

_____ d. After the earthquake was over, officials realized why some buildings were destroyed while others suffered hardly any damage at all.

Exercise 2   **Distinguishing a Supporting Detail from a Restatement of the Main Idea**

Each of the following topic sentences is followed by four additional sentences. Three of these additional sentences contain acceptable supporting details, but one of the sentences is simply a restatement of the topic sentence. In the space provided, identify each sentence as *SD* for *supporting detail* or *R* for *restatement*.

1. In the last 30 years, the number of people living alone in Canada has increased by 400 percent.

_____ a. People are living alone because the number of divorces has dramatically increased.

_____ b. Many young people are putting off marriage until they are financially more secure or emotionally ready.

_____ c. More and more Canadians are finding themselves living alone.

_____ d. An increasing percentage of our population is the age group over 65, among whom are many widows and widowers.

2. More and more people are realizing the disadvantages of using credit cards too often.

_____   a. People should think twice before using their cards.

_____   b. Interest rates on credit cards have been rising at an alarming rate.

_____   c. Credit cards make it possible to buy on impulse, rather than plan a budget carefully.

_____   d. Many credit card companies charge an annual fee for the privilege of using cards.

3. Writing as Sandra Field and Jocelyn Haley, Jill MacLean makes love pay the bills.

_____   a. Her first book, *To Trust My Love*, was published by Harlequin.

_____   b. Jill received a royalty cheque of about $1800 for her first book.

_____   c. She is the author of 36 full-fledged romance novels.

_____   d. Jill MacLean writes love stories under two pen names.

4. Since World War II, the status of women in Japan has changed.

_____   a. In 1947, women won the right to vote.

_____   b. The women's position in Japanese society has altered over the past 35 years.

_____   c. Many Japanese women now go on to higher education.

_____   d. Women can now own property in their own name and seek divorce.

5. Certain factors that cannot be changed have been shown to contribute to heart attacks and strokes.

_____   a. Three out of four heart attacks and six out of seven strokes occur after the age of 65, so age is definitely a factor.

_____   b. Heart attacks and strokes have many causes, some of which we can do nothing about.

_____   c. Heart disease is by far the greatest killer of both males and females in Canada.

_____   d. Men are at greater risk than women in their chance of suffering from cardiovascular disease.

How Do You Make Supporting Details Specific?

Students often write paragraphs that are made up only of general statements. When you read such paragraphs, you doubt the author's knowledge and you suspect that the point being made may have no basis in fact. Here is one such paragraph that never gets off the ground.

Doctors are terrible. They cause more problems than they solve. I don't believe most of their treatments are necessary. History is full of the mistakes doctors have made. We don't need all those operations. We should never ingest all those drugs doctors prescribe. We shouldn't allow them to give us all those unnecessary tests. I've heard plenty of stories that prove my point. Doctors' ideas can kill you.

Here is another paragraph on the same topic. This paragraph is much more interesting and convincing because the general statements throughout the essay have been changed to supporting details.

Evidence shows that "medical progress" has been the cause of tragic consequences and even death for thousands of people. X-ray therapy was thought to help patients with tonsillitis. Now many of these people are found to have developed cancer from these X-rays. Not so long ago, women were kept in bed for several weeks following childbirth. Unfortunately, this cost many women their lives, since they developed fatal blood clots from being kept in bed day after day. One recent poll estimates that 30 000 people each year die from the side effects of drugs that were prescribed by doctors. Recently, the Center for Disease Control reported that 25 percent of the tests done by clinical laboratories were done poorly. All this is not to belittle the good done by the medical profession, but to impress on readers that it would be foolish to rely totally on the medical profession to solve all our health problems.

This second paragraph is much more likely to be of real interest. Even if you would like to disprove the author's point, it would be very hard to dismiss these supports, which are based on facts and information that can be researched. Because the author sounds reasonable, you can respect him even if you have a different position on the topic.

In writing effectively, the ability to go beyond the general statement and get to the accurate pieces of information is what counts. A writer tries to make his or her reader an expert on the subject. Readers should go away excited to share with the next person they meet the surprising information they have just learned. A writer who has a statistic, a quotation, an anecdote, a historical example, or a descriptive detail has the advantage over all other writers, no matter how impressive these writers' styles may be.

Good writing, therefore, is filled with supporting details that are specific, correct, and appropriate for the subject. Poor writing is filled with generalizations, stereotypes, vagueness, untruths, and even sarcasm and insults.

Exercise 1   Creating Supporting Details

Below are five topic sentences. Supply three supporting details for each one. Be sure each detail is specific and not general or vague.

1.   Your first semester in college can be overwhelming.

   a. _____

   b. _____

   c. _____

2.   Clothing is a bad investment of your money.

   a. _____

   b. _____

   c. _____

3.   Dr. Kline is an easy teacher.

   a.   _____

   b.   _____

   c.   _____

4.   It is difficult to stop eating junk food.

   a.   _____

   b.   _____

   c.   _____

5.   My sister is the sloppiest person I know.

   a.   _____

   b.   _____

   c.   _____

Exercise 2   Creating Supporting Details

Below are five topic sentences. Supply three supporting details for each one. Be sure each detail is specific and not general or vague.

1.   December has become a frantic time at our house.

   a.   _____

   b.   _____

   c.   _____

2.   My best friend can often be very immature.

   a.   _____

   b.   _____

   c.   _____

3.   Each sport has its own peculiar injuries associated with it.

   a.   _____

   b.   _____

   c.   _____

4.   My car is on its "last wheels."

   a.   _____

   b.   _____

   c.   _____

5.   Watching too much television has serious effects on family life.

   a.   _____

   b.   _____

   c.   _____

Exercise 3 Creating Supporting Details

Below are five topic sentences. Supply three supporting details for each one. Be sure each detail is specific and not general or vague.

1. Maintaining a car is a continual drain on one's budget.

   a. _____

   b. _____

   c. _____

2. Travelling by train has several advantages over travelling by car.

   a. _____

   b. _____

   c. _____

3. Last year I redecorated my bedroom.

   a. _____

   b. _____

   c. _____

4. Banff, Alberta, is a great place for a family vacation.

   a. _____

   b. _____

   c. _____

5. The amateur photographer needs to consider several points when selecting a camera.

   a. _____

   b. _____

   c. _____

Developing Paragraphs: Description

What Is Description?

Description is one of the basic building blocks of good writing. When you are able to write an effective description of a person, an object, a place, or even an idea, you are in control of your writing. Good description also makes you able to control what your reader sees and does not see.

The key to writing a good description is the choice of the **specific details** you will use. Specific details make your descriptions real and help your reader remember what you have written. A careful writer always pays special attention to specific details in any piece of writing.

A second important aspect of good description is the use of **sensory images.** Sensory images are details that relate to your sense of sight, smell, touch, taste, or hearing. When you use at least some of these five senses in your descriptive writing, your reader will be able to relate directly to what you are saying. Sensory images also help your reader remember what you have written.

A third important aspect of good description is the **order** in which you place the details you have chosen. The combination of specific details, sensory images, and the order in which you present these details and impressions will help your reader form a **dominant impression** of what you are describing.

The following example of descriptive writing shows all of the elements of a good description. As you read this description of a typical neighbourhood delicatessen, note the specific details and the sensory images the writer uses. After you have read the whole description, ask yourself what dominant impression the writer wanted us to have of the place.

The delicatessen was a wide store with high ceilings that were a dark brown colour from many years of not being painted. The rough wooden shelves on both sides of the store were filled from floor to ceiling with cans of fruits and vegetables, jars of pickles and olives, and special imported canned fish. A large refrigerator case against one wall was always humming loudly from the effort of keeping milk, cream, and several cases of pop and juice cool at all times. At the end of the store was the main counter with its gleaming white metal scale on top and its cold cuts and freshly made salads inside. Stacked on top of the counter beside the scale today were baskets of fresh rolls and breads that gave off an aroma that contained a mixture of onion, caraway seed, and pumpernickel. Behind the scale was the friendly face of Mr. Rubino, who was in his store seven days a week, fourteen hours or more each day. He was always ready with a smile or a friendly comment, or even a sample piece of cheese or smoked meat as a friendly gesture for his "growing customers," as he referred to us kids in the neighbourhood.

Working with Description: Selecting the Dominant Impression

When you use a number of specific, sensory images as you write a description, you should do more than simply write a series of sentences that deal with a single topic. You should also create a dominant impression in your reader's mind. Each individual sentence that you write is part of a picture that becomes clear when the reader finishes the paragraph.

For example, when you describe a place, the dominant impression you create might be of a place that is warm, friendly, or comfortable; or it could be a place that is formal, elegant, or artistic. When you write a description of a person, your reader could receive the dominant impression of a positive, efficient person who is outgoing and creative, or of a person who appears to be cold, distant, or hostile. All the sentences should support the dominant impression you have chosen.

Here is a list for you to use as a guide as you work through this unit. Picking a dominant impression is essential in writing the descriptive college paragraph.

Possible Dominant Impressions for Descriptions of Places

crowded	cozy	inviting	cheerful	dazzling
romantic	restful	dreary	drab	uncomfortable
cluttered	ugly	tasteless	unfriendly	gaudy
stuffy	eerie	depressing	spacious	sunny

Possible Dominant Impressions for Descriptions of People

creative	angry	independent	proud	withdrawn
tense	shy	aggressive	generous	sullen
silent	witty	pessimistic	responsible	efficient
snobbish	placid	bumbling	bitter	easygoing

Exercise 1   Selecting the Dominant Impression

Each of the following places could be the topic for a descriptive paragraph. First, the writer must decide on a dominant impression. Fill in each blank to the right of the topic with an appropriate dominant impression. Use the guide above if you need help.

Topic	*Dominant Impression*
1. A high school gym on prom night	_____
2. Your barber or hairdresser's shop	_____
3. The room where you are now sitting	_____

4. The grocery store nearest you   _____

5. A hardware store   _____

6. The post office on Saturday morning   _____

7. An overcrowded waiting room   _____

8. The Okanagan Valley in the spring   _____

9. The home of your best friend   _____

10. The kitchen in the morning   _____

Exercise 2   **Selecting the Dominant Impression**

Each of the following persons could be the topic for a descriptive paragraph. First, the writer must decide on a dominant impression. Fill in each blank to the right of the topic with an appropriate dominant impression. Use the list on page 200 if you need help.

Topic	*Dominant Impression*
1. An actor or actress being interviewed on television	_____
2. An old woman in a nursing home	_____
3. A librarian	_____
4. A bank clerk on a busy day	_____
5. A farmer	_____
6. A politician running for office	_____
7. A cab driver	_____
8. A shoe salesman	_____
9. A bride	_____
10. A police officer	_____

Exercise 3   **Selecting the Dominant Impression**

Choose your own dominant impression for each of the following persons or places. In the space following each example, write the dominant impression you have chosen.

Topic	*Dominant Impression*
1. A city park	_____
2. A favourite aunt or uncle	_____
3. A large department store at Christmas	_____
4. A truck driver	_____
5. A school cafeteria	_____

6.   A nurse   _____

7.   A used-car salesman   _____

8.   A beach in the late afternoon   _____

9.   A movie theatre on Friday evening   _____

10. A student late for class   _____

Revising Vague Dominant Impressions

Certain words in the English language have become so overused that they no longer have any specific meaning for a reader. Careful writers avoid these words because they are almost useless in descriptive writing. Here is a list of the most common overused words:

> good, bad
> nice, fine, okay
> normal, typical
> interesting
> beautiful

The following paragraph is an example of the kind of writing that results from the continued use of vague words:

> I had a typical day. The weather was nice and my job was interesting. The food for lunch was okay; supper was really good. After supper I saw my girlfriend, who is really beautiful. That's when my day really became fun.

Notice that all of the details in the paragraph are vague. The writer has told us what happened, but we cannot really see any of the details that are mentioned. This is because the writer has made the mistake of using words that have lost much of their meaning.

Practice   Rewrite this vague paragraph you have just read. Replace the vague words with details that are more specific.

_____

_____

_____

_____

_____

_____

_____

_____

The next group of exercises will give you practice in recognizing and eliminating overused words.

Exercise 1   Revising Vague Dominant Impressions

In each of the spaces provided, change the underlined word to a more specific dominant impression. An example has been done for you.

Vague: The tablecloth was <u>beautiful</u>.
Revised: The tablecloth was of <u>white linen with delicate blue embroidery</u>.

1. The sky was <u>beautiful</u>.   _____

2. The water felt <u>nice</u>.   _____

3. Walking along the beach was <u>fun</u>.   _____

4. The storm was <u>bad</u>.   _____

5. The parking lot was <u>typical</u>.   _____

6. The main street is <u>interesting</u>.   _____

7. The dessert tasted <u>good</u>.   _____

8. My brother is <u>normal</u>.   _____

9. Our house is <u>fine</u>.   _____

10. My job is <u>okay</u>.   _____

Exercise 2   Revising Vague Dominant Impressions

In each of the spaces provided, change the underlined word to a more specific dominant impression.

1. It was a really <u>nice</u> date.   _____

2. The window display was <u>beautiful</u>.   _____

3. The boat ride was <u>fine</u>.   _____

4. The circus was <u>fun</u>.   _____

5. The lemonade was <u>awful</u>.   _____

6. The play was <u>bad</u>.   _____

7. His new suit looked <u>okay</u>.   _____

8. The dance class was <u>fine</u>.   _____

9. Her new watch was <u>nice</u>.   _____

10. It was a <u>good</u> lecture.   _____

Exercise 3   Revising Vague Dominant Impressions

In each of the spaces provided, change the underlined word to a more specific dominant impression.

1. It was a <u>normal</u> Friday evening.   _____

2. It was an <u>interesting</u> ride through the country.   _____

3. She sang in a very <u>normal</u> voice.   _____

4. The cook served a very <u>typical</u> dinner.   _____
5. The customer bought a <u>nice</u> hat to go with her dress.   _____

6. Roberta told us she had read two <u>good</u> books.   _____

7. She married a <u>fine</u> young pilot.   _____

8. Our trip to the discount store was <u>okay</u>.   _____

9. It was a <u>bad</u> interview.   _____
10. The couple went to a <u>typical</u> resort last week-end.   _____

Working with Description: Sensory Images

One of the basic ways all good writers communicate experiences to their readers is by using sense impressions. We respond to writing that makes us *see* an object, *hear* a sound, *touch* a surface, *smell* an odour, or *taste* a flavour. When a writer uses one or more of these sensory images in a piece of writing, we tend to pay more attention to what the writer is saying, and we tend to remember the details of what we have read.

For example, if you come across the word *door* in a sentence, you might or might not pay attention to it. However, if the writer tells you it was a *brown wooden* door that was *rough to the touch* and that *creaked loudly* when it opened, you would hardly be able to forget it. The door would stay in your mind because the writer used sensory images to make you aware of it.

Practice   The following sentences are taken from the description of Mr. Rubino's delicatessen, a description that you read on pages 199–200 . Notice how in each sentence the writer uses at least one sensory image to make the details of that sentence remain in our minds. As you read each of the sentences, identify the physical sense the writer is appealing to by the use of one or more sensory images.

1. A large refrigerator case against one wall was always humming loudly from the effort of keeping milk, cream, and several cases of pop and juice cool at all times.

   Physical sense: _____

2. Stacked on top of the counter were baskets of fresh rolls and breads that gave off an aroma that contained a mixture of onion, caraway seed, and pumpernickel.

   Physical sense: _____

3. He was always ready with a sample piece of cheese or smoked meat as a friendly gesture.

   Physical sense: _____

When you use sensory images in your own writing, you will stimulate your readers' interest, and these images created in their minds will be remembered.

Exercise 1   Recognizing Sensory Images

The following paragraph contains examples of sensory images. In the spaces following the paragraph, identify the sensory images used by the writer.

   Hear it! The crunching smash of twenty-four bottles of beer, all splintering against each other as I misdeal on the packing machine. Smell the stink of warm beer pouring over my clothes, washing over the sour sweat of my body. I can feel the unheard curse as I toss the wet, mangled carton down the rollers for some poor bastard to sort out. And back to the mother-eating machine where the bottles are already starting to pile up on the conveyor belt. The ten second delay bell starts ringing. The jangling vibrations echo in my skull, and the foreman comes running over, screaming incoherently. How the hell can I hear him over the roar of four acres of machinery, and the teeth-jarring rattle of 25,000 bottles, all clinking against each other as they ride down the hundred yards of clanking metal conveyor belts.

From Ian Adams,
Living with Automation in Winnipeg

Sensory Images

Sight: _____

_____

_____

Sound: _____

_____

Smell: _____

_____

Exercise 2   Recognizing Sensory Images

The following paragraph contains examples of sensory images. In the spaces following the paragraph, identify the sensory images used by the writer.

The temperature in Winkler at 7 p.m. on Thursday, January 20, 1972, is 35 below zero and dropping. The air is frozen into little slivers of glass which pierce the lungs. The light from the full moon reflected in the crystallized air makes the night fluorescent. People scurry through the neon streets beneath small white clouds of congealed breath like balloons in comic strips. Tears run down their cheeks. The cold freezes hands and feet to blocks of wood. It hurts to walk more than a few feet; even the cars scream and groan.

From Heather Robertson,
Sale Night

Sensory Images

Sight: _____

_____

Sound: _____

_____

Touch: _____

_____

Exercise 3   Recognizing Sensory Images

The following paragraph contains examples of sensory images. In the spaces following the paragraph, identify the sensory images used by the writer.

> When I was a boy, my most prized possession was a stamp my father had given me for my collection. It was a deep blue on one side, colouring the word CANADA and a picture of a sailing ship. I often dreamed that I stood on the deck of this ship, listening to the wind howling through the rigging, salt spray on my lips. The stamp felt brittle, like old parchment, and had a slight air of mustiness to it. It's gone now, lost somewhere, like so much of my youth.

Sensory Images

Sight: _____

_____

Sound: _____

_____

Touch: _____

_____

Taste: _____

_____

Smell: _____

_____

Exercise 1   Creating Sensory Images

Each of the following topic sentences contains an underlined word that names a physical sense. For each topic sentence, write three sentences that give examples of sensory images. For example, in the first sentence the sensory image of hearing in the vicinity of a hospital could be explained by writing sentences that describe ambulance sirens, doctors being called over loudspeaker systems, and the voices of people in the waiting room.

1. I knew I was walking past the hospital emergency room from the sounds I could <u>hear</u>.

    Three sentences with sensory images:

    a. _____

       _____

    b. _____

       _____

    c. _____

       _____

2. I can't help stopping in the bakery every Sunday morning because the <u>smells</u> are so good.

   Three sentences with sensory images:

   a. _____

   _____

   b. _____

   _____

   c. _____

   _____

3. The best part of my vacation last year was the <u>sight</u> that greeted me when I got up in the morning.

   Three sentences with sensory images:

   a. _____

   _____

   b. _____

   _____

   c. _____

   _____

4. Our team won the game because we fans kept <u>showing</u> the players our support.

   Three sentences with sensory images:

   a. _____

   _____

   b. _____

   _____

   c. _____

   _____

5. Thanksgiving always makes me think of the delicious <u>tastes</u> of my grandmother's Thanksgiving dinner.

   Three sentences with sensory images:

   a. _____

   _____

   b. _____

   _____

   c. _____

   _____

Exercise 2   **Creating Sensory Images**

Each of the following topic sentences contains an underlined word that names a physical sense. For each topic sentence, write three sentences that give examples of sensory images.

1. It is a luxury to wear clothing made with natural fibres because the <u>feeling</u> is quite different from polyesters.

    Three sentences with sensory images:

    a. _____
        _____

    b. _____
        _____

    c. _____
        _____

2. I knew the garbage strike had gone on for a long time when I had to <u>hold my nose</u> walking down some streets.

    Three sentences with sensory images:

    a. _____
        _____

    b. _____
        _____

    c. _____
        _____

3. A lake in the summertime is a relaxing place to be because the <u>sounds</u> you hear all day are so subdued.

    Three sentences with sensory images:

    a. _____
        _____

    b. _____
        _____

    c. _____
        _____

4. As the child walked through the field, she <u>touched</u> the different plants.

    Three sentences with sensory images:

    a. _____
        _____

    b. _____
        _____

c.   _____

_____

5. Fred drives a very old car, but you can <u>see</u> it is in good condition.

Three sentences with sensory images:

a.   _____

_____

b.   _____

_____

c.   _____

_____

Exercise 3   Creating Sensory Images

Each of the following topic sentences contains an underlined word that names a physical sense. For each topic sentence, write three sentences that give examples of sensory images.

1. Going to a nightclub is an overwhelming experience because of the different sounds you <u>hear</u> there.

Three sentences with sensory images:

a.   _____

_____

b.   _____

_____

c.   _____

_____

2. My friend Bill says he loves the <u>feel</u> of the chocolate, the nuts, and the coconut when he eats that candy bar.

Three sentences with sensory images:

a.   _____

_____

b.   _____

_____

c.   _____

_____

3. I could <u>see</u> that the old woman standing on the corner was very poor.

Three sentences with sensory images:

a.   _____

_____

b. _____

_____

c. _____

_____

4. When you visit a delicatessen you want to <u>taste</u> a great many things at once.
    Three sentences with sensory images:

a. _____

_____

b. _____

_____

c. _____

_____

5. I could <u>see</u> from her reaction that the coffee was too hot.
    Three sentences with sensory images:

a. _____

_____

b. _____

_____

c. _____

_____

Coherence in Description: Putting Details in Space Order

In descriptive paragraphs, the writer often chooses to arrange supporting details according to space. With this method, you place yourself at the scene and then use a logical order such as moving from nearby to farther away, right to left, or top to bottom. Often you move in such a way that you save the most important detail until last in order to achieve the greatest effect.

In the paragraph on the delicatessen given on pages 199–200, the writer first describes the ceilings and walls of the store, then proceeds to the shelves and large refrigerator, and ends by describing the main counter of the deli with its owner, Mr. Rubino, standing behind it. The ordering of details has been from the outer limits of the room to the inner area, which is central to the point of the paragraph. A description of a clothes closet might order the details differently. Perhaps the writer would begin with the shoes standing on the floor and finish with the hats and gloves arranged on the top shelf, an arrangement that goes from the ground up.

Here is a paragraph from Thierry Mallet's description of his travels through the Canadian Arctic, *Glimpses of the Barren Lands:*

Our camp had been pitched at the foot of a great, bleak, ragged hill, a few feet from the swirling waters of the Kazan River. The two small green tents, pegged down tight with heavy rocks, shivered and rippled under the faint touch of the northern breeze. A thin wisp of smoke rose from the embers of the fire.

Notice that the writer begins with a description of the landscape, then gives a description of the camp, and ends with a picture of the small fire. We are able to follow the writer through the description because there is a logic or plan. No matter which method of space order you choose in organizing details in a descriptive paragraph, be sure the results allow your reader to see the scene in a logical order.

Exercise 1   Working for Coherence: Using Space Order

Each of the following topic sentences is followed by four descriptive sentences that are out of order. Put these descriptive sentences in order by placing the number 1, 2, 3, 4, or 5 in the space provided before each sentence.

1. Charlottetown, P.E.I., the smallest provincial capital, has become a major tourist centre because of its favourable climate and many nearby beaches. *(Order the material from past to present.)*

    _____   When P.E.I. entered Confederation in 1873, Charlottetown was the eleventh-largest city in Canada, although it has failed to keep pace with the urban growth in the rest of Canada.

    _____   Incorporated in 1885, the area of the present city was actually settled in 1720 by the French, when the island was known as Île Saint-Jean.

    _____   Although declining in the order of Canadian municipalities in size, Charlottetown offers a quality of life far richer than its size would suggest.

    _____   The Confederation Centre, a large performing arts and museum complex, was opened in 1964.

    _____   The Charlottetown Conference of 1864 was held here, an event that give the city its title, "The Cradle of Confederation."

2. The old wallet lay on the nightstand. *(Order the material from the outside to the inside.)*

    _____   A clear plastic insert held photographs and necessary items such as a driver's licence and credit cards.

    _____   The secret compartment, which could hold extra money for emergencies, was visible when a small flap of leather was turned up.

    _____   Behind the photographs and other papers was a small pocket for postage stamps.

    _____   The rich brown leather of the wallet, worn smooth from years of hard use, faintly showed the owner's name stamped in gold.

    _____   The wallet seemed to double in size when it was opened, and the colour inside was a lighter brown.

3. The young woman was a teen of the eighties. *(Order the material from top to bottom.)*

    _____   She wore an oversized sweater that she had borrowed from her father.

_____ Her shoes were white tennis sneakers.

_____ Her dangling earrings, which were red and green, matched her outfit.

_____ Her short blond hair was clean and feathered attractively.

_____ Her jeans, which were the latest style, had a faint paisley print.

4. My aunt's kitchen is a very orderly place.
   (Order the material from near to far.)

   _____ As usual, in the centre of the table sits a vase with a fresh yellow daffodil.

   _____ Nearby on the refrigerator, a magnet holds the week's menu.

   _____ Sitting at the kitchen table, I am struck by the freshly pressed linen tablecloth.

   _____ Looking across the room through the stained-glass doors of her kitchen cupboards, I can see neat rows of dishes, exactly eight each, matching the colours of the tablecloth and wallpaper.

5. The dashboard of most cars has a standard order.
   (Order the material from the left to the right.)

   _____ The radio, which the driver can reach with his or her right hand without stretching too far, is a standard item in most cars today.

   _____ Another item on the typical dashboard, usually right in front of the passenger's seat, is the glove compartment.

   _____ The dashboard of a car contains the instruments needed to operate the car, beginning with the directional signals and light switches often located to the left of the steering wheel.

   _____ Just to the right of the steering wheel are the controls for the heating vents.

   _____ The main instrument panel directly in front of the driver indicates the distance driven, the speed the car is going, and the condition of the battery.

Exercise 2   Working for Coherence: Using Space Order

Each of the following topic sentences could be expanded into a fully developed paragraph. In the spaces provided, give the appropriate supporting details for the topic sentence. Be sure to give your supporting details in a particular order. That is, the details should go from top to bottom, from outside to inside, from close to far, or around the area you are describing.

1. The airport terminal was as busy inside as it was outside.

   a. _____

   _____

b. _____

_____

c. _____

_____

d. _____

_____

2. The cafeteria is a large and often deserted area of our school.

a. _____

_____

b. _____

_____

c. _____

_____

d. _____

_____

3. The picnic area was shady and inviting.

a. _____

_____

b. _____

_____

c. _____

_____

d. _____

_____

4. The motel lobby was obviously once very beautiful, but it was beginning to look shabby.

a. _____

_____

b. _____

_____

c. _____

_____

d. _____

_____

5. The night I had tickets to see my favourite rock group perform was a night to remember.

a. _____

_____

b. _____

_____

c. _____

_____

d. _____

_____

Exercise 3   Working for Coherence: Using Space Order

Each of the following topic sentences could be expanded into a fully developed paragraph. In the spaces provided, give the appropriate supporting details for the topic sentence. Be sure to give your supporting details in a particular order. That is, the details should go from top to bottom, from outside to inside, from close to far, or around the area you are describing.

1. The shopping mall was supposed to be restful, but the noise and the bright lights gave me a headache.

a. _____

_____

b. _____

_____

c. _____

_____

d. _____

_____

2. The swimming pool looked like a fish tank crowded with exotic fish.

a. _____

_____

b. _____

_____

c. _____

_____

d. _____

_____

3. We took our final examination in the chemistry laboratory.

   a. _____

   _____

   b. _____

   _____

   c. _____

   _____

   d. _____

   _____

4. The pizza shop is so tiny that people are not likely to stay and eat.

   a. _____

   _____

   b. _____

   _____

   c. _____

   _____

   d. _____

   _____

5. The bus was filled with a strange assortment of people.

   a. _____

   _____

   b. _____

   _____

   c. _____

   _____

   d. _____

   _____

Writing the Descriptive Paragraph Step by Step

To learn a skill with some degree of ease, it is best to follow a step-by-step approach so that various skills are isolated. This will ensure that you are not missing a crucial point or misunderstanding a part of the whole. There certainly are other ways to go about writing an effective paragraph, but here is one method you can use to get good final results. You will learn that writing, like most skills, can be developed by using a logical process.

Steps for Writing the Descriptive Paragraph

1. Study the given topic, and then plan your topic sentence, especially the dominant impression.
2. List at least ten details that come to your mind when you think about the topic.
3. Then choose the five or six most important details from your list. Be sure these details support the dominant impression.
4. Put your list in order.
5. Write one complete sentence for each of the details you have chosen from your list.
6. Write a concluding statement that offers some reason for describing this topic.
7. Finally, copy your sentences into standard paragraph form.

Exercise 1   Writing the Descriptive Paragraph Step by Step

The following exercise will guide you through the construction of a descriptive paragraph. Start with the suggested topic. Use the seven steps to help you work through each stage of the writing process.

Topic: A place you have lived

1. Topic sentence: _____

    _____

2. Make a list of possible supporting details.

    a. _____   f. _____

    b. _____   g. _____

    c. _____   h. _____

    d. _____   i. _____

    e. _____   j. _____

3. Circle the five or six details you believe are the most important for the description.
4. Put your final choices in order by numbering them.
5. Using your final list, write at least one sentence for each detail you have chosen.

    a. _____

    _____

    b. _____

    _____

    c. _____

    _____

    d. _____

    _____

    e. _____

    _____

f.   _____

_____

g.   _____

_____

6.   Write a concluding statement. _____

_____

7.   Copy your sentences into standard paragraph form.

_____

_____

_____

_____

_____

_____

_____

_____

_____

_____

_____

_____

_____

_____

_____

_____

_____

Exercise 2   **Writing the Descriptive Paragraph Step by Step**

The following exercise will guide you through the construction of a descriptive paragraph. Start with the suggested topic. Use the seven steps to help you work through each stage in the writing process.

Topic: A person you admire

1.   Topic sentence: _____

_____

2.   Make a list of possible supporting details.

a.   _____   c.   _____

b.   _____   d.   _____

e. _____   h. _____

f. _____   i. _____

g. _____   j. _____

3. Circle the five or six details you believe are the most important for the description.

4. Put your choices in order by numbering them.

5. Using your final list, write at least one sentence for each detail you have chosen.

a. _____

_____

b. _____

_____

c. _____

_____

d. _____

_____

e. _____

_____

f. _____

_____

g. _____

_____

6. Write a concluding statement. _____

_____

_____

7. Copy your sentences into standard paragraph form.

_____

_____

_____

_____

_____

_____

_____

_____

_____

_____

_____

_____

_____

_____

_____

_____

Exercise 3   Writing the Descriptive Paragraph Step by Step

The following exercise will guide you through the construction of a descriptive paragraph. Start with the suggested topic. Use the seven steps to help you work through each stage of the writing process.

Topic: A treasured possession

1. Topic sentence: _____

    _____

2. Make a list of possible supporting details.

    a. _____   f. _____

    b. _____   g. _____

    c. _____   h. _____

    d. _____   i. _____

    e. _____   j. _____

3. Circle the five or six details you believe are the most important for the description.
4. Put your final choices in order by numbering them.
5. Using your final list, write at least one sentence for each detail you have chosen.

    a. _____

    _____

    b. _____

    _____

    c. _____

    _____

    d. _____

    _____

    e. _____

    _____

    f. _____

    _____

g. _____

_____

6. Write a concluding statement. _____

_____

_____

7. Copy your sentences into standard paragraph form.

_____

_____

_____

_____

_____

_____

_____

_____

_____

_____

_____

_____

_____

_____

_____

_____

_____

On Your Own: Writing Descriptive Paragraphs from Model Paragraphs

A Description of a Home

ASSIGNMENT 1: Write a paragraph in which you describe a house or room that you remember clearly. Choose your dominant impression carefully and then make your sensory images support that impression. You may want to include in your description the person who lives in the house or room. Notice, in the model paragraph from Farley Mowat's *People of the Deer*, the importance of the last sentence, in which the writer gives his paragraph added impact by indicating that the igloo was certainly a less than desirable accommodation.

Model Paragraph

As I grew to know the People, so my respect for their intelligence and ingenuity increased. Yet it was a long time before I could reconcile my feelings of respect with the poor, shoddy dwelling places that they constructed. As with most Eskimos, the winter homes of the Ihalmiut are the snow-built domes we call igloos. (Igloo in Eskimo means simply "house" and thus an igloo can be built of wood or stone, as well as of snow.) But unlike most other Inuit, the Ihalmiut make snow houses which are cramped, miserable shelters. I think the people acquired the art of igloo construction quite recently in their history and from the coast Eskimos. Certainly they have no love for their igloos, and prefer the skin tents.

TEN SUGGESTED TOPICS

1. A student's apartment
2. A vacation cottage
3. A dormitory
4. The house of your dreams
5. Your bedroom
6. A kitchen
7. The messiest room you ever saw
8. The strangest room you ever saw
9. A house you will never forget
10. A house that did not fit the character of the person living there

A Description of a Person

ASSIGNMENT 2: Describe a person you have observed more than once. If you saw this person only once, indicate the details that made him or her stay in your mind. If you choose to describe a person with whom you are more familiar, select the most outstanding details that will help your reader have a single, dominant impression. In the model paragraph, from Alistair MacLeod's story "The Lost Salt Gift of Blood," the author describes his mother in Nova Scotia.

Model Paragraph

My mother ran her house as her brothers ran their boats. Everything was clean and spotless and in order. She was tall and dark and powerfully energetic. In later years, she reminded me of the women of Thomas Hardy, particularly Eustacia Vye, in a physical way. She fed and clothed a family of seven children, making all of the meals and most of the clothes. She grew miraculous gardens and magnificent flowers and raised broods of hens and ducks. She would walk miles on berry-picking expeditions and hoist her skirts to dig for clams when the tide was low. She was fourteen years younger than my father, whom she had married when she was twenty-six, and had been a local beauty for a period of ten years. My mother was of the sea as were all of her people, and her horizons were the very literal ones she scanned with her dark and fearless eyes.

TEN SUGGESTED TOPICS

1. An elderly relative
2. A hardworking student
3. An outstanding athlete
4. A loyal friend
5. An overworked waitress
6. A cab driver
7. A fashion model
8. A gossipy neighbour
9. A street vendor
10. A rude salesperson

A Description of a Time of Day

ASSIGNMENT 3: Write a paragraph in which you describe the sights, sounds, and events of a particular time of day in a place you know well. In the model paragraph that follows, from John Riley's "Growing Up in Cleveland," the writer has chosen to describe an especially busy time of day, namely, the morning hours, when activity can be frantic in a household.

Model Paragraph

I remember the turmoil of mornings in our house. My brothers and sisters rushed about upstairs and down trying to get ready for school. Mom would repeatedly tell them to hurry up. Molly would usually scream down from her bedroom, "What am I going to do? I don't have any clean underwear!" Amy, often in tears, sat at the kitchen table still in her pajamas trying to do her math. Paul paced back and forth in front of the mirror angrily combing his unruly hair which stuck up in all directions while Roland threatened to punch him if he didn't find the pen he had borrowed the night before. Mother was stuffing sandwiches into bags while she sighed, "I'm afraid there isn't anything for dessert today." No one heard her. Then came the yelling up the stairs, "You should have left ten minutes ago." One by one, these unwilling victims were packed up and pushed out the door. Mother wasn't safe yet. Somebody always came back frantic and desperate. "My flute, Mom, where's my flute, quick! I'll get killed if I don't have it today." Every crisis apparently meant the difference between life and death. Morning at our house was like watching a troop preparing for battle. When they had finally gone, I was left in complete silence while my mother slumped on a chair at the kitchen table. She paid no attention to me.

TEN SUGGESTED TOPICS
1. A Saturday filled with errands
2. The dinner hour at my house
3. Lunchtime in a cafeteria
4. A midnight raid on the refrigerator
5. Christmas morning
6. TGIF (Thank God It's Friday)
7. Getting ready to go out on a Friday night
8. My Sunday-morning routine
9. Coming home from school or work
10. Watching late-night movies

A Description of a Place

ASSIGNMENT 4: Write a paragraph in which you describe a place you know well or remember clearly. The model paragraph that follows is from John Kenneth Galbraith's book *The Scotch*, in which the author relates stories of his boyhood in southern Ontario.

Model Paragraph

It was a pleasant community with a sound basic plan. At one side of town, where Hogg Street met the Townline, and a little apart from both the commercial and industrial areas, was the religious and cultural centre. North along the principal street, one came first to the residential section and then the main shopping centre with the service industries conveniently close. After that came the railroads, the railroad stations, stockyard, another small residential area, another shopping centre and a small manufacturing establishment. A good half mile north of town, intelligently removed from all urban influences, was the school. Maples shaded the mercantile, manufacturing and residential areas alike; people walked not on harsh asphalt but on grass. No activity or function in the town intruded itself on any other save that, of a night, people might be momentarily aroused by a passing train.

TEN SUGGESTED TOPICS
1. A large department store
2. A delicatessen
3. A coffee shop
4. A pizza parlour
5. A shoe store
6. A shopping mall
7. A lively street corner
8. A college bookstore
9. A gymnasium
10. A student lounge

A Description of a Time of Year

ASSIGNMENT 5: Write a paragraph in which you describe a particular time of year. Make sure that all of the details you choose relate specifically to that time of year. In the model paragraph that follows, from the journal of Catharine Parr Traill, *The Backwoods of Canada*, the description of a sleigh ride during the grip of winter is a vivid picture of a natural phenomenon.

Model Paragraph

Nothing can surpass the loveliness of the woods after a snowstorm has loaded every bough and sprig with its feathery deposit. The face of the ground, so rough and tangled with a mass of uptorn trees, broken boughs, and timbers in every stage of decay, seems by the touch of some powerful magician's wand to have changed its character. Unrivalled purity, softness, and brilliancy, has taken the place of confusion and vegetable corruption. It is one of the greatest treats this country affords me, to journey through the thick woods after a heavy snowfall.

TEN SUGGESTED TOPICS
1. A winter storm
2. A summer picnic
3. Summer in the city
4. A winter walk
5. Jogging in the spring rain
6. Sunbathing on a beach
7. Signs of spring in my neighbourhood
8. The woods in autumn
9. Ice skating in winter
10. Halloween night

15 Developing Paragraphs: Narration

What Is Narration?

Narration is the oldest and best-known form of verbal communication. It is, quite simply, the telling of a story. Every culture in the world, past and present, has used narration to provide entertainment as well as information for the people of that culture. Since everyone likes a good story, the many forms of narration, such as novels, short stories, soap operas, and full-length movies, are always popular.

The following narrative paragraph, taken from an essay by Al Purdy titled "The Iron Road," tells the story of Purdy's trip westward in 1937, the height of the Great Depression, when he was looking for work. In this passage, Purdy had been caught illegally riding a freight train by the railway police, and he is imprisoned in a caboose.

When returned to my prison-on-wheels I felt panicstricken. I was only seventeen, and this was the first time I'd ventured far away from home. I examined the caboose-prison closely, thinking: two years. Why, I'd be nineteen when I got out, an old man! And of course it was hopeless to think of escape. Other prisoners had tried without success, and windows were broken where they'd tried to wrench out the bars. And the door: it was wood, locked on the outside with a padlock, opening inward. It was a very springy door, though. I could squeeze my fingertips between sill and door, one hand at the top and the other a foot below. That gave me hope, blessed hope, for the first time. My six-foot-three body was suspended in air by my hands, doubled up like a coiled spring, and I pulled. Lord, how I pulled! The door bent inward until I could see a couple of daylight inches between door and sill. Then Snap! and screws fell out of the steel hasp outside. I fell flat on my back.

Working with Narration: Using Narration to Make a Point

At one time or another you have met a person who loves to talk on and on without making any real point. This person is likely to tell you everything that happened in one day, including every cough and sideways glance. Your reaction to the seemingly needless and endless supply of details is probably one of fatigue and hope for a quick getaway. This is not narration at its best! A good story is almost always told to make a point: it can make us laugh, it can make us understand, or it can change our attitudes.

When Al Purdy tells the story of his escape from the caboose, he is careful to use only those details that are relevant to his story. For example, the way the door is constructed is important. Had it not been made of wood and springy, he might never have been able to get his fingertips in and force an opening. He might had had to spend two years in prison. Then Purdy would have had a different story to tell.

Exercise 1   **Using Narration to Make a Point**

Each of the following examples is the beginning of a topic sentence for a narrative paragraph. Complete each sentence by providing a controlling idea that could be the point for the story.

1. Since my family is so large (or small), I have had to learn to _____

    _____

2. When I couldn't get a job, I realized _____

    _____

3. After going to the movies every Saturday for many years, I discovered _____

    _____

4. When I arrived at the room where my business class was to meet, I found

    _____

5. When my best friend got married, I began to see that _____

    _____

    _____

Exercise 2   **Using Narration to Make a Point**

Each of the following examples is the beginning of a topic sentence for a narrative paragraph. Complete each sentence by providing a controlling idea that could be the point for the story.

1. When I looked more closely at the man, I realized that _____

    _____

2. When the prime minister finished his speech, I concluded that _____

    _____

3. By the end of the movie, I decided that _____

    _____

4. After I changed the course as well as the teacher, I felt _____

_____

5. When I could not get past the office secretary, I realized that _____

_____

Exercise 3   Using Narration to Make a Point

Each of the following examples is the beginning of a topic sentence for a narrative paragraph. Complete each sentence by providing a controlling idea that could be the point for the story.

1. When the art teacher tore up my sketches in front of the class, I decided

_____

_____

2. When there were no responses to my ad, I concluded _____

_____

3. After two days of trying to sell magazine subscriptions, I knew _____

_____

4. After I had actually performed my first experiment in the lab, I understood

_____

_____

5. The first time I tried to cook a dinner for a group of people, I found out

_____

_____

Coherence in Narration: Placing Details in Order of Time Sequence

Ordering details in a paragraph of narration usually follows a time sequence. That is, you tell what happened first, then next, and next, until finally you get to the end of the story. An event could take place in a matter of minutes or over a period of many years.

In the following paragraph, the story takes place in a single day. The six events that made the day a disaster are given in the order in which they happened. Although some stories flash back to the past or forward to the future, most use the natural chronological order of the events.

My day was a disaster. First, it had snowed during the night, which meant I had to shovel before I could leave for work. I was mad that I hadn't gotten up earlier. Then I had trouble starting my car, and to make matters worse, my daughter wasn't feeling well and said she didn't think she should go to school. When I eventually did arrive at school, I was twenty minutes late. Soon I found out the secretary had forgotten to type the exam I was supposed to give my class that day. I quickly had to make another plan. By three o'clock, I was looking forward to getting my paycheque. Foolish woman! When I went to pick it up, the girl in the office told me that something had gone wrong with the computers. I would not be able to get my cheque until Tuesday. Disappointed, I walked down the hill to the parking lot. There I met my final defeat. In my hurry to park the car in the morning, I had left my parking lights on. Now my battery was dead. Even an optimist like me had the right to be discouraged!

Exercise 1 Working for Coherence: Using Details in Order of Time Sequence

Each of the topics below is followed by five supporting details. These supporting details are not given in any order. Order the events according to time sequence by placing the appropriate number in the space provided.

1. A fight in my apartment building

    _____ Some of the neighbours became so frightened that they called the police.

    _____ The man and the woman began to fight around six o'clock.

    _____ When the police came, they found the couple struggling in the kitchen.

    _____ The neighbours heard the man's voice shouting angrily.

    _____ There were no arrests, but the police warned both individuals not to disturb the peace again.

2. A night patrol

    _____ Their uniforms were soaking wet from hours in the rain.

    _____ The captain ordered the soldiers to prepare for a special night patrol.

    _____ Grumbling, the men got up and dressed in the dark.

    _____ As they marched in single file through the woods, it began to rain.

    _____ The captain barked his orders to the men who were sleeping in the barracks.

3. An important invitation

    _____ On the day of the party, Louise asked her boss if she could leave an hour or two early in order to have time to get ready.

    _____ When Louise was invited to the party, she was very excited.

    _____ Four days before the party, she finally got up enough nerve to call Bob and ask him to go with her.

    _____ One week before the party she bought a new dress even though she could not afford one.

    _____ Still holding the invitation, she searched through her closet, but all her dresses looked so dull and unfashionable.

4. The driving test

    _____ She had her last lesson with Mr. Johnson on Saturday morning.

    _____ As she ate breakfast Monday morning, Melinda read the driver's manual one more time because she knew it was her last chance to review.

_____ Melinda's driving test was scheduled for Monday morning.

_____ On Sunday afternoon her father gave her some advice on what to be careful of when she took her road test.

_____ As her mother drove her to the motor vehicle bureau, Melinda tried to relax and not think about the test.

_____ The night before her test, Melinda had phone calls from two friends who wished her good luck.

5. Making up my mind

_____ By the time I saw the dean for final approval of the change, I knew I had made the right decision.

_____ When I registered for my new courses for the next semester, I knew that I was doing what I should have done all along.

_____ I spent the summer of my sophomore year thinking about the career I really wanted to follow.

_____ I suppose the experience taught me that you should always make a change in your life after you have thought it through completely.

_____ When I finally did decide to change majors, my friends acted as though I had decided to change my citizenship.

_____ When I told my favourite professor about my change of mind, he was very supportive, even though I had begun my major with him.

Exercise 2 **Working for Coherence: Using Details in Order of Time Sequence**

Each of the following topics is followed by supporting details. These supporting details are not in any order. Place a number in the space provided before each sentence to show the order according to time sequence.

1. From the life of Amelia Earhart, pioneer aviator and writer

_____ Amelia Earhart was born in Atchison, Kansas, in 1897.

_____ Toward the end of World War I, she worked as a nurse's aide.

_____ When she was sixteen, her family moved to St. Paul, Minnesota.

_____ Four years after her history-making flight across the Atlantic, she made her solo flight across that same ocean.

_____ After learning to fly in the early 1920s, she became, in 1928, the first woman to cross the Atlantic in an airplane, although on that trip she was a passenger and not a pilot.

_____ Three years after her solo Atlantic flight, she became the first person to fly from Hawaii to California.

_____ On her last flight, in 1937, she was lost at sea; no trace of her was ever found.

2. From the life of Pauline Johnson, Métis poet and entertainer

_____ Pauline Johnson was born on the Six Nations Indian Reserve, Upper Canada, in 1861.

_____ The daughter of a Mohawk chief and an Englishwoman, she adopted the native name Tekahionwake.

_____ After her poetry was published, she crisscrossed Canada, giving poetry readings in many remote settlements.

_____ Dressed as a native princess, she acted as a Canadian cultural representative in her travels.

_____ Pauline Johnson is best known for her poetry celebrating her native heritage.

_____ Her first collection of poems, *White Wampum*, was published in 1895.

_____ Between 1892 and 1910, she undertook a series of speaking tours across Canada, the United States, and England.

3. From the life of Réne Lévesque, journalist, politician, and founder of the separatist Parti Québécois

_____ Réne Lévesque began life in Campbelltown, N.B., in 1922, but he grew up in New Carlisle, Quebec.

_____ He broke with the Liberals in 1967 to found an independent political party, which became the Parti Québécois.

_____ Lévesque's party won a majority of 71 seats over Robert Bourassa in the 1976 election.

_____ After working as a journalist during World War II, he became one of Quebec's most influential radio and later television comentators when he joined the CBC in 1946.

_____ Lévesque was first elected to politics as the Liberal member for Montreal-Laurier in 1960.

_____ Much of Canada was unhappy with Lévesque's majority because he had promised a referendum on sovereignty-association.

_____ In 1980, the referendum took place, but Lévesque suffered a personal defeat when the separatists took only 40 percent of the vote.

4. From the life of Emily Carr, painter and writer

_____ Emily was born in Victoria, B.C., in 1871.

_____ Largely unrecognized, she visited eastern Canada when she was 57 and met members of the Group of Seven.

_____ In 1908, she continued a program to visit sites of native people and paint a record of the vanishing civilization.

_____ Orphaned in her teens, she went to California to study art.

_____ Slowly, from 1928 onwards, she gained critical recognition and her paintings began to sell nationally.

_____   On her return home two and a half years later, Emily set up an art studio and started art classes for children.

_____   Later in her life, nature themes replaced native subjects in her art.

5.   From the life of Joseph-Henri-Maurice "Rocket" Richard, hockey player

_____   Maurice Richard, born in Montreal in 1921, became a legend in the National Hockey League.

_____   He collected 32 goals in his first full year of playing for the Montreal Canadiens.

_____   Injuries restricted his scoring in his last two years of amateur competition and his first year in the NHL.

_____   After retiring, Richard was seen occasionally on television endorsing commercial products.

_____   Richard was an outstanding playoff scorer, once scoring five goals in a playoff game against Toronto.

_____   In 1944-45, he scored 50 goals in 50 games, becoming the first hockey player to do so.

_____   His 544 goals was a record in the NHL when he retired.

Exercise 3   **Working for Coherence: Using Details in Order of Time Sequence**

Each of the following topics is followed by supporting details. These supporting details are not in any order. Place a number in the space provided before each sentence to show the order according to time sequence.

1.   The novel *Frankenstein* by Mary Shelley

_____   The monster turns on Victor Frankenstein and kills his younger brother, William.

_____   While at college in Ingolstadt, Victor Frankenstein learns the secret of creating life.

_____   Victor Frankenstein chases the monster to the frozen North, where he dies and the monster escapes.

_____   In revenge, the monster kills Victor Frankenstein's new bride.

_____   By raiding butcher shops and medical labs, Victor Frankenstein is able to make an enormous monster and give it life.

_____   Suspicious after discovering his brother, Victor Frankenstein tries to find the monster; when he finds him, the monster demands that he make a mate for him.

_____   Victor Frankenstein is born in Geneva, Switzerland, and from an early age has a deep interest in science.

_____   If Victor Frankenstein agrees, the monster and his bride will go to South America, never to be seen again; if he refuses, the monster will continue to kill people at random.

_____   Victor Frankenstein agrees, but at the last moment destroys the monster's mate.

2. The novel *The Time Machine* by H. G. Wells

    _____ The Eloi hide his time machine and refuse to give it back.

    _____ He travels 30 million years into the future, but he finds only a barren landscape.

    _____ The Time Traveller goes forward in time and finds himself in a strange country where everyone is a vegetarian—animals have become extinct. The people of this land are the Eloi, who are soft and sensual; because the world is at peace, there is no need to struggle and people have lost their strength.

    _____ The Eloi live in the year 802 701.

    _____ He returns to the present.

3. The novel *Great Expectations* by Charles Dickens

    _____ Pip realizes Miss Havisham has had nothing to do with his inheritance.

    _____ Pip, an orphan, is raised by a blacksmith, Joe Gargery, and his sister.

    _____ After his adventure with the convict, Pip works in a mansion near his home for a Miss Havisham, a crazed old woman who still wears the wedding dress she wore on the day her bridegroom failed to show up for the wedding.

    _____ One day, Pip sees a stranger in the marshes near his home. The man asks Pip to bring him food and a filing iron—he is an escaped convict.

    _____ Pip is contacted by a lawyer, who tells him that a nameless person has arranged for him to go to London, all expenses paid, to begin life as a gentleman.

    _____ On his twenty-first birthday, Pip receives a visitor; it is the convict, Abel Magwitch, whom he had helped years before—it is he who has given Pip the money.

4. The story *Gulliver's Travels* by Jonathan Swift

    _____ He helps Lilliput in a war with a neighbouring country. However, he has a disagreement with the emperor, leaves the country, and sails back to England.

    _____ On his way to his native country, the ship is blown off course and Gulliver is captured by giants. He is put on show. After two years in the country of the Brobdingnag, he escapes and returns to England.

    _____ Lemuel Gulliver finds himself shipwrecked on the shore of a strange country and he wakes up to find himself held to the ground by hundreds of small ropes. This is Lilliput, the land of small humans, and this is his first adventure.

    _____ Perhaps his most famous voyage is to the land of the Houyhnhnms, intelligent horses who are the masters of the Yahoos, humanlike creatures who also live in that country.

5. The novel *1984* by George Orwell

    _____ Julia and Winston meet O'Brien, a member of the Inner Party.

_____   Winston is tortured; he confesses.

_____   Winston Smith works at the Ministry of Truth, where his job is to revise facts to suit the needs of the ruling party of Oceania, an imaginary future society.

_____   Julia and Winston are arrested by the Thought Police.

_____   He meets Julia and they have a love affair.

_____   Winston Smith loves Big Brother, the ruler of Oceania who is never seen.

Transitions and Time Order

Writers who deal with time order in their work find themselves using words and phrases to help their readers get from one part of their work to another. These words and phrases are called transitions, and they are an important tool for every writer. Here is a passage from Frederick Philip Grove's "A Storm in July," which describes a violent summer storm on the prairies. The transitional words and phrases are printed in boldface.

> The **first day** it had died down towards evening; and we had a quiet night; but **the second morning** it had sprung up again, bringing with it their waves of vapor and a suggestion of smoke in the air which grew stronger **as the day advanced**; till **at last** towards noon the wind seemed to blow from a huge conflagration in the south. Down there the big marsh which stretches north of the open prairie was on fire **as it often is**. The speed of the wind was increasing, too, **on this second day**. The leaves strained at their stalks; the small aspens stood vibrating at an angle; the large black poplars huddled their tops together on the north side of their trunks; **while** the wind pulled and snatched at the edges of their green garments. A rag tied to a pole to mark off a neighbouring homestead claim cracked and crackled with the slight changes in the direction of the blast; and in the kitchen-garden behind the house the cucumber vines were lying helpless, belly up, with their foliage ragged and dusty and worn by the sand which even in this country of the northern bush began to blow.

Notice how the time transitions used in this paragraph make the order of events clear. "_The first day_ it had died down towards evening" gives the reader the sense that the story of the storm is being told on a daily basis, and that the description actually begins late in the day when the worst of the storm was over for the day and there was a lull toward evening. "_The second morning_ it had sprung up again" continues the action into the next day, but this time the wind carried a hint of smoke, which hadn't been there before. The smoke "grew stronger _as the day advanced_," then, "_at last_," it was obvious that the big marsh in the south was on fire, "_as it often is_," which adds to the awesome power of the natural elements, still being described by Grove in a sequential fashion. The storm is still building "_on this second day_," "_while_" the remainder of the paragraph goes on to describe the effects of this storm on the second day to the Grove homestead.

Frederick Philip Grove has used time words and phrases to give us an idea of how long the storm lasted and what other elements in the prairie environment were at work. His use of transitions helps to make his meaning clear.

Exercise 1   Working with Transitions

Using the transitions given in the list below or using ones you think of yourself, fill in each of the blanks in the following student paragraph.

at once	later, later on	after a little while
immediately	now, by now	first, first of all
soon afterward	finally	then
suddenly	in the next moment	next

      I arrived at Aunt Lorinda's in the middle of a heat wave. It was 40 degrees in the shade and very humid. Aunt Lorinda as usual greeted me with the list of activities she had scheduled for the day. _____ we went to the attic to gather old clothes for the Salvation Army. I nearly passed out up in the attic. Sweat poured down my face. Aunt Lorinda, in her crisp cotton sundress, looked cool and was obviously enjoying herself. "If you see something you want, take it," she said graciously. "It's so nice of you to give me a hand today. You're young and strong and have so much more energy than I." _____ her plans included the yard work. I took off my shirt and mowed the lawn while my 80-year-old aunt trimmed hedges and weeded the flower beds. _____ it was time to drive into the dusty town and do errands. Luckily, Auntie stayed behind to fix lunch and I was able to duck into an air-conditioned coffee shop for ten minutes' rest before I dropped off the old clothes at the Salvation Army. I wasn't anxious to find out what help I could be to my aunt in the afternoon. I hoped it wouldn't be something like last year when I had to put a new roof on the old shed in the backyard. I could feel the beginning of a painful sunburn.

Exercise 2   Working with Transitions

Below is a narrative paragraph from the famous story "The Overcoat" by Nikolai Gogol. Make a list below of all the transitions of time that give order to the paragraph.

      In the meantime Akakii Akakiievich walked along feeling in the most festive of moods. He was conscious every second of every minute that he had a new overcoat on his shoulders, and several times even smiled slightly because of his inward pleasure. In reality he was a gainer on two points: for one, the overcoat was warm; for the other, it was a fine thing. He did not notice the walk at all and suddenly found himself at the Bureau; in the porter's room he took off his overcoat, looked it all over, and entrusted it to the particular care of the doorman. None knows in what manner everybody in the Bureau suddenly learned that Akakii Akakiievich had a new overcoat, and that the *negligee* was no longer in existence. They all immediately ran out into the vestibule to inspect Akakii Akakiievich's new overcoat. They fell to congratulating him, to saying agreeable things to him, so that at first he could merely smile, and in a short time became actually embarrassed. And when all of them, having besieged him, began telling him that the new overcoat ought to be baptized and that he ought, at the least, to get up an evening party for them, Akakii Akakiievich was utterly at a loss, not knowing what to do with himself, what answers to make, nor how to get out of inviting them. It was only a few minutes later that he began assuring them, quite simpleheartedly, that it wasn't a new overcoat at all, that it was just an ordinary overcoat, that in fact it was an old overcoat. Finally one of the bureaucrats — some sort of an Assistant to a Head of a Department actually — probably in order to show that he was not at all a proud stick and willing to mingle even with those beneath him, said: "So be it, then; I'm giving a party this evening and ask all of you to have tea with me; today, appropriately enough, happens to be my birthday."

_____   _____

_____   _____

_____   _____

Exercise 3   Working with Transitions

Below is a narrative paragraph from a story by the Russian writer Ivan Turgenev. Make a list of all the transitions of time that give order to the paragraph.

> I went to the right through the bushes. Meantime the night had crept close and grown up like a storm cloud; it seemed as though, with the mists of evening, darkness was rising up on all sides and flowing down from overhead. I had come upon some sort of little, untrodden, overgrown path; I walked along it, gazing intently before me. Soon all was blackness and silence around — only the quail's cry was heard from time to time. Some small nightbird, flitting noiselessly near the ground on its soft wings, almost flapped against me and scurried away in alarm. I came out on the further side of the bushes, and made my way along a field by the hedge. By now I could hardly make out distant objects; the field showed dimly white around; beyond it rose up a sullen darkness, which seemed moving up closer in huge masses every instant. My steps gave a muffled sound in the air, that grew colder and colder. The pale sky began again to grow blue — but it was the blue of night. The tiny stars glimmered and twinkled in it.

_____   _____

_____   _____

_____   _____

Writing the Narrative Paragraph Step by Step

To learn a skill with some degree of ease, it is best to follow a step-by-step approach so that various skills can be worked on one skill at a time. This will ensure that you are not missing a crucial point or misunderstanding a part of the whole. There certainly are other ways to go about writing assignments, but here is one logical process you can use to get good results.

Steps for Writing the Narrative Paragraph

1. Study the given topic and then plan your topic sentence with its controlling idea.
2. List the sequence of events that come to your mind when you think about the story you have chosen.
3. Then choose the five or six most important events from your list.
4. Put your list in order.
5. Write one complete sentence for each of the events you have chosen from your list.
6. Write a concluding statement that gives some point to the events of the story.
7. Finally, copy your sentences into standard paragraph form.

Exercise 1   Writing the Narrative Paragraph Step by Step

The following exercise will guide you through the construction of a complete narrative paragraph. Start with the suggested topic. Use the seven steps above to help you work through each stage of the writing process.

Topic: Every family has a favourite story they like to tell about one of their members, often something humorous that happened to one of them. There are also crises and tragic moments in the life of every family. Choose a story, funny or tragic, from the life of a family you know.

1.   Topic sentence: _____

     _____

2.   Make a list of events.

     a. _____   f. _____

     b. _____   g. _____

     c. _____   h. _____

     d. _____   i. _____

     e. _____   j. _____

3.   Circle the five or six events you believe are the most important for the point of the story.

4.   Put your final choices in order by numbering each of them.

5.   Using your final list, write at least one sentence for each event you have chosen.

     a. _____

        _____

     b. _____

        _____

     c. _____

        _____

     d. _____

        _____

     e. _____

        _____

     f. _____

        _____

     g. _____

        _____

6.   Write a concluding statement. _____

     _____

     _____

7.   Copy your sentences into standard paragraph form.

     _____

     _____

     _____

_____

_____

_____

_____

_____

_____

_____

_____

_____

_____

Exercise 2   **Writing the Narrative Paragraph Step by Step**

The following exercise will guide you through the construction of a complete narrative paragraph. Start with the suggested topic. Use the seven steps on page 234 to help you work through each stage of the writing process.

Topic: Recount the plot of a book you have read recently or a movie you have seen within the last few weeks.

1. Topic sentence: _____

_____

2. Make a list of events.

    a. _____   f. _____

    b. _____   g. _____

    c. _____   h. _____

    d. _____   i. _____

    e. _____   j. _____

3. Circle the five or six events you believe are the most important for the point of the story.
4. Put your choices in order by numbering them.
5. Using your final list, write at least one sentence for each event you have chosen.

    a. _____

    _____

    b. _____

    _____

    c. _____

    _____

d. _____

_____

e. _____

_____

f. _____

_____

g. _____

6. Write a concluding statement. _____

_____

_____

7. Copy your sentences into standard paragraph form.

_____

_____

_____

_____

_____

_____

_____

_____

_____

_____

_____

_____

_____

_____

_____

_____

_____

Exercise 3 Writing the Narrative Paragraph Step by Step

The following exercise will guide you through the construction of a complete narrative paragraph. Start with the suggested topic. Use the seven steps on page 234 to help you work through each stage of the writing process.

Topic: Tell a story that you have heard one of your parents tell about his or her past.

1. Topic sentence: _____

_____

2. Make a list of possible supporting details.

a. _____   f. _____

b. _____   g. _____

c. _____   h. _____

d. _____   i. _____

e. _____   j. _____

3. Circle the five or six details you believe are the most important for the point of the story.
4. Put your final choices in order by numbering them.
5. Using your final list, write one sentence for each detail you have chosen.

a. _____

_____

b. _____

_____

c. _____

_____

d. _____

_____

e. _____

_____

f. _____

_____

g. _____

_____

6. Write a concluding statement. _____

_____

_____

7. Copy your sentences into standard paragraph form.

_____

_____

_____

_____

_____

_____

_____

_____

_____

_____

_____

_____

_____

_____

On Your Own: Writing Narrative Paragraphs from Model Paragraphs

The Story of How You Faced a New Challenge

ASSIGNMENT 1: Write a paragraph telling the story of a day or part of a day in which you faced an important challenge of some kind. It could have been a challenge you faced in school, at home, or on the job. The following paragraph is an example of such an experience.

Model Paragraph

I hate to be late. So, when I began my new job, I was determined to be on time for my first day. I awoke early, had a leisurely breakfast, and gave myself lots of time to get through the traffic. I entered my new office building and sat down at my new desk a good fifteen minutes before starting time. My boss noticed me, smiled, and came over to my desk. "I'm glad you're early," she said. "In fact, you're a week early. You start *next* Monday."

TEN SUGGESTED TOPICS
1. The day I started a new job
2. My first day in history class
3. The day I began my first term paper
4. The day I tried to wallpaper my bedroom
5. The morning of my big job interview
6. Facing a large debt
7. Trying to re-establish a friendship gone sour
8. The day I started driving lessons
9. Coping with a death in the family
10. The day I faced a deadline

The Story of an Unpleasant Fight or Argument

ASSIGNMENT 2: Write a paragraph in which you tell the story of a fight or confrontation you either witnessed or became involved in. Choose an experience that left a deep impression on you. What are the important details of the incident that remain most clearly in your mind? The following paragraph is from George Gabori's "Coming of Age in Putnok."

Model Paragraph

By now a crowd had gathered around us and there was nothing for it but to fight it out. There were tears and laughter as Tivadar hit me in the nose before I got my jacket off. It was not the first time I had tasted my own blood, but it was the first time a Christian had made it flow. Tivadar was flushed with pleasure and excitement at the applause and not at all expecting it when I lashed out with my fist and sent him sprawling backward on the cobbles. The crowd of boys groaned and shouted to Tivadar to get up and kill the Jew, but poor Tivadar did not move. Frightened, I grabbed my jacket and shoved my way through the crowd stunned into silence by this overturning of the laws of nature.

TEN SUGGESTED TOPICS
A confrontation between
1. A police officer and a guilty motorist
2. A teacher and a student
3. An angry customer and a store clerk
4. A frustrated parent and a child
5. A manager and an unhappy employee
6. A judge and an unwilling witness
7. A museum guard and a careless tourist
8. A politician and an angry citizen
9. A mugger and a frightened victim
10. An engaged couple about to break up

The Beginning of a Special Relationship

ASSIGNMENT 3: Write a paragraph that tells the story of how you became close to another person. Select one particular moment when the relationship changed from casual friendliness to something deeper and more lasting. Perhaps you shared an experience that brought you together. The following paragraph is taken from Morley Callaghan's short story "One Spring Night."

Model Paragraph

Bob had taken her out a few times when he had felt like having some girl to talk to who knew him and liked him. And tonight he was leaning back good-humoredly, telling her one thing and then another with the wise self-assurance he usually had when with her; but gradually, as he watched her, he found himself talking more slowly, his voice grew serious and much softer, and then finally he leaned across the table toward her as though he had just discovered that her neck was full and soft with her spring coat thrown open, and that her face under her little black straw hat tilted back on her head had a new, eager beauty. Her warm, smiling softness was so close to him that he smiled a bit shyly.

TEN SUGGESTED TOPICS
1. My relationship with a teacher
2. My relationship with a fellow student
3. A moment when I understood my clergyman in a new way
4. When I learned something new about a neighbourhood merchant
5. When I shared an experience with a fellow worker
6. When I made friends with someone older or younger than myself
7. When my relationship with my brother or sister changed
8. The moment when my attitude about a grandparent changed
9. When a stranger became a friend
10. When a relationship went from bad to worse

You Won't Believe What Happened to Me Today!

ASSIGNMENT 4: Tell the story of a day you found yourself in a difficult or frustrating situation. The following example is from Max Ferguson's "The Birth of Rawhide."

Model Paragraph

At last I was able to ask Syd what the problem was. He took two full minutes to babble out his message, but when I'd mentally pruned all the extraneous and profane prefixes and suffixes it was reduced to a rather concise skeletal form — "The Yodelling Ranger is not only a local Halifax boy but also the most popular idol in the Maritimes!" Syd further advised that, to avoid being lynched the moment I stepped out onto Sackville Street, I should hastily make the most abject apology I could think of. There wasn't much program time left, so I faded down the record that was playing, opened my microphone, and said, still in the Rawhide voice, "I just made a very unfortunate mistake in calling that previous singer the Yodelling Idiot. I certainly didn't mean to be disparaging and was obviously confusing him with another Yodelling Idiot I once knew in Upper Canada. This is the Canadian Broadcasting Corporation." Kennedy showed great restraint, waiting till the very last word of the corporation cue was finished and the microphone cut before he clapped both hands to his head, emitted an anguished groan, and vanished from the studio.

TEN SUGGESTED TOPICS
1. When I ran out of money
2. When I ran out of gas
3. When I was accused of something I didn't do
4. When I was stopped by the police (or by some other authority)
5. When I was guilty of . . .
6. When something terrible happened just before a big date
7. When the weather didn't co-operate
8. When I locked myself out of the house
9. When I couldn't reach my family by phone
10. When my typewriter broke down the night before a paper was due

A Memorable Experience from Childhood

ASSIGNMENT 5: Write a paragraph in which you remember a special moment from your childhood. The following example is from George Orwell's novel *Coming Up for Air*.

Model Paragraph

It was an enormous fish. I don't exaggerate when I say it was enormous. It was almost the length of my arm. It glided across the pool, deep under water, and then became a shadow and disappeared into the darker water on the other side. I felt as if a sword had gone through me. It was by far the biggest fish I'd ever seen, dead or alive. I stood there without breathing, and in a moment another huge thick shape glided through the water, and then another and then two more close together. The pool was full of them. They were carp, I suppose. Just possibly they were bream or tench, but more probably carp. Bream or tench wouldn't grow so huge. I knew what had happened. At some time this pool had been connected with the other, and then the stream had dried up and the woods had closed round the small pool and it had just been forgotten. It's a thing that happens occasionally. A pool gets forgotten somehow, nobody fishes in it for years and decades and the fish grow to monstrous sizes. The brutes that I was watching might be a hundred years old. And not a soul in the world knew about them except me. Very likely it was twenty years since anyone had so much as looked at the pool, and probably even old Hodges and Mr. Farrel's bailiff had forgotten its existence.

TEN SUGGESTED TOPICS

1. The first time I went swimming
2. My first time on a roller coaster (or on another ride)
3. A frightening experience when I was home alone
4. My most memorable Halloween (or other holiday)
5. The best birthday party I ever had
6. My first bicycle (or car)
7. The greatest present I ever received
8. A memorable visit to a favourite relative
9. My first time travelling alone
10. The first time I went camping

16

Developing Paragraphs: Process

What Is Process?

Process is the method that explains how to do something or that shows how something works.

When Do We Use Process?

There are two kinds of process writing: **directional** and **informational**. A process that is directional actually shows you, step by step, how to do something. For example, if you want to show someone how to brew a perfect cup of coffee, you would take the person through each step of the process, from selecting and grinding the coffee beans to pouring the finished product. Instructions on a test, directions on how to get to a wedding reception, or your favourite spaghetti recipe are a few examples of the kinds of process writing you see and use regularly. You can find examples of directional process writing everywhere you look, in newspapers, magazines, and books, as well as on the containers and packages of products you use every day.

On the other hand, a process that is informational tells you how something is or was done. This is for the purpose of informing you about the process. For example, in a history course, it might be important to understand how the process of Confederation joined Upper and Lower Canada. Of course, you would not use this process yourself. The purpose is for information.

The following paragraph describes the various steps that the medical researcher Hans Selye suggests a person can go through to avoid the harmful effects of stress. Notice that each step in the process is given in its proper sequence. Words such as *consequently* and *however* can be used to show that a writer is developing an idea by using process.

You should not and cannot avoid stress, because to eliminate it completely would mean to destroy life itself. If you make no more

243

demands upon your body, you are dead. Whatever we do — run up a flight of stairs, play tennis, worry or fight starvation — demands are made upon us. A lash of the whip and a passionate kiss can be equally stressful! Although one causes distress and the other eustress, both make certain common demands, necessitating adaptation to change in our normal resting equilibrium. Even while we sleep, the heart must continue to beat, we must move the muscles that help the lungs to breathe, we continue to digest last night's meal and even the brain does not cease to function as we dream. Consequently, it would be quite unthinkable that anyone could, or would, or would even want to, avoid stress. However, the more we learn about conditioning and the ways to deal with the stress of life, the more we can enjoy eustress, which is the spice of our existence. It gives us the only outlet we have to express our talents and energies, to pursue happiness.

Working with Process: Don't Overlook Any of the Steps

The writer of the process essay is almost always more of an authority on the subject than the person reading the essay. In giving directions or information on how something is to be done or was done, it is possible to leave out a step that you think is so obvious that it is not worth mentioning. The reader, on the other hand, does not necessarily fill in the missing step as you did. An important part of process writing, therefore, is understanding your reader's level of ability. All of us have been given directions that, at first, seemed very clear. However, when we actually tried to carry out the process, something went wrong. A step in the process was misunderstood or missing. The giver of the information either assumed we would know certain parts of the process or didn't stop to think through the process completely. The important point is that directions must be complete and accurate. Here is one further consideration: if special equipment is required in order to perform the process, the directions must include a clear description of the necessary tools.

Exercise 1   **Is the Process Complete?**

In each of the following processes, try to determine what important step or steps of information have been omitted. Try to imagine yourself going through the process using only the information provided.

Making Popovers
1. Preheat the oven.
2. Sift 250 mL of flour and 1 mL of salt into a mixing bowl.
3. Using another mixing bowl, combine the eggs, 250 mL of milk, and 5 mL of melted butter.
4. Stir until well blended and smooth.
5. Lightly oil ovenproof glass custard cups.
6. Fill the cups a little more than half full.
7. Place the cups on a baking sheet and place in the oven.
8. Bake the popovers until done.

Missing step or steps: _____

_____

_____

How to Use the Copying Machine
1. Open the top of the copier.
2. Position the paper you are copying on the glass surface.

3. Set the copier to the kind of copying you are going to do (light, normal, or dark).
4. Check the size of the paper. Most copiers have a setting for two sizes of paper.
5. Put your money into the copier machine.

Missing step or steps: _____

_____

_____

Exercise 2   Is the Process Complete?

In each of the following processes, try to determine what important step or steps of information have been omitted. Try to imagine yourself going through the process using only the information provided.

How to Install and Run an Air Conditioner
1. Clean the air conditioner's filter or replace it if necessary.
2. Clean the window frame by removing any loose dirt.
3. Make sure the air conditioner is tilted to allow excess water to drain off and to prevent buildup of any moisture in the unit.
4. Use caulking or other material to make the space between the air conditioner and the window airtight.
5. Place pieces of wood or metal in the window frame to prevent the weight of the air conditioner from forcing the window open.

Missing step or steps: _____

_____

_____

How to Plan a Wedding
1. Make an appointment with the minister or other authority involved, to set a date for the wedding.
2. Discuss plans with both families as to the budget available for the wedding; this will determine the size of the party and where it is to be held.
3. Reserve the banquet hall as much as eight months in advance.
4. Choose members of the wedding party and ask them whether they will be able to participate in the ceremony.
5. Begin to choose the clothing for the wedding party, including your own wedding gown or suit.
6. Enjoy your wedding!

Missing step or steps: _____

_____

_____

Exercise 3   Is the Process Complete?

In each of the following processes, try to determine what important step or steps of information have been omitted. Try to imagine yourself going through the process using only the information provided.

How to Prepare for an Essay Exam
1. Read the chapters well in advance of the test as they are assigned.
2. Take notes in class.
3. If the teacher has not described the test, ask the teacher what format the test will take.
4. Get a good night's sleep the night before.
5. Bring any pens or pencils that you might need.
6. Arrive at the classroom a few minutes early in order to get yourself settled and to keep yourself calm.

Missing step or steps: _____

_____

_____

How to Balance Your Chequebook with the Monthly Bank Statement
1. Put your returned cheques in order by number or date.
2. Check them off in your chequebook, making sure the amount of each cheque agrees with each amount listed in your chequebook.
3. Subtract from your chequebook balance any amounts that are automatically deducted from your account (loan payments, for example).
4. Add to your bank statement balance the amounts of deposits you made after the date on the statement.
5. Subtract from the bank statement balance the total number of cheques still outstanding.
6. The balance you get should agree with your chequebook balance.

(Do you see now why so many people cannot balance their chequebooks?)

Missing step or steps: _____

_____

_____

Coherence in Process: Order in Logical Sequence

When you are working with process, it is important not only to make sure the steps in the process are complete; you must also make sure they are given in the right sequence. For example, if you are describing the process of cleaning a mixer, it is important to point out that you must first unplug the appliance before you actually remove the blades. The importance of this step is clear when you realize that a person could lose a finger if this part of the process were missing. Improperly written instructions could cause serious injuries or even death.

Exercise 1 Coherence in Process: Order in Logical Sequence

The following steps describe the process of refinishing hardwood floors. Put the steps into their proper sequence.

_____ Keep sanding until you expose the hardwood.

_____ Apply a coat of polyurethane finish.

_____ When the sanding is done, clean the floor thoroughly with a vacuum sweeper to remove all the sawdust.

_____ Allow the finish to dry for three days before waxing and buffing.

_____ Take all furnishings out of the room.

_____ Do the initial sanding with a coarse sandpaper.

_____ The edger and hand sander are used after the machine sanding to get to those hard-to-reach places.

_____ Put the second coat of polyurethane finish on the following day, using a brush or a roller.

_____ Change to a fine sandpaper for the final sanding.

_____ Any nails sticking out from the floor should be either pulled out or set below the surface of the boards before you start the sanding machine.

Exercise 2 Coherence in Process: Order in Logical Sequence

The following steps describe the process of moving a household. Put the steps into their proper sequence.

_____ List the contents of every carton, including what room the carton should be brought to.

_____ A few days before moving, seal the cartons with heavy-duty gummed tape.

_____ Before you seal the cartons, be sure no carton weighs more than 25 kilograms.

_____ About two months before the scheduled move, begin collecting boxes. Liquor stores are a particularly good source, since their boxes are often cushioned and sturdy.

_____ Allow young children on the day of the move to take with them one or two favourite toys for comfort.

_____ The day before the move, make the beds with clean linen so the next morning you can roll up the bedclothes like a camp bedroll and have them all ready to put on the beds at the new home.

_____ Also, buy a variety of thick felt-tip pens with which to mark the cartons.

Exercise 3 Coherence in Process: Order in Logical Sequence

The following steps describe the process of making a filing system that works. Put the steps into their proper sequence.

_____ When your mind begins to blur, stop filing for that day.

_____ Now label the file folder and slip the piece of paper in.

_____ Gather together all materials to be filed so that they are all in one location.

_____ Alphabetize your file folders and put them away into your file drawer, and you are finished for that session.

_____ Add to these materials a wastebasket, folders, labels, and a pen.

_____ Pick up the next piece of paper and go through the same procedure, the only variation being that this new piece of paper might fit into an existing file, rather than one with a new heading.

_____ Pick up an item on the top of the pile and decide whether this item has value for you. If it does not, throw it away. If it does, go on to the next step.

_____ Finally, to maintain your file once it is established, each time you consult a file folder, riffle through it quickly to pick out and throw away the dead wood.

_____ If the piece of paper is worth saving, ask yourself the question, "What is this paper about?"

Transitions for Process

Writers of process, like writers of narration, usually order their material by time sequence. Although it would be tiresome to use "and then" for each new step, a certain number of transitions are necessary for the process to read smoothly and be coherent. Here is a list of transitions frequently used in process.

Transitions

the first step	while you are . . .	the last step
in the beginning	as you are . . .	the final step
to start with	next	finally
to begin with	then	at last
first of all	the second step	eventually
	after you have . . .	

Exercise 1   Using Transitions to Go from a List to a Paragraph

Select one of the six processes listed on pages 244–246. Change this list into a process paragraph that uses enough transitional devices so that the paragraph is coherent and flows smoothly.

_____

_____

_____

_____

_____

_____

_____

_____

_____

_____

_____

_____

_____

_____

_____

_____

_____

_____

_____

Exercise 2 Using Transitions to Go from a List to a Paragraph

Select one of the six processes listed on pages 244–246. Change this list into a process paragraph that uses enough transitional devices so that the paragraph is coherent and flows smoothly.

Exercise 3 Using Transitions to Go from a List to a Paragraph

Select one of the six processes listed on pages 244–246. Change this list into a process paragraph that uses enough transitional devices so that the paragraph is coherent and flows smoothly.

_____

_____

_____

_____

_____

_____

_____

_____

_____

_____

_____

_____

_____

_____

_____

_____

_____

_____

_____

Writing the Process Paragraph Step by Step

To learn a skill with some degree of ease, it is best to follow a step-by-step approach so that various skills are isolated. This will ensure that you are not missing a crucial point or misunderstanding a part of the whole. There certainly are other ways to go about writing an effective paragraph, but here is one step-by-step method you can use to get good final results. You will learn that writing, like most other skills, can be developed by using a logical process.

Steps for Writing the Process Paragraph

1. Write a topic sentence.
2. List as many steps or stages in the process as you can.
3. Eliminate any irrelevant points; add equipment needed or special circumstances of the process.
4. Put your list in order.
5. Finally, write at least one complete sentence for each of the steps you have chosen from your list.
6. Write a concluding statement that says something about the results of completing the process.
7. Copy your sentences into standard paragraph form.

Exercise 1   **Writing the Process Paragraph Step by Step**

The following exercise will guide you through the construction of a complete process paragraph. Start with the suggested topic. Use the seven steps to help you work through each stage of the writing process.

Topic: How to lose weight

Perhaps no topic has filled more bookstores or magazine pages than the "lose five kilograms in two days" promise. The wide variety of diet plans boggles the mind. Here is your chance to add your own version.

1. Topic sentence: _____

    _____

2. Make a list of possible steps.

    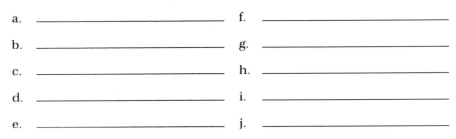

    a. _____   f. _____

    b. _____   g. _____

    c. _____   h. _____

    d. _____   i. _____

    e. _____   j. _____

3. Circle the five or six steps you believe are the most important.
4. Put your final choices in order by numbering them.
5. Using your final list, write at least one sentence for each step you have chosen.

    a. _____

    _____

    b. _____

    _____

    c. _____

    _____

    d. _____

    _____

    e. _____

    _____

    f. _____

    _____

    g. _____

    _____

6. Write a concluding statement. _____

    _____

    _____

7. Copy your sentences into standard paragraph form.

_____

_____

_____

_____

_____

_____

_____

_____

_____

_____

_____

_____

_____

_____

_____

_____

_____

_____

_____

_____

_____

Exercise 2   Writing the Process Paragraph Step by Step

The following exercise will guide you through the construction of a complete process paragraph. Start with the suggested topic. Use the seven steps to help you work through each stage of the writing process.

Topic: How to pick a college

Sometimes an individual goes through an agonizing process before he or she is finally seated in a college classroom. The factors that go into selecting a college can be extremely complicated. Give advice to a prospective college student on how to go about finding the right college.

1. Topic sentence: _____

_____

2. Make a list of possible steps.

    a. _____   d. _____

    b. _____   e. _____

    c. _____   f. _____

g. ——————————————   i. ——————————————

h. ——————————————   j. ——————————————

3. Circle the five or six steps you believe are the most important.
4. Put your final choices in order by numbering them.
5. Using your final list, write at least one sentence for each step you have chosen.

a. ————————————————————————————
————————————————————————————

b. ————————————————————————————
————————————————————————————

c. ————————————————————————————
————————————————————————————

d. ————————————————————————————
————————————————————————————

e. ————————————————————————————
————————————————————————————

f. ————————————————————————————
————————————————————————————

g. ————————————————————————————
————————————————————————————

6. Write a concluding statement. ————————————————
————————————————————————————
————————————————————————————

7. Copy your sentences into standard paragraph form.
————————————————————————————
————————————————————————————
————————————————————————————
————————————————————————————
————————————————————————————
————————————————————————————
————————————————————————————
————————————————————————————
————————————————————————————
————————————————————————————

_____

_____

_____

_____

_____

_____

_____

_____

_____

_____

Exercise 3   Writing the Process Paragraph Step by Step

The following exercise will guide you through the construction of a complete process paragraph. Start with the suggested topic. Use the seven steps to help you work through each stage of the writing process.

Topic: How to manage a budget
Imagine you are the expert who has been hired by a couple to help them sort out their money problems. They bring in a reasonable income, but still they are always spending more than they earn.

1.   Topic sentence: _____

_____

2.   Make a list of possible steps.

a.   _____   f.   _____

b.   _____   g.   _____

c.   _____   h.   _____

d.   _____   i.   _____

e.   _____   j.   _____

3.   Circle the five or six steps you believe are the most important.
4.   Put your final choices in order by numbering them.
5.   Using your final list, write one sentence for each step you have chosen.

a.   _____

_____

b.   _____

_____

c.   _____

_____

d.   _____

_____

e. _____

_____

f. _____

_____

g. _____

_____

6. Write a concluding statement. _____

_____

_____

7. Copy your sentences into standard paragraph form.

_____

_____

_____

_____

_____

_____

_____

_____

_____

_____

_____

_____

_____

_____

_____

_____

_____

_____

On Your Own: Writing Process Paragraphs from Model Paragraphs

Directional: How to Accomplish a Physical Task

ASSIGNMENT 1: Write a paragraph in which you describe the process of doing a physical task of some kind, or the process of doing a task in order to accomplish something else. For example, you might have learned how to antique an old piece of furniture in order to save money, or you might have learned how to drive so that you would be in a better position to get a job. The following paragraph, taken from a publication of the Public Records Office in London, England, describes how to trace your family tree if you think that you have ancestors who came from England or Wales.

> Anyone of English or Welsh descent who wishes to trace his family tree may come to St. Catharines House and make searches to establish the last three or four generations. The records are, however, concerned with individual events and not with pedigrees. It may therefore be necessary to make a series of searches to trace the lines of descent back to 1837. For example, if a person wishes to trace the record of his father's birth but does not know when he was born it may be necessary first to search for the record of his father's marriage (working backward from the date of birth of the eldest child in the family). A certificate of the marriage should give the bridegroom's age and the name of his father, and so will give a starting point for tracing and identifying the record of the birth concerned.

TEN SUGGESTED TOPICS
1. How to move from one city to another
2. How to install your own telephone
3. How to install a stereo system
4. How to lay a carpet
5. How to make homemade ice cream
6. How to prepare a package for mailing
7. How to pack a suitcase
8. How to furnish an apartment inexpensively
9. How to wallpaper a room
10. How to care for a lawn

Informational: How Something Scientific Works

ASSIGNMENT 2: Write a paragraph in which you describe a scientific process. You could tell how a simple radio works, or you could describe how a snake sheds its skin. The following paragraph gives a description of a modern scientific process that increases the world's supply of drinking water. After you have chosen a topic, look for specific information in encyclopedias, textbooks, or other sources to help you explain the process.

> The Anse method of converting sea water to fresh water is a cheap and efficient way to produce drinkable water from the sea. First, you cover an area of water with a sheet of black plastic. Air-filled channels in the plastic keep it raised slightly above the water. Underneath this plastic is another sheet of plastic that floats on the water; this plastic has small holes that allow sea water to seep up between the two layers of plastic. The heat of the sun, striking the upper layer of the plastic, causes the water to evaporate, leaving the salt behind. The hot air, filled with water, is then forced through a pipe and into an underground collection chamber by wind that is channeled between the plastic sheets by air ducts built on top of the plastic. When the hot air enters the collection chamber, the water in the air condenses, leaving fresh water on the bottom of the submerged chamber. This fresh water can then be pumped out of the chamber and used.

TEN SUGGESTED TOPICS
1. How leather is made

2. How metamorphosis happens
3. How an airplane flies
4. How stars are formed
5. How an eclipse occurs
6. How the human heart works
7. How a bee makes honey
8. How a camera works
9. How a piano works
10. How a book is produced

Directional: How to Care for Your Health

ASSIGNMENT 3: Write a paragraph in which you give the major steps in some area of caring for your health, mentally or physically. Concern for health and physical fitness is enjoying great popularity, bringing in big profits to health-related magazines, health clubs, health-food producers, and sports equipment manufacturers. The following paragraph tells us how to get a good night's sleep.

> The process of getting a good night's sleep depends on several factors. First, the conditions in your bedroom must be correct. Be sure that the room temperature is around eighteen degrees and that the room is as quiet as possible. Next, pay attention to your bed and how it is furnished. A firm mattress is best and wool blankets are better than blankets made of synthetic material. In addition, pillows that are too soft can cause stiffness of the neck and lead to a poor night's sleep. Also, keep in mind that what you eat and how you eat are part of the process of preparing for bed. Do not go to bed hungry, but do not overeat, either. Avoid candy bars or cookies; the sugar they contain acts as a stimulant. Finally, do not go to bed until you are sleepy; do something relaxing until you are tired.

TEN SUGGESTED TOPICS
1. How to plan a healthful diet
2. How to care for someone who is ill
3. How to plan a daily exercise program
4. How to choose a sport that is suitable for you
5. How to live to be 100
6. How to pick a doctor
7. How to make exercise and diet foods fun
8. How to stop eating junk food
9. How to deal with depression
10. How to find a spiritual side to life

Informational: How to Accomplish an Important Task

ASSIGNMENT 4: Write a paragraph in which you show how an important task is accomplished. The task may be something that is frequently done in human society, or that occurs in the world of nature. The following paragraph, which describes how an insect builds a nest, is an example of this kind of process.

> The insect known as the hunter wasp goes through a regular procedure when it builds a nest. First, it digs a small tunnel into the earth. Then it goes in search of a cicada, a large insect that resembles a cricket. After stinging and paralyzing the cicada, the hunter wasp brings it to the tunnel, lays an egg on the helpless insect, and seals the tunnel. The hunter wasp then leaves. When the egg hatches, it uses the cicada as a source of food.

TEN SUGGESTED TOPICS
1. How cheese is made
2. How a piece of farm machinery works
3. How a school yearbook is produced
4. How people obtain a divorce
5. How Madame Curie discovered radium
6. How the ancient Egyptians built the pyramids
7. How a bill becomes a law
8. How penicillin was discovered
9. How the snowmobile was developed
10. How glass is made

Directional: How to Write School Assignments

ASSIGNMENT 5: Your writing in school takes many forms. Write a paragraph in which you show the process of writing a specific assignment related to school. The following paragraph, from Mary Finlay's *Communication at Work*, shows the several steps you need to keep in mind when determining the length of an oral presentation.

Ascertain how long your presentation is expected to take. Normally, a speech is delivered at about 150 words a minute. Make sure your material is adequate for the time allotted. Of course, this does not mean that a 10-minute oral report will be as dense as a 1500-word essay. You will need to build in much more repetition to ensure that you are getting your point across. But planned repetition is one thing. Rehashing points you have already made in order to fill up your time is a sure-fire way to annoy and frustrate your listeners. Leave time for questions and feedback. If there are none, don't fill in the time by answering questions nobody asked. This suggests that you are having second thoughts about the organization and planning of your report.

TEN SUGGESTED TOPICS
1. How to prepare a term paper
2. How to write a résumé
3. How to write a letter of application (for a school or for a job)
4. How to write a science experiment
5. How to write a book review
6. How to revise an essay
7. How to take classroom notes
8. How to take notes from a textbook
9. How to write a letter home, asking for money
10. How to write a story for the school newspaper

Developing Paragraphs: Comparison or Contrast

What Is Comparison or Contrast?

Comparison and contrast are two related methods of explaining subjects. When we use comparison, we emphasize the similarities between two subjects. When we use contrast, we emphasize the differences between two subjects. We sometimes use the word *comparison* to refer to both similarities and differences between people or things, but it is more exact to use *comparison* for similarities and *contrast* for differences. For example, if you were to write about twin sisters you know, and how close they are in appearance and personality, the similarities you would include would make up a comparison. On the other hand, if you wanted to emphasize some important differences between the two sisters, the result of your work would be a contrast.

When Do We Use Comparison or Contrast?

We use comparison or contrast in a variety of ways every day. We put similar products side by side in the grocery store before we decide to buy one of them; we listen to two politicians on television and think about the differences between their positions before we vote for one of them; and we read college catalogues and talk to our friends before we make a final choice as to which school we should attend.

When we compare two items, we are able to judge which is better. In addition, when we use comparison we are able to see each individual item more clearly. For example, if you were trying to decide whether to buy a small computer or upgrade your typewriter, you should find someone who often uses typewriters and computers. This person could compare or contrast the two machines: show you the similarities or the differences. Today many people are trying to decide whether they would use the computer enough to justify the difference between the cost of a computer and the cost of a typewriter. If the person decides to buy a computer, then the comparison or contrast process begins again: finding out the similarities or differences among the many different makes and sizes. One must consider price, capability, availability of service, compatibility with other equipment, and clarity of the screen. Even the wisest shopper would find such a purchase a complicated procedure.

Working with Comparison or Contrast: Choosing the Two-Part Topic

The problem with writing a good comparison or contrast paragraph usually centres on the fact that you now have a two-part topic. This demands very careful attention to the topic sentence. While you must be careful to choose two subjects that have enough in common to make them comparable, you must also not choose two things having so much in common that you cannot possibly handle all the comparable points in one paragraph or even ten paragraphs. For example, a student trying to compare the French word *chaise* with the English word *chair* might be able to come up with only two sentences of material. With only a dictionary to consult, it is unlikely that the student would find enough material for several points of comparison. On the other hand, contrasting Canada with Europe would present such an endless supply of points to compare that the tendency would be to give only general facts that your reader would already know. When the subject is too broad, the writing is often too general. A better two-part topic might be to compare travelling by train in Europe with travelling by train in Canada.

Once you have chosen a two-part topic that you feel is not too limiting and not too broad, you must remember that a good comparison or contrast paragraph should devote an equal or nearly equal amount of space to each of the two parts. If the writer is only interested in one of the topics, the danger is that the paragraph will end up being very one-sided.

Here's an example of a one-sided contrast:

> While Canadian trains go to only a few towns, are infrequent, and are often shabby and uncomfortable, the European train is much nicer.

The following example is a better-written contrast that gives attention to both topics:

> While Canadian trains go to only a few large cities, run very infrequently, and are often shabby and uncomfortable, European trains go to virtually every small town, are always dependable, and are clean and attractive.

Exercise 1 Evaluating the Two-Part Topic

Study the following topics and decide whether each topic is *too broad* for a paragraph, or whether it is *suitable* as a topic for a paragraph of comparison or contrast. Mark your choice in the appropriate space to the right of each topic.

Topic	Too Broad	Suitable
1. Australia and England	_____	_____
2. Indian elephants and African elephants	_____	_____
3. Canadian wine and French wine	_____	_____
4. Wooden furniture and plastic furniture	_____	_____

5. Wood and plastic   _____ _____

6. Photography and oil painting   _____ _____

7. Heart surgeons and plastic surgeons   _____ _____

8. Taking photographs with a flash and taking photographs using available light   _____ _____

9. Doctors and lawyers   _____ _____

10. Community colleges and universities   _____ _____

Exercise 2   Working with Comparison or Contrast

Each of these suggested comparison or contrast topics is followed by a more specific topic that has not been completed. Complete each of these specific topics by supplying details of your own. Each topic you complete should be one that you could develop as an example of comparison or contrast.

1. Compare two friends:

   My friend _____ with my friend _____

2. Compare two kinds of coats:

   _____ coats with _____ coats

3. Compare two kinds of diets:

   The _____ diet and the _____ diet

4. Compare two kinds of floors:

   _____ floors with _____ floors

5. Compare two kinds of entertainment:

   Watching _____ with looking at _____

6. Compare two kinds of rice:

   _____ rice with _____ rice

7. Compare two places where you can study:

   Studying in the _____ with studying in the _____

8. Compare the wedding customs of two groups:

   What _____ do at a wedding with what _____ do at a wedding

9. Compare two textbooks:

   A textbook that has _____ with a textbook that contains

   _____

10. Compare two politicians:

    A local politician who _____ with a federal politician who

    _____

Exercise 3   Working with Comparison or Contrast

Each of these suggested comparison or contrast topics is followed by a more specific topic that has not been completed. Complete each of these specific topics by supplying details of your own. Each topic you complete should be one that you could develop as an example of comparison or contrast.

1. Compare two kinds of popular board games people play:

   Playing _____ with playing _____

2. Compare two ways of looking at movies:

   Watching movies on _____ with going to

   _____

3. Compare two careers:

   A career in _____ with a career as a _____

4. Compare two ways of paying for a purchase:

   Using _____ to buy something with using _____ to buy something

5. Compare two different lifestyles:

   Living the life of a _____ with living as a _____

6. Compare two places to go swimming:

   Swimming in a _____ with swimming in a _____

7. Compare a no-frills product with the same product sold under a standard brand name (such as no-frills corn flakes with Kellogg's corn flakes):

   A no-frills _____ with _____

8. Compare two popular magazines:

   _____ with _____

9. Compare two hobbies:

   Collecting _____ with _____

10. Compare two kinds of tests given in school:

    The _____ kind of test with the _____ kind of test

Coherence in Comparison or Contrast: Two Approaches to Ordering Material

The first method for ordering material in a paragraph or an essay of comparison or contrast is known as the **point-by-point method.** When you use this method, you compare a point of one topic with a point of the other topic. For example, here is a paragraph from Julius Lester's *All Is Well*. In the paragraph, the writer uses the point-by-point method to compare the difficulties of being a boy with the difficulties of being a girl:

> Now, of course, I know that it was as difficult being a girl as it was a boy, if not more so. While I stood paralyzed at one end of a dance floor trying to find the courage to ask a girl for a dance, most of the girls waited in terror at the other, afraid that no one, not even I, would ask them. And while I resented having to ask a girl for a date, wasn't it also horrible to be the one who waited for the phone to ring? And how many of those girls who laughed at me making a fool of myself on the baseball diamond would have gladly given up their places on the sidelines for mine on the field?

Notice how, after the opening topic sentence, the writer uses half of each sentence to describe a boy's situation growing up and the other half of the same sentence to describe a girl's experience. This technique is effective in such a paragraph, and it is most often used in longer pieces of writing in which many points of comparison are made. This method helps the reader keep the comparison or contrast carefully in mind at each point.

The second method for ordering material in a paragraph of comparison or contrast is known as the **block method.** When you use this approach, you present all of the facts and supporting details about your first topic, and then you give all of the facts and supporting details about your second topic. Here, for example, is another version of the paragraph you studied above, but this time it is written according to the block method:

> Now, of course, I know that it was as difficult being a girl as it was being a boy, if not more so. I stood paralyzed at one end of the dance floor trying to find the courage to ask a girl for a dance. I resented having to ask a girl for a date, just as I often felt foolish on the baseball diamond. On the other hand, most of the girls waited in terror at the other end of the dance floor, afraid that no one, not even I, would ask them to dance. In addition, it was a horrible situation for the girls who had to wait for the phone to ring. And how many of those girls who waited on the sidelines would have traded places with me on the baseball diamond?

Notice how the first half of this version presents all of the details about the boy, while the second part of the paragraph presents all of the information about the girls. This method is often used in shorter pieces of writing because with a shorter piece it is possible for the reader to keep the blocks of information in mind.

Looking at the above two paragraphs in outline form will help you see the shape of their development:

Point-by-Point Method

Topic sentence: "Now, of course, I know that it was as difficult being a girl as it was a boy, if not more so."

First point, first topic: "While I stood paralyzed at one end of a dance floor trying to find the courage to ask a girl for a dance . . ."

First point, second topic: ". . . most of the girls waited in terror at the other, afraid that no one, not even I, would ask them."

Second point, first topic: "And while I resented having to ask a girl for a date, . . ."

Second point, second topic: ". . . wasn't it also horrible to be the one who waited for the phone to ring?"

Third point, first topic: "And how many of those girls who laughed at me making a fool of myself on the baseball diamond . . ."

Third point, second topic: ". . . would have gladly given up their places on the sidelines for mine on the field?"

Block Method

Topic sentence: "Now, of course, I know that it was as difficult being a girl as it was a boy, if not more so."

First topic, points one, two, and three:

"I stood paralyzed at one end of the dance floor trying to find the courage to ask a girl for a dance. I resented having to ask a girl for a date, just as I often felt foolish on the baseball diamond."

Second topic, points one, two, and three:

"On the other hand, most of the girls waited in terror at the other end of the dance floor, afraid that no one, not even I, would ask them to dance. In addition, it was a horrible situation for the girls who had to wait for the phone to ring. And how many of those girls who waited on the sidelines would have traded places with me on the baseball diamond?"

You will want to choose one of these methods before you write a comparison or contrast assignment. Keep in mind that although the block method is most often used in shorter writing assignments, such as a paragraph, you will have the chance to practise the point-by-point method as well.

Exercise 1   Working for Coherence: Recognizing the Two Approaches to Ordering Material

Each of the following passages is an example of comparison or contrast. Read each paragraph carefully and decide whether the writer has used the point-by-point method or the block method. Indicate your choice in the spaces provided after each example. Also indicate whether the piece emphasizes similarities or differences.

1.   Female infants speak sooner, have larger vocabularies, and rarely demonstrate speech defects. (Stuttering, for instance, occurs almost exclusively among boys.) Girls exceed boys in language abilities, and this early linguistic bias often prevails throughout life. Girls read sooner, learn foreign languages more easily, and, as a result, are more likely to enter occupations involving language mastery. Boys, in contrast, show an early visual superiority. They are also clumsier, performing poorly at something like arranging a row of beads, but excel at other activities calling on total body co-ordination. Their attentional mechanisms are also different. A boy will react to an inanimate object as quickly as he will to a person. A male baby will often ignore the mother and babble to a blinking light, fixate on a geometric figure, and, at a later point, manipulate it and attempt to take it apart.

——— Point-by-point   ——— Block

——— Similarities   ——— Differences

2.   Canadians have always been great inventors, and while some of their inventions have contributed to civilization, others have faded into obscurity. On one hand, Canadians have invented the chainsaw, the paint roller, the power mower, Pablum, the zipper, the snowmobile, the Jolly Jumper for babies, and the pop-up carrying handle for beer cases. On the other hand, Canadians have also come up with such ingenious ideas as the cast iron airship, the reverse cooking stove, a mechanical skirt lifter (to keep women's frocks clean while crossing muddy streets), and a medical patent designed to cure all common ailments with carrots. Whatever else, Canadians are creative!

_____ Point-by-point   _____ Block

_____ Similarities   _____ Differences

3. The Stratford and Shaw festivals have both blossomed into internationally acclaimed drama festivals over the past quarter century. The Stratford Festival, located in Stratford, Ontario, and dedicated initially to Shakespearian drama, opened in July, 1953, for a six-week season. The first plays were performed in a tent and included, under the artistic direction of Tyrone Guthrie, *Richard III*, with Alec Guinness in the lead, and *All's Well That Ends Well*. In 1957 the tent was replaced with the Festival Theatre, designed by Canadian architect Robert Fairfield. The Stratford Festival now offers a program of classical and modern plays, and musical productions. Recent offerings have included *The Comedy of Errors* and *Henry V*, with Geraint Wyn Davies appearing in both, as well as Cole Porter's *Kiss Me Kate* and Tennesee Williams's *Cat on a Hot Tin Roof*. The Shaw Festival, on the other hand, was founded in Niagara-on-the-Lake, Ontario, in 1962 and is the only festival in the world devoted to the plays of George Bernard Shaw. During its initial season, the Shaw offered eight amateur performances, but under Barry Morse, the Festival was transformed into a major event. Queen Elizabeth II inaugurated a new 860-seat theatre in 1973, but revues and musicals are still staged at the Royal George Theatre and the historic Niagara-on-the-Lake courthouse, the site of the original playhouse. In addition to Shavian offerings, audiences can now see musical comedies, lunch-time theatre, European farces, and various revues, from *Peter Pan* and *Cyrano de Bergerac* to *Saint Joan* and *Camille*.

_____ Point-by-point   _____ Block

_____ Similarities   _____ Differences

4. We went fishing the first morning. I felt the same damp moss covering the worms in the bait can, and saw the dragonfly alight on the tip of my rod as it hovered a few inches from the surface of the water. It was the arrival of this fly that convinced me beyond any doubt that everything was as it always had been, that the years were a mirage and there had been no years. The small waves were the same, chucking the rowboat under the chin as we fished at anchor, and the boat was the same boat, the same colour of green and the ribs broken in the same places, and under the floor-boards the same freshwater leavings and debris—the dead helgramite, the wisps of moss, the rusty discarded fishhook, the dried blood from yesterday's catch. We stared silently at the tips of our rods, at the dragonflies that came and went. I lowered the tip of mine into the water, tentatively, pensively dislodging the fly, which darted a metre away, poised, darted a metre back, and came to rest again a little farther up the rod. There had been no years between the ducking of this dragonfly and the other one—the one that was part of memory. I looked at the boy, who was silently watching his fly, and it was my hands that held his rod, my eyes watching. I felt dizzy and didn't know which rod I was at the end of.

_____ Point-by-point   _____ Block

_____ Similarities   _____ Differences

5. The streets are littered with cigarette and cigar butts, paper wrappings, particles of food, and dog droppings. How long before they become indistinguishable from the gutters of medieval towns when slop pails were emptied from the second-storey windows? Thousands of New York women no longer attend evening services in their churches. They fear assault as they walk the few steps from bus or subway station to their apartment houses. The era of the medieval footpad has returned, and, as in the Dark Ages, the cry for help brings no assistance, for even grown men know they would be cut down before the police could arrive.

_____ Point-by-point   _____ Block

_____ Similarities   _____ Differences

Exercise 2   **Using the Point-by-Point and Block Methods for Comparison or Contrast**

The passage below uses the block method to make its points of contrast. Rewrite the material using the point-by-point approach.

The Stratford and Shaw festivals have both blossomed into internationally acclaimed drama festivals over the past quarter century. The Stratford Festival, located in Stratford, Ontario, and dedicated initially to Shakespearian drama, opened in July, 1953, for a six-week season. The first plays were performed in a tent and included, under the artistic direction of Tyrone Guthrie, *Richard III*, with Alec Guinness in the lead, and *All's Well That Ends Well.* In 1957 the tent was replaced with the Festival Theatre, designed by Canadian architect Robert Fairfield. The Stratford Festival now offers a program of classical and modern plays, and musical productions. Recent offerings have included *The Comedy of Errors* and *Henry V*, with Geraint Wyn Davies appearing in both, as well as Cole Porter's *Kiss Me Kate* and Tennesee Williams's *Cat on a Hot Tin Roof.* The Shaw Festival, on the other hand, was founded in Niagara-on-the-Lake, Ontario, in 1962 and is the only festival in the world devoted to the plays of George Bernard Shaw. During its initial season, the Shaw offered eight amateur performances, but under Barry Morse, the Festival was transformed into a major event. Queen Elizabeth II inaugurated a new 860-seat theatre in 1973, but revues and musicals are still staged at the Royal George Theatre and the historic Niagara-on-the-Lake courthouse, the site of the original playhouse. In addition to Shavian offerings, audiences can now see musical comedies, lunch-time theatre, European farces, and various revues, from *Peter Pan* and *Cyrano de Bergerac* to *Saint Joan* and *Camille.*

_____

_____

_____

_____

_____

_____

Exercise 3   **Using the Point-by-Point and Block Methods**

Use the list below to write a comparison or contrast paragraph on life in the city compared with life in a suburban area. Review the list provided and add to it any of your own ideas. Omit any you do not wish to use. Then, selecting either the block method or the point-by-point method, write a comparison or contrast paragraph.

Topic sentence: If I could move back to the city from the suburbs, I know I would be happy.

The following points provide details that relate to living in the city and living in a suburban community:

Topic I *Advantages of the City*	*Topic II* *Disadvantages of the Suburbs*
A short ride on the bus or subway gets you to work.	Commuting to work in the city is often long and exhausting.
Less time spent commuting leaves more time to get involved in the community.	More time commuting means less time to get involved in neighbourhood activities.
Variety is more stimulating.	Sameness of people and streets is monotonous.
Families and single people.	Mostly families.
Local shopping for nearly everything.	Mostly highway shopping.
Mingle with people walking in the neighbourhood daily	Little walking, use cars to go everywhere.

Notice that the maker of this list centred only on the disadvantages of the suburbs in contrast to the city. No mention, for instance, has been made of crime. One could also present the contrast from the point of view of someone who prefers the suburbs.

_____

_____

_____

_____

_____

_____

_____

Working for Coherence: Using Transitions

A number of words and phrases are useful to keep in mind when writing the comparison or contrast paper. Some of them are used in phrases, some in clauses.

My sister is just <u>like</u> me.

Like is a preposition and is used in the prepositional phrase "like me."

My sister is a good cook *as* is my mother.

As is a subordinate conjunction and is used in a clause with a subject and a verb.

Common Transitions

Transitions for Comparison	*Transitions for Contrast*	
similar to	on the contrary	though
similarly	on the other hand	unlike
like	in contrast with	even though
likewise	in spite of	nevertheless
just like	despite	however
just as	instead of	but
furthermore	different from	otherwise
moreover	whereas	except for
equally	while	and yet
again	although	still
also		
too		
so		

Exercise 1   Using Transitions in Comparisons and Contrasts

Each of the following examples is made up of two sentences. Read both sentences and decide whether the idea being expressed is one of comparison or contrast. Next, combine the two sentences by using a transition you have chosen from one of the above lists. Then write your new sentence on the lines provided. You may find you have to reword your new sentence slightly in order to make it grammatically correct. An example has been done for you.

Mr. Johnson is a teacher.

His wife is a teacher.

First you decide that the two sentences show a comparison. Then you combine the two by using an appropriate transition:

Mr. Johnson is a teacher just like his wife.

or

Mr. Johnson is a teacher; so is his wife.

1. Dr. Rappole has a reputation for excellent bedside manners.

   Dr. Connolly is very withdrawn and speaks so softly that it is almost impossible to understand what he has said.

   Your combined sentence: _____

   _____

   _____

2. In Canada, interest in soccer has become apparent only in recent years.

   Soccer has always been immensely popular in Brazil.

   Your combined sentence: _____

   _____

   _____

3. Robertson Davies' novel *Fifth Business* is part of the Deptford Trilogy.

   The same writer's novel *The Manticore* is also part of the Deptford Trilogy.

   Your combined sentence: _____

   _____

   _____

4. Amy is carefree and fun-loving, with little interest in school.

   Janet, Amy's sister, is so studious and hardworking that she is always on the honour roll.

   Your combined sentence: _____

   _____

   _____

5. The apartment had almost no furniture, was badly in need of painting, and felt chilly even though I was wearing a coat.

   The other apartment was attractively furnished, had been freshly painted, and was warm enough so that I had to take off my coat.

   Your combined sentence: _____

   _____

   _____

Exercise 2   **Using Transitions in Comparisons and Contrasts**

First, identify each of the following examples as comparison or contrast. Then combine the two sentences by using a transition from the list on page 269. Finally, write your new sentence on the lines provided.

1. English-speaking Canadians have numbered about 67 percent of the population over the past 30 years.

    The number of French-speaking Canadians declined from 19 percent of the population in the 1960s to 16 percent in the 1980s.

    Your combined sentence: _____

    _____

    _____

2. Canada has never won an Olympic gold medal in men's springboard diving.

    Sylvie Bernier won Canada's first-ever gold medal in women's springboard diving in the 1984 Olympics.

    Your combined sentence: _____

    _____

    _____

3. The French Revolution was directed by the common people.

    The Russian Revolution was directed by an elite group of thinkers.

    Your combined sentence: _____

    _____

    _____

4. Some scientists believe that dinosaurs became extinct because they ran out of food.

    Some scientists think that dinosaurs were victims of radiation from a meteor from outer space.

    Your combined sentence: _____

    _____

    _____

5. Canada's entry into the Space Age was initiated with the launch of the satellite Alouette I in 1962.

    The satellite Radarsat, to be launched in 1994, will be used to explore the world's mineral resources.

    Your combined sentence: _____

    _____

    _____

Exercise 3   Using Transitions in Comparisons and Contrasts

First, identify each of the following examples as comparison or contrast. Then combine the two sentences by using a transition from the list on page 269. Finally, write your new sentence on the lines provided.

1. A ballet dancer trains for years in order to master all aspects of dancing.

    A hockey player puts in years of practice in order to learn the game from every angle.

    Your combined sentence: _____

    _____

    _____

2. The University of Toronto is a large urban university that has the resources of a big city as part of its attraction for faculty and students.

    Mount Allison University is a small rural university that overlooks the Tantramar marshes of New Brunswick.

    Your combined sentence: _____

    _____

    _____

3. Ice cream, a popular dessert for many years, has many calories and added chemicals to give it more flavour.

    Tofuti is a dessert made of processed soybeans that is low in calories and contains no harmful additives.

    Your combined sentence: _____

    _____

    _____

4. Benny Cooperman, a fictional private eye created by Howard Engel, operates in small-town Ontario.

    Eric Wright's Charlie Salter is a big-city investigator.

    Your combined sentence: _____

    _____

    _____

5. *Lazaro*, a novel of revenge, was written by David Kendall.

    Where the River Runs Black, a movie based on the novel, contains scenes of action and adventure in exotic settings.

    Your combined sentence: _____

    _____

    _____

Writing the Comparison or Contrast Paragraph Step by Step

To learn a skill with some degree of ease, it is best to follow a step-by-step approach so that various skills are isolated. This will ensure that you are not missing a crucial point or misunderstanding a part of the whole. Of course, there are other ways to approach writing assignments, but here is one step-by-step approach you can use to achieve good results while at the same time learning how paragraphs can be developed through a logical process.

Steps for Writing the Comparison or Contrast Paragraph

1. Study the given topic, and then plan your topic sentence, especially the dominant impression.
2. List all your ideas for points that could be compared or contrasted.
3. Then choose the three or four most important points from your list.
4. Decide whether you want to use the point-by-point method or the block method of organizing your paragraph.
5. Write at least one complete sentence for each of the points you have chosen from your list.
6. Write a concluding statement that summarizes the main points, makes a judgement, or emphasizes what you believe is the most important point.
7. Finally, copy your sentences into standard paragraph form.

Exercise 1 Writing the Comparison or Contrast Paragraph Step by Step

The following exercise will guide you through the construction of a comparison or contrast paragraph. Start with the suggested topic. Use the seven steps to help you work through each stage of the writing process.

Topic: Compare or contrast how you spend your leisure time with how your parents or a friend spends leisure time.

1. Topic sentence: _____

   _____

2. Make a list of possible comparisons or contrasts.

   a. _____   f. _____

   b. _____   g. _____

   c. _____   h. _____

   d. _____   i. _____

   e. _____   j. _____

3. Circle the three or four comparisons or contrasts that you believe are most important, and put them in order.
4. Choose either the point-by-point method or the block method.
5. Using your final list, write at least one sentence for each comparison or contrast you have chosen.

   a. _____

   _____

   b. _____

   _____

c. _____

_____

d. _____

_____

e. _____

_____

f. _____

_____

g. _____

_____

6. Write a concluding statement. _____

_____

_____

7. Copy your sentences into standard paragraph form.

_____

_____

_____

_____

_____

_____

_____

_____

_____

_____

_____

_____

_____

_____

_____

_____

_____

Exercise 2   **Writing the Comparison or Contrast Paragraph Step by Step**

The following exercise will guide you through the construction of a comparison or contrast paragraph. Start with the suggested topic. Use the seven steps to help you work through each stage of the writing process.

Topic: Compare or contrast going to work with going to college immediately after high school.

1. Topic sentence: _____

    _____

    _____

2. Make a list of possible comparisons or contrasts.

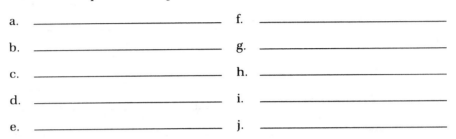

    a. _____   f. _____

    b. _____   g. _____

    c. _____   h. _____

    d. _____   i. _____

    e. _____   j. _____

3. Circle the three or four comparisons or contrasts that you believe are most important, and put them in order.
4. Choose either the point-by-point method or the block method.
5. Using your final list, write at least one sentence for each comparison or contrast you have chosen.

    a. _____

    _____

    b. _____

    _____

    c. _____

    _____

    d. _____

    _____

    e. _____

    _____

    f. _____

    _____

    g. _____

    _____

6. Write a concluding statement. _____

    _____

    _____

7. Copy your sentences into standard paragraph form.

_____

_____

_____

_____

_____

_____

_____

_____

_____

_____

_____

_____

_____

_____

_____

_____

_____

_____

_____

_____

_____

_____

Exercise 3 Writing the Comparison or Contrast Paragraph Step by Step

The following exercise will guide you through the construction of a comparison or contrast paragraph. Start with the suggested topic. Use the seven steps to help you work through each stage of the writing process.

Topic: Compare or contrast the styles of two television personalities (or two public figures often in the news).

1. Topic sentence: _____

_____

_____

2. Make a list of possible comparisons or contrasts.

   a. _____   f. _____

   b. _____   g. _____

   c. _____   h. _____

   d. _____   i. _____

   e. _____   j. _____

3. Circle the three or four comparisons or contrasts that you believe are most important, and put them in order.
4. Choose either the point-by-point method or the block method.
5. Using your final list, write at least one sentence for each comparison or contrast you have chosen.

a. _____

_____

b. _____

_____

c. _____

_____

d. _____

_____

e. _____

_____

f. _____

_____

g. _____

_____

6. Write a concluding statement. _____

_____

_____

7. Copy your sentences into standard paragraph form.

_____

_____

_____

_____

_____

_____

_____

_____

_____

_____

_____

_____

_____
_____
_____
_____
_____
_____
_____

On Your Own: Writing Comparison or Contrast Paragraphs from Model Paragraphs

Comparing Two Places

ASSIGNMENT 1: Write a paragraph in which you compare or contrast two places you know, either from personal experience or from your reading. The following paragraph contrasts the East Coast and a major urban centre as they appear to a person who has been to both places.

Model Paragraph

Since I travel East so often, I am usually asked to compare the life-styles of the East Coast with those of the big city where I live. That's easy. Both places leave a distinct impression, and readers will have to decide for themselves which lifestyle is more desirable. When I was riding a bus between Louisbourg and Sydney, Nova Scotia, an old man waved the bus down, boarded, and handed the driver a large fish to pay for his fare. In the city, exact change is the rule on the bus, and that only in coin of the realm. In St. John's, Newfoundland, I found that some nightclubs and bars remained open until the last customer had left, and that the best time was had when patrons brought their own musical instruments and set up some Down East foot-stompin' music. Back home, you sit, behave yourself, and drink your beer, or out you go. Incidentally, the best pizza I ever had was from a small shop on the St. John's waterfront, with a Volcano pizza from Windsor, Ontario, a close second. The cardboard pizzas from the fast food joints in Toronto and Montreal don't even rate. On the other hand, my favourite hamburger came from Montreal, and nothing can beat Prince Edward Island for seafood. Do I sound biased toward the East? If you're not from the East, take your next vacation there. You'll see what I mean.

TEN SUGGESTED TOPICS

Compare or contrast two places you have lived in, visited, or read about:

1. Two neighbourhoods
2. Two towns or cities
3. Two vacation spots
4. Two provinces
5. Two countries
6. Two streets
7. Two schools
8. Two shopping areas
9. Two favourite (or least favourite) spots
10. Two regions with very different scenery and atmosphere

Comparing Two Cultures

ASSIGNMENT 2: Write a paragraph in which you compare two cultures, or an aspect of culture that may be observed in two societies. The following paragraph is from an essay, "Gender Apartheid," by Emil Sher. An edited version was broadcast on "Open House," CBC, in 1989.

Model Paragraph

A little more than a year ago in South Africa a black labourer became another statistic scratched into the wall of apartheid. He got on his tractor to do some ploughing and accidentally ran over two dogs lying underneath. The white farmer he worked for beat him to death. The courts found the farmer guilty of culpable homicide, but suspended the sentence. A little earlier, a Canadian court suspended the sentence of another man. He'd sexually assaulted an 11-year-old girl. What does one incident have to do with the other? The attitude of the white minority in South Africa isn't all that different from the way many men treat women. The underlying assumption in both sets of relationships is one of presumed value. When a white is let off for beating a black to death, and a man is set free for assaulting an 11-year-old girl, the message is clear: the black farmhand and the young girl are second-class citizens, somewhat less than completely human. Through white eyes and in male hands, black skin and a woman's body become disposable property. The more I thought about the links between racism and sexism, the more similarities began to surface. Black and white miners work in the same shafts, but blacks are paid less. Come payday, Canadian women often take home smaller paycheques than their male counterparts. Black miners earn less in white-ruled South Africa simply because they're black. What's our excuse for women's wages?

TEN SUGGESTED TOPICS
Compare or contrast:

1. Mexican cooking with Chinese cooking
2. Marriage customs in Africa and in Canada
3. Attitudes toward women's roles in Saudi Arabia and in Canada
4. Folk dancing in two countries
5. Raising children in Asia with raising them in Canada
6. Urban people with small-town people
7. The reputation of a place with the reality of the place as you found it
8. The culture of your neighbourhood with the general culture of our society
9. The culture you live in now with the culture in which your parents were raised
10. Medical care in our society with the medical care of any other society

Comparing a Place Then and Now

ASSIGNMENT 3: Write a paragraph in which you compare the appearance of a place you knew when you were growing up with the appearance of that same place now. The following paragraph compares a small city as it was some years ago and how it appeared to the writer on a recent visit.

Model Paragraph

As I drove up Swede Hill, I realized that the picture I had in my mind all these years was largely a romantic one. It was here that my father had boarded, as a young man of eighteen, with a widow who rented rooms in her house. Now the large old wooden frame houses were mostly two-family homes; no single family could afford to heat them in the winter. The porches which had once been beautiful and where people had passed their summer evenings had peeling paint and were in poor condition. No one now stopped to talk; the only sounds to be heard were those of cars whizzing past. The immigrants who had come to this country, worked hard, and put their children through school were now elderly and mostly alone, since their educated children could find no jobs in the small upstate city. From the top of the hill I looked down fondly upon the town built on the hills and noticed that a new and wider highway now went through the town. My father would have liked that; he would not have had to complain about Sunday drivers on Foote Avenue. In the distance I could see the large shopping mall which now had most of the business in the surrounding area and which had forced several local businesses to close. Now the center of town no longer hummed with activity, as it once had. My town was not the same place I had known, and I could see that changes were taking place that would eventually transform the entire area.

TEN SUGGESTED TOPICS

Compare or contrast a place as it appears now with how it appeared some years ago:

1. A barbershop or beauty salon
2. A house of worship
3. A local "corner store"
4. A friend's home
5. Your elementary school
6. A local bank
7. A downtown shopping area
8. A restaurant or diner
9. An undeveloped place such as an open field or wooded area
10. A favourite local gathering place

Comparing Two Approaches to a Subject

ASSIGNMENT 4: Write a paragraph in which you compare two ways of considering a particular topic. The following paragraph compares two approaches to the art of healing—the traditional medical approach and the approach that involves less dependence on chemicals and more reliance on the body's natural defence system.

Model Paragraph

Natural healing is basically a much more conservative approach to health care than traditional medical practice. Traditional medical practice aims for the quick cure by means of introducing substances or instruments into the body which are highly antagonistic to whatever is causing the disease. A doctor wants to see results, and he or she wants you to appreciate the fact that traditional medicine is what is delivering those results to you. Because of this desire for swift, decisive victories over disease, traditional medicine tends to be dramatic, risky, and expensive. Natural healing takes a slower, more organic approach to the problem of disease. It first recognizes that the human body is superbly equipped to resist disease and heal injuries. But when disease does take hold or an injury occurs, the first instinct in natural healing is to see what might be done to strengthen that natural resistance and those natural healing agents so that they can act against the disease more effectively. Results are not expected to occur overnight, but neither are they expected to occur at the expense of the body, which may experience side effects or dangerous complications.

TEN SUGGESTED TOPICS
Compare or contrast:

1. Retiring or working after age 65
2. Owning your own business or working for someone else
3. Two views on abortion
4. Two attitudes toward divorce
5. Two political viewpoints
6. Your lifestyle today and your lifestyle five years ago
7. Working mothers and mothers who stay home
8. Buying Canadian-made products or buying foreign-made goods
9. Two attitudes on the "right to die" issue
10. Two attitudes toward religion

Comparing Male Attitudes and Female Attitudes

ASSIGNMENT 5: Some observers believe that males share similar attitudes toward certain subjects, while females seem to have a similar way of thinking on certain other topics. Other observers believe that such conclusions are nothing more than stereotypes and that people should not be divided in this way. The following paragraph reports that recent studies indicate a possible biological basis for some of the differences between males and females.

Model Paragraph

Recent scientific research has shown that differences in behavior between males and females may have their origins in biological differences in the brain. Shortly after birth, females are more sensitive than males to certain types of sounds, and by the age of five months a female baby can recognize photographs of familiar people, while a boy of that age can rarely accomplish this. Researchers also found that girls tend to speak sooner than boys, read sooner than they do, and learn foreign languages more easily than boys do. On the other hand, boys show an early visual superiority over girls and they are better than girls at working with three-dimensional space. When preschool girls and boys are asked to mentally work with an object, the girls are not as successful as the boys. In this case, as in several others, the girls are likely to give verbal descriptions while the boys are able to do the actual work in their minds.

TEN SUGGESTED TOPICS
In a paragraph, compare what you believe are male and female attitudes on one of the following topics:

1. Cooking
2. Sports
3. The nursing profession
4. Child care
5. The construction trade
6. Military careers
7. A career in science
8. Hobbies
9. Friendship
10. Clothing

18 Developing Paragraphs: Definition, Classification, and Cause and Effect

What Is Definition?

You define a term in order to explain its meaning or significance. The starting point for a good definition is to group the word into a larger category. For example, the trout is a kind of fish; a doll is a kind of toy; a shirt is an article of clothing. Here is a dictionary entry for the word *family*.

> **family** (fam'ə -le, fam'le) *n., pl.* **-lies.** *Abbr.* **fam.** 1. The most instinctive, fundamental social or mating group in man and animal, especially the union of man and woman through marriage and their offspring; parents and their children. 2. One's spouse and children. 3. Persons related by blood or marriage; relatives; kinfolk. 4. Lineage; especially, upper-class lineage. 5. All the members of a household; those who share one's domestic home.

To what larger category does the word *family* belong? The family, according to this entry, is a kind of *social group*. Once the word has been put into a larger class, the reader is ready to understand the identifying characteristics that make it different from other members in the class. What makes a *trout* different from a *bass*, a *doll* different from a *puppet*, a *shirt* different from a *sweater*? Here a definition can give examples. The dictionary definition of *family* identifies the family as a married man and woman and their children. Four additional meanings provide a suggestion of some variations.

When you write a paragraph or an essay that uses definition, the dictionary entry is only the beginning. In order for your reader to understand a difficult term or idea, you will need to expand this definition into what is called **extended definition**. It is not the function of a dictionary to go into great depth. It can only provide the basic meanings and synonyms. Extended definition, however, seeks to analyze a concept so that the reader will have a more complete understanding. For instance, you might include a historical perspective. When or how did the concept begin? How did the term change or evolve over the years, or how do different cultures understand the term? You will become involved in the word's connotations. Extended definition, or analysis as it is sometimes called, uses more than one method to arrive at an understanding of a term.

The following paragraph, taken from *Sociology: An Introduction* by John E. Conklin, is the beginning of a chapter on the family. The author's starting point is very similar to the dictionary entry.

> In every society, social norms define a variety of relationships among people, and some of these relationships are socially recognized as family or kinship ties. A *family* is a socially defined set of relationships between at least two people who are related by birth, marriage, or adoption. We can think of a family as including several possible relationships, the most common being between husband and wife, between parents and children, and between people who are related to each other by birth (siblings, for example) or by marriage (a woman and her mother-in-law, perhaps). Family relationships are often defined by custom, such as the relationship between an infant and godparents, or by law, such as the adoption of a child.

The author begins this definition by putting the term into a larger class. "Family" is one type of social relationship among people. The writer then identifies the people who are members of this group. Family relationships can be formed by marriage, birth, adoption, or custom, as with godparents. The author does not stop here. The extended definition explores the functions of the family, conflicts in the family, the structure of the family, and the special characteristics of the American family.

The writer could also define *family* by **negation**. That is, he could describe what a family is *not*:

> A family is not a corporation.
> A family is not a formal school.
> A family is not a church.

When a writer defines a concept using negation, the definition should be completed by stating what the subject *is:*

A family is not a corporation, but it is an economic unit of production and consumption.

A family is not a formal school, but it is a major centre for learning.

A family is not a church, but it is where children learn their moral values.

Exercise 1   Working with Definition: Class

Define each of the following terms by placing it in a larger class. Keep in mind that when you define something by class, you are placing it in a larger category so that the reader can see where it belongs. Use the dictionary if you need help. An example has been done for you.

> Chemistry is *one of the branches of science* that deals with a close study of the natural world.

1. Mythology is _____

_____

2. Nylon is _____

_____

3. Amoeba is _____

_____

4. Tricycle is _____

_____

5. Cabbage is _____

_____

6. Democracy is _____

_____

7. Asbestos is _____

_____

8. Piccolo is _____

_____

9. Poetry is _____

_____

10. University is _____

_____

Exercise 2   Working with Definition: Distinguishing Characteristics

Using the same terms as in Exercise 1, give one or two identifying characteristics that differentiate your term from other terms in the same class. An example is done for you.

Chemistry studies the structure, properties, and reactions of matter.

1. Mythology _____

_____

2. Nylon _____

_____

3. Amoeba _____

_____

4. Tricycle _____

_____

5. **Cabbage** _____

_____

6. Democracy _____

_____

7. Asbestos _____

_____

8. Piccolo _____

_____

9. Poetry _____

_____

10. University _____

_____

Exercise 3   **Working with Definition: Example**

Help define each of the following terms by providing one example. Examples always make writing more alive. An example has been done for you.

     Term: Chemistry
     Example: Chemistry studies an element like hydrogen. This element is the simplest in structure of all the elements, with only one electron and proton; it is colourless, highly flammable, the lightest of all gases, and the most abundant element in the universe.

1. Mythology

_____

_____

2. Friendship

_____

_____

3. Philanthropist

_____

_____

4. Planet

_____

_____

5. Success

_____

_____

6. Greed

_____

_____

7. Sportsmanship

_____

_____

8. Patriotism

_____

_____

9. Terrorism

_____

_____

10. Equality

_____

_____

Exercise 4 Working with Definition: Negation

Define each of the following by using negation to construct your definition. Keep in mind that such a definition is not complete until you have also included what the topic you are defining *is*.

1. A *disability* is not _____,

   but it is _____.

2. The *perfect car* is not _____,

   but it is _____.

3. *Drugs* are not _____,

   but they are _____.

4. *Freedom* is not _____,

   but it is _____.

5. A *good job* is not _____,

   but it is _____ .

6. *Exercise* is not _____,

   but it is _____.

7. A *university* is not _____,

   but it is _____.

8. A *politician* is not _____,

   but he or she is _____.

9. The *ideal pet* is not _____,

   but it is _____.

10. A *boring person* is not _____,

    but he or she is _____.

Writing a Paragraph Using Definition

Choose one of the following topics and write a complete paragraph of definition. For the topic that you choose to write about, develop your definition by using one or more of the techniques you have studied — class, identifying characteristics, example, and negation — as well as any further analysis, historical or cultural, that will help the reader.

Topics
1. Photosynthesis
2. Ecology
3. Coma
4. Football
5. Paranoia
6. Courage
7. Algebra
8. Democracy
9. Masculinity or femininity
10. Justice

What Is Classification?

When you place items into separate groups, you are able to think more clearly about the groups you have created, and you are better able to understand individual items in each group. This is classification, a skill that helps you control information that you are given when you read and helps you control the way other people receive information that you give them when you write.

In order to classify things properly, you must always take the items you are working with and put them into *distinct categories*, making sure that each item belongs in only one category. For example, if you were to classify computers into imported computers, Canadian-made computers, and used computers, this would not be an effective use of classification because an imported computer or a Canadian-made computer could also be a used computer. When you classify, you want each item to belong in only one category.

A classification should also be *complete*. For example, if you were classifying computers into the two categories of new and used, your classification would be complete because any item can only be new or used. Finally, a classification should be *useful*. If you are thinking of buying a computer, or if a friend is thinking of buying one, then it might be very useful to classify them in this way because you or your friend might save a great deal of money by deciding to buy a used machine.

The following paragraph shows the writer classifying different kinds of neighbours.

> To me, there are only two kinds of neighbours: those with cats and those without cats. I refuse to get along with cat owners, regardless of how pleasant either the cats or their owners happen to be. I take great exception to having cats on my property, fighting with each other in the middle of the night, dirtying my flower beds, and chasing the birds that come to my feeder. I don't have a great deal to say to neighbours who let their cats out at night to get into my garbage, and when I point out the mess that these cats leave, I'm told, "There's no law against it." As far as those neighbours who don't have cats are concerned — they can borrow my lawnmower anytime.

In this paragraph, the writer presents two distinct types of neighbours, cat owners and those who don't own cats. These are the only types that have any significance for the author. The author's classification is complete because it covers the entire range of neighbours for the author — there are, in the author's opinion, no other kinds of neighbours. This is a useful classification, because many of us have neighbours with cats; perhaps you are that neighbour.

Exercise 1   **Working with Classification: Finding the Basis for Classification**

For each of the following topics, pick three different ways it could be classified. An example has been done for you.

> *Topic:* Ways to choose a vacation spot
> *Basis for classification:* By price (first class, medium price, economy), by its special attraction (the beach, the mountains, the desert, etc.), by the accommodations (hotel, motel, cabin, trailer)

1. **Topic:** Cars

   Basis for classification: _____

   _____

2. **Topic:** Houses

   Basis for classification: _____

   _____

3. **Topic:** Neighbourhoods

   Basis for classification: _____

   _____

4. **Topic:** Religions

   Basis for classification: _____

   _____

5. **Topic:** Soft drinks

   Basis for classification: _____

   _____

6. **Topic:** Dates

   Basis for classification: _____

   _____

7. **Topic:** Floor coverings

   Basis for classification: _____

   _____

8. **Topic:** Medicines

   Basis for classification: _____

   _____

9. **Topic:** Snack foods

   Basis for classification: _____

   _____

10. **Topic:** Relatives

    Basis for classification: _____

    _____

Exercise 2 **Working with Classification: Making Distinct Categories**

First pick a basis for classifying each of the following topics. Then break it down into distinct categories. Divide the topic into as many distinct categories as you think the classification requires.

Keep in mind that when you divide your topic, each part of your classification will belong only to one category. For example, if you were to classify cars, you would not want to make *sports cars* and *international cars* two of your categories because several kinds of sports cars are also international cars.

1. Clothing stores

    Distinct categories:

    _____ _____ _____

    _____ _____ _____

2. Television commercials

    Distinct categories:

    _____ _____ _____

    _____ _____ _____

3. College sports

    Distinct categories:

    _____ _____ _____

    _____ _____ _____

4. Doctors

    Distinct categories:

    _____ _____ _____

    _____ _____ _____

5. Hats

    Distinct categories:

    _____ _____ _____

    _____ _____ _____

6. Courses in the English department of your college

    Distinct categories:

    _____ _____ _____

    _____ _____ _____

7. Pens

    Distinct categories:

    _____ _____ _____

    _____ _____ _____

8. Dances

   Distinct categories:

   _____   _____   _____

   _____   _____   _____

9. Mail

   Distinct categories:

   _____   _____   _____

   _____   _____   _____

10. Music

    Distinct categories:

    _____   _____   _____

    _____   _____   _____

Writing a Paragraph Using Classification

Choose one of the following topics and write a paragraph using classification. As you plan your paragraph, keep in mind the following points. Is there some purpose for your picking the basis for your classification? (For example, will it help someone make a decision or understand a concept better?) Are you sure the classification is complete and that no item could belong to more than one category? Does the classification help to organize your material?

Topics
1. Parents
2. Governments
3. Dogs
4. Careers
5. Parties
6. Summer jobs
7. Movies
8. Classmates
9. Co-workers
10. Restaurants

What Is Cause and Effect?

When we use cause and effect, we are asking the basic question "Why?" about something. Children ask this question so often that they drive their parents crazy, but adults ask the same kinds of questions almost as often: Why do we have recessions? Why did my car break down just after I got it back from the garage? Why don't I ever win the lottery?

Some of the questions children and adults ask cannot be answered, but when causes or effects can be explained, it is important to make a complete investigation and give the underlying causes or the long-term effects of what you are discussing. For example, if a plane crashed because it lost an engine in flight, the cause of the crash might be blamed on a mechanical failure. However, if it could be shown that the plane crashed because a mechanic did a sloppy job of attaching the plane's engines after a tune-up, then the real cause of the crash might be better described as a mechanic's failure.

Another important consideration when dealing with cause and effect is to be careful not to jump to conclusions. For example, if you find it hard to sleep every time you have worked late, the work itself may not be the reason. There could be another factor causing the problem. Were you also drinking coffee while you worked? A genuine cause-and-effect relationship is the result of a real connection between facts, and not simply coincidence.

Looking at a Model Paragraph: Cause

The following paragraph discusses some of the causes of a widespread medical problem, the common headache.

> Headaches can have several causes. Many people think that the major cause of headache is nervous tension, but there is strong evidence that suggests diet and environment as possible factors. Some people get headaches because they are dependent on caffeine. Other people may be allergic to salt, or they may have low blood sugar. Still other people are **allergic to household chemicals, including polishes, waxes, bug killers,** and paint. If they can manage to avoid these substances, their headaches tend to go away. When a person has recurring headaches, it is worthwhile to look for the underlying cause, especially if the result of that search is freedom from pain.

Writing a Paragraph Using Causes

Choose one of the following topics and write a paragraph that deals with cause. Use the above paragraph as your model. As you plan your paragraph, keep in mind that the writer of the paragraph on headaches was careful to note as many causes for headaches as possible. This gave the paragraph a sense of completeness. Your paragraph will also be successful if you include as many specific causes for your topic as possible.

Topics
1. The causes of war
2. The causes of senility
3. The causes of social unrest in many countries
4. The causes of the teenage runaway problem
5. The causes of income tax cheating
6. The causes of the feminist movement
7. The causes of drug abuse
8. The causes of divorce
9. The causes of prostitution
10. The causes of the backup in our legal system

Looking at a Model Paragraph: Effect

The following paragraph by a student writer describes some of the effects on children when both parents in a family work.

> The most noticeable change for most families is that Mum is no longer home during the day—not there to fix hot lunches or to soothe scraped knees and bruised egos. So who does? The answer, unfortunately, often is "No one." Countless numbers of children have become "latchkey children," left to fend for themselves after school because there

aren't enough dependable, affordable baby-sitters or after-school pro- grams for them. Some children are able to handle this early indepen- dence quite well and may even become more resourceful adults because of it, but many are not. Vandalism, petty thievery, and alcohol and drug abuse may all be products of this unsupervised life, problems that society in general must deal with eventually. Some companies (although too few) have adapted to this changing lifestyle by instituting on-site child-care fa- cilities and/or "flextime" schedules for working mothers and fathers. Schools have begun to provide low-cost after-school activities during the school year, and summer day camps are filling the need during those months.

Writing a Paragraph Using Effects

Choose one of the following topics and write a paragraph that will illustrate effects. Use the above paragraph as your model. As you plan your paragraph, keep in mind that the writer of the model paragraph was careful to include both the short-term and long-term effects on children of having both parents work. Your paragraph will also be successful when you are careful to include both the short-term and the long-term effects of the topics you have chosen.

Topics

1. The effects of children on a marriage
2. The effects of a water shortage in the summer
3. The effects of unemployment on a family
4. The effects of having too much time on your hands
5. The effects of television on children
6. The effects of pornography
7. The effects of drunk drivers on our society
8. The effects of imported products on our economy
9. The effects of TV political commercials on how people vote
10. The effects of AIDS on our society

19

The Student Essay: Developing the Paragraph

Paragraph Review

Back in Chapter 12, the reader was introduced to the idea of the topic sentence. A topic sentence, you will recall, is the sentence in a paragraph that states the main idea of that paragraph. It is the most general sentence of the paragraph. All the other sentences in the paragraph serve to explain, describe, extend, or support this main-idea sequence.

Reproduced below are a number of introductory paragraphs submitted by students at Canadian colleges or universities for the HBJ-Holt College Essay Contest. Each of these paragraphs has a topic sentence, but the topic sentence is not necessarily the first sentence in the paragraph. See if you can identify the topic sentence in the following paragraphs:

> "You can't pinch an inch. No you can't pinch an inch on me." This little ditty has become a rule of life rather than a catchy jingle for a cereal company. It demonstrates how women have been conditioned to think thin is best. Protruding tummies are not acceptable —unless you are a male and then the rules change. Although many people diet and exercise to lose weight for health reasons or to feel more attractive, many continue to a level below their recommended weight, and the majority of those people are women. The feeling is, the thinner the better.

From "Pressure to Be Thin,"
Linda Blore, Mt. St. Vincent University

The topic sentence in this paragraph is found in the third sentence — "It demonstrates how women have been conditioned to think thin is best." Why is this the topic sentence? Because it is the main idea of the paragraph, and indeed of the entire essay, and all of the other ideas in the paragraph support this idea.

Here are more paragraphs with topic sentences contained in them. Following this selection, you will be asked to identify the topic sentences from each selection.

Wherever I go in the world — whether it is to Toronto, to England, or down the road to the mall — I am continually fascinated by people. When I watch people, though, I do not just give them a casual perusal; I genuinely study them, guessing things about what kind of people they are, pretending I know them, and making up stories about them. I occasionally receive withering glares from people who catch me studying them, but I never mind. As Flannery O'Connor said, "The writer should never be ashamed of staring. There is nothing that does not require his attention." As a writer, I see four types of people in the world who seem to be caricatures of themselves (people who fill the backgrounds of every novel): crazy people, serious people, old people, and children. I am not attempting to classify all the people in the world, but merely those who attract my attention as a writer and a human being.

From "Four Types of Interesting People,"
Mark Young, King's College, University of Western Ontario

Topic sentence: _____

_____

When Dr. Frederick Banting researched human blood sugar levels, he worked extensively with dogs. He made liver extracts, injected and monitored the dogs, and often had to perform postmortem examinations. The cure for diabetes was found. Had experimentation on animals been banned, insulin would not have been discovered, and none of the present-day medicine or surgical techniques would have existed. In the quest for new cures for incurable diseases, animals are the only research subjects alternative to man. Animal experimentation is essential to the advancement of medical science.

From "Experimentation on Animals: Justified,"
Grace Soo, Erindale College, University of Toronto

Topic sentence: _____

_____

I grew up in the city enjoying the comfort of paved streets, gas lamps, and a catered environment. When I married a farmer in 1934, I exchanged this urban existence for the wide-open country where a person talked more to animals than to people. Until this time, I had never been privileged enough to possess a cat or dog, much less a large animal and the only live horse I saw, conceivably enough, was drawing a milk wagon over hard, uneven streets. Consequently, it could not be construed as strange that in this quiet atmosphere inhabited mostly by farm creatures, I was compelled to appreciate these dumb beasts that not only provided our means of livelihood but in return demanded that we give them food and care for their usefulness.

From "My Animal Kingdom,"
Margaret Fisher, North Island College

Topic sentence: _____

_____

After two years of marriage, and a job that wasn't going anywhere, I decided to go back to school. My husband and I wanted to start our family, so in order to break myself into the academic life and the maternal one slowly, I started part time at university.

From "From a Mature Student's Perspective,"
S. L. Armstrong, St. Mary's University

Topic sentence: _____

_____

Supporting details are essential in any paragraph. In Chapter 13, we learned that a supporting detail is a piece of evidence used by the writer to make the controlling idea of the topic sentence convincing to the reader. These details will convince your reader that what you are claiming in the topic sentence is believable or reasonable.

In Linda Blore's essay "Pressure to Be Thin," there are a number of supporting details in the opening paragraph that support her topic sentence. If "women have been conditioned to think thin is best," the author explains why this is so:

1. The ditty she quotes "has become a rule of life."
2. "Protruding tummies are not acceptable" unless you are a man.
3. Many women diet below their recommended weights.
4. "The thinner the better."

Now look at the other paragraphs reproduced at the beginning of this chapter, and try to find the supporting details in each one.

1. "Four Types of Interesting People" supporting details:

_____

_____

_____

_____

2. "Experimentation on Animals: Justified" supporting details:

_____

_____

_____

_____

3. "My Animal Kingdom" supporting details:

_____

_____

_____

_____

4. "From a Mature Student's Perspective" supporting details:

_____

_____

_____

_____

Supporting details for the topic sentence appear throughout the essay. When Linda Blore established her topic in the opening paragraph of her essay "Pressure to Be Thin" and immediately offered supporting details to justify her point of view, she went on in the second paragraph of her essay both to offer more information that would support her belief that there is undue pressure on women to be thin, and to expand upon details she had offered in her opening paragraph.

> Throughout the day we receive subtle messages advocating slim bodies. Stores use skinny mannequins in their window displays and slender models in their fashion shows. Even the women on our favourite television programs are trim. Some of the messages we receive are not as subtle. Newspapers have huge advertisements for weight-loss clinics. The before and after pictures demonstrate the drastic effect of the program. In grocery stores things are not much better. The "keep thin" products have increased drastically on the grocery store shelves. There are diet pops, sparkling mineral waters claiming no calories, calorie-reduced yogurts, "lite" cheese whiz products, and even low-calorie kool-aid mix and sugar-free fudgsicles. We can now purchase Weight Watcher lasagna, Lean Cuisine cannelloni stuffed with cheese, and Weight Watcher carrot cakes and gooey desserts. While some of these foods are beneficial to certain people, we have gone too far. Everything has to be calorie reduced so we can eat and not gain weight, or better yet, eat and lose weight. At the checkout counter, we see magazines telling us about the new diets. They tell us how we can lose five kilograms and fit into a Christmas party dress or how we can tone up problem areas with only twenty minutes of exercise a day. For those who want to lose but do not like exercise, there are machines now to do the work for you.

Paragraph Practice: Narration

A narrative paragraph is one that tells a story. The following is an example of a student essay that uses the narrative approach.

> "Another Saturday night," I mumble quietly, "and I don't now how I got brainwashed into working again. I am going to have to tolerate the usual uninhibited drunks, the muddle of orders, and the harsh working conditions. O Lord, please help me survive the night without any hassles!" Straightening my apron and arming myself with a tray, I push open the doors and enter the "weekender zone."
>
> From "I Have the Bar Waitress Blues,"
> Christine Thomson, Centennial College

Imagine the situation that Christine describes. Why do you think she feels as she does? On the lines following, describe what you think happens next.

_____

_____

_____

_____

_____

_____

_____

_____

_____

_____

_____

_____

_____

_____

Paragraph Opportunity: Narration

In a paragraph, tell the story of a job you once had or now have. Describe a situation you encountered in your job. What happened to you or to someone you worked with?

_____

_____

_____

_____

_____

_____

_____

_____

_____

_____

_____

_____

_____

_____

_____

_____

_____

_____

_____

_____

Paragraph Practice: Description

A descriptive paragraph is one that describes something. The following example
is taken from a student essay in which a description is given of an outfit worn
by a girl on vacation in Italy. Even though the paragraph begins as a narrative,
the descriptive elements are dominant.

> "We're leaving tomorrow so don't do anything stupid like fall in love
> with him," my sister screamed from the shower.
> "I only said yes because he would make a great guide. He does live
> in Venice," I bellowed back as I finished dressing.
> I looked in the mirror. I wore what I called the outfit for the mod-
> ern explorer, suitable for all the adventures of a tourist: a cotton top and
> skirt and a pair of sneakers. The top had two wide straps, the ends of
> which scooped down to form an oval neckline. The skirt was gathered at
> the waist so that it flared, swirling just above my knees when I walked.
> Blotches of dirt marred my once-white sneakers. I always felt comfortable
> in this outfit, for it portrayed me exactly as I was: a young traveller able
> to go where I wanted (the worn sneakers did not give me blisters), see
> what I wanted (the skirt and a big shawl even allowed my entrance into a
> mosque), and flirt whenever I wanted (as the strap of the top sometimes
> fell off my shoulder). But today, before I left, I wore a T-shirt over my top,
> thinking that my shoulders, already rosy, would burn under the scorch-
> ing Italian sun. Now I was ready to meet Franco. I stuffed my camera into
> my purse and yelled goodbye to Sophie.

> From "Sunblock,"
> Ann Palantzas, Innis College, University of Toronto

What do you learn about this girl as she is described? From what is given
in the paragraph, attempt to describe the girl more fully. Can you describe her
facial features, her personality? What picture do you have in mind about this
tourist?

_____

_____

_____

_____

_____

_____

_____

_____

_____

_____
_____
_____
_____
_____
_____
_____
_____
_____
_____
_____
_____
_____
_____
_____
_____
_____

Paragraph Opportunity: Description

Describe a fellow student as you have observed him or her reading, either in class, in the library, or in some other place. First, describe what the student was wearing, and then describe how he or she held the book or magazine that was being read. Be sure to use such details as the expression on the student's face and whether or not the student was concentrating on what was being read. Did the student ignore distractions?

_____
_____
_____
_____
_____
_____
_____
_____
_____
_____
_____

_____

_____

_____

_____

_____

_____

_____

_____

_____

Paragraph Practice: Process

A process paragraph is one that describes how to do something. The following selection is taken from a student essay in which the author argues in favour of immortality through freezing the body.

After the body has been cooled and the blood has been replaced, it could be held at a constant temperature of 4 degrees centigrade, where water is at its densest and therefore at the lowest temperature before crystallization. Then the body is plunged into a large volume of helium II to freeze it super-quickly before ice crystals have time to form. Helium II is normal liquid helium which has been cooled below a certain critical point where it ceases to behave either like helium or any other liquified gases. At this temperature, helium becomes superconductive; in fact, it conducts heat so quickly that it doesn't even have time to boil. It is just this property that I propose will cool a person quickly enough so that crystallization will not be a problem. After quick freezing is accomplished, the body can be allowed to warm and be easily stored at liquid nitrogen temperatures until needed.

From "Batteries Not Included,"
Fred Murphy, Memorial University

It is well within the realm of modern technology to freeze a body and preserve it for an extended period of time in the hope that a cure can be found for what whatever the person died from, and the person brought back to life. This process has, in fact, been the subject of many movies over the past number of years, in particular _2001_, where people are put into suspended animation for years while the space ship in which they are travelling crosses the vast distances to the stars. Do you think that the process of freezing bodies, or of suspended animation, is realistic?

_____

_____

_____

_____

_____

_____

_____

_____

_____

_____

_____

_____

_____

_____

Paragraph Opportunity: Process

In a paragraph, describe the process you went through in order to obtain something and put it in working order. You might have bought a bicycle and had to assemble it before it could be used, or you might have bought an unfinished piece of furniture that you had to stain and varnish.

_____

_____

_____

_____

_____

_____

_____

_____

_____

_____

_____

Paragraph Practice: Comparison or Contrast

Back in Chapter 17, it was stated that when we use comparison, we emphasize the similarities between two subjects, and that when we use contrast, we emphasize the differences between two subjects. Read the following student paragraph.

> Native children are taught that not speaking is a form of respect for an older person. Should a native child be required to speak to an adult, that child must speak quietly and moderately. Boldness, in children, is frowned upon in the native culture. For a child to make continual eye

contact with an older person while conversing is considered bold and very rude. In the non-native culture children are taught to speak up and ask questions when they do not understand something. Not making eye contact with the person that a child is conversing with is usually a sign of inattentiveness or, worse still, guilt! Naturally, a non-native teacher understands these non-verbal cues and attaches the same meanings to the native children. This, of course, leads to misunderstandings and confusion, with both the native children and teacher being alienated from each other. The native child considers the teacher stupid and ignorant, which is a correct impression, from his or her (the child's) perspective. The non-native teacher considers the native child unresponsive, shy, reserved, a slow learner, and so on. This impression is also correct, from the teacher's perspective, because both the native student and the non-native teacher are judging each other from their own perspective.

From "Native Communication Styles,"
Rena Kinney, College of New Caledonia

Is this a paragraph of comparison or contrast? Why? What is being compared or contrasted?

_____

_____

_____

_____

_____

_____

_____

_____

_____

_____

_____

_____

_____

Paragraph Opportunity: Comparison or Contrast

In a paragraph, compare or contrast your way of thinking about a topic with another person's way of thinking about the same topic.

_____

_____

_____

_____

_____

_____

_____

_____

_____

_____

_____

_____

_____

_____

_____

_____

_____

_____

_____

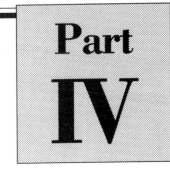

Part IV

Structuring the College Essay

20 Moving from the Paragraph to the Essay

When you learned to write a well-developed paragraph in Part III, you were creating the basic support paragraph for the college essay. An essay is a longer piece of writing, usually five or more paragraphs, in which you can develop a topic in much more depth than you could in a single paragraph. In college, this longer piece of writing is usually called the college essay, although you may also hear it called a composition, theme, or paper. In most schools, such writing is an important part of almost every course, not only the English composition class.

You learned in Part III that the paragraph with its topic sentence and supporting details must have an organization that is both unified and coherent. The college essay must also have these characteristics. Furthermore, since the essay develops a topic at greater length or depth, making all the parts work together becomes an added challenge.

What Kinds of Paragraphs Are in an Essay?

In addition to the support paragraphs that you studied in Part III, the essay has two new kinds of paragraphs:

1. The **introductory paragraph** is the first paragraph of the essay. Its purpose is to be so inviting that the reader will not want to stop reading. In most essays, and in all college essays, this introduction contains a **thesis statement**.

2. **Support paragraphs** (sometimes called body paragraphs) provide the evidence that shows your thesis is valid. A college essay must have at least three well-developed support paragraphs. (You have studied these kinds of paragraphs in Part III.) One paragraph must flow logically into the next. This is accomplished by the careful use of **transitional devices**.

3. The **concluding paragraph** is the last paragraph of the essay. Its purpose is to give the reader a sense of coming to a satisfying ending, that everything has been said that needed to be said.

Before you begin the process of writing your own college essays, this chapter will prepare you to understand and work with these special essay features:

> Thesis statement
> Introductory paragraph
> Transitions between body paragraphs
> Concluding paragraph

What Is a Thesis?

The **thesis** of an essay is a statement of the main idea of that essay. It is the statement of what you are going to explain, defend, or prove about your topic. It is usually placed at the end of the introductory paragraph.

How to Recognize the Thesis Statement

1. The thesis statement is a complete sentence. Students sometimes confuse a title for a thesis. Remember that titles are usually phrases rather than complete sentences.

    > *Title:*   The advantages of all-day kindergarten
    >
    > *Thesis:*   Schools should offer parents the option of an all-day kindergarten program for their children, not only for the benefit of the working mother but also because of the advantages for the children.

2. The thesis statement presents a viewpoint about the topic that can be defended or shown in your essay. Students sometimes think that a simple statement of fact can be a thesis. A fact, however, is either true or false. It is not a topic that is debatable. Such a sentence could not be the focus of an essay, since there is no apparent purpose for providing the factual information.

    > *Fact:*   Nearly all kindergartens in Canada offer a half day of instruction.
    >
    > *Thesis:*   Parents know there is more than one reason why most children at five years of age should only be in school for half a day.

Practice: Read each of the following statements. If you think the statement is a fact, mark it with an *F*. If you think the statement is a thesis, mark it with a *T*.

———— 1. In Canada, kindergarten is not compulsory.

———— 2. Children should begin learning to read in kindergarten.

———— 3. Putting a child into kindergarten before he or she is physically or emotionally ready can have several unfortunate effects on a child.

———— 4. In some European countries, children do not begin formal schooling until age seven or eight.

Exercise 1   Recognizing the Thesis Statement

In the space provided, identify each of the following as (1) a *title*, (2) a *thesis*, or (3) a *fact* that could be used to support a thesis.

_____   1.   The personal interview is the most important step in the employment process.

_____   2.   Looking for a job

_____   3.   Sixty percent of all jobs are obtained through newspaper advertisements.

_____   4.   The best time to begin a foreign language is in grade school.

_____   5.   The importance of learning a foreign language

_____   6.   In the 1970s, the number of students studying foreign languages declined dramatically.

_____   7.   Most Canadians doing business with Japan do not know a word of Japanese.

_____   8.   Working and studying at the same time

_____   9.   Many students in community colleges have part-time jobs while they are going to school.

_____   10.   Working at a part-time job while going to school puts an enormous strain on a person.

Exercise 2   Recognizing the Thesis Statement

In the space provided, identify each of the following as (1) a *title*, (2) a *thesis*, or (3) a *fact* that could be used to support a thesis.

_____   1.   It is estimated that between 5000 and 9000 grizzly bears live in the Yukon.

_____   2.   The survival of grizzly bears in our country should be a top priority.

_____   3.   When bears are young cubs, there are twice as many males as females.

_____   4.   Only about 60 percent of bear cubs survive the first few years of life.

_____   5.   Bears, a precious natural resource

_____   6.   The average life span of a bear today is only five or six years.

_____   7.   The sad plight of the grizzly bear

_____   8.   Five actions need to be taken to save the grizzly bear from extinction.

_____   9.   To save the grizzly bear, we need laws from Parliament, the co-operation of hunters and campers, and an educated general public.

_____   10.   A decision to save the grizzly bear

Exercise 3   Recognizing the Thesis Statement

In the space provided, identify each of the following as (1) a *title*, (2) a *thesis*, or (3) a *fact* that could be used to support a thesis.

———————   1. It is not known whether these people expanded farther into North America.

———————   2. There are three small caves overlooking a wide basin.

———————   3. People lived in these caves more than 10 000 years ago.

———————   4. The Bluefish caves in the Yukon are an important source of information about the ancient people of North America.

———————   5. The way ancient people lived

———————   6. A few chipped stone articles have been found along with the skeletons of extinct animals.

———————   7. Learning about the diet of an ancient people of North America

———————   8. The Bluefish caves are discovered.

———————   9. The discovery of artifacts in the Bluefish caves has led archeologists to believe that they represent the expansion of Asian hunting peoples across the Bering Strait.

———————   10. The Bluefish caves are the oldest known home of human beings in Canada.

Writing the Effective Thesis Statement

An effective thesis statement has the following parts:

1. **A topic that is not too broad:** Broad topics must be narrowed down in scope. You can do this by *limiting the topic* (changing the term to cover a smaller part of the topic), or *qualifying the topic* (adding phrases or words to the general term that will narrow down the topic).

    Broad topic: Swimming
    Limited topic: Learning to float (Floating is a kind of swimming, more specialized than the term *swimming*.)
    Qualified topic: Swimming two hours a week (The use of the phrase "two hours a week" narrows the topic down considerably. Now the topic concentrates on the fact that the *time* spent swimming is an important part of the topic.)

    There are an endless number of ways to narrow a topic in order to make it fit into a proper essay length as well as make it fit your experience and knowledge.

2. **A controlling idea that you can defend:** The controlling idea is what you want to show or prove about your topic; it is your attitude about that topic. Often the word is an adjective such as *beneficial*, *difficult*, or *maddening*.

    Learning to float at the age of twenty was a *terrifying* experience.

    Swimming two hours a week brought about a *dramatic change* in my health.

3. **An indication of what strategy for development is to be used:** (Often you can use words such as the following: *description, steps, stages, comparison, contrast, causes, effects, reasons, advantages, disadvantages, definition, analysis, persuasion.*)

   Although not all writers include the strategy in the thesis statement, they must always have in mind what major strategy they plan to use to prove their thesis. Professional writers often use more than one strategy to prove the thesis. However, in this book, you are asked to develop your essays by using one major strategy at a time. By working in this way, you can concentrate on understanding and developing the skills needed for each specific strategy.

Study the following thesis statement:

> Although a date with the right person is marvellous, going out with a group can have many advantages.

Now look back and check the parts of this thesis statement.

General topic: Going out
Qualified topic: Going out in a group (as opposed to a single date)
Controlling idea: To give the advantages
Strategy for development: Contrast between the single date and the group date

Exercise 1   Writing the Thesis Statement

Below are four topics. For each one, develop a thesis sentence by (1) limiting or qualifying the general topic, (2) choosing a controlling idea (what you want to explain or prove about the topic), and (3) selecting a strategy that you could use to develop that topic. An example is done for you.

General topic: Senior citizens

a. *Limit or qualify the subject*:

Community services available to the senior citizens in my town

b. *Controlling idea*:

To show the great variety of programs

c. *Strategy for development* (narration, process, cause and effect, definition and analysis, comparison or contrast, classification, argument):

Classify the services into major groups.

Thesis statement:

The senior citizens of New Glasgow, Nova Scotia, are very fortunate to have programs available that help them deal with health, housing, and leisure time.

1. Saskatoon (or another city with which you are familiar)

   a. Limit or qualify the subject

   _____

   b. Controlling idea

   _____

   c. Strategy for development (narration, process, cause and effect, definition and analysis, comparison or contrast, classification, or argument)

_____

Thesis statement:

_____

_____

2. Terrorism

   a. Limit or qualify the subject

_____

   b. Controlling idea

_____

   c. Strategy for development (narration, process, cause and effect, definition and analysis, comparison or contrast, classification, or argument)

_____

Thesis statement:

_____

_____

3. Shopping

   a. Limit or qualify the subject

_____

   b. Controlling idea

_____

   c. Strategy for development (narration, process, cause and effect, definition and analysis, comparison or contrast, classification, or argument)

_____

Thesis statement:

_____

_____

4. The library

   a. Limit or qualify the subject

_____

   b. Controlling idea

_____

   c. Strategy for development (narration, process, cause and effect, definition and analysis, comparison or contrast, classification, or argument)

_____

Thesis statement:

_____

_____

Exercise 2 Writing the Thesis Statement

Below are five topics. For each one, develop a thesis sentence by (1) limiting or qualifying the general topic, (2) choosing a controlling idea (what you want to explain or prove about the topic), and (3) selecting a strategy that you could use to develop that topic. Review the example in Exercise 1 (page 311).

1. Television

    a. Limit or qualify the subject

    _____

    b. Controlling idea

    _____

    c. Strategy for development (narration, process, example, cause and effect, definition and analysis, comparison or contrast, classification, or argument)

    _____

    Thesis statement:

    _____

    _____

    _____

    _____

2. Soccer (or another sport)

    a. Limit or qualify the subject

    _____

    b. Controlling idea

    _____

    c. Strategy for development (narration, process, example, cause and effect, definition and analysis, comparison or contrast, classification, or argument)

    _____

    Thesis statement:

    _____

    _____

    _____

    _____

3.   Math (or another field of study)

   a.   Limit or qualify the subject

   _____

   b.   Controlling idea

   _____

   c.   Strategy for development (narration, process, example, cause and effect, definition and analysis, comparison or contrast, classification, or argument)

   _____

   Thesis statement:

   _____

   _____

   _____

   _____

4.   Guns

   a.   Limit or qualify the subject

   _____

   b.   Controlling idea

   _____

   c.   Strategy for development (narration, process, example, cause and effect, definition and analysis, comparison or contrast, classification, or argument)

   _____

   Thesis statement:

   _____

   _____

   _____

   _____

5.   Clubs

   a.   Limit or qualify the subject

   _____

   b.   Controlling idea

   _____

   c.   Strategy for development (narration, process, example, cause and effect, definition and analysis, comparison or contrast, classification, or argument)

   _____

   Thesis statement:

   _____

_____

_____

_____

_____

Ways to Write an Effective Introductory Paragraph

An introduction has one main purpose: to "grab" your readers' interest so that they will keep reading. There is no one way to write an introduction. However, since many good introductions follow the same common patterns, you will find it helpful to look at a few examples of the more typical patterns. When you are ready to create your own introductions, you can consider trying one of these patterns.

1. **Begin with a general subject that can be narrowed down into the specific topic of your essay.** Here is the introduction to a House of Commons speech given by Tommy Douglas during the debate on capital punishment:

    > There are times, Mr. Speaker, when the House of Commons rises to grandeur and becomes deeply conscious of its great traditions. I think this debate has been one of those occasions. There has been a minimum of rancour and there has been no imputation of motives because I think that the abolitionists and the retentionists alike have been sincerely searching their consciences to see if we can honestly resolve a moral problem. This problem is, how can we abolish a brutal punishment without endangering the safety of society?

    Then comes the specific topic of this speech:

    > I am in favour of a motion to abolish capital punishment.

2. **Begin with specifics (a brief anecdote, a specific example or fact) that will broaden into the more general topic of your essay.** Here is the introduction to an essay about a family of Russian Jews settling on a prairie farm just outside of Winnipeg.

    > The year that I was twelve my father came home one day and announced that he had bought a farm. My sister Helen and I could hardly wait to see the farm which, according to my father, consisted of twenty-six acres in St. Vital, just beyond the outskirts of Winnipeg. There were twenty acres of bush with buildings, and six acres of meadow beside the river. My father had dreamed of such a farm all the years he was shut up in the dark greasy machine shop where he earned his living.

    > From Miriam Waddington,
    > "The Hallowe'en Party"

    What follows is the topic of the story, a topic that is larger than the idea of merely buying a farm:

    > Now as I look back, I can understand my father's deep hunger for land.

3. **Give a definition of the concept that will be discussed.** Here is the introduction to an essay about the rising trend toward single motherhood.

They are a new breed of mother — single, self-sufficient, and in their thirties. They have opted for motherhood without marriage. Some call it a return to tribal times when women raised children on their own with the help of other women. Others see it as a dangerous trend, labelling them as "the most narcissistic group of people you will ever see." Regardless of how it's perceived, statistics show that in the past few years the number of single mothers in their thirties has increased dramatically.

From Lydia Bailey,
"Man, Woman and Child"

4. **Make a startling statement.**

Man is an inveterate meddler. An active curiosity is known as a measure of intelligence, but human meddling goes far beyond all normal bounds of rational behaviour. This compulsive hyperactivity has frequently been responsible for ecological disasters in all parts of the world. No aspect of human meddling has had more far-reaching effects than the importation and deliberate introduction of foreign species into strange environments.

From John A. Livingstone,
"Landed Immigrants"

5. **Start with an idea or statement that is a widely held point of view. Then surprise the reader by stating that this idea is false or that you hold a different point of view.**

Canadians live under the remarkable illusion that we are a technologically advanced people. Everything around us denies that assumption. We are, in many ways, a Third World country, selling our natural resources in exchange for the high technology of the industrialized world. Try going through your home and looking at the country of origin of your clothes, electrical appliances, books, car. The rare technological product that does have Canada stamped on it is usually from a branch plant of a multinational company centred in another country.

From David Suzuki,
"A Planet for the Taking"

6. **Start with a familiar quotation or a quotation by a famous person.**

Man does not live by bread alone, but by fantasy and daydream as well. Young men and women are sitting behind desks in downtown Toronto, Montreal, and Vancouver and thinking, when I get my grubstake I'm going to leave this scene for good. I'm heading for the country. Get a place ten miles from the nearest town and only come in on weekends for supplies, like lentils and Crunchy Granola. Yes. A little homestead far from the Great Urban Maw ... and at the same time as these visions are being entertained, the other men and women are flocking to Toronto and Montreal and Vancouver, from places like Marathon, Ont., and Gypsumville, Man., and Vanderhoof, B.C., for jobs in life-insurance offices and a comfortable nook in some monstrous high rise. It's not the popular dream, to settle down in the big city, but there you have it — real alternatives are simply too scarce.

From Philip Marchand,
"Learning to Love the Big City"

7. **Give a number of descriptive images that will lead to the thesis of your essay.**

When the British Columbia Supreme Court recently ordered that the $100 000 trust fund set up for the family of mass murderer Clifford

Olson be declared null and void, it threw a wrench into the whole legal system of plea-bargaining. The fund had been set up by the Crown in return for Mr. Olson telling the authorities where he had hidden the bodies of the children he murdered, and for giving the Crown full details of these crimes to ensure his conviction. This is not the first time that the Crown has made "deals." In Ontario, a Mafia enforcer named Cecil Kirby has been granted full immunity, protection, a new identity, a financial allowance and other benefits for helping the Crown prosecute the people who hired him to commit numerous crimes. Mr. Olson and Mr. Kirby are simply the two most graphic examples of plea-bargaining and the tactics used to gain convictions.

From Leo Adler,
"Is Plea-Bargaining So Bad?"

8. **Ask a question that you intend to answer.** Many essays you will read in magazines and newspapers use a question in the introductory paragraph to make the reader curious about the author's viewpoint. Some writing instructors prefer that students do not use this method. Check with your instructor for his or her viewpoint. Here is an example of such an introduction.

Human beings sustained in a state of technical "life" through complex machinery present to society and medicine a terribly and increasingly familiar dilemma. All the meaning and pleasure of ordinary life are absent and there's no hope of return to a dignified existence. Who has the authority to decide that the time has come to stop the machines?

From Vivian Rakoff,
"The Fatal Question"

9. **Use classification** to indicate how your topic fits into the larger class to which it belongs, or how your topic can be divided into categories that you are going to discuss. Here is how Robert Fulford began an essay on the destruction of Métis and native societies in the West:

They may never have seen each other's faces, but the two most famous non-whites in late nineteenth-century Canada — Louis Riel and Big Bear — were linked by history and by the events of the crisis year 1885. They were dissimilar in many ways — Riel a Montreal-educated Métis who travelled widely and was three times elected to the Canadian parliament, Big Bear a Plains Cree, who knew no world beyond the Prairies. But they were also alike: both were mystics and prophets and both were charismatic leaders of peoples doomed by the westward thrust of the Canadian empire.

From Robert Fulford,
"How the West Was Lost"

What *Not* to Say in Your Introduction

1. Avoid telling your reader that you are beginning your essay:

   In this essay I will discuss . . .
   I will talk about . . .
   I am going to prove . . .

2. Don't apologize:

   Although I am not an expert . . .
   In my humble opinion . . .

3. Do not refer to later parts of your essay:

By the end of this essay, you will agree . . .
In the next paragraph, you will see . . .

4. Don't use trite expressions. Since they have been so overused, they will lack interest. Using such expressions shows that you have not taken the time to use your own words to express your ideas. Some examples of trite expressions are

busy as a bee
you can't tell a book by its cover
haste makes waste

Using Transitions to Move the Reader from One Idea to the Next

Successful essays help the reader understand the logic of the writer's thinking by using transitional expressions when needed. Usually this occurs when the writer is moving from one point to the next. It can also occur whenever the idea is complicated. The writer may need to summarize the points so far; the writer may need to emphasize a point already made; or the writer may want to repeat an important point. The transition may be a word, a phrase, a sentence, or even a paragraph.

Here are some of the transitional expressions that might be used to help the reader make the right connections.

1. To make your points stand out clearly:

the first reason	second, secondly	finally
first of all	another example	most important
in the first place	even more important	all in all
	also, next	in conclusion
	then	to summarize

2. To show an example of what has just been said:

for example
for instance

3. To show the consequence of what has just been said:

therefore
as a result
then

4. To make a contrasting point clear:

on the other hand
but
contrary to current thinking
however

5. To admit a point:

of course
granted

6. To resume your argument after admitting a point:

nevertheless
even so

nonetheless
still

7. To call the reader's attention to your organization:

    Before attempting to answer these questions, let me . . .
    In our discussions so far, we have seen that . . .
    At this point, it is necessary to . . .
    It is beyond the scope of this paper to . . .

A more subtle way to link one idea to another in an essay is to repeat a word or phrase from the preceding sentence. Sometimes instead of the actual word, a pronoun will take the place of the word.

8. To repeat a word or phrase from a preceding sentence:

    I have many memories of my childhood in Cuba. These *memories* include the aunts, uncles, grandparents, and friends I had to leave behind.

9. To use a pronoun to refer to a word or phrase from a preceding sentence:

    Like all immigrants, my family and I have had to build a new life from almost nothing. *It* was often difficult, but I believe the struggle made us strong.

Exercise 1 Finding Transitional Devices

Below are the first three paragraphs of an essay on African art. Circle all the transitional devices or the repeating words that are used to link one sentence to another or one idea to the next.

Like language and social organization, art is essential to human life. As embellishment and as creation of objects beyond the requirements of the most basic needs of living, art has accompanied man since prehistoric times. Because of its almost unfailing consistency as an element of many societies, art may be the response to some biological or psychological need. Indeed, it is one of the most constant forms of human behaviour.

However, use of the word *art* is not relevant when we describe African "art" because it is really a European term that at first grew out of Greek philosophy and was later reinforced by European culture. The use of other terms, such as *exotic art*, *primitive art*, *art sauvage*, and so on, to delineate differences is just as misleading. Most such terms are pejorative—implying that African art is on a lower cultural level. Levels of culture are irrelevant here, since African and European attitudes toward the creative act are so different. Since there is no term in our language to distinguish between the essential differences in thinking, it is best then to describe standards of African art.

African art attracts because of its powerful emotional content and its beautiful abstract form. Abstract treatment of form describes most often—with bare essentials of line, shape, texture, and pattern—intense energy and sublime spirituality. Hundreds of distinct cultures and languages and many types of people have created over 1000 different styles that defy classification. Each art and craft form has its own history and its own aesthetic content. But there are some common denominators (always with exceptions).

Ways to Write an Effective Concluding Paragraph

A concluding paragraph has one main purpose: to give the reader the sense of reaching a satisfying ending to the topic discussed. Students often feel they have nothing to say at the end. A look at how professional writers frequently end their essays can ease your anxiety about writing an effective conclusion. You have more than one possibility. Here are some of the most frequently used patterns for ending an essay.

1. **Come full circle; that is, return to the material in your introduction.** Finish what you started there. Remind the reader of the thesis. Be sure to restate the main idea using a different wording. Here is an example from the essay on life-support machines (page 317).

    > We are involved in an unending process of questioning and adaptation — an adaptation that, with luck, will not fall into a simple-minded rejection of the machine as the work of the devil. It is at least equally valid to see the manufacture of machines and goods as the continuous unfolding of human endowment in a cumulative history. Man the toolmaker is man expressing an ancient and important component of his true nature.

2. **Summarize by repeating the main points.** This example is from the essay on African art (page 319):

    > In summary, African art explains the past, describes values and a way of life, helps man relate to supernatural forces, mediates his social relations, expresses emotions, and enhances man's present life as an embellishment denoting pride or status as well as providing entertainment such as with dance and music.

3. **Show the significance of your thesis by making predictions, giving a warning, giving advice, offering a solution, suggesting an alternative, or telling the results.** This example is from the essay by David Suzuki (page 316).

    > But Canadians do value the spiritual importance of nature and want to see it survive for future generations. We also believe in the power of science to sustain a high quality of life. And while the current understanding of science's power is, I believe, misplaced, in fact the leading edges of physics and ecology may provide the insights that can get us off the current track. We need a very profound perceptual shift and soon.

4. **End with an anecdote that illustrates your thesis.** This example is from Robert Fulford's essay on the Métis and native people (page 317).

    > The criminal trials of the Indians and the Métis in the autumn of 1885 seem, in retrospect, outrageously illogical — the rebels were convicted of treason against an empire that had conscripted them as citizens without consulting them. But the North-West Rebellion also produced a trial that was merely bizarre. Shortly after the rebellion ended, an article in the Toronto *News* said that Montreal's Sixty-fifth Battalion had conducted itself during the hostilities in a way that was mutinous, reckless, disorderly, and drunken. Officers of the battalion sued, and eventually the editor of the *News* — a notorious enemy of French Canadians and the French language — was summoned to Montreal to stand trial for criminal libel. Convicted and fined $200, he emerged from the courtroom, barely escaped with his life from a howling mob of outraged Montrealers, and went home to be treated to a torchlight parade of 4,000 cheering supporters in Toronto. Two years later, fed up with the stresses of daily newspaper work, the editor, Edmund E. Sheppard, founded a new periodical, *Saturday Night*.

What *Not* to Say in Your Conclusion

1. Do not introduce a new point.
2. Do not apologize.
3. Do not end up in the air, leaving the reader feeling unsatisfied. This sometimes happens if the very last sentence is not strong enough.

A Note about Titles

Be sure to follow the standard procedure for writing your title.

1. Capitalize all words except articles (*the*, *a*, *an*) and prepositions.
2. Do not underline the title or put quotation marks around it.
3. Try to think of a short and catchy phrase (three to six words). Often writers wait until they have written a draft before working on a title. There may be a phrase from the essay that will be perfect. If you still cannot think of a clever title after you have written a draft, choose some key words from your thesis statement.
4. Centre the title at the top of the page, and remember to leave about an inch of space between the title and the beginning of the first paragraph.

21

The Writing Process

What Is the Process for Writing a College Essay?

Writing is a craft. This means that a writer, no matter how good or how inexperienced, needs to follow a certain process in order to arrive at a successful finished product. Very few writers can "dash off" a masterpiece. We sometimes think that a person is "a born dancer" or "a born writer," but the reality is that the person has worked long hours for many years to achieve his or her level of skill.

Just as no two chefs or carpenters or painters approach their work in the same way, no two writers work in exactly the same way. In spite of this individuality, each writer goes through a surprisingly similar series of steps to reach the finished product.

Steps in the Writing Process

1. Getting the idea for developing a topic
2. Gathering the information (brainstorming, taking notes)
3. Selecting and organizing material
4. Writing the rough draft
5. Revising the rough draft (some writers work on many, many drafts that they revise before they are satisfied)
6. Writing the second draft
7. Proofreading
8. Typing the final copy
9. Checking for typing errors

Following this process will help you produce your best writing. You will feel more in control, since you will be working on one step at a time and not trying to do everything all at once. Careful preparation before writing and careful revisions after writing always pay off. You will see your initial idea change and develop into something much more detailed and organized than your first thoughts on the topic. Remember that writing, just like the other skills you develop in life, improves when you follow the same process used by those who have already been successful. If you take the time to practise using this process regularly, your writing will improve.

Many students believe that a writer somehow has a magical inspiration that allows him or her to sit down and produce the piece immediately. Although this very seldom happens, you may be lucky enough on occasion to have the exciting experience of being "turned on" to your topic, an experience in which the words flow easily from your pen. At such a time, you will feel how satisfying writing can be, for writing is a way to self-discovery. It is a method of finding within yourself the wealth of untapped ideas and thoughts that are waiting for expression.

Understanding the Writing Process

1. Getting the Idea

Usually a writer sits down to write knowing the general topic he or she wants to write about. You might have to write an essay on the political system in Canada for a history class. You might have to write a paper for psychology class on coping with stress. Maybe you are angry about a toxic waste site near your home, and you decide to write a letter to the newspaper. Perhaps your employer asks you to write a report to describe the ways in which productivity could be increased in your department. In all these cases, the topic is set before you. You do not have to say to yourself, "Now what in the world shall I write about?" Most students prefer to have a specific topic rather than have no direction at all. Furthermore, if the topic is of interest to you, your writing is much more likely to be interesting to your readers. When you enjoy your work, you will spend more time on it and use more of your inner resources.

Even though you will usually be assigned a particular topic or given a group of topics from which to choose, you will need to spend some time thinking of a possible approach that can make use of your experience or knowledge. In writing, this approach is called the "controlling idea." One of our students, for example, loved to play chess. He admitted to us in his senior year of college that he had tried to use his interest in and knowledge of this hobby to help him complete several of his college assignments. For an assignment in his psychology class, when the teacher asked for a paper titled "Stereotypes—Are They True?" he wrote about the characteristics of people who play chess. For a political science class, this same student discussed the importance of international games, including chess, of course. For a paper in his literature course, he wrote about four writers who used games in their writing to symbolize a struggle for power between two characters. You can see from these examples that this student was able to use his own special interests and knowledge to make his writing interesting for himself and undoubtedly interesting to the teachers who read his papers. Don't ever think that you have nothing to write about!

You should always keep in mind that your goal is to find an angle that will interest whoever is going to read your work. All writers write best about topics that are related to their own experience and knowledge. You cannot hope to interest the reader if the material does not first interest you! This section of the book will guide you in this important step of searching for the approach or controlling idea that will work for you.

A Student Essay in Progress: Getting the Idea for an Essay

A student is asked to write a personal-experience essay about fear or anxiety. She begins by making a list of the possibilities:

> Taking tests
> Speaking in front of a large group
> Going on a date with someone for the first time
> Performing on the piano
> Walking alone at night
> Having an argument with one's parents

Which one should she pick? She goes over the possibilities and discovers that when she comes to the one about the piano, she feels a tightness in her chest. Here is an experience in her life that makes her nervous just to think about it! Furthermore, she has had several experiences performing on the piano that she thinks could make an interesting piece of writing. She feels excited because she realizes that she does indeed have many thoughts and feelings about this traumatic experience in her life.

2. Gathering Information

Once you have found a topic, you still have many choices to make. What is going to be your point about the topic? What angle or strategy will you use? You might choose to tell a story, give several examples or anecdotes to prove your point, define and analyze, or compare or contrast. In other words, you can choose from these several different strategies the one that best suits your knowledge or experience.

To make these choices, writers usually need to gather some information to find out what they have to work with. If the assignment calls for your own experience, you will not need to conduct outside research—in the library or in interviews, for instance—to get information. In such a case, you can begin with the technique known as **brainstorming**. Writers use brainstorming to discover what they already know and feel about a given topic.

When you brainstorm, you allow your mind to roam freely around the topic, letting one idea lead to another, even if the ideas seem unrelated or irrelevant. You jot down every word and phrase that pops into your mind when you think about your topic. Sometimes it helps to brainstorm with another person or a group of people. Since this list will only be for your own use, you can jot down single words, phrases, or entire sentences. Your thoughts will be listed in the order in which you originally think of them, or in some other order that makes sense to you. The important point about brainstorming is that it helps to stimulate your thinking on the topic, and as well it gives you the opportunity to write down your first thoughts on the topic. Once you have some ideas jotted down on paper, you will begin to feel less anxious, and perhaps even pleasantly surprised that you have discovered so many possibilities for your essay.

A Student Essay in Progress: Brainstorming the Topic

Topic: Performing on the piano
Approach (or controlling idea): Makes me frightened, anxious, nervous

stage fright	my teacher
strange pianos	lack of self-confidence
parents in the audience	dread of recitals
embarrassed if I make a mistake	being the oldest in the group but not
my shyness	the best
memorizing music	Mrs. Stuart's performance classes

forgetting a chord in the left hand
hands and legs shaking
wanting to please my teacher
fingers get sweaty
Leonard always plays better than the rest of us
contest in June
trills in my piece
finding time to practise in the spring

the performance class last year
playing the sonata
Leonard's playing
jealous
computer programming
always late
feel stupid
Michelle's poor playing
some people don't appreciate classical music

3. Selecting and Organizing Details

When you brainstorm, ideas come from your mind in no particular order, and you jot them down as they come. Your next step in the writing process is to give a sense of organization to these ideas. You do this when you place the results of your brainstorming in an order that helps you see a sequence of events, or logical order for the ideas. This need not be the final order, but it will help you plan an order for your first draft.

As you select and organize the details on your list, do not hesitate to cross out items you know you cannot use. This is an important part of the writing process at this stage. If you are careful in your choice of items, your essay will eventually have more, not less, to offer your reader.

A Student Essay in Progress: Organizing the Material

The student writer strikes out the ideas that do not seem useful and then begins to group the other ideas that she can use. As she works with the words and phrases, she is considering what she should do with all this material. What she determines is that she could write the essay in many ways: analyze her fears, give several examples of performances and describe her fears, or tell one special story that would reveal how she feels. She chooses the last possibility because she thinks an actual incident will be the most interesting. Furthermore, if she does this, she will have the chance to use many specific details.

She begins to work out an order. Some teachers ask students to make this order into an informal outline. Here is how this student grouped her material:

Introduction
  My problems
    shyness
    lacking self-confidence
    older than the others
    not enough time to practise such long pieces
    wanting to do well
    difficulty memorizing
    stage fright
      shaky hands and legs
    cold fingers
Supporting Details
  Coming to Mrs. Stuart's performance class
    her personality
    her house
    the other students
  My performance
    The difficulty of the sonata trills
    runs shaky, better than I thought
    wanting to please my teacher

Leonard's performance
    his appearance
    his talent
Conclusion
    My reaction
        feel stupid
        disappointed
        jealous
        still determined

Notice how some of the ideas on the brainstorming list have been omitted or have changed slightly. Since this essay will primarily use narration, ordering is not as difficult as in some other writing. The student will start by telling her problem, then give the story of one particular performance, and conclude with her reactions to the experience.

4. Writing the Rough Draft

After you have gone through the brainstorming process and you have organized the material into some kind of order, the time has come to write a rough draft.

A rough draft is just what its name implies: your first attempt to write your essay. The first attempt is "rough" because it will undoubtedly undergo many changes before it is finished: parts may be missing, some paragraphs will probably lack sufficient detail, or some parts may be repetitious or inappropriate. Some sentences are likely to sound awkward and need to be rewritten later. The experienced writer expects all this and does not worry. All that you should try to accomplish in the rough draft is to let your mind relax and to get down on paper all of your initial ideas. These first ideas will provide the seeds that can be better developed later on.

Armed with a first draft, you will now have something with which to work. No longer is there a blank paper staring you in the face. This accomplishment is a great relief to most writers, but remember, this is still the beginning!

A Student Essay in Progress: The Rough Draft

Performing on the Piano

1   Sometimes I wonder why I play the piano. It makes me so nervous when I have to play in front of people. I want to do well. But I can never play my best when I'm so nervous. I'm going to tell you about a typical performance I gave last Febuary. On a saturday afternoon I walked up the long driveway to my piano teachers house. My hands were already shaking and my stomach felt upset. I was not looking forward to this at all. In fact, I had been dreading this moment for over a month. This day would not be the end of my terror. In the Spring I would be playing in a special contest where I would be judged and given a score.

2   Today, as usual, I felt my piece was not securely memorized. I never had enough time to practise. Although I wanted to please my teacher. I felt funny being nearly the oldest student in her class. I should be the best, I thought.

3   Now I hoped I wouldn't make a fool of myself in front of the younger kids in my teacher's class, especially that little wizard, Leonard.

4   He was skinny with big glasses. When he looked at you it seemed to be with a laugh. He was as great at the violin, the computer, and everything else as he was at the piano. At least I could always count on Michelle to mess up her piece. She never practised but it didn't seem to

bother her. She always acted as if she was pleased with herself. At least I knew I sounded better than she did.

5 I was late as usual the class had begun. Mrs. Stuart was pleased to see me and she motioned to me to take a chair near the piano. The house was so nice. Filled with beautiful furniture and things on the shelves and tables.

6 Mrs. Stuart was kind to everyone, always trying to make us feel like "somebody." There was something about her looks and personality that made everybody who knew her like her. She had dark eyes and brown hair, was not too tall, and never seemed to wear makeup.

7 Before I knew it, it was my turn. Everyone was watching me. I said what piece I was going to play and sat down. Starting was always the worst. This piece had hard trills and runs and I was really scared. I counted to ten, took a deep breath, and began.

8 It went better than I thought. The trills weren't so great, my runs were shaky, but at least I got through it without forgetting any part. What a relief when it was over.

9 My teacher seemed pleased. She says a few nice words and then moves on to the next student. People were begining to get tired of sitting. One little girl yawned. Then it was Leonard's turn. He got up and announced that he was going to play the same piece as me. My heart started to beat faster. I was really upset. This little kid was going to play my piece.

10 You can guess what happened. He played better than me. The teacher praised him to the sky and I ended up feeling like a jerk. Why should I even bother to play piano when there are kids like Leonard?

5. Revising the Rough Draft

If you have time, put aside your rough draft for a day or two. Then, when you reread it, you will look at it with a fresh mind. In this important revision stage, you should be concerned with how you have organized your ideas into paragraphs. At this point, do not worry about grammar, spelling, and punctuation.

Begin this important revision stage by asking these major questions:

a. Is the essay unified? Do you stick to the topic you have announced? Go through the essay and take out irrelevant material.

b. Do you repeat yourself? Look back over your essay to determine whether or not you have given the same information more than once. Even if you find you have used only some different words, you should delete the repetitious material.

c. Does the essay make sense? Can a reader follow your logic or train of thought? (Giving the rough draft to someone else to read will often answer this question for you.) If the essay is confusing to the reader, you must find out where it goes wrong and why. Sometimes when you read your writing out loud, you will hear a strange sentence or feel that one paragraph has leaped to some point that doesn't follow from the sentence before.

d. Are the paragraphs roughly the same length? If you see one sentence presented as a paragraph, you know something is wrong. Usually each paragraph should develop its point by the use of at least five sentences. Check through your essay. Do you need to change the paragraphing? You may need to develop one paragraph more fully, or a one-sentence paragraph may really belong with the paragraph that comes before or with the paragraph that follows.

e. Do you have all the types of paragraphs essential to an essay: the introduction with its thesis, at least three well-developed body paragraphs with transitional devices used to connect ideas, and a concluding paragraph?

f. Can you add more specific details? Most writing teachers agree that nearly every paper they read could be improved by adding more details, more descriptive verbs, and more sensory images to make the writing come alive.

g. Can you add dialogue or a quote from someone?

h. Could you make the introduction, conclusion, or title more creative?

A Student Essay in Progress: Revising the Rough Draft

a more creative title? **Performing on the Piano**

Student has another idea for an intro-duction. This is the end of the intro-duction. Should begin a new ¶.

1   Sometimes I wonder why I play the piano. It makes me so nervous when I have to play in front of people. I want to do well, but I can never play my best when I'm so nervous. I'm going to tell you about a typical performance I gave last Febuary. On a saturday afternoon I walked up the long driveway to my piano teachers house. My hands were already shaking and my stomach felt upset. I was not looking forward to this at all. In fact, I had been dreading this moment for over a month. This day would not be the end of my terror. In the Spring I would be playing in a special contest where I would be judged and given a score.

¶ 2 is too short.

2   Today, as usual, I felt my piece was not securely memorized. I never had enough time to practise. Although I wanted to please my teacher. I felt funny being nearly the oldest student in her class. I should be the best, I thought.

¶ 3 is too short. Belongs to ¶ 2.

3   Now I hoped I wouldn't make a fool of myself in front of the younger kids in my teacher's class, especially that little wizard, Leonard.

needs to be a new ¶.

4   He was skinny with big glasses. When he looked at you it seemed to be with a laugh. He was as great at the violin, the computer, and everything else as he was at the piano. At least I could always count on Michelle to mess up her piece. She never practised but it didn't seem to bother her. She always acted as if she was pleased with herself. At least I knew I sounded better than she did.

Be more specific.
Be more specific.

5   I was late as usual the class had begun. Mrs. Stuart was pleased to see me, and she motioned to me to take a chair near the piano. The (house was so nice.) Filled with beautiful furniture and things on the shelves and tables.

Use a quote here.

6   Mrs. Stuart was kind to everyone, always trying to make us feel like "somebody." There was (something) about her looks and personality that made everybody who knew her like her. She had dark eyes and brown hair, was not too tall, and never seemed to wear makeup.

7   Before I knew it, it was my turn. Everyone was watching me. I said what piece I was going to play and sat down. Starting was always the worst. This piece had hard trills and runs and I was really scared. I counted to ten, took a deep breath and began.

¶ too short. Give more details.

8   It went better than I thought. The trills weren't so great, my runs were shaky, but at least I got through it without forgetting any part. What a relief when it was over.

use a quote here.

9   My teacher seemed pleased. She says a few nice words and then moves on to the next student. People were beginning to get tired of sitting. One little girl yawned. Then it was Leonard's turn. He got up and announced that he was going to play the same piece as me. My heart started to beat faster. I was really upset. This little kid was going to play my piece.

slang—not appropriate.

10   You can guess what happened. He played better than me. The teacher praised him to the sky and I ended up feeling like a jerk. Why should I even bother to play piano when there are kids like Leonard?

Give more thought to your reactions.

6. Writing the Second Draft

If you have worked hard in revising the rough draft, you will be delighted with the improvements as you write the second draft.

Feedback is an important aid in each of the final stages of writing an essay. A good way to help yourself see your own work better is to put the writing aside for a few days, if you can. Then read what you have written aloud to someone else or yourself if no one is available. You will be very surprised at the number of places in your writing where you will hear a mistake and make a change even as you read.

A Student Essay in Progress: The Second Draft

Sonata in C Major, Opus 35

1   Have you ever been to a children's piano recital? The little seven-year-olds walk eagerly up to the piano, play their 30-second piece that is sixteen bars long, feel very pleased with themselves, and walk back to their seats to wait for everyone else to finish. All they are thinking about is the cookies and punch. I, on the other hand, sit pale and still, twisting my hands, dreading the moment when I must take my place at the piano. I must play well. What if I don't play well? What if I make a mess? The thought of forgetting the piece or stumbling through a difficult passage in front of an audience would be so embarrassing. My experience last month at a class recital still makes me shudder.

2   It was a bleak saturday afternoon in Febuary. I trudged up the long driveway to my piano teachers house. My hands were already shaking and my stomach felt upset. I had been dreading this moment all week. I had to perform my contest piece in front of my teacher and fifteen other talented students. Later in the spring I would be performing the same piece for a judge who would give me a score.

3   Today, as usual, I felt my piece was not securely memorized. I never had enough time to practise. Even though I practised one hour a day, I really needed to spend at least two hours to get the Mozart sonata that I was playing in good shape. To make matters worse, I was the oldest student. This made me feel that I should be the best even though I knew that several of the others had been playing much longer than I had. Now I could only hope I didn't make a fool of myself in front of the younger kids in my teacher's class. They never seemed to make any mistakes when they played, especially that little Leonard.

4   Leonard was a skinny little kid with a mat of black hair slicked smoothly back against his egg-shaped head. His thick glasses made him look like the stereotype of a brainy kid. When he looked at anyone, it was always with a look of amusement. I guess he knew his gray matter was far superior to whatever was in the rest of our brains! He was as good in computer programming, creative writing, and chemistry as he was at the piano. He had been taking lessons for only three years and was already playing pieces at an advanced level. What's more, I heard his mother complaining once that Leonard didn't spend much time at the piano. The worst part of performing in the same room with Leonard was his age. He was only nine!

5   Now, a student like Michelle made me feel better about myself. I

could always count on her to break down in the middle of her piece. She seldom practised. Nevertheless, she was content to do what she could. At least I knew I sounded better than she sounded.

6   I entered the large Victorian house through the back door as the sound of a familiar Bach prelude drifted out from the heavy doors of the music room. As usual I was late. I took off my shoes and crept noiselessly into the room, where I slipped into an armchair near the door.

7   Oh, if only I could sit here and just listen. My eyes wandered across the large room filled with beautiful antique furniture and treasures from around the world. In the far corner stood the black ebony grand piano. How much more beautiful its tone was than the old spinet on which I practised. Children ranging in age from five to twelve sat motionless in the rows of sturdy wooden folding chairs set up across a large Oriental rug.

8   Mrs. Stuart looked over and smiled, seeming to know how nervous I was. She had tried for years to assure me of my talent, yet I still tended to doubt it—particularly on these occasions. Mrs. Stuart was not your typical overbearing piano instructor. She was kind and always encouraging. She was in her mid-thirties, yet appeared younger. Her face was free of makeup, yet her high cheekbones and large dark eyes seemed not to need it. She radiated a warmth that was felt by all of her students.

9   As soon as the music ceased, I was jolted back into the reality of my situation. I was next. I approached the piano cautiously, feeling the eyes of the younger children riveted upon me. "Uhm . . . this piece is a Mozart sonata," I murmured quietly. Filled with difficult runs and countless trills, it was the kind of piece that could easily fall apart. Specially when the performer is nervous. I counted to ten in an attempt to calm my nerves, and with one deep breath I began.

10   To my surprise, I played the first movement smoothly, hardly missing a note. In the second movement I made a small memory slip, but I managed to keep going. The third movement gave me some trouble. My fingers didn't seem to be able to move fast enough for the trills. I had to slow down. I missed two of the hard runs. Finally, I reached the last notes of the sonata, heaved a great sigh of relief, and stood up from the bench.

11   "Beautiful, Suzanne. I think that was the best I've heard you play this piece. By April you will sound more secure." The reassuring voice of Mrs. Stuart broke the silence and I started to relax. The younger students were begining to get restless. One girl yawned and two boys in the back were poking at each other. Then it was Leonard's turn.

12   Leonard marched up to the piano with the posture of a Westpoint cadet. In a high, somewhat nasal voice he announced, "This afternoon I will perform the Mozart Sonata in C Major, Opus 35."

13   My heart started to beat faster. I was disgraced! Leonard was going to play my piece. How could Mrs. Stuart have given us both the same piece?

14   Of course all of my hopes were shattered as he began to play. The sound of the music took everyone by surprise. I stared at my teacher in disbelief. I could hardly recognize this as the same piece. The evenness of the trills, the beauty of the melody, the flawless technique on the runs—I had to admit the piece was more beautiful than I had imagined. I was thrilled and devastated. The piece was gorgeous, but my performance had been mediocre and I felt discouraged.

15   So now I ask myself, "What keeps me going back to the piano? How can all this misery be worth it?" It's the thrill and challenge of hearing a beautiful piece and then trying to re-create that beauty myself.

7. Proofreading

An important step still remains. The student must check each sentence to see that the sentence is correct, including grammar, spelling, and punctuation. In the rush to get a paper in on time, this is a step that is often overlooked. If you take each sentence, starting with the last and going sentence by sentence back toward the beginning, you will be able to look at the sentence structure apart from the other aspects of the essay. Taking the time to look over a paper will usually result in your spotting several sentence-level errors.

At this point, you might want to correct errors of grammar, spelling, and punctuation in the first and second drafts of the student essay (pp. 326–27 and 329–30).

8. Typing the Final Copy

Use 8 ½-by-11-inch paper.

Type on one side of the paper only.

Double-space.

Leave approximately 3.5 centimetre margins on each side of the paper.

Do not hyphenate words at ends of lines unless you consult a dictionary to check how to divide the word into syllables.

Centre the title at the top of the page.

Put your name, the date, and the title of your paper on a separate title page or on the back of the last page.

If you have more than one page, staple or clip them together so they are not lost.

9. Checking for Typing Errors

If possible, you should type your paper. Many teachers require typed papers mainly because they are much easier to read than handwritten ones. Don't forget that if you type your paper or have it done for you, you are still responsible for errors. Remember also that you can make corrections (if there are not too many) neatly in ink on your typed copy before handing it in.

Writing the Narrative Essay

At one time or another, you have undoubtedly been in a position in which you felt uncomfortable, nervous, or intimidated by an authority figure such as a teacher, a doctor, or an official of some kind. You might have felt overwhelmed or powerless facing an organization with its regulations.

This first essay is the chance to tell a story, the kind of writing that is probably most fun because you can base it on your own experience. You are the expert on this topic!

Exploring the Topic

1. In your opinion, do most people feel at ease or uncomfortable when they enter a bank? What is it about the way a bank is built or furnished that makes people feel the way they do?

   Most people feel _____ in a bank because _____

   _____

   _____

2. What is the best way to handle a bank clerk or a clerk in a store who is rude or unhelpful?

   _____

   _____

   _____

3. Where is the best place to save your money?

   _____ a savings account

   _____ a Christmas club

_____ a mattress

_____ other

Explain your answer:

_____

_____

_____

4. What office or school situations do you find yourself in that make you feel uncomfortable?

_____

_____

_____

_____

_____

5. How do you react in a situation when you become nervous? How many different reactions can you name?

_____

_____

_____

_____

_____

_____

The Model Essay: Stephen Leacock, "My Financial Career"

confused

windows in the bank

jaybird

When I go into a bank I get **rattled**. The clerks rattle me; the **wickets** rattle me; the sight of the money rattles me; everything rattles me.

The moment I cross the threshold of a bank I am a hesitating **jay.** If I attempt to transact business there I become an irresponsible idiot.

I knew this beforehand, but my salary had been raised to fifty dollars a month, and I felt that the bank was the only place for it.

So I shambled in and looked timidly round at the clerks. I had an idea that a person about to open an account must consult the manager.

I went up to a wicket marked "Accountant." The accountant was a

gloomy

tall, cool devil. The very sight of him rattled me. My voice was **sepulchral.**

"Can I see the manager?" I said, and added solemnly, "alone."

"Certainly," said the accountant, and fetched him.

The manager was a grave, calm man. I held my fifty-six dollars clutched in a crumpled ball in my pocket.

"Are you the manager?" I said. God knows I didn't doubt it.

"Yes," he said.

"Can I see you?" I asked. "Alone?" I didn't want to say "alone" again, but without it the thing seemed self-evident.

The manager looked at me in some alarm. He felt that I had an awful secret to reveal.

"Come in here," he said, and led the way to a private room. He turned the key.

"We are safe from interruption here," he said, "sit down."

We both sat down and looked at one another. I found no voice to speak.

famous detective agency

"You are one of **Pinkerton's** men, I presume," he said.

He had gathered from my mysterious manner that I was a detective. I knew what he was thinking and it made me worse.

"No, not from Pinkerton's," I said, seemingly to imply that I came from a rival agency. "To tell the truth," I went on, as if I had been prompted to lie about it, "I am not a detective at all. I have come to open an account. I intend to keep all my money in this bank."

famous wealthy families

The manager looked relieved, but still serious; he concluded now that I was a son of Baron **Rothschild,** or a young **Gould.**

"A large account, I suppose," he said.

"Fairly large," I whispered. "I propose to deposit fifty-six dollars now, and fifty dollars a month regularly."

The manager got up and opened the door. He called to the accountant.

"Mr. Montgomery," he said, unkindly loud, "this gentleman is opening an account; he will deposit fifty-six dollars. Good-morning."

I rose.

A big iron door stood open at the side of the room.

"Good-morning," I said, and stepped into the safe.

"Come out," said the manager coldly, and showed me the other way.

a quick, nervous movement

magic

I went up to the accountant's wicket and poked the ball of money at him with a quick, **convulsive** movement as if I were doing a **conjuring** trick.

My face was ghastly pale.

"Here," I said, "deposit it." The tone of the words seemed to mean, "Let us do this painful thing while the fit is on us."

He took the money and gave it to another clerk. He made me write the sum on a slip and sign my name in a book. I no longer knew what I was doing. The bank swam before my eyes.

"Is it deposited?" I asked, in a hollow, vibrating voice.

"It is," said the accountant.

"Then I want to draw a cheque."

My idea was to draw out six dollars of it for present use. Someone gave me a cheque-book through a wicket, and someone else began telling me how to write it out. The people in the bank had the impression that I was an invalid millionaire. I wrote something on the cheque and thrust it in at the clerk. He looked at it.

"What! Are you drawing it all out again?" he asked in surprise. Then I realized that I had written fifty-six instead of six. I was too far gone to reason now. I had a feeling that it was impossible to explain the thing. All the clerks had stopped writing to look at me.

Reckless with misery, I made a plunge.

"Yes, the whole thing."

"You withdraw your money from the bank?"

"Every cent of it."

"Are you not going to deposit any more?" said the clerk astonished.

"Never."

An idiot hope struck me that they might think something had insulted me while I was writing the cheque and that I had changed my mind. I made a wretched attempt to look like a man with a fearfully quick temper.

The clerk prepared to pay the money.

"How will you have it?" he said.

"What?"

"How will you have it?"

"Oh," I caught his meaning and answered without even trying to think, "in fifties."

He gave me a fifty-dollar bill.

"And the six?" he asked dryly.

"In sixes," I said.

He gave it to me and I rushed out.

As the big doors swung behind me I caught the echo of a roar of laughter that went up to the ceiling of the bank. Since then I bank no more. I keep my money in cash in my trousers pocket, and my savings in silver dollars in a sock.

Analyzing the Writer's Strategies

1. Look at the introduction. What is the thesis?
2. When do you first realize that this is a humorous essay? In what places were you most amused? Why?
3. Why is dialogue such a big part of this narration?
4. How many different incidents happen to Leacock in the bank?
5. What are some of the descriptive words the author uses to describe the clerks' and manager's reactions to him?
6. What are some of the words the author uses to describe how the main character looks or talks?

Suggested Topics for Writing

Choose one of the following topics and write a narrative essay of at least five paragraphs to develop that topic. Use the section that follows this list to help you work through the various stages in the writing process.

1. Trying to make a teacher understand my situation
2. Trying to get a parent to listen to my point of view
3. Trying to talk a police officer out of giving me a ticket
4. Trying to convince an interviewer that I should be hired for the job
5. Dealing with an aggressive salesperson
6. Trying to use a pay telephone
7. A mix-up with a friend
8. Trouble at the post office
9. Trying to fill out a complicated application or tax return
10. Trouble dealing with my doctor
11. How my nervousness made matters worse
12. Wanting an evening to go perfectly
13. Making a fool of myself in front of an audience (or class)
14. An embarrassing experience
15. How people make fools of themselves

Writing a Narrative Essay: Being Intimidated by a Person in Authority

1. Getting the Idea

Using the above list of fifteen topics, and/or using ideas of your own, jot down two or three different topics that appeal to you.

_____

_____

_____

From this list of possibilities, select the topic you think would give you the best opportunity for writing. Which one do you feel strongest about? Which one are you the most expert in? Which one is most likely to interest your readers? Which one is best suited to being developed into a college essay?

Your next step is to decide what your controlling idea should be. What is the point you want to make about the experience? Was the confrontation humiliating, absurd, or hilarious?

_____

_____

_____

2. Gathering Information (Brainstorming, or Taking Notes)

Take at least fifteen minutes and jot down everything about your topic that comes into your mind. If your topic is one that you can easily share, brainstorm with other people who can help you think of additional material, including specific details or additional vocabulary words that you will be able to use to give your writing more accuracy, completeness, and depth. If you can, go to the spot where the story takes place and jot down some details, particularly the sensory images that you may have forgotten.

_____

_____

_____

_____

_____

_____

_____

_____

_____

_____

_____

_____

_____

_____

_____

---

3. Selecting and Organizing Material

Review your brainstorming list and cross out any ideas that you decide are not appropriate. Prepare to build on the ideas that you find promising. Put these remaining ideas into an order that will serve as your temporary guide. Keep in mind that in a narrative essay, the order is usually determined by chronology.

Some instructors may require you to work this material into an outline so you can see which ideas are subsidiary to the main points.

---

4. Writing the Rough Draft

At this point in your work, you should not feel that every phrase is set in final form. Many writers feel it is more important to let your mind be relaxed and allow the words to flow freely even if you are not following your plan exactly. Sometimes a period of "free writing" can lead you on to new ideas, ideas that are better than the ones you had in your brainstorming session. Keep in mind that you are free to add ideas, drop others, or rearrange the order of your details at any point. There are an infinite number of possibilities, so it is natural that you will make changes.

5. Revising or Editing

As you work on your rough draft, you may work alone, with a group, with a peer tutor, or directly with your instructor. Here are some of the basic questions you should consider at this most important stage of your work.

a. Does the rough draft **satisfy the conditions for essay** form? Is there an introductory paragraph, **at least three well-developed paragraphs in the body, and a concluding paragraph?** Remember that one sentence is not a developed paragraph. **(One exception to this rule is when you have dialogue** between two people, as you saw in the Stephen Leacock essay. Then each line of dialogue is written as a separate paragraph.)

b. Is your essay a narration? Does it tell a story of one particular incident rather than talk about incidents in general? Where does the action take place? Can the reader see it? What time of day, week, or year is it?

c. Have you put the details of the essay in a certain time order? Find the expressions that show the time sequence.

d. Can you think of any part of the story that is missing and should be added? Is there any material that is irrelevant and should be omitted?

e. Are there sentences or paragraphs that seem to be repetitious?

f. Find several places where you can substitute better verbs or nouns. Add adjectives to give the reader better sensory images.

g. Find at least three places where you can add details, perhaps even a whole paragraph that will more fully describe the person or place that is central to your story.

h. Can you think of a better way to begin or end?

i. Show your draft to at least two other readers and ask for suggestions.

6. Writing the Second Draft

If you have worked hard in revising the rough draft, you will be delighted with the improvements as you write the second draft.

Feedback is an important aid in each of the final stages of writing an essay. A good way to help yourself see your own work better is to put the writing aside for a few days, if you can. Then read what you have written aloud to someone else, or to yourself if no one else is available. You may be very surprised at the number of places in your writing where you will hear the need for a change and indeed make changes even as you read.

7. Proofreading

Check your second draft for

>   misspellings
>   fragments or run-ons
>   incorrect punctuation
>   consistency of voice, tense
>   verb problems
>   agreement
>   parallel structure

8. Typing the Final Copy (see page 331)

9. Checking for Typing Errors (see page 331)

23 Writing the Process Essay

It is your sister's birthday. You have bought her a gift that you must first put together. Carefully following the instructions, you try to assemble the item, but something is wrong. It does not work. Either you have not followed the instructions properly, or the instructions themselves are not clear. All of us have found ourselves in this situation at one time or another. It takes careful thought to write about a process. The writer must not assume the reader knows more than he or she is likely to know.

One example of a "How to . . ." process essay is the one following, by Florence H. Pettit, titled "How to Sharpen Your Knife." The reader can see the amount of explanation needed for this seemingly simple manual process.

If you have never done any whittling or wood carving before, the first skill to learn is how to sharpen your knife. You may be surprised to learn that even a brand-new knife needs sharpening. Knives are never sold honed (finely sharpened), although some gouges and chisels are. It is essential to learn the firm stroke on the stone that will keep your blades sharp. The sharpening stone must be fixed in place on the table, so that it will not move around. You can do this by placing a piece of rubber inner tube or a thin piece of foam rubber under it. Or you can tack four strips of wood, if you have a rough worktable, to frame the stone and hold it in place. Put a generous puddle of oil on the stone — this will soon disappear into the surface of a new stone, and you will need to keep adding more oil. Press the knife blade flat against the stone in the puddle of oil, using your index finger. Whichever way the cutting edge of the knife faces is the side of the blade that should get a little more pressure. Move the blade around three or four times in a narrow oval about the size of your fingernail, going *counterclockwise* when the sharp edge is facing right. Now turn the blade over in the same spot on the stone, press hard, and move it around the small oval *clockwise*, with more pressure on the cutting edge that faces left. Repeat the ovals, flipping the knife blade over six or seven times, and applying lighter pressure to the blade the last two times. Wipe the blade clean with a piece of rag or tissue and rub it flat on the piece of leather strop at least twice on each side. Stroke *away* from the cutting edge to remove the little burr of metal that may be left on the blade.

In the following selection, author Pierre Berton gives an unusually detailed recipe for making what he calls "Klondike Baked Beans."

Exploring the Topic

1. Think of a time when you had to put something together, but you were not given good directions. What did you do?

   _____

   _____

   _____

2. When people write instructions or give directions, what do they usually neglect to keep in mind?

   _____

   _____

   _____

3. Recall a time when you had to explain a process to someone. You might have had to show someone how to get somewhere, or you might have had to write a detailed description of how you did a science experiment. What was the process? Was it hard to explain? Why or why not?

   _____

   _____

   _____

4. What was your worst experience with trying to follow a process? You could have been trying to work something out yourself, or you could have been trying to follow someone else's directions. How did you overcome your difficulty?

   _____

   _____

   _____

The Model Essay: Pierre Berton, "Klondike Baked Beans"

Now we come to my famous (or infamous) formula for Klondike baked beans, the one that disturbed so many people because of its complexity. Well, winter is coming on and these beans will be needed, no matter how complex they seem to be. There is nothing quite like them. They are guaranteed to melt the frostiest heart, bring warmth to the palest cheeks, satisfy the most gnawing hunger, and rekindle the spark of hope in the coldest breast.

The Klondikers carried baked beans frozen solid in their packs and, when the trail grew weary and the stomach cried out for succour, they would chop pieces off with a knife and gnaw at them as they plunged onward. For beans carry a warmth locked within them, and when the human fire burns low, they act as hot coals to send the blood coursing through the veins.

My beans are more exotic than the 1898 variety, and they are not meant to be frozen, but the principle is exactly the same.

I warn you that this is a lengthy task, so fortify yourself in any of the several ways known to cooks the world over. Step One is the simplest: simply take the quantity of navy beans that you require and soak them overnight in cold water.

The next morning, early, Step Two begins: simmer these soaked beans very lightly. Put them over a low heat and throw in a couple of crushed bay leaves, a handful of finely chopped parsley, some crushed garlic, orégano, thyme, chili powder, cloves, and salt. The idea here is to get the beans soft and to impregnate them with a basic flavour.

Let them simmer gently for an hour or two while you go over to the butcher's for some salt pork. Have him cut the pork — or good side bacon will do as well — into large cubes or chunks, the size of marsh-mallows. Get lots of pork; the makers of tinned beans skimp on the stuff, but we don't have to. There's nothing quite so good as pork or bacon cooked to a soft succulence in a frothing mass of beans and molasses.

You can tell if your beans are soft enough by picking a couple out of the pot and blowing on them. If the skins break, you're ready for Step Three. Turn off the heat and drain away the liquid, but for heaven's sake don't throw it away. It is nectar. What you don't use in the finished dish you can always save as soup stock.

Pour the drained beans in a big earthenware casserole and throw in the salt pork. I often serve beans at a party along with a good smoked ham; if you do this throw some of the ham fat in with the beans. Pour it right out of the pan, if you like.

Now we are into Step Three, and it is here that the boys are separated from the men, and the men from the women. Take a few cups of the liquid you poured from the beans and put it in a pot to simmer. Chop up some tomatoes and throw them in the pot with a few shots of chili sauce and a tin of tomato paste. Chop several onions, half of them very fine, so they'll disappear in the brew, and half in chunks, and throw them in. Green onion tops, chopped up, go well, too, if you can get them.

Now season this mixture, tasting carefully as you go, with dry mustard, freshly ground black pepper, Worcestershire sauce, crushed garlic, celery seed, a few squirts of tabasco, and some monosodium glutamate.

When it tastes pungent and hot (remember that the pungency will be cut by the beans) stir in a large quantity of molasses. Most people don't put in enough molasses, and yet this is the essence of all good baked bean dishes. For there comes a critical moment when the sweet-ness of the molasses is wedded to the sharpness of the vegetables and herbs, and it is this subtle flavour, baked indelibly into the beans and mingling with the pork fat, that brings a sparkle to the eyes.

Now pour this bubbling and fragrant syrup over the pot of pork and beans. Put a lid on the pot and bake the beans for several hours in a 250 degree oven. They should bake for at least six hours, but you can bake them much longer if you want. The longer they bake, the better they taste. This gives you time to work up an appetite, shovelling snow, chop-ping logs for the fire and so on.

About half-way through the baking, pull out the pot and taste the beans. *Taste*, I said! Don't eat them all up — they're nowhere near done.

But at this point you ought to check the bouquet. Is it right? Are they too sweet or not sweet enough? Do they need more liquid? Don't let them get too dry.

Fix them up and put them back in for some more baking. One hour before they're ready you perform another important rite. Pour a cup of good sherry over them. Not cooking sherry — but the kind you drink yourself.

Do I see a small bird-like woman in the back row rise and denounce me for spreading debauchery and intoxication through the land? Control yourself, madam. I give you my bond that before this dish is done the alcoholic content of that fortified wine will have vanished, leaving only its delicate flavour behind, fused inseparably with a dish which supplies its own intoxication.

Now take some bacon strips and cover the entire top of the beans. Fifteen minutes before serving, take the lid off the pot so the bacon crispens into a thick crust.

By now you should be close to starvation, for the beans are meant to be devoured only when the tortured stomach pleads for sustenance. Call in your friends. Get some fresh bread with a hard crust. Tear open these loaves and rip out the soft insides. Now open the steaming pot, plunge a ladle through the bacon crust, spoon the bubbling brown beans, the soft globes of pork, and all the attendant juices, into the containers of bread.

Notice that the pork is sweet to the tooth, that the beans while still firm and round are infused with a delirious flavour, and that the simmering sauce is maddening to the palate.

Provide the company with mugs of steaming coffee. Now as you tear ravenously at the bread and feel the piping hot beans begin to woo your taste buds, accept the homage of your friends, for you have earned it. And, as your tired muscles lose their tensions, and the beans begin to come out of your ears, and the day passes into history, give thanks to your Maker for putting beans on this earth and giving men the wit to bake them as they deserve.

Analyzing the Writer's Strategies

1. What method did the writer use for the introduction?
2. What method did he use for the conclusion?
3. How many steps are there to the process as the writer described it?
4. Where, at each step of the process, does the writer give specific examples to make each part of his process clear?

Suggested Topics for Writing

Choose one or more of the following topics and write a process essay of at least six paragraphs to develop that topic.

1. How to get good grades in college
2. How to do well in a job interview
3. How to plan a budget
4. How to buy a used car
5. How to study for a test
6. How to choose the right college
7. How to redecorate a room
8. How to buy clothes on a limited budget
9. How to find the right place to live
10. How to make new friends

Writing the Process Essay: How to . . .

Thousands of books and articles have been written that promise to help us accomplish some goal in life: how to start your own business, how to cook, how to lose weight, how to install your own shower, how to assemble a bicycle. In the essay you are about to write, you will have the opportunity to describe how you once went through a process to achieve a goal of some kind.

1. Getting the Idea

Using the above list of ten topics, and/or using ideas of your own, jot down two or three different topics that appeal to you.

_____

_____

_____

_____

From these two or three topics, select the one that promises to give you the best opportunity for writing. Which one do you feel strongest about? Which one are you the most expert in? Which one is most likely to interest your readers? Which one is best suited to being developed into a college essay?

Your next step is to decide what your controlling idea should be. What is the point you want to make about the process? Is the process tedious, useful, unpredictable, or complicated?

_____

_____

_____

2. Gathering Information (Brainstorming, or Taking Notes)

Take at least fifteen minutes and jot down everything about your topic that comes into your mind. If your topic is one that you can easily share, brainstorm with other people who can help you think of additional material, including specific details or additional vocabulary words that you will be able to use to give your writing more accuracy, completeness, and depth.

_____
_____
_____
_____
_____
_____
_____
_____
_____
_____
_____

3. Selecting and Organizing Material

Review your brainstorming list and cross out any ideas that you decide are not appropriate. Prepare to build on the ideas that you find promising. Put these remaining ideas into an order that will serve as your temporary guide. Keep in mind that in a process essay, the order and completeness of the steps are essential. Some instructors may require you to work this material into an outline so you can see which ideas are subsidiary to the main points.

_____
_____
_____
_____
_____
_____
_____
_____
_____
_____
_____
_____
_____
_____
_____

_____

_____

_____

4. Writing the Rough Draft

At this point in your work, you should not feel that every phrase is set in final form. Many writers feel it is more important to let your mind be relaxed and allow the words to flow freely even if you are not following your plan exactly. Sometimes a period of "free writing" can lead you on to new ideas, ideas that are better than the ones you had in your brainstorming session. Keep in mind that you are free to add ideas, drop others, or rearrange at any point the order of your details. By re-evaluating the logic of your ideas, you will undoubtedly make changes in content and approach.

_____

_____

_____

_____

_____

_____

_____

_____

_____

_____

_____

_____

_____

_____

_____

_____

_____

_____

_____

_____

_____

_____

_____

5. Revising or Editing

As you work on your rough draft, you may work alone, with a group, with a peer tutor, or directly with your instructor. Here are some of the basic questions you should consider at this most important stage of your work.

a.   Does the rough draft satisfy the conditions for essay form? Is there an introductory paragraph, at least three well-developed paragraphs in the body, and a concluding paragraph? Remember that one sentence is not a developed paragraph.
b.   Does this essay show us how to do something specific?
c.   Are the steps in the process in the correct order?
d.   Is any step or important piece of information left out? Is any of the material included irrelevant?
e.   Are there sentences or paragraphs that seem to be repetitious?
f.   Find several places where you can substitute better verbs or nouns. Add adjectives to give the reader better sensory images.
g.   Can you think of a better way to begin or end?
h.   Does the paper flow logically from one idea to the next? Could you improve the paper with better use of transitional devices?
i.   Show your draft to at least two other readers and ask for suggestions.

6. Writing the Second Draft

If you have worked hard in revising the rough draft, you will be delighted with the improvements as you write the second draft.

Feedback is an important aid in each of the final stages of writing an essay. A good way to help yourself see your own work better is to put the writing aside for a few days, if you can. Then read what you have written aloud to someone else or to yourself if no one else is available. You may be very surprised at the number of places in your writing where you will hear a mistake and make a change even as you read.

7. Proofreading

Check your second draft for

> misspellings
> fragments or run-ons
> incorrect punctuation
> consistency of voice, tense
> verb problems
> agreement
> parallel structure

8. Typing the Final Copy (see page 331)

9. Checking for Typing Errors (see page 331)

Writing the Comparison or Contrast Essay

Computer technology is advancing so rapidly that scientists are already discussing the possibility of creating what they call "artificial intelligence," a computer that will be able to duplicate the thinking process of the human mind. In fact, scientists in this country and abroad are now actively designing such a computer. In the following selection from his book *The Morningside Papers*, Peter Gzowski deals with one of the advances in technology by comparing working on a modern word processor with writing using a typewriter.

Exploring the Topic

1. What are some of the jobs that computers can already do better and faster than human beings can?

   _____

   _____

   _____

2. What are some of the jobs you have to do now that you would like a computer to do for you? How many of these jobs do you think a computer will take over in your lifetime?

   _____

   _____

   _____

3. Do you think a computer could ever be programmed to be as creative as the human mind?

   _____

4. In your opinion, are there any dangers in the advanced computer technology we see all around us today?

The Model Essay: Peter Gzowski, "People and Their Machines and Vice Versa"

If I have remembered my own history correctly, it is exactly thirty years ago this week that I arrived in Timmins, Ontario, to begin my life as a newspaperman. Almost every day for those thirty years, I have opened my working procedures the same way, I have cranked a piece of paper into my typewriter, banged out what newspapermen call a slug at the top of the page, usually followed, for reasons I don't know but by a habit I can't break, by the page number typed four or five times, and started pounding away with as many fingers as seemed to fit. Like most old newspapermen, I am as fast as a Gatling gun at my machine, and almost as noisy. I make mistakes — which is like saying Wayne Gretzky gets scoring points — but I strike them out: xxxxxxx or, if I'm really flying, mnmnmnmnmnmn, *m* with the right forefinger, *n* with the left. Afterward, I go over what I've done with the heaviest pencil I can find, changing a word here, a phrase there. I cross out some more, with a bold, black stroke and a flourishing delete sign. I add. Sometimes I make what one of my editors called chicken tracks from the place I had the first thought out into the margin. Out there, I create anew. I scribble up into the bare space at the top, up by the stammering page numbers, and on good days, when my juices are flowing and the ghost of Maxwell Perkins is looking over my shoulder, I carry on from there, turning the page under my pencil, down the outer edges, filling the bottom and off, off into virgin territories, leaving my inky spoor behind me. When I am pleased with what I have done, or when the chicken tracks get too dense to follow, I put a new page in the typewriter and start again. This is not the way anyone taught me to work. But it is the way I have done things. It has served me through five books, more magazine articles than you could shake an art director's ruler at and enough newspaper pieces to line the cage of every eagle that ever flew.

But no more. I am a word-processor man now, or trying to become one. I made the change at the end of this summer. The words I am reading to you now first appeared to my eye etched in green on a dark screen. Or, rather, some *version* of the words I am reading to you now so appeared. "Green," for instance, was "gereen," or perhaps "jereen," until I danced my cursor around the screen (the "screeen?") and obliterated the extra *e*. "Etched," too, is probably the wrong word. The process by which these words appear is too sophisticated for my manually operated mind, and I no more understand it than I understand what really happens when I turn on the ignition of my car. All I know, in fact, are two things: one, I can do it. If I take my time, and think my way through such delicate differences as that between the "control" key and the shift lock, and resist the urge to hit the space bar (which makes sense to me) and instead hit a simultaneous "control" and *d* (which doesn't) when I want to move my little cursor over one notch, I can, however painstakingly, make the words come out in prose. That's one. Two is that I hate doing it. Over the years, the relationship I have built up with my various manuals is an emotional one. I pound them and they respond, as the Steinway responded to Glenn Gould. I knew I was working because I could hear it, and the measure of what I had accomplished in a working day was often the pile of out-takes that grew in my wastepaper basket, like tailings at a mine. Now, I work silently. I wrote what you are hearing now while my daughter slept in the next room. This was convenient for Alison, but it did not seem to me to be what I have always done for a living. It neither sounded nor felt like *writing*. God, it seems to me, no more meant words to appear in fluorescent electronic letters than he meant pool tables to be pink, or golf balls orange.

Analyzing the Writer's Strategies

1. An essay of comparison usually emphasizes the similarities between two subjects, while an essay of contrast emphasizes the differences. With this in mind, is the essay you have just read an essay of comparison or contrast?
2. Does the writer use the alternating method or the block method in writing this essay?
3. Does the writer provide an equal number of details that relate to both the word processor and the typewriter?
4. Specifically, how does the writer compare the word processor with the typewriter?

Suggested Topics for Writing

Compare or contrast:

1. High school classes with college classes
2. Shopping in a mall with shopping in a downtown area
3. Two movies (the acting, the photography, the quality of the story)
4. A friend from your childhood with a present friend
5. Two items you have owned (cars, bicycles, radios)
6. Two stores that sell the same kind of merchandise
7. Two vacation spots
8. Two apartments or houses where you have lived
9. Watching television with reading a book
10. Cooking dinner at home with eating out

Writing the Comparison or Contrast Essay

Every time you go to the grocery store or look in your closet to decide what to wear, you are involved in making comparisons or contrasts. When you have to make a big decision in life, usually the problem involves weighing the advantages and disadvantages of one choice against the advantages and disadvantages of another choice. Should you go to college or get a job? Should you get married now or wait another year? Should you tell that person how upset you are by what he or she did? In all cases, you must compare the two choices to see which seems to be the better one. Making a decision is not easy, just as writing a good comparison or contrast essay is not easy. You have to consider two topics rather than one.

1. Getting the Idea

Using the list of ten topics, and/or using ideas of your own, jot down two or three different topics that are appealing to you.

_____

_____

_____

From these two or three possibilities, select the topic you think would give you the best opportunity for writing. Which one do you feel strongest about? Which one are you the most expert in? Which one is most likely to interest your readers? Which one is best suited to being developed into a college essay?

Your next step is to decide what your controlling idea should be. What is the point you want to make about the comparison or contrast? Is your conclusion that one is better than the other?

_____

_____

_____

2. Gathering Information (Brainstorming or Taking Notes)

Take at least fifteen minutes to jot down everything about your topic that comes into your mind. If your topic is one that you can easily share, brainstorm with other people who can help you think of additional material, including specific details or additional vocabulary words that you will be able to use to give your writing more accuracy, completeness, and depth.

_____

_____

_____

_____

_____

_____

_____

_____

_____

_____

_____

_____

_____

_____

_____

_____

_____

_____

_____

3. Selecting and Organizing Material

Review your brainstorming list and cross out any ideas that you decide are not appropriate. Prepare to build on the ideas that you find promising. Put these remaining ideas into an order that will serve as your temporary guide. Keep in mind that in a comparison or contrast essay, the order is important because it helps the reader to keep the points in mind. Use the block method or the point-by-point method. Some instructors may require you at this point to make an outline. This will help you see which ideas are subsidiary to the main points.

_____

_____

_____

_____

_____

_____

_____

_____

_____

_____

_____

_____

_____

_____

_____

_____

_____

4. Writing the Rough Draft

At this point in your work, you should not feel that every phrase is set in final form. Many writers feel it is more important to let your mind be relaxed and allow the words to flow freely even if you are not following your plan exactly. Sometimes a period of "free writing" can lead you on to new ideas, ideas that are better than the ones you had in your brainstorming session. Keep in mind that you are free to add ideas, drop others, or rearrange at any point the order of your details. By re-evaluating the logic of your ideas, you will undoubtedly make changes in content and approach.

5. Revising or Editing

As you work on your rough draft, you may work alone, with a group, with a peer tutor, or directly with your instructor. Here are some of the basic questions you should consider at this most important stage of your work.

a. Does the rough draft satisfy the conditions for essay form? Is there an introductory paragraph, at least three well-developed paragraphs in the body, and a concluding paragraph? Remember that one sentence is not a developed paragraph. (One exception to this rule is when you have dialogue between two people, as you saw in the Stephen Leacock essay. Then each line of dialogue is written as a separate paragraph.)

b. Did you use the point-by-point method or the block method?

c. What is the point of your comparison or contrast?

d. Is any important comparison or contrast left out? Is any of the material included irrelevant?

e. Are there sentences or paragraphs that seem to be repetitious?

f. Find several places where you can substitute better verbs or nouns. Add adjectives to give the reader better sensory images.

g. Can you think of a better way to begin or end?

h. Does the paper flow logically from one idea to the next? Could you improve the paper with better use of transitional devices?

i. Show your draft to at least two other readers and ask for suggestions.

6. Writing the Second Draft

If you have worked hard in revising the rough draft, you will be delighted with the improvements as you write the second draft.

Feedback is an important aid in each of the final stages of writing an essay. A good way to help yourself see your own work better is to put the writing aside for a few days, if you can. Then, read what you have written aloud to someone else or to yourself if no one else is available. You may be very surprised at the number of places in your writing where you will hear a mistake and make a change even as you read.

7. Proofreading

Check your second draft for

> misspellings
> fragments or run-ons
> incorrect punctuation
> consistency of voice, tense
> verb problems
> agreement
> parallel structure

8. Typing the Final Copy (see page 331)

9. Checking for Typing Errors (see page 331)

Writing Persuasively

What Is Persuasion?

So far, your purpose in various writing assignments in this text has been to describe, narrate, or explain by using various strategies for development. Still another purpose in writing is to persuade. **Persuasion** is the attempt to change the reader's present viewpoint, or at least to convince him or her that your viewpoint is a valid one. Every time you write a paper for a course, you are trying to persuade your teacher that what you are presenting is the correct view of the subject matter. You might want to show that Canadian airlines are among the safest in the world, or that the crime novel is becoming Canada's favourite form of fiction, with many novels set in actual Canadian locales. As you approach such types of assignments, you need to be aware of each part of the persuasion process so that you will be able to use it effectively in your own writing.

You could view all writing as persuasion, since one of the writer's main goals is always to get the reader to see, think, and believe in a certain way. However, **formal persuasion** follows certain guidelines. If you were ever a member of a high school debating team, you would have spent a good deal of time studying this special form. Learning to recognize techniques of persuasion and to use them in your own writing is the subject of this chapter.

Guide to Writing the Persuasive Essay

1. State a clear thesis. Use words such as *must, ought,* or *should.*

We should not ban all handguns.
Canada must reform its prison system.
All provinces should have the same legal drinking age.

2. Use examples. Well-chosen examples are the heart of any essay. Without them, the piece of writing would be flat, lifeless, and unconvincing. Providing a good example for each of your main points will help make a much stronger argument. Examples help your reader *see* what you are talking about.

3. Use opinions from recognized authorities to support your points. One of the oldest methods of supporting an argument is to use one or more persons of authority to support your particular position. People will usually believe what well-known experts claim. You should use carefully chosen experts to help make your position on a topic more persuasive. However, be sure that your authority is someone who is respected in the area you are discussing. For example, if you are arguing that we must end the nuclear arms race, your argument will be stronger if you quote a respected scientist who can accurately predict the consequences of a nuclear war. A famous movie star giving the same information might be more glamorous and get more attention, but he or she would not be as great an authority as the scientist.

4. Answer your critics in advance. When you point out, beforehand, what your opposition is likely to say in answer to your argument, you will be writing from a position of strength. You are letting your reader know that there is another side to the argument you are making. By pointing out this other side and then answering its objections in advance, you are strengthening your own position.

5. Point out the results. Here, you help your reader see what will happen if your argument is (or is not) believed or acted upon as you believe it should be. You should be very specific and very rational when you point out results, making sure that you avoid exaggerations of any kind. For example, if you are arguing against the possession of handguns, it would be an exaggeration to say that "everyone is going to be murdered if the opposition's point of view is listened to" instead of your position.

The following essay concerns physical abuse against women. As you read the essay, look for the major parts of an effective argument: strong thesis, carefully chosen examples, quotations from authorities, answers to the opposition, and predictions. Can you find any weaknesses in the argument?

The Model Essay: Emil Sher, "There Is No Excuse for Physical Abuse"

Last week, Kirby Inwood was given 30 days in jail for assaulting his baby son Misha, and a suspended sentence for assaulting his wife, Tatyana Sidorova. He also received three years' probation.

The storm of publicity surrounding the lengthy trial has left in its wake serious concerns about violence against women and the way the issue is treated by the justice system. But still standing after the storm, with barely a scratch, are men's unshakeable attitudes toward women.

Judge Gordon Hachborn ordered Mr. Inwood to take psychiatric treatment for alcoholism and for his chronic violent tendencies toward women. For those men who have given thought to the issue, it's easy and comforting to portray Mr. Inwood as aberrant, one of the boys who's just a little more wild than most.

That's small comfort to women. In Canada, one in every 10 women who are either married or in a marital-type relationship is assaulted by her husband or partner. The difference between Mr. Inwood and other violent men must seem academic to a woman with a hand around her throat.

But for all our differences, Mr. Inwood and all other men, myself included, are members of the same fraternity. Initiation is painless. The benefits are enormous. Women, we quickly learn, are here to serve all our needs. If we want sexual gratification, we know whom to call. If we need to be nurtured emotionally, we know whom to lean on. If there's a ring around our collar, we know whom to blame.

"I just don't know how much I can take physically before my health breaks," Mr. Inwood stated at the thought of a protracted trial, unaware of his ironic choice of words. Had he lived in England in the nineteenth century, he would have had an easier time of it. Under English law it was legal for a husband to beat his wife, provided the instrument was "a rod not thicker than his thumb."

The laws have changed, but the spirit continues. "Under my thumb," The Rolling Stones' Mick Jagger sang in the song of the same name, "is the squirming dog who's just had her day."

He can hardly be blamed for the abuse of women that occurs in teen relationships, but his lyrics are part of a larger message that is so readily accepted. It's difficult to imagine Mick Jagger singing about the black or the Jew who once pushed him around but is now under his thumb.

They may be just lyrics, but words are an essential part of the artillery men carry in their assault against women. Verbal abuse takes its own toll and leaves a different type of scar. Some men hurl verbal arrows dipped in venom. Most of us use more subtle weapons: there are ten times as many words for a sexually promiscuous female as for a similarly inclined male. Just spend a few minutes in the proverbial locker room.

When defence lawyer Edward Greenspan raised the issue of Ms. Sidorova's past relationships, you could hear the words to a favourite rallying cry of men: she was a loose woman who got what she deserved. So once again it's the woman's fault. It's another version of the song belted out by men who rape: I was provoked. When will men realize that the cuts, welts, and bruises that cover a battered woman's body are not self-inflicted?

From schoolyards to boardrooms, we are taught that might — physical, political, financial — makes right. And we need not fear the consequences. Any man we would have to face — a police officer, lawyer, or judge — would almost certainly share our patronizing attitude toward women.

A man's home, we'd all agree, is his castle. The moat around it ensures that no outsiders interfere with such family concerns as keeping a woman in her place.

In the book *No Safe Place: Violence Against Women and Children* (The Women's Press), a lawyer speaks of our court system and notes that those who sit on the bench might, in fact, hold the very same attitudes as other men who regard women as "second-class citizens, the purveyors of family disharmony and their problems probably lie in the fact that they are just not adequate wives, mothers and women."

Thirty days in jail will not change Mr. Inwood's attitude toward women. Psychiatric treatment may help him. But the institutions that allow him to beat women will remain intact.

It is these economic, political and religious institutions that shape men's attitudes and give tacit approval to the way they behave.

The Kirby Inwood assault trial should not be seen in isolation. Assault must become a "men's issue." Men have a lot to answer for, and must begin to question the assumptions that allow violence against women to happen in the first place. If we don't, little Misha will grow up in a world no different from his father's.

Analyzing the Writer's Strategies

Because Emil Sher's essay deals with a controversial topic, many people may take exception to some of the points Sher makes. However, the writer combines the results of his own experience, his observations, and his reports of facts to convince us that we should take a stand against the physical abuse of women.

The writer first gains our attention by referring to the Kirby Inwood trial in 1988, and uses this trial as a central theme throughout the essay. He summarizes the trial by stating that we should have serious concerns about the social mechanisms that appear to tacitly approve of, or at least allow, violence in the family.

Sher then shifts to a broader perspective, delineating male myths about women, before moving to a historical overview of the problem, and ends this section with a discussion of the image of women conveyed in modern song lyrics. Combined with this is an overtone of moral outrage at traditional attitudes toward women and their roles in society. Even more incredible, to the author, is the attitude conveyed by the Western judicial system toward women. To give credence to his position, Sher quotes from a book written by a lawyer, who comments on the lax attitude of the judicial system toward those who abuse women.

Finally, having made his point clear and having offered a mixture of clearly labelled fact and opinion to support his position, the author concludes by saying that "assault must become a men's issue. Men have a lot to answer for, and must begin to question the assumptions that allow violence against women to happen in the first place."

After reading this essay, do you see any weaknesses or oversights in Sher's logic?

Exercise 1   Using Research Material to Write the Persuasive Essay

Below are several pieces of information on the controversial topic of pollution. Use this information as the basis for your own essay on the topic. You may choose to rely on as many facts as you want, or you may adapt the opinions to agree with your own way of thinking. As you study the list, try to decide in which of your paragraphs you would use each of the facts or opinions you have been given.

1. We are polluting our environment at an alarming rate.
2. Governments and industries appear to be doing little to reduce the pollution levels in the environment.
3. One government scientist criticized most levels of pollution judged acceptable in Canada as "usually far too high."
4. The garbage glut has produced a frantic search for dumps.
5. Metro Toronto dumps 5000 tonnes of garbage daily and is running out of dump space.
6. Hazardous chemicals are still entering the Niagara River from the American side.
7. In 1989, the tanker *Exxon Valdez* ran aground in Prince William Sound near Alaska, spewing massive amounts of oil into the water.
8. Ozone is created when other pollutants, such as those from automobile exhausts, interact with the air in the sun's heat.
9. In its natural state, fifteen to 25 kilometres above the earth, ozone protects us from the sun's ultraviolet rays.

10. Austria, which ran out of dumps years ago and now ships its garbage to Hungary, prohibits packaging that can't be recycled.
11. In the summertime, more and more beaches are being closed because they are polluted.
12. Ear, nose, eye, and throat infections are common reactions after a person swims in polluted water.
13. Newcastle, New Brunswick, has an unusually high cancer rate, thought to be caused by poison in the town's water supply.
14. The U.S. Congress has passed a bill promising cuts in acid rain emissions of between 40 and 50 percent.
15. The United States currently dumps about 10 million tonnes of sulphur dioxide emissions into the atmosphere.

_____

_____

_____

_____

Exercise 2   Writing the Persuasive Essay

Choose one of the following ten topics and write a persuasive essay of at least five paragraphs. Use the guide to persuasive writing on pages 356–57.

Plan your essay on scratch paper. Use the lines that follow the essay topics to write your rough draft.

Essay Topics
Write an argument for or against

1. Females playing on male sports teams
2. Required courses in college
3. Tenure for teachers
4. Expense accounts for business people
5. The use of grades in school
6. **Cancelling a driver's licence for drunk driving**
7. Socialized medicine
8. Hunting for sport
9. The right to commit suicide
10. Violence on television

_____

_____

_____

_____

_____

_____

_____

_____

_____

_____

_____

_____

_____

_____

_____

_____

_____

_____

_____

_____

_____

_____

_____

_____

_____

_____

_____

_____

_____

_____

_____

_____

_____

_____

_____

_____

_____

_____

_____

_____

_____

_____

_____

_____

_____

_____

        Canada's first prime minister, Sir John A. Macdonald (1815–1891), was born in Glasgow, Scotland, and came to Canada in 1820. Even in school he was recognized as a student with rare abilities. A successful lawyer and businessman, he was elected to the Legislative Assembly in 1844 and became a member of the Cabinet in 1847. His political ingenuity, constitutional expertise, and his clear vision of a country united under a strong federal government combined to make him the central player in the deliberations that eventually made Canada a nation. As prime minister (1867–73, 1878–91), he built the country, and proceeded to make it secure by imposing high tariffs on imported American goods and by encouraging westward expansion with the building of the transcontinental railway. The following excerpt from a speech in the Legislative Assembly,

February 6, 1865, displays Macdonald's political and oratorical skills as he pleads the case for the union of the colonies he had worked so hard to bring about.

Model Essay: Sir John A. Macdonald, "Confederation"

The whole scheme of Confederation, as propounded by the Conference, as agreed to and sanctioned by the Canadian Government, and as now presented for the consideration of the people, and the Legislature, bears upon its face the marks of compromise.

Of necessity there must have been a great deal of mutual concession. When we think of the representatives of five colonies, all supposed to have different interests, meeting together, charged with the duty of protecting those interests and of pressing the views of their own localities and sections, it must be admitted that had we not met in a spirit of conciliation, and with an anxious desire to promote this union; if we had not been impressed with the idea contained in the words of the resolution — "That the best interests and present and future prosperity of British North America would be promoted by a Federal Union under the Crown of Great Britain," — all our efforts might have proved to be of no avail. If we had not felt that, after coming to this conclusion, we were bound to set aside our private opinions on matters of detail, if we had not felt ourselves bound to look at what was practicable, not obstinately rejecting the opinions of others nor adhering to our own; if we had not met, I say, in a spirit of conciliation, and with an anxious, overruling desire to form one people under one government, we never would have succeeded. With these views, we press the question on this House and the country.

I say to this House, if you do not believe that the union of the colonies is for the advantage of the country, that the joining of these five peoples into one nation, under one sovereign, is for the benefit of all, then reject the scheme. Reject it if you do not believe it to be for the present advantage and future prosperity of yourselves and your children. But if, after a calm and full consideration of this scheme, it is believed, as a whole, to be for the advantage of this province — if the House and country believe this union to be one which will ensure for us British laws, British connection, and British freedom — and increase and develop the social, political and material prosperity of the country, then I implore this House and the country to lay aside all prejudices, and accept the scheme which we offer. I ask this House to meet the question in the same spirit in which the delegates met it. I ask each member of this House to lay aside his own opinions as to particular details, and to accept the scheme as a whole if he think it beneficial as a whole.

As I stated in the preliminary discussion, we must consider this scheme in the light of a treaty. By a happy coincidence of circumstances, just when an Administration had been formed in Canada for the purpose of attempting a solution of the difficulties under which we laboured, at the same time the Lower Provinces, actuated by a similar feeling, appointed a Conference with a view to a union among themselves, without being cognizant of the position the government was taking in Canada. If it had not been for this fortunate coincidence of events, never, perhaps, for a long series of years would we have been able to bring this scheme to a practical conclusion.

But we did succeed. We made the arrangement, agreed upon the scheme, and the deputations from the several governments represented at the Conference went back pledged to lay it before their governments, and to ask the legislatures and people of their respective provinces to assent to it. I trust the scheme will be assented to as a whole. I am sure this House will not seek to alter it in its unimportant details; and, if altered in any important provisions, the result must be that the whole will be set aside, and we must begin *de novo*. If any important changes are made, every one of the colonies will feel itself absolved from the implied obligation to deal with it as a Treaty, each province will feel itself at liberty to amend it *ad libitum* so as to suit its own views and interests; in fact, the whole of our labours will have been for nought, and we will have to renew our negotiations with all the colonies for the purpose of establishing some new scheme.

I hope the House will not adopt any such a course as will postpone, perhaps for ever, or at all events for a long period, all chances of union. All the statesmen and the public men who have written or spoken on the subject admit the advantages of a union, if it were practicable: and now when it is proved to be practicable, if we do not embrace this opportunity the present favorable time will pass away, and we may never have it again. Because, just so surely as this scheme is defeated, will be revived the original proposition for a union of the Maritime Provinces, irrespective of Canada; they will not remain as they are now, powerless, scattered, helpless communities; they will form themselves into a power, which, though not so strong as if united with Canada, will, nevertheless, be a powerful and considerable community, and it will be then too late for us to attempt to strengthen ourselves by this scheme, which, in the words of the resolution, "is for the best interests, and present and future prosperity of British North America."

If we are not blind to our present position, we must see the hazardous situation in which all the great interests of Canada stand in respect to the United States. I am no alarmist. I do not believe in the prospect of immediate war. I believe that the common sense of the two nations will prevent a war; still we cannot trust to probabilities. The Government and Legislature would be wanting in their duty to the people if they ran any risk. We know that the United States at this moment are engaged in a war of enormous dimensions — that the occasion of a war with Great Britain has again and again arisen, and may at any time in the future again arise. We cannot foresee what may be the result; we cannot say but that the two nations may drift into a war as other nations have done before. It would then be too late when war had commenced to think of measures for strengthening ourselves, or to begin negotiations for a union with the sister provinces.

At this moment, in consequence of the ill-feeling which has arisen between England and the United States — a feeling of which Canada was not the cause — in consequence of the irritation which now exists, owing to the unhappy state of affairs on this continent, the Reciprocity Treaty, it seems probable, is about to be brought to an end — our trade is hampered by the passport system, and at any moment we may be deprived of permission to carry our goods through United States channels— the bonded goods system may be done away with, and the winter trade through the United States put an end to. Our merchants may be obliged to return to the old system of bringing in during the summer months the supplies for the whole year. Ourselves already threatened, our trade interrupted, our intercourse, political and commercial, destroyed, if we do not take warning now when we have the opportunity, and while one avenue is threatened to be closed, open another by taking advantage of the present arrangement and the desire of the Lower Provinces to draw closer the alliance between us, we may suffer commercial and political disadvantages it may take long for us to overcome.

The Conference having come to the conclusion that a legislative union, pure and simple, was impracticable, our next attempt was to form a government upon federal principles, which would give to the General Government the strength of a legislative and administrative union, while at the same time it preserved that liberty of action for the different sections which is allowed by a Federal Union. And I am strong in the belief — that we have hit upon the happy medium in these resolutions, and that we have formed a scheme of government which unites the advantages of both, giving us the strength of a legislative union and the sectional freedom of a federal union, with protection to local interests.

Analyzing The Writer's Strategies

Sir John A. Macdonald's speech is a model of effective persuasion. He begins by stating the situation, that in a spirit of compromise, representatives of the five colonies (only four joined Confederation in 1867 — Nova Scotia, New Brunswick, Quebec, and Ontario; Prince Edward Island joined in 1873), have met to discuss a union of the colonies, a union that would promote "the best interests and future prosperity of British North America . . . under the Crown of Great Britain."

Macdonald issues a challenge, that anyone who does not believe that a union could be advantageous should reject the idea of Confederation. But Macdonald gives a number of reasons why, in answer to his own challenge, the colonies should join together, and effectively puts down any argument that his detractors may have been thinking of.

He also plays on the fears of his listeners. He tells them that if they don't act quickly, a confederation of the Atlantic provinces may be formed that would, while weak, be an effective barrier against a united Canada, and that once this Atlantic union was formed, it would be too late for Canada to include these colonies in Confederation.

Macdonald also plays on another great fear of many people in the colonies at that time, the fear of an invasion by the United States. There were two reasons for people to anticipate an invasion. In the first place, the Civil War was raging in the United States, and there was fear that, because of the American "Manifest Destiny" concept, the northern army would march into British North America.

This was possible because the British were actively supporting the southern states during the Civil War, and an invasion of Canada would have been an effective means of having the British cease their support of the southern enemy. In addition to these concerns, Britain had adopted free trade in 1846, and Canada was no longer a preferred trading partner. An economic as well as a political union with the United States would not have been out of the question.

As well, there was a serious political problem in the colony of Canada. The union of Upper and Lower Canada (Upper Canada became Canada West, then became Ontario after Confederation; Lower Canada was known as Canada East, then Quebec) in 1841 had resulted in the creation of a single legislature for the new colony, Canada. By the 1860s, however, the legislature was barely functioning. No single party could gain enough support from both Anglophones and Francophones to gain a majority. There had been twelve different governments in fifteen years, and Canadian politicians were desperate for a solution.

With this background, it is nothing short of a miracle that Macdonald was able to bring all parties together to discuss the concept of Confederation. If two colonies could not function effectively as a union, how could four or five get along? It was a prime opportunity for the Americans to take advantage of, and had the Civil War not been raging, the Americans might well have moved north.

Therefore, when Macdonald stated that he believed that the form of government agreed upon at that time — a confederation of the five colonies

— was advantageous to all, he had the support of the colonial representatives because of his persuasive argument based on the factual realities of the time. Union would forestall an Atlantic union, the creation of which would effectively block Confederation; union would prevent an American invasion; and union would establish an effective form of government.

We all know how effective Macdonald was. On July 1, 1867, Confederation was achieved through the British North America Act, laying the foundation for the Canada we have today.

Exercise 1 **Using Research Material to Write the Persuasive Essay**

Below are several pieces of information on the controversial topic of mercy killing. Who should make the life-and-death decisions in such matters? Use this information as the basis for your own essay on the topic. You may choose to rely on as many facts as you want, or you may adapt the opinions to agree with your own way of thinking. As you study the list, try to decide in which of your paragraphs you could make use of several of the facts or opinions you have been given.

1. Nearly 4000 Canadians commit suicide every year.
2. The idea of suicide has been rejected by society for many centuries.
3. Some societies discourage suicide by enacting strict laws against it.
4. Mercy killing is an act of charity when there is no hope that the sick person will ever enjoy a healthy life.
5. In the famous Karen Anne Quinlan case, when the life-support system was turned off, she remained alive for nearly ten years.
6. As our technical ability to extend life increases, the pressure on us to make life-and-death decisions will also increase.
7. "Suicide," the famous German poet Goethe said, "is an incident in human life which, however much disputed and discussed, demands the sympathy of every man, and in every age must be dealt with anew."
8. In 1962, Corinne van de Put was born without arms and with deformed feet. Eight days after she was born, her mother killed her.
9. If we had laws that encouraged mercy killing, we would not have the lives of such people as Helen Keller to show the world what handicapped people can do.
10. The general reaction to mercy killing will change as people realize that life should not always go on no matter what the cost may be.
11. The Canadian Medical Association does not support mercy killing.
12. The worst tragedy in life is to live without dignity.
13. People often make "living wills" stating that they should be allowed to die naturally.
14. Years ago, people seldom spoke openly about suicide; now there are organizations that openly advocate it.
15. A very common form of mercy killing occurs when parents and doctors agree not to give retarded newborn children needed medical attention, eventually causing their deaths.

_____

_____

_____

_____

_____

Exercise 2 Writing the Persuasive Essay: Essay Topics

Choose one of the following ten topics and write an essay of at least five paragraphs. Use the five points discussed on **pages 356–57 as a guide** for your writing.

1. Write a strong thesis statement.
2. Provide examples for each of your reasons.
3. Use at least one authority to support your thesis.
4. Admit that others have a different point of view.
5. Indicate the results or predictions in the conclusion.

   Plan your essay on scratch paper, and use the following lines to write your rough draft.

Essay Topics
Argue for or against:

1. Capital punishment
2. Censorship of books or movies
3. Legalized prostitution
4. Continuation of the manned space program
5. Gambling casinos
6. Stricter immigration laws
7. Prayer in the public schools
8. Single-parent adoption
9. Abortion
10. Tax exemptions for religious organizations

_____

_____

_____

_____

_____

_____

_____

_____

_____

_____

_____

_____

_____

_____

_____

The Student Essay: Developing the Essay

Back in Chapter 19 you saw a number of student paragraphs that gave examples of narration, description, comparison and contrast, and process writing. Reprinted below are three student essays, all submitted for the HBJ-Holt College Essay Contest. The first, by Morris Yee from the University of Regina, is an example of a narrative essay. Each essay is followed by a number of questions that ask you to analyze its various components. You will then be given an opportunity to write a narrative essay of your own.

The Model Essay: Morris Yee, "Say Something in Chinese"

"Say something in Chinese." I have yet to comply. I think my refusal stems from the manner in which the question is usually asked. Often it is stated as a command, like "Rover, roll over," or "Spot, fetch the stick." I feel that a reply would debase my intelligence and expose my differences. Perhaps I do not want to reveal my lack of fluency in Chinese, especially my failure to use profanity in another language. Yet, whenever I hear this request to speak Chinese, I remember instantly my Saturday afternoons in Chinese school.

Chinese school was not a real institution. It was a hole in the base-ment of the Chinese Alliance Church on 13th Avenue in Regina. Every Saturday, it was transformed from a sanctuary into a dungeon for every known Chinese-Canadian child in the city. The torture lay not in our forced learning of the secret language, but in the extension of the school week to six days (seven if you include Sunday school.)

Our teacher was Mrs. Pon. Her knowledge of Chinese was limited but her patience was unlimited. She did not speak English but she spoke in our home dialect, which instilled in us a little more respect for her person. However, in class, Cantonese became her game. It was amazing how few students ever won. There were exceptions such as Louie, who broke out and never came back. If memory serves me, he actually advanced to a higher-level class. But the rest of us, out of habit, imitated Mrs. Pon in speech and manner. We really did not grasp the language, since it was all a game consisting of stalemates.

Generally, teaching Chinese meant vigourous repetition. We were taught to copy characters without an inkling of "why" or "how come." Writing became a set pattern of stroke, dot, left, right, up and down. With such ignorance, it was no wonder that illiteracy ran high in China.

Yet even today I remember many of those lessons, although their meaning is as obscure now as it was back then. "Up on the mountain there are cows and sheep. Down from the mountain there are flowers and grass." No one questioned why the cows and sheep were up on the mountain when the flowers and grass were below.

For three hours, we absorbed such absurdity. But no matter how little we managed to memorize, there was always homework assigned. With good intentions, we all promised to do the work during the following week. But somewhere, between Monday and Friday, there was never any time or desire to complete our Chinese studies. It all seemed irrelevant to public school and our pale weekday friends. So by Saturday, we never achieved any further progress in Chinese than that made on any other previous Saturday.

However, by age twelve I began to question this ritual brain thrashing. One Saturday evening, I meekly suggested to my parents that Chinese school was basically a waste of time. Dad replied, "You look Chinese. You can't change that. What are you going to do when someone asks you to say something in Chinese?" I did not answer. I simply quit Chinese school.

Questions

Why can Morris Yee's essay be classified as a narrative?

_____

_____

_____

What is the topic sentence?

_____

_____

What are some supporting details for the topic sentence?

_____

_____

_____

How is the essay structured to convey the main ideas effectively?

_____

_____

_____

What are some of the devices that the author uses to make transitions between paragraphs?

_____

_____

_____

How does the author summarize his essay? Is it effective?

_____

_____

_____

Essay Opportunity: Narration

Relate the events of a particular day when your family faced a crisis. What happened? Give the sequence of events in chronological order. How did different family members react to the situation? What did each one do to resolve the issue? Begin your narration with a setting that establishes the time and place.

_____

_____

_____

_____

_____

_____

_____

_____

_____

_____

_____

_____

_____

_____

_____

_____

_____

_____

_____

_____

_____

_____

_____

_____

_____

_____

_____

_____

_____

_____

_____

_____

_____

_____

_____

_____

The next essay, by Kathleen Darlington from Concordia University, is an example of a comparison/contrast essay.

The Model Essay: Kathleen Darlington, "How to Write an Essay"

After puzzling over the problem of explaining how to write an essay, I thought I might do so most easily by using analogy. Eating is a commonly understood activity, and since I enjoy both eating and cooking, I decided to liken writing an essay to preparing a meal. Now, a meal to some might be a microwave TV dinner, which would be similar, I suppose, to writing for the *Daily News*; however, for this occasion, I will aspire to slightly more literary fare and equate an essay with a least a five-course dinner.

The procedures for making a dinner are much the same as the steps to writing an essay: planning, physical preparation, serving the courses in sequence, and attention to presentation.

A well-prepared meal appears simple and effortless. All serious cooks know this is not so. The illusion of effortlessness is a triumph of planning and organization. First, menus are created around the special tastes of dinner guests; then foods are chosen to complement each other and provide variety of flavour, texture, and visual appeal. Recipes are ferreted out, grocery lists scribbled, utensils and cooking times deliberated, and shopping is done.

A well-prepared essay is also deceptively simple. Similar planning determines a successful piece of writing: content and tone are defined by the prospective reader; then the theme and sequence of the essay are decided. Notes are made, references and writing materials are readied, and time required to complete the project is carefully allotted.

To actually cook food or write an essay takes time. Either one requires familiarity with the material being prepared, the imagination to add variety and originality, and a light touch with additives. A dish, obfuscated under heavy sauces or flavours, is not nearly as delightful as food with its own best qualities revealed by delicate seasoning. So, too, writing may be muddied by too many ideas or tortuous descriptions, and although over-spiced food, alas, cannot be redeemed, writing can.

Dinners and essays follow the same sequences, each having a beginning, middle, and end. The first course, or opening paragraph, is offered as a prelude, to whet the appetite. Following this, a dinner guest may be served a number of substantial main dishes; a reader is given the meat of the essay. Here both cook and writer try to satisfy without satiation, achieving a balance between quantity and variety. Finally dessert and a savoury round out the meal and signal conclusion, lightly enough so the guests will be sorry it's done, while an essay's conclusion is summary, with, hopefully, a similar result.

A beautiful meal is a work of art and deserves an appropriate setting, so to present a suitably aesthetic atmosphere, the paper serviettes are hidden and the table is set with smooth linen, gleaming china, polished silver, and glasses of wine that shine like jewels in the candlelight. Similarly, a good essay is crowned with careful punctuation, graceful description, orderly thought, and legible neatness.

An incidental likeness exists between food and words; or, rather, cooks and essayists: it is possible but unnecessary to possess natural talent. Cooking or writing well can be learned by reading manuals and studying the work of experts. Almost anyone, with practice, can become proficient and may, indeed, achieve a literary feast.

Questions

Is Kathleen Darlington's essay an essay of comparison or contrast? Why?

_____

_____

_____

Normally essays beginning with "how to" or with "how to" in the title might be considered process essays. Could this be considered a process essay as well as a comparison or contrast essay?

_____

_____

_____

_____

What things are compared or contrasted in this essay?

_____

_____

Is the use of analogy effective? Why?

_____

_____

_____

_____

How are transitions between paragraphs used by the author?

_____

_____

_____

Is the conclusion of the essay effective? Why or why not?

_____

_____

_____

Essay Opportunity: Comparison or Contrast

Write an essay in which you compare or contrast two people you know, or two people you have observed in a peculiar situation. In addition to people, your subjects could include comparison or contrast of two kinds of schools, two political parties, two jobs, or two hobbies.

_____

_____

_____

_____

_____

_____

_____

_____

_____

_____

_____

_____

_____

_____

_____

_____

_____

_____

_____

_____

_____

_____

_____

_____

_____

_____

_____

_____

_____

_____

This essay, by Carol Marsel of the University of Victoria, is a persuasive essay, intended to convince the reader of something.

The Model Essay: Carol Marsel, "Environmentalism"

Our environment includes land, sea, and air, and all things that inhabit them. With the growing populations of the earth, the balance of our ecological system is becoming more and more difficult to maintain. It is this fragile balance of nature I am concerned with, and would like to discuss.

Nature consists of plants and animals, and their relationships with people. Plants and animals, when free from interference by people, seem to have a well-balanced interdependence. Animals that graze on plants fertilize the soil with their waste products, as well as their bodies when they die. In a sense, they feed one another. In this manner, both survive and contribute to each's life cycle. Too little plant life will result in too little food for the animals, which, in turn, results in fewer animals surviving and, eventually, less stress on plants. This then allows the plants to replenish their numbers and once again become abundant.

Natural disasters and diseases account for significant upsets in the ecosystem. Such infestations by pine bark beetles and spruce budworms can take a tremendous toll on trees. Forest fires can alter the habitat so greatly that it takes several decades for growth to resume. These occurrences are part of nature and contribute to the way in which our environment is balanced or unbalanced.

The more complex component of the ecological system is the human race, and there are three ways in which it interacts with nature. The first is people living. We need air to breathe, food to eat, clothing to wear, and shelter to keep us warm. These are necessities. Other activities, such as driving cars, may be desirable, but not essential. Just to maintain our biological functions is complex. We must find ways to dispose of garbage and sewage. Environmentalists are exploring the ways in which we can do this, without harming the components of nature. Disposing of garbage in large cities, such as Vancouver, poses a difficult problem. Because of the tremendous amount of wastes accumulated, its citizens must find alternate areas in which to place its garbage. Many citizens of Cache Creek are not at all pleased that their town has been chosen as a dumping site for Vancouver's garbage. Vancouver long ago ran out of places to bury its waste. Burning of most garbage is no longer acceptable, because we are now discovering that harmful chemicals and other pollutants are often released into the atmosphere.

Sewage disposal is also becoming more difficult. Just recently, Victoria's newspaper was filled with pre-election promises by political candidates who vowed to look into better sewage treatment systems. Raw sewage being pumped out to sea, which is current practice in many ports like Victoria, has contributed to an upset in the balance of the oceanic ecosystem. In addition to the harmful effects the raw sewage has on aquatic life, the temperature of the ocean has been affected, and the inclusion of various chemicals and nutrients has altered the living conditions on the ocean floor.

The second way in which people interact with the environment is in how we earn our living. To have money to buy the things we need to survive, we eke out our livelihood by performing a variety of tasks. When we thoughtlessly perform our jobs, disregarding the environment around us, we often change drastically, or even destroy, elements in nature. A logger who clear-cuts large tracts of land, leaving it barren, can damage the area so that the soil may be irreversibly depleted, leaving it vulnerable to erosion. Valuable nutrients are carried away, leaving the soil unable to support plant life. Devoid of plants, the area does not attract animals which may carry seeds in their excrement. The cycle continues until the land will no longer support plants or animals. People who practise these same irresponsible habits in mining harm the ecosystem in much the same way. Thousands of hectares of land are gouged away, leaving gaping holes and mounds of unproductive rock. Environmentalists focus their attention on problems such as these.

Factories and industrial firms are often not aware of, or not concerned with, the disposal of their wastes. Some are buried. Some are stockpiled, waiting for a better place to be stored. More often than not, we find that harmful toxins have escaped into the soil from these storage systems. Many production methods in factories result in the release of harmful air pollutants, which have contributed to the breakdown of our protective ozone layer and effected a "green-house," or warming tendency. This heating of the earth will have a great impact on ports and shorelines as some of the ice caps melt and the oceans rise. The warming alone will alter the growing season of crops, like apples, for example, which need a short cold spell at the end of their growth to produce crisp, red fruit. These changes, too, are environmentalism.

The third manner in which people co-exist with nature is what we do for recreation. We hike, ski, bike, and ride through the woods. In carrying out our activities, we do not always consider the needs of nature. We ride our snow machines over the dens of sleeping bears, often disturbing their hibernation, sometimes causing premature birth of cubs or aborted fetuses. We build ski tows and sky trains high into the realm of birds who are unused to the noise and intrusion. We thoughtlessly drive our all-terrain vehicles through previously inaccessible destinations, to disturb and disrupt the quietude of elk, deer, and grizzly bear. Examining how we play is also environmentalism.

There is nothing that does not contribute to the balance of our ecological system. Nothing we do is not involved with the way the world turns. What we eat, where we sleep, how we play, and how we work, all contribute to the operation of our planet. Eating, playing, and working in greater and greater numbers affects the earth more quickly, and in greater ways, but all we do, in some small way, touches our environment. If there are too many of us, and we breathe too much air, the system will cease to support us. If we grow too much of one crop, we deplete the soil of one set of nutrients, eventually affecting all other growing systems. If we release too much of one chemical, from our factories, into the air, we upset the balance in the atmosphere. There is nothing that we do, nothing that we eat or breathe, that does not contribute to the state of our planet, and therefore to environmentalism.

Questions

Does the thesis statement reveal the author's position on the subject she is going to write about?

_____

_____

_____

How does the author reinforce her thesis statement?

_____

_____

_____

Does the author use any authorities to reinforce her position?

_____

_____

_____

Are any objections to the author's position pointed out and dealt with in the essay?

_____

_____

_____

Does the author convince you that her position on the matter of environmentalism is the right one? Why or why not?

_____

_____

Essay Opportunity: Writing Persuasively

Write an essay in which you convince another person that a particular decision or a certain action is the right thing to do. For example, you might want to persuade a teacher to extend the deadline for a term paper, or you might want to convince a friend not to drop out of school.

_____

_____

_____

27 Writing under Pressure

Most people prefer to do their writing when they have the time to develop their subject, but it often happens that you do not have the chance to write and revise as you would like. Sometimes you have to write under pressure. For example, you may be given a last-minute assignment that must be done right away, or what is even more likely, you have to produce an in-class written examination for a course you are taking.

No matter what the circumstances are, you want to be able to do the best writing you can with the time you are given. For example, if you are given an essay question for a final examination in a course, your first step should *not* be to begin writing. Instead, you should take a few moments to analyze the question you have been given. What does the question require you to do? Is there more than one part to the question? Does the professor want you to *define* a term or *compare* two historical figures or *narrate* the story of your search for the right part-time job? Furthermore, how many points is the question worth? How much time do you have to spend on the question?

Study the following sample essay question to determine exactly what is being asked for:

> Describe the rise of the feminist movement in the 1960s in Canada. Be specific.

If this were one of five short essay questions on a final examination, the following answer would probably be adequate.

> The late 1960s saw, in Canada as throughout the Western world, the emergence of a new women's movement. This new feminism rejected all limits to the equality of women's rights and showed that equality in daily life could not be obtained through simple legal, political, or institutional modifications. Discovering that "sisterhood is powerful," women from Vancouver to Halifax began forming groups. The Vancouver Women's Caucus was organized in 1968. The Montreal Women's Liberation Move-

ment was founded in 1969, and the Front de libération des femmes du Québec published a feminist manifesto in 1970. At first, some were consciousness-raising groups, but others quickly turned to concrete action, providing abortion services, health centres, militant theatre, day-care, shelters for battered women, rape crisis centres, and they began agitating for equal pay. By the end of the 1960s, Canada had begun to adjust to the rebirth of a major social movement.

Guide to Answering the Essay Question

1. Read the question over again. How many points is it worth? Decide how much time you should spend answering it.
2. What is the method of development asked for?
3. From key words in the question, compose your thesis statement.
4. Answer the question using several specific details (include names and dates of important facts).
5. Check the question again to be sure all parts of the question have been answered. (A question can have more than one part.)

Frequently Used Terms in Essay Questions

Definition: A definition is the precise meaning of a word or term. When you define something in an essay, you usually write an *extended definition*, in which you select an appropriate example or examples to illustrate the meaning of a term.

Comparison or Contrast: When you *compare* two people or things, you point out the similarities between them. When you *contrast* two items, you point out the differences. Sometimes you may find yourself using both comparison and contrast in an essay.

Narration: Narration is the telling of a story by the careful use of a sequence of events. The events are usually (but not always) told in chronological order.

Summary: When you write a summary, you are supplying the main ideas of a longer piece of writing.

Discussion: This is a general term that encourages you to analyze a subject at length. Inviting students to discuss some aspect of a topic is a widely used method of asking examination questions.

Of course, answering an essay question correctly depends largely on the work you have done preparing for the test. To study for an essay exam, you should try to anticipate questions the teacher is likely to ask. Then prepare the information you need to have in order to answer these questions. Unlike the multiple-choice or true/false test, the essay examination requires that you have absorbed the material so well that you can give it back in your own words.

Exercise 1   Methods of Development

Each of the following college essay questions deals with the single topic of computers. Use the above list of explanations to help you decide which method of development is being called for in each case. In the space provided after each question, identify the method being required.

1. Tell the story of the first time you encountered a computer. Did you first see a computer at school, at work, or in a friend's home? What was your

reaction to this new technology? What did you learn about computers at this first encounter?

Method of development: _____

2. Point out the similarities and differences between computer use in the home and at school. In how many ways are these uses similar? In how many ways are they different?

Method of development: _____

3. Analyze the present role of computers in society.

Method of development: _____

4. List and explain the uses of computers in school, at work, and at home.

Method of development: _____

5. Write a condensed account of the history of computers, from the time they were invented up to the present day.

Method of development: _____

Exercise 2 Methods of Development / Parts of a Question

Each of the following questions is an example of an essay question that could be asked in different college courses. In the spaces provided after each question, indicate: (a) what method of development (definition, comparison or contrast, narration, summary, or discussion) is being called for; (b) how many parts there are to the question. This indicates how many parts there will be in your answer.

1. What does the term *sociology* mean? Include in your answer at least four different meanings the term *sociology* has had since this area of study began.

Method of development: _____

The different parts of the question: _____

_____

_____

2. Compare the reasons Canada entered the Korean War with the reasons it entered World War II.

Method of development: _____

The different parts of the question: _____

_____

_____

3. Trace the history of our knowledge of the planet Jupiter, from the time it was first discovered until the present day. Include in your answer at least one nineteenth-century discovery and three of the most recent discoveries that have been made about Jupiter through the use of unmanned space vehicles sent near that planet.

Method of development: _____

The different parts of the question: _____

_____

4. Contrast baseball and soccer.

   Method of development: _____

   The different parts of the question: _____

   _____

5. Explain the three effects of high temperatures on space vehicles as they re-enter the earth's atmosphere.

   Method of development: _____

   The different parts of the question: _____

   _____

6. What was the complete process of building the transcontinental railway? Include in your answer six different aspects of the construction, from laying the rails across the Canadian Shield to the effects of the Riel Rebellion.

   Method of development: _____

   The different parts of the question: _____

   _____

7. Trace the history of the English language from its beginnings to the present day. Divide the history of the language into at least three different parts, using Old English, Middle English, and Modern English as your main divisions.

   Method of development: _____

   The different parts of the question: _____

   _____

8. Discuss the events that led up to World War I. Be sure to include both the political and social problems of the time that directly and indirectly led to the war.

   Method of development: _____

   The different parts of the question: _____

   _____

9. Summarize the four theories that have been proposed as to why dinosaurs became extinct 65 million years ago.

   Method of development: _____

   The different parts of the question: _____

   _____

   _____

10. Define the term *monarchy* and discuss the relevance or irrelevance of this form of government in today's world.

    Method of development: _____

    The different parts of the question: _____

    _____

    _____

Using the Thesis Statement in Essay Questions

One of the most effective ways to begin an essay answer is to write a thesis statement. Your thesis statement should include the important parts of the question and should also give a clear indication of the approach you intend to take in your answer. Writing your opening sentence in this way gives you a real advantage as your professor begins to read your work because from the beginning of your essay, it is clear *what* you are going to write about and *how* you are going to treat your subject.

For example, suppose you were going to write an essay on the following topic:

> A woman prime minister could handle the demands of the most stressful job in the country.

An effective way to write your opening sentence would be to write the following thesis sentence:

> I agree that a woman prime minister could handle the demands of the most stressful job in the country.

The reader would then know that this was indeed the topic you had chosen and would also know how you intended to approach that topic.

Exercise 3 **Writing Thesis Statements**

Rewrite each of the following essay questions in thesis statement form. Read each question carefully and underline the important words or phrases in it. Then decide on the approach you would take in answering that question. An example has been done for you.

> *Essay question:* How does one learn another language?

> *Thesis statement:* The process of learning another language is complicated but usually follows four distinct stages.

1. Essay question: Discuss the effects of free trade on Canada's economy.

    Thesis statement: _____

    _____

2. Essay question: What are the effects of TV violence on children?

    Thesis statement: _____

    _____

3. Essay question: Trace the development of portrait painting from the Middle Ages to today.

   Thesis statement: _____

   _____

4. Essay question: What are the major causes for the economic crisis facing the African nations today?

   Thesis statement: _____

   _____

5. Essay question: What have we recently learned from ocean exploration, and what remains to be done?

   Thesis statement: _____

   _____

6. Essay question: Is it harmful or beneficial to adopt a child from one culture and raise that child in another culture?

   Thesis statement: _____

   _____

7. Essay question: In what ways does the new Japan differ from the old Japan?

   Thesis statement: _____

   _____

8. Essay question: What four countries depend on tourism for the major part of their national income and why is this so?

   Thesis statement: _____

   _____

9. Essay question: What factors should a college use when judging the merits of a particular student for admission?

   Thesis statement: _____

   _____

10. Essay question: What is Alzheimer's disease, its sequence of characteristic symptoms, and the current methods of treatment?

    Thesis statement: _____

    _____

Appendices

A Parts of Speech

Words can be divided into eight categories called **parts of speech.** Understanding these categories will help you work with language more easily, especially when it comes to revising your own writing.

1. A **noun** is a word that names persons, places, or things.

Common Nouns	Proper Nouns
officer	Michael Johnson
station	Union Station
magazine	*Canadian Geographic*

    Nouns are said to be **concrete** if you can see or touch them.

    > window
    > paper
    > river

    Nouns are said to be **abstract** if you cannot see or touch them. These words can be concepts, ideas, or qualities.

    > meditation
    > honesty
    > carelessness

    To test for a noun, it may help to ask these questions.

    - Can I make the word plural? (Most nouns have a plural form.)
    - Can I put the article *the* in front of the word?
    - Is the word used as the subject or object of the sentence?

2. A **pronoun** is a word used to take the place of a noun. Just like a noun, it is used as the subject or object of a sentence. Pronouns can be divided into several classes. Here are some of them:

Pronouns

Personal Pronouns	Relative Pronouns
I, me	who, whom, whose
you	which
he, she, it	that
we, us	what
they, them	whoever, whichever

Demonstrative Pronouns	Indefinite Pronouns
this	all, both, each, one
that	nothing, nobody, no one
these	anything, anybody, anyone
those	something, somebody, someone
	everything, everybody, everyone

3. An **adjective** is a word that modifies a noun or pronoun. Adjectives usually come before the nouns they modify, but they can also come after the verb.

> The *unusual* package was placed on my desk.
> The package felt *cold*.

4. A **verb** is a word that tells what a subject is doing as well as the time (past, present, or future) of that action. Verbs can be divided into three classes:

Action Verbs

> The athlete *runs* ten kilometres every morning.
> (The action takes place in the present.)

> The crowd *cheered* for the oldest runner.
> (The action takes place in the past.)

Linking Verbs

A linking verb joins the subject of a sentence to one or more words that describe or identify the subject.

> He *was* a dancer in his twenties.
> She *seemed* disappointed with her job.

Common Linking Verbs

be (am, is, are, was, were, have been)	
act	grow
appear	look
become	seem
feel	taste

Helping Verbs (also called "auxiliaries")

A helping verb is any verb used before the main verb.

It could show the tense of the verb:

> It *will* rain tomorrow. (Shows future tense.)

It could show the passive voice:

> The new civic centre *has been* finished.

It could give a special meaning to the verb:

> Anne Murray *may be* singing there tonight.

Common Helping Verbs

can, could
may, might, must
shall, should
will, would
forms of the irregular verbs *be*, *have*, and *do*

5. An **adverb** is a word that modifies a verb, an adjective, or another adverb. It often ends in *-ly*, but a better test is to ask yourself if the word answers the question how, when, or where.

    The student walked *happily* into the classroom.

- The adverb *happily* answers the question "How?"
- It ends in *-ly*, and it modifies the verb *walked*.

    It will be *very* cold tomorrow.

- The adverb *very* answers the question "How?"
- It modifies the adjective *cold*.

    Winter has come *too* early.

- The adverb *too* answers the question "How?"
- It modifies the adverb *early*.

    Here are some adverbs to look out for:

Adverbs of Frequency	*Adverbs of Degree*
often	even
never	extremely
sometimes	just
seldom	more
always	much
ever	only
	quite
	surely
	too
	very

6. A **preposition** is a word used to relate a noun or pronoun to some other word in the sentence. The preposition with its noun or pronoun is called a prepositional phrase.

    The letter is *from* my father.
    The envelope is addressed *to* my sister.

    Read through the following list of prepositions several times so that you will be able to recognize them. Your instructor may ask you to memorize them.

Common Prepositions

about	below	in	since
above	beneath	inside	through
across	beside	into	to
after	between	like	toward
against	beyond	near	under
along	by	of	until
among	down	off	up
around	during	on	upon
at	except	outside	with
before	for	over	within
behind	from	past	without

7. A **conjunction** is a word that joins or connects other words, phrases, or clauses.

    Connecting two words:

    Sooner *or* later, you will have to pay.

    Connecting two phrases:

    The story was on the radio *and* in the newspaper.

    Connecting two clauses:

    Dinner was late *because* I had to work overtime at the office.

Conjunctions

Co-ordinating Conjunctions	*Subordinating Conjunctions*
and	after
but	although
or	as, as if, as though
nor	because
for (meaning "because")	before
yet	how
so	if, even if
	provided that
	since
	unless
	until
	when, whenever
	where, wherever
	while

Correlative Conjunctions

either . . . or
neither . . . nor
both . . . and
not only . . . but also

Adverbial Conjunctions (also known as "conjunctive adverbs")

To add an idea: furthermore
                moreover
                likewise
To contrast: however
             nevertheless
To show results: consequently
                 therefore
To show an alternative: otherwise

8. An **interjection** is a word that expresses a strong feeling and is not connected grammatically to any other part of the sentence.

    Oh, I forgot my keys.
    Well, that means I'll have to sit here all day.

•   Since one word can function differently or have different forms or meanings, you must often study the context in which the word is found to be sure of its part of speech.

    The parent makes sacrifices *for* the good of the children.

    In this sentence, *for* is a preposition.

    The parent sacrificed, **for** the child needed a good education.

    In this sentence, *for* is a conjunction meaning "because."

Exercise 1   Parts of Speech

In the sentences below, identify the part of speech for each underlined word. Choose from the following list:

a.   noun
b.   pronoun
c.   adjective
d.   verb
e.   adverb
f.   preposition
g.   conjunction

_____   1.   The young man <u>pocketed</u> the change.

_____   2.   Unfortunately, he had a hole in his <u>pocket</u>.

_____   3.   He lost his <u>pocket</u> knife as well as his change.

_____   4.   Agatha changed her mind <u>rather</u> suddenly.

_____   5.   She slipped <u>quietly</u> out of the room.

_____   6.   Driving <u>fast</u>, she arrived home before her friend.

_____   7.   <u>Everyone</u> agrees with the basic concept.

_____   8.   <u>Between</u> you and me, I don't think the idea will work.

_____   9.   The young doctor tried to help the <u>victims</u> of the fire.

_____   10.   His hands were numb, <u>for</u> the air was frigid.

Exercise 2   Parts of Speech

Below are three words. Each word can function differently. Write sentences using the given words in the ways suggested. An example is done for you.

corrupt

Noun: The <u>corruption</u> of the local police caused a scandal.

Adjective: The entire force was not <u>corrupt</u>.

Verb: One individual <u>corrupted</u> two others.

1.   spot

Noun: _____

Verb: _____

Adjective: _____

2.   time

Noun: _____

Verb: _____

Adverb: _____

3.   like

Preposition: _____

Verb: _____

Adjective: _____

Adverb: _____

Exercise 3 Parts of Speech

In the following sentences, identify the part of speech for each underlined word. Choose from:

a. noun
b. pronoun
c. adjective
d. verb
e. adverb
f. preposition
g. conjunction

_____ 1. Smiling cautiously <u>at</u> us, the child accepted the gift.

_____ 2. The toy was <u>inexpensive</u>.

_____ 3. Everyone was waiting for the <u>decision</u> of the committee.

_____ 4. The director <u>looked</u> as if he had the answer.

_____ 5. A <u>feeling</u> of anticipation was in the air.

_____ 6. The manager is finishing his <u>monthly</u> report.

_____ 7. <u>For</u> your own sake, eat a good breakfast.

_____ 8. The authorities managed to capture the criminal, <u>but</u> they may not be able to convict him.

_____ 9. Alisha is <u>seldom</u> late for class.

_____ 10. This detective book is <u>thrilling</u> from beginning to end.

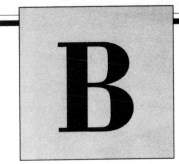

B Solving Spelling Problems

Learning to Spell Commonly Mispronounced Words

Several common English words are often mispronounced or pronounced in such a way that the result is incorrect spelling. Below are 60 common words that are often misspelled. As you study them, be careful to spell each of the underlined syllables correctly.

I. The Common Omission of Vowels

1. Do not omit the underlined syllable with the *a*:

accident<u>al</u>ly	liter<u>a</u>ture
basi<u>cal</u>ly	mini<u>a</u>ture
bound<u>a</u>ry	sep<u>a</u>rate
extra<u>or</u>dinary	temper<u>a</u>ment
incident<u>al</u>ly	temper<u>a</u>ture

2. Do not omit the underlined syllable with the *e*:

consid<u>e</u>rable	math<u>e</u>matics
diff<u>e</u>rence	num<u>e</u>rous
fun<u>e</u>ral	scen<u>e</u>ry
int<u>e</u>resting	

    However, notice the following words in which the *e* should be omitted:

disaster	*becomes*	disast<u>r</u>ous
enter	*becomes*	ent<u>r</u>ance
hinder	*becomes*	hind<u>r</u>ance
hunger	*becomes*	hung<u>r</u>y
launder	*becomes*	laund<u>r</u>y
monster	*becomes*	monst<u>r</u>ous
remember	*becomes*	rememb<u>r</u>ance

3. Do not omit the underlined syllable with the *i*:

asp<u>i</u>rin
fam<u>i</u>ly
sim<u>i</u>lar

4. Do not omit the underlined syllable with the *o*:

choc<u>o</u>late   hum<u>o</u>rous
envir<u>o</u>nment   lab<u>o</u>ratory
fav<u>o</u>urite   soph<u>o</u>more

5. Do not omit the underlined syllable with the *u*:

lux<u>u</u>ry
acc<u>u</u>racy

6. Do not omit the underlined syllable with the *y*:

stud<u>y</u>ing

II. Omission of Consonants

1. ***b***   5. ***n***
proba<u>b</u>ly   gover<u>n</u>ment

2. ***c***   6. ***r***
ar<u>c</u>tic   Feb<u>r</u>uary
library
3. ***d***   su<u>r</u>prise
can<u>d</u>idate
han<u>d</u>kerchief   7. ***t***
han<u>d</u>some   authen<u>t</u>ic
suppose<u>d</u> to   iden<u>t</u>ical
use<u>d</u> to   iden<u>t</u>ity
par<u>t</u>ner
4. ***g***   promp<u>t</u>ly
reco<u>g</u>nize   quan<u>t</u>ity

III. Common Addition of a Syllable:

athlete
athletic

IV. Common Transposition of Letters.

tra<u>ge</u>dy
p<u>er</u>form
p<u>er</u>suade
p<u>re</u>fer

Exercise 1 Words Commonly Mispronounced

Circle the correct spelling for each of the following words.

1. seperate   seprate   separate
2. probably   probaly   probly
3. ardic   arctic   artic
4. suprise   saprize   surprise
5. tragedy   tradgedy   trajedy
6. quantity   quantidy   quanity
7. litrature   literature   literture

8.	hungery	hungary	hungry
9.	handsome	hansome	handsom
10.	favourite	faverite	favrite

Exercise 2 Words Commonly Mispronounced

Fill in each of the following blanks with an appropriate word from the list of commonly mispronounced words.

1. The first free public _____ was in Saint John, New Brunswick.

2. The second month of the year is _____.

3. The federal _____ collects taxes.

4. Are these emeralds _____ or are they just glass?

5. Never go swimming alone; always have a _____.

6. The orchestra will _____ a Beethoven symphony.

7. Madame Curie was doing research in her _____ when she heard the news about the discovery.

8. Jessica and Jill are _____ twins.

9. He is never late; he arrives _____.

10. The _____ was made of Irish linen.

Exercise 3 Words Commonly Mispronounced

Fill in the correct letters to complete the spelling of these words commonly mispronounced.

1. asp____in
2. disast____ous
3. fam____ly
4. ath____ete
5. math____matics
6. bound____ry
7. mini____ture
8. reco____nize
9. soph____more
10. use____ to

Learning to Spell *ie* or *ei* Words

Use this rhyme to help you remember how to spell most *ie* and *ei* words:

> *i* before *e*
> except after *c*
> or when sounded like *a*
> as in *neighbour* or *weigh*.

i before *e*
  The majority of all the *ie* or *ei* words use *ie*.

> believe
> chief
> friend
> shriek
> yield

except after *c*

> ceiling
> conceit
> conceive
> receipt
> receive

or when sounded like *a*

> beige
> eight
> reins
> sleigh
> vein

Once you have learned the rhyme, concentrate on learning the following groups of words that are the exceptions to this rhyme.

caffeine	leisure	ancient
codeine	seizure	conscience
protein	seize	efficient
		sufficient
neither	height	
either	Fahrenheit	
	counterfeit	
sheik	foreign	
stein		
their		
weird		

Exercise 1   *ie* and *ei* Words

Choose the correct combination of *ie* or *ei* in the following words.

1. sl____gh
2. bel____ve
3. s____ge
4. v____l
5. l____sure
6. dec____t
7. n____ce
8. w____ght
9. prot____n
10. anc____nt

Exercise 2   *ie* and *ei* Words

Choose the correct combination of *ie* or *ei* in the following words.

1. for____gn
2. r____ndeer
3. perc____ve
4. f____nd
5. br____fcase
6. ach____ve
7. misch____f
8. rel____ve
9. h____ght
10. y____ld

Exercise 3   *ie* and *ei* Words

Choose the correct combination of *ie* or *ei* in the following words.

1. p____ce
2. p____
3. fr____ght
4. dec____ve
5. effic____nt
6. rec____pt

7. n_____ther   9. th_____f
8. n_____ghbour   10. Fahrenh_____t

Forming the Plurals of Nouns

Almost all nouns can be made plural by simply adding -s to the singular form:

| girl | *becomes* | girls |
| dinner | *becomes* | dinners |

However, each of the following groups of words has its own special rule for forming the plural.

1. **Words ending in -y:**

   In words ending in -y preceded by a *consonant*, change the y to i and add *es*.

   | lady | *becomes* | la*dies* |
   | ceremo*ny* | *becomes* | ceremo*nies* |

   Words ending in -y preceded by a *vowel* form their plurals in the regular way by just adding -s.

da*y*	*becomes*	days
monke*y*	*becomes*	monkeys
valle*y*	*becomes*	valleys

   Practice   In the spaces provided, write the plural form of each of these singular nouns:

   turkey   _____

   candy   _____

   play   _____

   gypsy   _____

   delivery   _____

2. **Words ending in -o:**

   Most words ending in -o preceded by a consonant add -es to form the plural.

her*o*	*becomes*	her*oes*
potat*o*	*becomes*	potat*oes*
ech*o*	*becomes*	ech*oes*

   However, musical terms or names of musical instruments add only -s.

pian*o*	*becomes*	pianos
sol*o*	*becomes*	solos
sopran*o*	*becomes*	sopranos

   Words ending in -o preceded by a *vowel* add -s.

pat*io*	*becomes*	patios
rad*io*	*becomes*	radios
rod*eo*	*becomes*	rodeos

   Some words ending in -o may form their plural with -s or -es.

memen*to*	*becomes*	mementos	or	memen*toes*
pin*to*	*becomes*	pintos	or	pin*toes*
zer*o*	*becomes*	zeros	or	zer*oes*

If you are uncertain about the plural ending of a word ending in -*o*, it is best to use the dictionary. The dictionary gives all the endings of irregular plurals. If no plural form is given, you know the word will form its plural in the regular way by adding only -*s*.

Practice In the spaces provided, write the plural form of each of these singular nouns:

banjo _____

stereo _____

torpedo _____

studio _____

embargo _____

3. **Words ending in -*ch*, -*sh*, -*s*, -*x*, and -*z*:**
   For words ending in -*ch*, -*sh*, -*s*, -*x*, and -*z*, add -*es*.

   witch*es*
   dish*es*
   dress*es*
   tax*es*
   buzz*es*

Practice In the spaces provided, write the plural form for each of these singular nouns:

dish _____

success _____

flash _____

box _____

peach _____

4. **Words ending in -*fe* or -*f*:**
   Some words ending in -*fe* or -*f* change the *f* to *v* and add -*es*. You can hear the change from the *f* sound to the *v* sound in the plural.

   wi*fe*   *becomes*   *wives*
   lea*f*   *becomes*   leaves

   Other words ending in -*fe* or -*f* keep the *f* and just add -*s*.

   sheri*ff*   *becomes*   sheri*ff*s
   belie*f*   *becomes*   belie*f*s

   Again, you can hear that the *f* sound is kept in the plural. Some words can form their plural either way. If so, the dictionary will give the preferred way first.

Practice In the spaces provided, write the plural form of each of these singular nouns:

hoof _____

scarf _____

tariff _____

chief _____

self _____

5. **Foreign words:**

Some words borrowed from other languages keep the plurals from those other languages to form the plural in English.

cris*is*	*becomes*	cris*es*
phenomen*on*	*becomes*	phenomen*a*
alumn*us*	*becomes*	alumn*i*
alumn*a*	*becomes*	alumn*ae*
al*ga*	*becomes*	al*gae*

6. **Compound nouns:**

Compound nouns make their plurals by putting the *-s* on the end of the main word.

brother-in-law	*becomes*	brothers-in-law
passer-by	*becomes*	passers-by

7. **Irregular plurals:**

Some nouns in English have irregular plurals.

Singular	*Plural*
child	children
deer	deer
foot	feet
goose	geese
man, woman	men, women
moose	moose
mouse	mice
ox	oxen
sheep	sheep
tooth	teeth

Exercise 1   Forming the Plurals of Nouns

Using the rules you have learned, make the following words plural.

1. puppy   _____

2. mother-in-law   _____

3. tooth   _____

4. cameo   _____

5. phenomenon   _____

6. loaf   _____

7. match   _____

8. mix   _____

9. enemy   _____

10. bag   _____

Exercise 2   Forming the Plurals of Nouns

Using the rules you have learned, make the following words plural.

1. attorney   _____

2. watch   _____

3. tango   _____

4. letter   _____

5. library   _____

6. echo   _____

7. glass   _____

8. deer   _____

9. hypothesis _____

10. ratio   _____

Exercise 3   Forming the Plurals of Nouns

Using the rules you have learned, make the following words plural.

1. woman   _____

2. company   _____

3. calf   _____

4. alumnus   _____

5. address   _____

6. ox   _____

7. wish   _____

8. melody   _____

9. zero   _____

10. key   _____

Should the Final Consonant Be Doubled?

The answer to this question involves the most complicated spelling rule. However, the rule is well worth learning because once you know it, you will suddenly be able to spell thousands of words correctly.

In order to understand the rule, remember first the difference between vowels (*a, e, i, o, u,* and sometimes *y*) and consonants (all the other letters in the alphabet).

The problem in spelling occurs when you want to add an ending that begins with a vowel such as *-ed, -er, -est,* or *-ing.* Sometimes the word will double the last letter before adding an ending:

trap + ing = trapping   The fur traders spent their time trapping animals.

Sometimes the word will *not* double the last letter before adding the ending:

turn + er = turner   He dropped the pancake turner.

How do you know when to double the final consonant?

Rule for Doubling One-Syllable Words

Double the final consonant of a one-syllable word when adding an ending that begins with a vowel only if the last three letters of the word are a consonant-vowel-consonant combination.

Since *rap* in the word *trap* is a consonant-vowel-consonant combination, this one-syllable word will double the final consonant when adding an ending beginning with a vowel. Since the last three letters *urn* in the word *turn* are a vowel-consonant-consonant combination, this one-syllable word does not double the final consonant when adding an ending beginning with a vowel.

Study the list of words that follows. For each of these one-syllable words, determine whether or not the word will double the final consonant when adding an ending beginning with a vowel.

One-Syllable Word	*Consonant-Vowel-Consonant Combination?*	*Double?*	*Add* -ing *Ending*
drag	yes	yes	dragging
drain	no	no	draining
slip			
crack			
broil			
win			

NOTE: In words with *qu* like *quit* or *quiz*, think of the *qu* as a consonant. (The *u* does have a consonant *w* sound.) *quit* + ing = *quitting*

Rule for Doubling Words of More than One Syllable

For words of more than one syllable, the rule adds one more condition: if the first syllable is accented in the newly formed word you do not double the final consonant.

pre fer′ + ed   = pre ferred′

but

pre fer′ + ence = pref′ er ence

(The accent has changed to the first syllable.)

Try these two-syllable words:

con *trol*′   +   ing   =   _____

fe′*ver*   +   ish   =   _____

Study the list of words that follow. For each of these words of more than one syllable, determine whether or not the word will double the final consonant when adding an ending beginning with a vowel.

com *pel*′   +   ed   =   _____

dif′ *fer*   +   ence   =   _____

de *sign*′   +   er   =   _____

be *gin*′   +   ing   =   _____

Exercise 1 **Doubling the Final Consonant When Adding Endings That Begin with Vowels**

Decide whether or not to double the final consonant when adding the endings to the following words.

	Word		*Ending*	*New Word*
1.	bit	+	-en	_____
2.	oc cur'	+	-ence	_____
3.	wa'ver	+	-ing	_____
4.	pre fer'	+	-ed	_____
5.	pre' fer	+	-ence	_____
6.	thin	+	-er	_____
7.	trans fer'	+	-ed	_____
8.	sail	+	-ing	_____
9.	ex cel'	+	-ent	_____
10.	o mit'	+	-ed	_____

Exercise 2 **Doubling the Final Consonant When Adding Endings That Begin with Vowels**

Decide whether or not to double the final consonant when adding the endings to the following words.

	Word		*Ending*	*New Word*
1.	stop	+	-ed	_____
2.	com mit'	+	-ee	_____
3.	com mit'	+	-al	_____
4.	big	+	-est	_____
5.	e quip'	+	-ed	_____
6.	tap	+	-ing	_____
7.	suc ceed'	+	-ing	_____
8.	hid	+	-en	_____
9.	lis' ten	+	-er	_____
10.	god	+	-ess	_____

Exercise 3 **Doubling the Final Consonant When Adding Endings That Begin with Vowels**

Decide whether or not to double the final consonant when adding the endings to the following words.

	Word	Ending	New Word
1.	soil	+ ing	_____
2.	for got'	+ en	_____
3.	rag	+ ed	_____
4.	ben' e fit	+ ed	_____
5.	wrap	+ er	_____
6.	plan	+ ing	_____
7.	fi' nal	+ ize	_____
8.	trans mit'	+ er	_____
9.	wed	+ ing	_____
10.	sup port'	+ ive	_____

Words Ending in -y

1. When a *y* at the end of a word is preceded by a consonant, change *y* to *i* and add the ending.

carry	+	er	=	car*rier*
merry	+	ment	=	mer*riment*
fun*ny*	+	er	=	_____
bu*sy*	+	ness	=	_____
va*ry*	+	es	=	_____

   Exceptions: Do not change the *y* to *i* if the ending starts with an *i*. In English we seldom have two *i*'s together.

stu*dy*	+	ing	=	stud*ying* not studiing
rea*dy*	+	ing	=	_____

   Some long words drop the *y* when adding the ending. You can hear that the *y* syllable is missing when you pronounce the word correctly.

milita*ry*	+	ism	=	militar*ism*
accompa*ny*	+	ist	=	_____

2. When *y* at the end of a word is preceded by a vowel, do *not* change the *y* when adding the ending. Simply add the ending.

sur*vey*	+	s	=	sur*veys*
enj*oy*	+	ment	=	_____

Exercise 1   Adding Endings to Words That End in -y

Add endings to the following words, being sure to change the *y* to *i* wherever necessary.

1. key   +   s   = _____
2. lonely   +   ness   = _____
3. cry   +   ing   = _____
4. cry   +   s   = _____
5. pray   +   er   = _____
6. cray   +   fish   = _____
7. monkey   +   ing   = _____
8. beauty   +   ful   = _____
9. theory   +   es   = _____
10. ceremony   +   al   = _____

Exercise 2 Adding Endings to Words That End in *-y*

Add endings to the following words, being sure to change the *y* to *i* wherever necessary.

1. day   +   care   = _____
2. carry   +   ing   = _____
3. mercy   +   ful   = _____
4. valley   +   s   = _____
5. category   +   ize   = _____
6. bury   +   ed   = _____
7. bury   +   ing   = _____
8. ally   +   es   = _____
9. chimney   +   s   = _____
10. try   +   ed   = _____

Exercise 3 Adding Endings to Words That End in *-y*

Add endings to the following words, being sure to change the *y* to *i* wherever necessary.

1. easy   +   ly   = _____
2. marry   +   age   = _____
3. attorney   +   s   = _____
4. hurry   +   ing   = _____
5. destroy   +   er   = _____
6. baby   +   ish   = _____
7. baby   +   ed   = _____

8.   lucky   +   est   =   _____

9.   story   +   es   =   _____

10. monopoly   +   ize   =   _____

Is It One Word or Two?

There is often confusion about whether certain word combinations should be joined together to form compound words. Study the following three groups of words to avoid this common confusion.

These words are always written as one word:

another	everything	playroom
bathroom	grandmother	schoolteacher
bedroom	nearby	southeast, northwest, etc.
bookkeeper	nevertheless	roommate
cannot	newspaper	yourself
downstairs		

These words are always written as two words:

a lot	living room
all right	no one
dining room	good night
high school	

These words are written as one or two words depending on their use:

all ready *(pronoun and adj.)*   completely prepared

already *(adv.)*   previously; before

He was _____ there by the time I arrived.

I have _____ read that book.

We were _____ for the New Year's Eve party.

all together *(pronoun and adj.)*   in a group

altogether *(adv.)*   completely

Our family was _____ at Thanksgiving.

I am _____ too upset to concentrate.

Have you gathered your papers _____?

all ways *(adj. and noun)*   every road or path

always *(adverb)*   on every occasion

Be sure to check _____ before you cross that intersection.

She tried _____ she could think of before she gave up on the problem.

She _____ figures out the homework.

any one *(adj. and pronoun)*   one person or thing in a specific group

anyone *(indef. pronoun)*   any person at all

Did _____ ever find my gloves?

She will talk to _____ who will listen to her.

I would choose _____ of those sweaters if I had the money.

every one *(adj. and pronoun)*   every person or thing in a specific group

everyone *(indef. pronoun)*   all of the people

_____ of the books we wanted was out of stock.

_____ was so disappointed.

_____ of the workers disapproved of the new rules.

may be *(verb)*   might be

maybe *(adv.)*   perhaps

The news broadcast said that there _____ a storm tomorrow.

If it's bad, _____ I won't go to work.

_____ my car won't start.

Exercise 1   One Word or Two?

Fill in the blank in each of the following sentences by choosing the correct word to complete that sentence.

1.   The blue rug looks beautiful in the white _____.
     (bed room, bedroom)

2.   The room is usually occupied by _____, but she is not
     (grandmother, grand mother)
     here right now.

3.   She has _____ left for a winter vacation.
     (all ready, already)

4.   Last night we all called her and _____ we sang
     (all together, altogether)
     "Happy Birthday" over the phone.

5.   We _____ remember her birthday, no matter where
     (all ways, always)
     we are.

6.   _____ likes to be remembered on special days, partic-
     (Every one, Everyone)
     ularly a birthday.

7.   Next year, _____ all the members of the family will be
     (may be, maybe)
     able to celebrate her birthday with us.

8.   If she _____ come to us, we will drive up and surprise
     (cannot, can not)
     her.

9.   Most families have members who do not live _____.
     (near by, nearby)

10. _____, we can keep in touch by letter, phone, or visits.
     (Never the less, Nevertheless)

Exercise 2 **One Word or Two?**

Fill in the blank in each of the following sentences by choosing the correct word to complete that sentence.

1. When you rent a place to live, you must ask _____
    (yourself, your self)
    several important questions.

2. First, you have to make sure the _____ is big enough
    (living room, livingroom)
    for your needs.

3. Next, if you plan to have people over for dinner very often, you might need

    a _____.
    (dining room, diningroom)

4. If _____ in your family is going to stay with you, you
    (anyone, any one)
    have to take that into account.

5. If you are going to rent a house, think of the advantages of having a

    _____ on the first floor.
    (bathroom, bath room)

6. When there are several young children in a family, having a

    _____ is an important consideration.
    (play room, playroom)

7. Also, where will you spend most of the time in your house—will you be in

    the upper rooms or _____?
    (down stairs, downstairs)

8. _____ ever has enough space.
    (No one, Noone)

9. Finally, after you have thought about what you hope to find, consider what

    percent of your salary you _____ paying for rent.
    (maybe, may be)

10. If the rent is too high, you might want to consider looking for a

    _____.
    (roommate, room mate)

Exercise 3 **One Word or Two?**

Fill in the blank in each of the following sentences by choosing the correct word to complete that sentence.

1. A major problem facing _____ of people these days is
    (a lot, alot)
    how to get a good education and how to get a good job.

2. Some people would like to look for a job right after they graduate from

    _____.
    (high school, highschool)

3. _____ should make a quick decision about this, since
    (No one, Noone)
    it will have a long-term effect on one's life.

4. If you want to be a _____ , you will have a
    (book keeper, bookkeeper)
    certain amount of college education in addition to specific training.

5. It is certainly _____ to take off a year to think about
    (all right, alright)
    your future plans.

6. It often happens that one of the best sources of advice is a
    _____ you had in high school.
    (school teacher, schoolteacher)

7. A further career consideration is the area of the country where you would
    like to live—the _____, for example.
    (south west, southwest)

8. _____ important point about a career is whether or
    (Another, An other)
    not it will be in demand five or ten years from now.

9. One way to get some good information about the best jobs now and in the
    future is to carefully read the _____ for details on eco-
    (newspapers, news papers)
    nomic trends.

10. In the end, such important decisions about education and career depend
    on _____ you can find out about them.
    (every thing, everything)

Spelling 200 Tough Words

Word List 1: Silent Letters

b	*h*	*p*
crum*b*	ex*h*ibit	*p*neumonia
clim*b*	r*h*etoric	*p*sychology
de*b*t	r*h*ythm	
dou*b*t	sc*h*edule	*s*
su*b*tle		aisle
	l	island
c	co*l*onel	debris
indi*c*t		
	n	*t*
d	autum*n*	depo*t*
knowle*d*ge	colum*n*	lis*t*en
We*d*nesday	condem*n*	mor*t*gage
	w	
	answer	

Word List 2: Double Letters

accidenta*ll*y	a*r*rangement	nece*ss*ary
acco*mm*odate	co*mm*i*tt*ee	o*cc*asiona*ll*y
acro*ss*	emba*rr*ass	omi*ss*ion
add*r*ess	exa*gg*erate	posse*ss*ion
a*nn*ual	fina*ll*y	prefe*rr*ed
a*pp*arently	guarant*ee*	questio*nn*aire

recommend   suggest   tomorrow
succeed   summarize   written *but* writing
success

Word List 3: *-able* or *-ible*

-able

Usually, when you begin with a complete word, the ending is *-able*.

acceptable
agreeable

*   These words keep the *e* when adding the ending:

peaceable   manageable
noticeable   knowledgeable

*   These words drop the *e* when adding the ending:

conceivable   indispensable
desirable   inevitable
imaginable   irritable

-ible

Usually, if you start with a root that is not a word, the ending is *-ible*.

audible   permissible
compatible   plausible
eligible   possible
feasible   sensible
illegible   susceptible
incredible   tangible

Word List 4: *de-* or *di-*

de-	*di-*
decide	dilemma
decision	dilute
delinquent	discipline
descend	discuss
describe	disease
despair	disguise
despicable	dispense
despise	dispute
despite	dissent
despondent	divide
destructive	division
develop	divine
device	

Word List 5: The *-er* Sound

Most words ending with the *-er* sound are spelled with *-er*, as in the words *prisoner*, *customer*, and *hunger*. Words that are exceptions to this should be learned carefully.

-ar

beggar	grammar
burglar	pillar
calendar	polar
collar	similar
dollar	vulgar

-or
actor
author
bachelor
doctor
emperor
governor
motor
professor
sailor
scissors

-ur
murmur

-yr
martyr

-our
humour
labour
neighbour

-re
theatre
centre
litre

Word List 6: *-ance* or *-ence*

Most words with the *-ence* sound at the end are spelled *-ence*. Here are a few examples:

audience
correspondence
excellence
existence
intelligence
presence
reference
licence (noun)

Learn these exceptions:

-ance
allowance
ambulance
appearance
assistance
attendance
balance
dominance
guidance
ignorance
nuisance
observance
resistance
significance
tolerance

-ense
license (verb)

-eance
vengeance

Word List 7: Problems with *s, c, z, x,* and *k*

absence
alcohol
analyze
auxiliary
awkward
biscuit
complexion
concede
consensus
criticize
ecstasy
emphasize
especially
exceed
exercise
fascinate
magazine
medicine
muscle
prejudice
recede
sincerely
supersede
vacillate
vicious

Word List 8: Twenty-four Demons

acquire
argument
benefit
cafeteria
cemetery
category
conquer
corroborate
courageous
extremely
frightening
grateful
inoculate
lightning
ninety
ninth
occurred
occurrence
privilege
ridiculous
secretary
truly
until
village

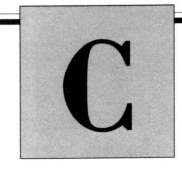

Capitalization

Many students are often confused or careless about the use of capital letters. Sometimes these students capitalize words without thinking, or they capitalize "important" words without really understanding what makes them important enough to deserve a capital letter. The question of when to capitalize words becomes easier to answer when you study the following rules and carefully apply them to your own writing.

Ten Basic Rules for Capitalization

1. Capitalize the first word of every sentence.
2. Capitalize the names of specific things and places.

Specific buildings:

I went to the Jamestown Post Office.

but

I went to the post office.

Specific streets, cities, states, countries:

She lives on Elam Avenue.

but

She lives on the same street as my mum and dad.

Specific organizations:

He collected money for the Canadian Cancer Society.

but

Janice joined more than one club at the school.

413

Specific institutions:

> The loan is from the Royal Bank of Canada.

> > *but*

> The loan is from one of the banks in town.

Specific bodies of water:

> My uncle fishes every summer on Lake Winnipeg.

> > *but*

> My uncle spends every summer at the lake.

3. Capitalize days of the week, months of the year, and holidays. Do *not* capitalize the names of seasons.

> The second Monday in October is Thanksgiving Day.

> > *but*

> I cannot wait until spring.

4. Capitalize the names of all languages, nationalities, races, religions, deities, and sacred terms.

> My friend who is Ethiopian speaks very little English.

> The Koran is the sacred book of Islam.

5. Capitalize the first word and every important word in a title. Do *not* capitalize articles, prepositions, or short connecting words in the title.

> *World of One* is a novel by Charles Templeton.

> Her favourite short story is "We Have to Sit Opposite" by Ethel Wilson.

6. Capitalize the first word of a direct quotation.

> The teacher said, "You have been chosen for the part."

> > *but*

> "You have been chosen," she said, "for the part."

NOTE: *for* is not capitalized because it is not the beginning of the sentence in quotation marks.

7. Capitalize historical events, periods, and documents.

> The Rebellion of 1837

> The Depression

> The Charter of Rights and Freedoms

8. Capitalize the words *north, south, east,* and *west* when they are used as places rather than as directions.

> He comes from the East.

> > *but*

> The farm is about 40 kilometres west of Weyburn.

9. Capitalize people's names.

Proper names:

> George Hendrickson

Professional titles when they are used with the person's proper name:

Judge Samuelson	*but*	the judge
Professor Shapiro	*but*	the professor

Term for a relative (like *mother, sister, nephew, uncle*) when it is used in the place of the proper name:

I told Grandfather I would meet him later.

- Notice that terms for relatives are not capitalized if a pronoun, article, or adjective is used with the name.

I told my grandfather I would meet him later.

10. Capitalize brand names.

Laura Secord Candies	*but*	candies
Weston Bread	*but*	bread

Exercise 1 Capitalization

Capitalize wherever necessary.

1. The italian student got a job in the school cafeteria.
2. Our train ride through the canadian rockies was fabulous.
3. The author often made references in his writing to names from the bible.
4. A student at the university of alberta was chosen for the national award.
5. My uncle's children always have a party on halloween.
6. I met the president of bell canada last friday at a convention in winnipeg, manitoba.
7. The cobalt 60 cancer therapy unit was invented by a canadian, dr. donald green.
8. My niece said, "why don't you consider moving farther south if you hate the winter so much?"
9. The canadian auto workers voted not to go on strike over the new contract.
10. A very popular radio program in the west is called a prairie home companion.

Exercise 2 Capitalization

Capitalize wherever necessary.

1. Every tuesday the general visits the hospital.
2. On one level, the book *the lord of the rings* can be read as a fairy tale; on another level, the book can be read as a christian allegory.
3. The thousand islands international bridge over the st. lawrence river may be the most beautiful bridge in canada.
4. She is the sister of my french teacher.
5. I've always wanted to take a trip to the far east in spring.
6. The kremlin houses the soviet government and is located in moscow.
7. I needed to see dr. Madison, but the nurse told me the doctor would not be in until next week.
8. He shouted angrily, "why don't you ever arrive at your history class on time?"
9. The graduate record examination will be given on january 18.

10. Before confederation, mesopelagia, albertonia, and efisga were all suggested as names for the country we now call canada.

Exercise 3 Capitalization

Capitalize wherever necessary.

1. The lawyer's office is located on south pleasant street.
2. My uncle lives farther south than grandmother.
3. I'd like to move to the south if I could find a job there.
4. The amount of public funding for the national ballet, the toronto and montreal symphony orchestras, the royal winnipeg ballet, and les grands ballets canadiens is determined by the federal government.
5. In a recent national geography test, only 55 percent of those tested were able to locate ottawa on an outline map of canada.
6. The ontario northland railway's polar bear express travels from cochrane to moosonee.
7. Since 1971, the canadian brass has released more than twenty albums, including selections of gershwin and dixieland.
8. I read the magazine article in *canadian business* while I was waiting in the dentist's office yesterday.
9. The tour took the retired teachers above the arctic circle.
10. Nabisco shredded wheat used a picture of niagara falls as a trademark.

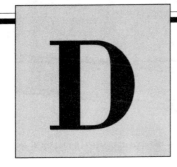

The Apostrophe

Three Uses for the Apostrophe

I.   To form the possessive:

   A.   Add *'s* to singular nouns:

   the pen of the teacher = the teacher*'s* pen

   the strategy of the boss = the boss*'s* strategy

   the work of the week   = the week*'s* work

   • Watch out that you choose the right noun to make possessive. Always ask yourself *who* or *what* possesses something. In the sentences above, the teacher possesses the pen, the boss possesses the strategy, and the week possesses the work.

   Note these unusual possessives:

   Hyphenated words: mother-in-law*'s* advice

   Joint possession: Lucy and Desi*'s* children

   Individual possession: John*'s* and Steve*'s* ideas

   B.   Add *'s* to irregular plural nouns that do not end in *-s.*

   the hats of the children = the children*'s* hats

   the harness for the oxen = the oxen*'s* harness

   C.   Add *'s* to indefinite pronouns:

   everyone's responsibility

   somebody's wallet

Indefinite Pronouns

anyone	everyone	no one	someone
anybody	everybody	nobody	somebody
anything	everything	nothing	something

- Possessive pronouns in English (his, hers, its, ours, yours, theirs, whose) do *not* use an apostrophe.

    Whose key is this?

    The key is *his*.

    The car is *theirs*.

    D. Add an apostrophe only to regular plural nouns ending in -*s*.

    the coats of the ladies   =   the ladies' coats

    the store of the brothers =   the brothers' store

- A few singular nouns ending in the *s* or *z* sound are awkward-sounding if another *s* sound is added. You may in these cases drop the final *s*. Let your ear help you make the decision.

    Jesus' robe   *not*   Jesus's robe

II. To form certain plurals in order to prevent confusion, use *'s*.

    Numbers: 100's

    Letters: *a*'s and *b*'s

    Years: 1800's or 1800s

    Abbreviations: Ph.D.'s

    Words referred to in a text: He uses too many *and's* in his writing.

- Be sure *not* to use the apostrophe to form a plural in any case other than these.

III. To show where letters have been omitted in contractions, use an apostrophe.

    cannot   = can't

    should not = shouldn't

    will not   = won't (the only contraction that changes its spelling)

    I am   = I'm

    she will   = she'll

Exercise 1   Using the Apostrophe

Fill in each of the blanks below using the rules you have just studied for uses of the apostrophe.

1. rays of the sun   the _____ rays

2. sleeve of the dress   the _____ sleeve

3. width of the feet   the _____ width

4. the house of Antony and Maria (joint possession)   _____ house

5. the idea of nobody   _____ idea

6. The book belongs to him.   The book is _____.

7. in the century of 1700   in the _____

8. That is her opinion.   _____ her opinion.

9. shirts for boys   _____ shirts

10. the cover of the book   the _____ cover

Exercise 2   Using the Apostrophe

Fill in each of the blanks below using the rules you have just studied for uses of the apostrophe.

1. clarity of the ice   the _____ clarity

2. the flight of the geese   the _____ flight

3. the work of Ann and Chris
   (individual possession)   _____ work

4. the plan of someone   _____ plan

5. The drums belong to her.   The drums are _____.

6. the terrible year of two   the terrible _____

7. We cannot leave yet.   We _____ leave yet.

8. the leaves of the tree   the _____ leaves

9. the cheese of the farmers   the _____ cheese

10. the lifestyle of my brother-in-law   my _____ **lifestyle**

Exercise 3   Using the Apostrophe

Fill in each of the blanks below using the rules you have just studied for uses of the apostrophe.

1. the engine of the train   the _____ engine

2. the spirit of the class   the _____ spirit

3. the centre for women   the _____ **centre**

4. the wish of everybody   _____ wish

5. The toys belong to them.   The toys are _____.

6. The child mixes up *b* and *d*. The child mixes up his

                                     _____.

7. I will not leave this house.   I _____ leave this house.

8. the grain of the wood   the _____ grain

9. the story of the owners   the _____ story

10. the policies of Ridge School and   _____ policies
    Orchard School (individual pos-
    session)

E Irregular Verbs

Principal Parts of Irregular Verbs

Simple Form	*Past Form*	*Past Participle*

1. Principal parts are the same.

beat	beat	beat or beaten
bet	bet	bet
burst	burst	burst
cast	cast	cast
cost	cost	cost
cut	cut	cut
fit	fit	fit
hit	hit	hit
hurt	hurt	hurt
let	let	let
put	put	put
quit	quit	quit
read	*read	*read
rid	rid	rid
set	set	set
shut	shut	shut
split	split	split
spread	spread	spread
wet	wet	wet

2. The past form and past participle are the same.

bend	bent	bent
lend	lent	lent

*Pronunciation changes.

send	sent	sent
spend	spent	spent
build	built	built
creep	crept	crept
feel	felt	felt
keep	kept	kept
sleep	slept	slept
sweep	swept	swept
deal	dealt	dealt
mean	meant	meant
leave	left	left
bleed	bled	bled
feed	fed	fed
flee	fled	fled
lead	led	led
speed	sped	sped
cling	clung	clung
dig	dug	dug
spin	spun	spun
stick	stuck	stuck
sting	stung	stung
strike	struck	struck
swing	swung	swung
wring	wrung	wrung
win	won	won
lay (to put)	laid	laid
pay	paid	paid
say	said	said
sell	sold	sold
tell	told	told
bind	bound	bound
find	found	found
grind	ground	ground
wind	wound	wound
bring	brought	brought
buy	bought	bought
fight	fought	fought
find	found	found
think	thought	thought
seek	sought	sought
teach	taught	taught
catch	caught	caught
have	had	had
sit	sat	sat
hear	heard	heard
hold	held	held
shoot	shot	shot
stand	stood	stood

Simple Form	Past Form	Past Participle

3. All forms are different.

Simple Form	Past Form	Past Participle
draw	drew	drawn
fall	fell	fallen
shake	shook	shaken
take	took	taken
bear	bore	borne
swear	swore	sworn
tear	tore	torn
wear	wore	worn
blow	blew	blown
fly	flew	flown
grow	grew	grown
know	knew	known
throw	threw	thrown
begin	began	begun
drink	drank	drunk
ring	rang	rung
shrink	shrank	shrunk
sink	sank	sunk
sing	sang	sung
spring	sprang	sprung
swim	swam	swum
bite	bit	bitten (or bit)
hide	hid	hidden (or hid)
drive	drove	driven
ride	rode	ridden
stride	strode	stridden
rise	rose	risen
write	wrote	written
break	broke	broken
freeze	froze	frozen
speak	spoke	spoken
steal	stole	stolen
weave	wove	woven
get	got	gotten
forget	forgot	forgotten
choose	chose	chosen
give	gave	given
forgive	forgave	forgiven
forbid	forbade	forbidden
do	did	done
eat	ate	eaten
go	went	gone
lie (to recline)	lay	lain
see	saw	seen

Exercise 1   Irregular Verbs

Supply the past form or the past participle for each verb in parentheses.

1. We _____ four trout in the stream.
   (to catch)

2. The burglar _____ up the fire escape.
   (to creep)

3. The audience _____ when the singer attempted the
   (to flee)
   high notes.

4. The pipe _____ yesterday; we are waiting for a
   (to burst)
   plumber.

5. He has _____ aimlessly around the city for several
   (to ride)
   hours.

6. The firefighters _____ down the ladder.
   (to slide)

7. The elevator _____ quickly to the tenth floor.
   (to rise)

8. She had _____ her job before the baby was born.
   (to quit)

9. The pond was _____ enough for ice skating.
   (to freeze)

10. He had washed and _____ out all his clothes in the
    (to wring)
    bathtub.

Exercise 2   Irregular Verbs

Read the following paragraph and find all the mistakes in irregular verbs. Write the correct forms below.

Mr. Weeks, an alumnus of our university, had gave a large sum of money to the school just before he died. A committee was choosen to study how the money should be used. Each member thunk about the possibilities for several weeks before the meeting. Finally, the meeting begun in late November. Each member brung his or her ideas. One gentle man fealt the school should improve the graduate program by hiring two new teachers. Another committee member layed down a proposal for remodelling the oldest dormitory on campus. Janice Spaulding had a writen plan for increasing the scholarships for deserving students. A citizen unexpectedly swang open the door and strode into the room. She pleaded with the school to provide more programs for the community. After everyone had spoke, the committee was asked to make a more thorough study of each project.

1. _____   4. _____

2. _____   5. _____

3. _____   6. _____

7. _____   9. _____

8. _____   10. _____

Exercise 3   Irregular Verbs

Supply the past form or the past participle for each verb in parentheses.

1. We _____ in the lake last summer.
   (to swim)

2. The director _____ a solution to the problems.
   (to seek)

3. The family _____ bitterly over the death of the child.
   (to weep)

4. The clerk _____ the clock before going home.
   (to wind)

5. The door seemed to be _____.
   (to stick)

6. The dog _____ itself as it came out of the water.
   (to shake)

7. The youth _____ he was telling the truth.
   (to swear)

8. Yesterday, the food had _____ on the table all day
   (to lie)
   without being touched.

9. My friend _____ her first child in a taxicab on the way
   (to bear)
   to the hospital.

10. The hosts _____ their guests to drink in their home.
    (to forbid)

Documentation: MLA and APA Styles

When you write a research paper, you should document all facts, opinions, and ideas that you quote, paraphrase, or use as source material. Failure to do so is plagiarism. When you do research for your paper, it is a good idea to keep a good record of the books, magazines, and other sources that you use. You will be able to use this list when you prepare your bibliography.

There are two generally accepted systems of documentation: Modern Language Association (MLA) style, often used in the humanities, and American Psychological Association (APA) style, often used in the social sciences.

MLA Style: Setting Up the Works-Cited List

The MLA suggests that you entitle your bibliography "Works Cited." The examples below show how certain entries would appear in your list of works cited. There are three basic divisions in an entry: author, work, and publishing information. If you need any further information, consult Joseph Gibaldi and Walter S. Achtert, *MLA Handbook for Writers of Research Papers*, 3rd ed. (New York: Modern Language Association, 1988).

Books

One Author
Dryden, Ken. *The Game*. Toronto: Macmillan, 1983.

Notice that, for the sake of alphabetizing, the author's name is reversed. In addition, each entry is flush with the left margin and two spaces follow each period.

Two or Three Authors
Grant, Carl A., and Christine E. Sleeter. *After the School Bell Rings*. Philadelphia: Falmer, 1986.

When citing a book by two or three authors, reverse only the first author's name, and list the authors as they appear on the title page of the book. Notice that when an entry is more than one line long, the subsequent lines are indented five spaces from the left margin.

More than Three Authors, Second or Later Edition
Thomas, Gillian, et al. *Introduction to Literature.* 2nd ed. Toronto: Holt, 1989.

When citing a work by more than three authors, name only the first author and add *et al.* If the book you are citing is the second or a later edition, insert this information after the title. In addition, you may abbreviate the publisher's name provided that there will not be any confusion between publishers on the list of works cited (for example, the abbreviation above might not be acceptable in a list of works cited when another publisher has a similar name).

Corporation or Institution as Author
University of Windsor. *University Alumni Magazine.* Windsor: University of Windsor, Fall, 1989.

Encyclopedia
Kalman, Harold. "Airport Architecture." *The Canadian Encyclopedia.* Edmonton: Hurtig, 1988.

Edited Edition
Paikeday, Thomas M., ed. *Compact Dictionary of Canadian English.* Toronto: Holt, 1976.

Anthology
Leacock, Stephen. "My Financial Career." *Canadian Anthology.* Eds. Carl F. Klinck and R. E. Watters. Toronto: Gage, 1974.

Government Publication
Canada. Department of the Secretary of State. *The Canadian Family Tree.* Ottawa: Centennial Commission, 1967.

Magazines, Articles, and Journals

Article from a Magazine
Suzuki, David. "A Planet for the Taking." *Canadian Forum* February 1985: 6–8.

Unsigned Article
"Canada's National Parks and Sites." *The Canadian World Almanac.* Toronto: Global, 1987: 494–495.

Newspaper
Picton, John. "Canada's Great Inventions." *The Toronto Star* 2 July 1989:C9.

Non-Print Material

Lecture
Cutherbertson, George. "Introduction to Cabinetmaking." Lecture given in Basic Woodworking, Mohawk College, 13 September 1989.

Television or Radio Program
"Egypt Today." *Paula Ragheb's Voyages of Discovery.* MHWK, Mohawk College, Hamilton, Ont. 30 September 1987.

Interview
Gunn, Don. Personal Interview. 15 April 1988.

MLA Style: Citing Works in Your Essay

Now that you have a list of the works you have cited, you can document all the material that you will use in your essay. If you are quoting from a book listed in your Works Cited as follows:

> Smith, Fred. *A Concise Grammar*. Toronto: Falls, 1989.

then the citation in your essay would appear like this:

> One grammarian says that "a verb can be either transitive or intransitive" (Smith 72).

This citation indicates that a direct quotation is used from page 72 of Smith's book *A Concise Grammar*. However, a situation may occur when Smith's name is used with the quote, like the following:

> As Smith states, "A verb can be either transitive or intransitive" (72).

In this case, only the page number is necessary. On the other hand, if you use a source indirectly (paraphrasing), the entry would appear as follows:

> It has been stated that a verb can be either transitive or intransitive (Smith 72).

Should you have more than one book written by a person named Smith, you will want to distinguish between them by referring to the book as well as the author, as in the above case (Smith *Grammar* 72).

The Author-Date System of Citation

The MLA style also employs the author-date system, which is similar to the APA system of citation. Should you choose to use the author-date system, you must use it throughout your essay. Again, referring to the Smith text above, the proper citation for a reference to page 72 under the author-date system would be (Smith 1989, 72). The listing in your Works Cited would be altered slightly. The new entry would be as follows:

> Smith, Fred. 1989. *A Concise Grammar*. Toronto: Falls.

APA Style: Setting Up the References List

The APA prefers to give the bibliography the title "References." The style is similar to the MLA author-date system, but there are important differences. For further details on the APA style of documentation, consult American Psychological Association, *Publication Manual of the American Psychological Association*, 3rd ed. (Washington: American Psychological Assn., 1983).

Books

One Author
Dryden, K. (1983). *The Game*. Toronto: Macmillan.

Notice that the publication date is enclosed in parentheses and that there are two spaces after each period.

Multiple Authors

Roberts, J., Herman, W., Young, J. (1989). *Troubleshooting*. Toronto: Holt.

Notice that all of the authors' names are reversed, and that there is no "and" before the last author's name.

Journals

One Author

Suzuki, D. (1985). A planet for the taking. *Canadian Forum*, February, 6–8.

Notice that only the first letter of the first word of the article's title is capitalized.

Multiple Authors

Lahey, K., Salter, S. Corporate law in legal theory and legal scholarship: from classicism to feminism. *Osgoode Law Journal* 23.

APA Style: Citing Works in Your Essay

When citing sources using APA style, always include three elements: the author's name, the date of publication, and the page number(s). In a long, direct quotation, the author's name would appear first, followed by the quotation, finished with the page reference. For example:

According to Smith (1989):

Verbs can be either transitive or intransitive (p. 72).

If you were paraphrasing an author's work, it would appear like the following:

A verb has two states, transitive or intransitive (Smith, 1989, p. 72).

Finally, if you mention the author's name in a sentence in which you are using that author's work, it would appear like the following:

Smith (1989) once said that verbs have two states (p. 72).

Following the basic guidelines for either the MLA or the APA styles will aid you in writing a sound research essay. Remember to always be consistent and to document all material in your essay that is not yours.

Answer Key to Practices and Selected Exercises

Part I: Building Your Word Power

Chapter 1: Understanding Your Basic Sourcebook: The Dictionary

Using the Dictionary to Find the Correct Meaning of a Word

Exercise 1 (p. 8)
1. 14. An abbreviated list, as of contents; a synopsis
2. 9. The front part of a stringed instrument
3. 7. A plateau or tableland
4. 3. The food and drink served at meals
5. tr. v. *tabled*: 2. To postpone consideration of (a piece of legislation, for example)
6. 11. A horizontal rock stratum
7. 1. An article of furniture supported by one or more vertical legs
8. To reverse a situation and gain the upper hand
9. 13. An orderly written, typed, or printed display of data
10. 15. A slab or tablet, as of stone, bearing an inscription

Exercise 2 (p. 10)
1. 1. The supporting part; foundation
2. 5. One of the four corners of a baseball infield marked by a bag or plate

3. 3. The fundamental ingredient from which a mixture is prepared
4. 2. The fundamental principle or underlying concept of a system or theory
5. 8. The lowest part of a structure, considered as a separate architectural unit
6. 13. a. A compound that turns litmus blue
7. 7a. or 7b. A fortified centre of operations; a supply centre for a large force
8. 10. A morpheme or morphemes regarded as a form to which affixes or other bases may be added
9. 6. A centre of organization, supply, or activity; headquarters
10. 11a. The side or face of a geometric figure to which an altitude is or is thought to be drawn

Shades of Meaning: Denotation/Connotation

Exercise 1 (p. 13)
1. thin 2. inexpensive 3. active 4. unusual 5. things 6. committed 7. interested 8. eat 9. smart 10. fat

Exercise 2 (p. 13)
1. colleague: a co-worker in a given occupation
   confederate: a person who works with another in a suspicious venture
   ally: a person who supports another person, at least temporarily

   accomplice: someone who works with another person in a criminal activity
   associate: someone who works in the same field as another person and who is in direct contact with that other person
2. compassion: a feeling for the misfortune of others and a desire to help them
   commiseration: a more casual and superficial concern
   sympathy: an immediate, spontaneous emotion at the misfortune of another
   condolence: sympathy given on specific occasions, such as a death in the family
   empathy: the feeling a person has who can see himself or herself in the same place as the person who is suffering misfortune
3. scorch: surface contact with flame that results in discolouration or similar damage
   singe: momentary burning of edges as a result of nearness to a source of heat
   sear: surface burning of organic tissue by the use of intense heat
   char: blackening or disintegration of something as a result of fire
   parch: drying of the surface and the creation of cracks, due to long exposure to fire or to the sun
4. melancholy: a state of mind that re-

sults from a personality that dwells on sombre thoughts

downhearted: referring to a depressed mood that usually results from a specific reason and does not last a long time

sorrowful: showing an emotion of extreme sadness

doleful: a very mournful or gloomy reaction or appearance that sometimes gives a comic effect that is not intended

desolate: implies a reaction of great sorrow over the loss of someone or something that cannot be replaced

Recognizing Words with Special Limitations

Exercise 1 (p. 16)

1. My father gave me enough money last night to take a girl to the movies.
2. The police finally caught the narcotics pusher and put the man in jail.
3. The gullible person was tricked by the man he met in the street.
4. That child has failed every awful French test because she always fools around in class.
5. My older brother is excellent, but my younger brother is stupid; he is always bothering me.
6. Since I have no money, my friend will bring the food.
7. I'll sleep for a while in this run-down place if it's all right with you.
8. I don't have the courage to speak honestly with my professor.
9. Her bad leg is causing her a great deal of pain.
10. Frank's radio is terrific.

Exercise 2 (p. 17)

1. take a liking 2. infatuation 3. flustered 4. appreciate 5. stylish 6. failure 7. pistols 8. ideal, first-rate 9. daring, plucky 10. a stupid or silly person

Understanding Dictionary Entries

Exercise 1 (p. 19)

1. universal 2. on welfare or unemployment insurance 3. fleeting, temporary, provisional 4. British Columbian fish that resembles a trout 5. noun, adjective, adverb 6. prep. 7. te·na·cious 8. nich 9. adverb 10. a leather belt with a strap fastened diagonally over the right shoulder.

Exercise 2 (p. 20)

1. A North American Indian food made of meat, fat, and fruit 2. theater 3. condense, compress, constrict, and shrink 4. A Canadian secondary school that offers commercial, technical, and academic courses 5. rY-sĕt′ 6. councilor 7. penitentiary 8. late summer 9. mag·is·te·ri·al 10. noun, adjective, adverb, and verb

Chapter 2: Distinguishing between Words That Are Often Confused

Words That Sound Alike: Group I

Practice (pp. 21–25)

1. It's; its
2. it's; its
3. they're; their; there
4. they're; their; there
5. Whose; who's
6. Who's; whose
7. you're; your
8. your; you're
9. allowed; aloud
10. aloud; allowed
11. alter; altar
12. alter; altar
13. oral; aural
14. oral; aural
15. brake; breaking
16. brake; brake
17. capital; capital
18. capital; capital
19. capital; capitol
20. cords; cord
21. chord; cord
22. close; clothes; cloth
23. cloth; clothes; close
24. course; coarse
25. coarse; course
26. complement; compliment
27. compliment; complement
28. fair; fare
29. fair; fair
30. flower; flour
31. flower; flour
32. four (or forty); for
33. fore; for
34. fourth; forth
35. forth; fourth
36. foreword; forward
37. forward; foreword
38. grated; grate
39. grateful; grate
40. great; grateful
41. knew; new
42. knew; new
43. know; no
44. no; know

Exercise 1 (p. 25)

1. aloud 2. It's 3. Your 4. There 5. Who's 6. forward 7. alter 8. compliment 9. capital 10. course

Exercise 2 (p. 25)

1. brakes 2. fare 3. forward 4. forth 5. grate 6. know 7. flour 8. for 9. course 10. They're

Words That Sound Alike: Group II

Practice (pp. 26–31)

1. pane; pain
2. pain; pane

3. past; passed
4. past; past
5. patience; patients
6. patients; patience
7. piece; peace
8. peace; piece
9. plane; plain
10. plain; plane
11. presence; presents
12. presents; presents
13. principal; principles
14. principal; principal
15. rein; reign
16. rain; rein
17. raze; raise
18. raised; raise
19. rays; raised
20. cite; sight
21. site; cite
22. stare; stairs
23. stairs; stare
24. stake; steak
25. steak; stake
26. staked; stake
27. stationery; stationary
28. stationary; stationery
29. too; two
30. to; to; too
31. vane; vain
32. vain; vein
33. vain; vein
34. wasted; waist
35. waste; waist
36. waiting; weight
37. wait; weight
38. Whether; weather
39. weather; whether
40. wears; wares
41. where; wear
42. whole; hole
43. whole; hole
44. would; wood
45. would; would
46. right; rites
47. right; write
48. write; right; right
49. Yolks
50. yoke
51. yoke

Exercise 1 (p. 31)

1. whole 2. too 3. reign 4. weather 5. principal 6. sites 7. razed 8. rites 9. know 10. peace

Exercise 2 (p. 31)

1. reign 2. sight 3. weight 4. principal 5. stare 6. pane 7. steak 8. past 9. stationary 10. piece

Words That Sound or Look Almost Alike

Practice (pp. 33–39)

1. except; accept; accept
2. access; excess; access
3. advise; advise; advice
4. effects; affect; effects
5. illusion; illusion; allusions

6. breath; breath; breathe
7. cloths; clothes; cloths
8. conscience; conscious; conscience; conscientious
9. custom; costumes; customs
10. counsel; consul; counsel; council
11. deserted; deserted; dessert; desert
12. diner; dinner; diner
13. emigrated; immigrated; immigrants
14. farther; further; farther
15. locale; local; locale
16. moral; morale; moral
17. personnel; personal; personnel
18. preceded; proceed; proceed
19. quite; quiet; quit
20. recipe; receipt; receipts
21. special; especially; especially
22. then; than; than
23. thought; through; though; threw; thorough; through

Exercise 1 (p. 39)
1. personnel 2. conscious 3. desert
4. access 5. diner 6. locale 7. farther
8. illusion 9. though 10. costume

Exercise 2 (p. 39)
1. quite 2. counsel 3. than 4. accept
5. emigrate 6. morale 7. cloths 8. illusion
9. effect 10. further

Words That Sound or Look Almost Alike: *sit/set; rise/raise; lie/lay*

Practice (pp. 41–42)

set; set; sitting; sit
raised; rose; rose; raised
lie; lying; laid; lain; lays; lied; lay

Exercise 1 (p. 42)
1. lain 2. lie 3. rises 4. raised 5. laid
6. raised 7. sits 8. sat 9. sit 10. set

Exercise 2 (p. 43)
1. rising 2. lying 3. lain 4. set 5. raised
6. lay 7. raised 8. sit 9. rising 10. laid

Exercise 3 (p. 43)
1. risen 2. lain 3. sit 4. lay 5. raise 6. set
7. sat 8. laid 9. rose 10. lie

Words That Sound or Look Almost Alike: *choose/chose; lose/loose; lead/led; die/dye*

Practice (p. 45)
chose; chose; chooses
lost; lose; loses
led; lead; led
dying; died; died

Words That Sound or Look Almost Alike: *use/used; suppose; supposed*

Practice (p. 46)
use; used; used
supposed; suppose; supposed

Exercise 1 (p. 46)
1. choosing 2. led 3. supposed 4. choose
5. lose 6. died 7. used 8. use 9. lose 10. led

Exercise 2 (p. 47)
1. used 2. led 3. chose 4. choose 5. led
6. lose 7. supposed 8. dying 9. supposed
10. led

PART II: Developing the Complete Sentence

Chapter 3: Finding Subjects and Verbs in Simple Sentences

Finding the Subject of a Sentence

Exercise 1 (p. 61)
1. The <u>train</u> stopped.
2. <u>Stephen Laye</u> had arrived!
3. <u>He</u> was afraid.
4. <u>Everything</u> looked so strange.
5. The fearful <u>man</u> held his bag tightly.
6. The <u>tunnel</u> led up to the street.
7. <u>Buses</u> and <u>cars</u> choked the avenues.
8. <u>People</u> rushed everywhere.
9. The <u>noise</u> made his head ache.
10. <u>Loneliness</u> filled his heart.

Esercise 2 (p. 62)
1. The <u>road</u> twisted and turned.
2. A young <u>boy</u> hurried along briskly.
3. <u>He</u> carried an important message.
4. A red-winged <u>blackbird</u> flew overhead.
5. Dark <u>clouds</u> and a sudden <u>wind</u> encouraged him to hurry faster.
6. His <u>family</u> would be elated.
7. <u>Someone</u> was working in the yard.
8. His <u>father</u> called out his name.
9. The old <u>man</u> tore open the envelope.
10. The <u>message</u> was brief.

Finding Subjects in Sentences with Prepositional Phrases

Exercise 1 (p. 63)
Answers will vary.

Exercise 2 (p. 64)
1. A <u>child</u> arrived ~~at the house beside the church~~.
2. <u>She</u> knocked timidly ~~on the door~~.
3. ~~From his table~~, the Reverend Stephen Laye looked across the room.
4. The <u>girl</u> had brought a letter ~~from Johannesburg~~.
5. ~~In the hope of getting some food~~, she waited ~~by the side of the table~~.
6. The <u>letter</u> ~~in her hand~~ was dirty, especially ~~around the stamp~~.
7. <u>It</u> had obviously been handled ~~by many people~~.
8. The <u>pastor</u> feared the contents ~~of the letter~~.
9. ~~In Johannesburg~~ lived several <u>members</u> ~~of his family~~.
10. <u>All</u> ~~of these close relatives~~ seemed ~~like phantoms to him~~.

What Are the Other Problems in Finding Subjects?

Exercise 1 (p. 66)
1. <u>(You)</u> look ~~at a map of South America~~.
2. Where is the ancient <u>city</u> ~~of Chan Chan~~?
3. Here ~~on the coastal desert of northern Peru~~ stand the <u>remains</u> ~~of this city of the kings~~.
4. <u>Chan Chan</u>, ~~once the fabulously wealthy centre of the Chimor~~, is situated ~~in one of the driest, bleakest regions in the world~~.
5. <u>It</u> was the largest pre-Columbian city ~~in South America~~.
6. ~~In the ruins of this city~~, <u>scientists</u> have found fragments to piece together the mystery ~~of the past~~.
7. How could this <u>civilization</u> have survived this hostile environment and become so advanced?
8. There the <u>people</u> had engineered an astonishing irrigation system.
9. Unfortunately ~~for the Chimor~~, <u>Incas</u> captured the city ~~in the late fifteenth century~~ and carried away much ~~of its wealth~~.
10. Later, the Spanish <u>armies</u> brought disease and destruction ~~to this desert people~~.

How Do You Find the Verb of a Sentence?

Exercise 1 (p. 67)
1. <u>woman</u> ⟨told⟩ (past)
2. <u>she</u> ⟨lay⟩ (past)
3. <u>Confusion</u> and <u>noise</u> ⟨filled⟩ (past)
4. <u>woman</u> ⟨entered⟩ and ⟨gave⟩ (past)
5. <u>man</u> ⟨came⟩ and ⟨led⟩ (past)
6. <u>Scientists</u> ⟨asked⟩ (past)
7. <u>one</u> ⟨proposed⟩ (past)
8. <u>woman</u> ⟨suffered⟩ (past)
9. <u>dream</u> ⟨showed⟩ (past)
10. <u>therapist</u> ⟨predicted⟩ (past)

Exercise 2 (p. 68)
1. My <u>dream</u> last night ⟨was⟩ wonderful.
2. I ⟨had become⟩ middle-aged.
3. In a sunlit kitchen with a book in hand, I ⟨appeared⟩ relaxed and happy.
4. The <u>house</u> ⟨was⟩ empty and quiet.
5. In the morning light, the <u>kitchen</u> ⟨felt⟩ cozy.
6. The brewing <u>coffee</u> ⟨smelled⟩ delicious.
7. The <u>bacon</u> never ⟨tasted⟩ better.
8. I ⟨looked⟩ peaceful.
9. I ⟨seemed⟩ to have grown calmer.
10. I ⟨felt⟩ satisfied with life.

Chapter Review Exercises

Exercise 1 (p. 70)
1. Mother and Dad always (blame) me for any trouble with my sister.
2. My sister, the most popular girl in her class, (is) two years older than I.
3. Yesterday, for instance, she (was) (trying) on her new graduation dress.
4. Helpfully, I (took) out her new shoes and purse for her.
5. Margaret instantly (became) furious with me.
6. Then mother (walked) into the room with a necklace for Margaret.
7. Margaret's new shoes and purse (were) immediately put back in the closet.
8. Why (couldn't) they (have understood?)
9. I (was) only (sharing) Margaret's excitement about her new clothes.
10. Far from their assumptions, my intentions (had been) the best.

Exercise 2 (p. 70)
1. There (are) several kinds of journals.
2. Which (is) the right one for you?
3. Your personality and interests (will determine) your choice.
4. Some people (do) not (write) an entry in their journal every day.
5. A growing number of people (are) (keeping) dream journals.
6. In these journals, the writer (makes) his or her entry first thing in the morning.
7. Otherwise, the dream (might be forgotten.)
8. Busy people often (need) to keep an activity-oriented diary.
9. Another kind of journal, the writer's journal, (could benefit) every college student.
10. In such a notebook, one (would) (save) for future use any interesting phrases, overheard conversations, or quotes from books and magazines.

Chapter 4:   A First Look at Correcting the Fragment

Practice Putting a Conversation into Complete Sentences (p. 73)
1. You are early again.
2. I want to get a front-row seat.
3. Is your homework done yet?
4. It is nearly finished.
5. Do you think the professor will give us a quiz today?
6. I certainly hope not.
7. It looks like rain today.
8. It had better not rain. I haven't got a bag for these new books.

9. Are you going to the game on Saturday?
10. I will probably go.

What Is a Fragment?

Exercise 1 (p. 74)
1. a. subject 2. b. verb 3. c. both subject and verb 4. b. verb 5. b. verb 6. a. subject 7. b. verb 8. d. contains subject and verb but lacks a complete thought 9. a. subject 10. b. verb

Exercise 2 (p. 74)
1. a. subject 2. b. verb 3. c. subject and verb 4. b. verb 5. b. verb 6. c. subject and verb 7. b. verb 8. a. subject 9. a. subject 10. b. verb

How Many Kinds of Phrases Are There?

Exercise 1 (p. 77)
1. gerund 2. infinitive 3. prepositional 4. participial 5. noun 6. participial 7. verb 8. prepositional 9. verb 10. prepositional

Exercise 2 (p. 78)
1. prepositional 2. infinitive 3. prepositional 4. noun 5. verb 6. prepositional 7. gerund 8. verb 9. infinitive 10. prepositional

Using the Participial Phrase/ Participle

Exercises 1 and 2 (pp. 78–80)
Answers will vary.

Correcting the Fragment That Contains a Participle

Exercise 1 (p. 81)
Answers will vary. Below are sample answers.
1. The rooming houses are often catching fire.
   The rooming houses often catch fire.
   Often catching fire, the rooming houses are dangerous places to live.
2. The tenants are moving out of the house.
   The tenants move out of the house.
   Moving out of the house, the tenants said goodbye to their neighbours.
3. The dogs were howling in the night.
   The dogs howled in the night.
   Howling in the night, the dogs kept us awake.
4. The police are warning people not to panic.
   The police warned people not to panic.
   Warning people not to panic, the police hoped to save more lives.
5. The fire department is doing its best.
   The fire department does its best.

Doing its best, the fire department tried to save the building.

Exercise 2 (p. 82)
Answers will vary.

Correcting Fragments

Exercise 1 (p. 83)
Answers will vary.

Exercise 2 (p. 84)
1. gerund or participial 2. prepositional 3. infinitive 4. prepositional 5. gerund or participial 6. infinitive 7. prepositional 8. gerund or participial 9. prepositional 10. gerund or participial
Sentences will vary depending on student response.

Chapter Review Exercises

Exercise 1 (p. 86)
1. Fragment 2. complete 3. fragment 4. complete 5. fragment 6. fragment 7. complete 8. complete 9. fragment 10. complete

Exercise 2 (p. 87)
1. complete 2. fragment 3. fragment 4. fragment 5. complete 6. fragment 7. complete 8. fragment 9. fragment 10. fragment

Exercise 3 (p. 88)
Answers will vary.

Chapter 5: Combining Sentences Using Co-ordination

Combining Sentences Using Co-ordinating Conjunctions

Practice (p. 91)
1. The audience was packed (for) this was a man with an international reputation.
2. He could have told about all his successes, (but) instead he spoke about his disappointments.
3. His words were electric (so) the crowd was attentive.
4. I should have brought a tape recorder, (or) at least I should have taken notes.

Exercise 1 (p. 91)
1. The farmers in Canada want to work, but they are experiencing severe financial difficulty.
2. Some people are losing their farms, for the banks are refusing to make further loans.
3. The government programs have not been effective, nor can the public do anything.
4. The farmers feel neglected, so they are protesting to the government.
5. Some people think the farmers are to blame, for they went too heavily into debt in recent years.

6. There is an increased need for farm products, but the government pays farmers not to grow food.

7. The government has co-operated with farmers for years, yet the farmers are in more difficulty today than ever before.

8. Angry farmers watch their land and machinery being sold at auction, but they can do nothing about it.

9. Everyone needs what the farmers produce, so we should be concerned about their problems.

10. In the future, fewer people will become farmers, so the problem is likely to become increasingly serious.

Combining Sentences Using Adverbial Conjunctions

Practice (p. 94)

1. The <u>restaurant</u> <u>is</u> always too crowded on Saturdays; neverthe-less, it <u>serves</u> the best food in town.

2. The <u>land was</u> not for sale; however, the <u>house could be rented</u>.

3. The <u>lawsuit cost</u> the company several million dollars; consequently, the <u>company went</u> out of business a short time later.

4. The <u>doctor told</u> him to lose weight; furthermore, <u>she insisted</u> he also stop smoking.

Exercise 1 (p. 94)

1. Most people prefer to write with a pen or pencil; however, the computer is quickly becoming another favourite writing tool.

2. Computers provide a powerful way to create and store pieces of writing; furthermore, they will become even more important in the future.

3. Some people do not like the idea of using electronics to create words; however, they should realize that the modern typewriter is also an electronic tool.

4. Computers have already revolutionized today's offices; consequently, no modern business can afford to be without them.

5. Many schools are using computers in the classroom; therefore, these same schools are helping students prepare for their working careers.

6. The prices of many computers are coming down these days; consequently, more and more people see that owning a computer is a real possibility.

7. Some children know more about computers than many adults; therefore, some children are teaching the adults how to operate computers.

8. Professional writers have become enthusiastic about the use of computers; however, there are still some writers who will use only a ballpoint pen.

9. The electronic revolution has just begun; consequently, it is our responsibility to keep up with that revolution.

10. We have many technological aids to writing; however, let us not forget that the source for all our ideas is the human brain.

Combining Sentences Using the Semicolon

Exercises 1 and 2 (pp. 97–98)

Answers will vary.

Chapter Review Exercises

Exercises 1, 2, and 3 (pp. 98–101)

Answers will vary.

Chapter 6: Combining Sentences Using Subordination

Practice (p. 103)

1. a. Since the librarian took constant coffee breaks, the boss fired him.
   b. The boss fired the librarian, since he took constant coffee breaks.

2. a. After he won the wrestling match, he went out to celebrate.
   b. He went out to celebrate after he won the wrestling match.

3. a. When Donna returned from Europe this spring, the family was excited.
   b. The family was excited when Donna returned from Europe this spring.

Recognizing Dependent and Independent Clauses

Exercise 1 (p. 104)

1. DC 2. DC 3. IC 4. DC 5. IC 6. DC 7. DC 8. IC 9. DC 10. DC

Exercise 2 (p. 104)

1. DC 2. IC 3. DC 4. IC 5. IC 6. DC 7. DC 8. IC 9. IC 10. DC

Using Subordinating Conjunctions

Exercise 1 (p. 105)

Students will compose their own sentences.

Exercise 2 (p. 106)

Students will pick an appropriate subordinating conjunction. The following are possible answers.

1. While he was eating breakfast, the results of the election came over the radio.

2. The town council voted against the plan because they believed the project was too expensive.

3. I will see Shirley Carr tonight, since she is speaking at the university this evening.

4. Although not one person in the department was promoted last year, the worker hoped for a promotion.

5. Since the worker hoped for a promotion, he made sure all his work was done accurately and on time.

Using a Relative Pronoun to Create a Complex Sentence

Practice 1 (p. 107)

1. The chemistry lab that I attend is two hours long.

2. The student assistant who is always willing to help us is very knowledgeable.

3. The equipment that was purchased last year will make possible some important new research.

Practice 2 (p. 107)

1. Canada's first census, which was taken in 1667, showed 3215 non-native inhabitants in 668 families.

2. Most of these families were French Canadians who lived near the St. Lawrence River.

3. By the time of Confederation, the population of the country had risen to 3 463 000, which was an increase of 1077 percent over 200 years.

4. If the population, which is about 26 000 000 persons in Canada now, increases by a similar percentage, we'll have a population of 280 020 000 by the year 2167.

5. Where, do you think, will we put everyone who will live in Canada then?

Combining Sentences with a Subordinating Conjunction or a Relative Pronoun

Exercise 1 (p. 108)

Following are sample answers. There is often more than one way to combine these sentences.

1. People have been fascinated for centuries by the problem of stuttering even though modern science is only beginning to understand some of the underlying causes of the problem.

2. For some people, stuttering disappears by itself, while other people continue into adulthood as stutterers.

3. Stutterers usually keep their affliction unless they seek professional help.

4. Although many stutterers lose their impediment when they sing or whisper, under stress the impediment becomes worse.

5. Since stutterers become unable to

speak when they appear in public or when they find themselves on the phone, they try to avoid such situations.

6. Even though you see a stutterer chanting the school cheer with everyone else, that same person is usually tongue-tied when called on by a teacher.

7. It is true that there is some psychological basis for stuttering even though psychologists have not been able to solve the problem.

8. Although all kinds of scientists have looked at the problem from all different angles, there is no single answer to stuttering.

9. If stuttering runs in a family, a child's chances of becoming a stutterer increase.

10. If you hear someone say he or she knows the causes of stuttering, you know that person cannot be speaking scientifically.

Exercise 3 (p. 110)

Answers will vary. The following is one possibility.

Just what is a "sport"? I am not saying a "sportsman," because everyone knows what he is. Every now and then, he simply has to get out and kill something. Not that he's cruel; he wouldn't hurt a fly. It's not big enough. But he has the instinct from way back in the centuries, and he's got to get out on the water or in the bush and kill something. Or rather, not so much that he wants to kill it, he wants to crawl around after it. He wants to crawl under brush and stoop under branches, pretending that he's a bushman of 10 000 years ago. He wants to kill this thing and eat it. He *won't* eat it, really; he'll give it away or give it to his wife to clean, then forget about it. In my part of the country, Simcoe County, all the "keen sportsmen" go out after partridge every autumn, even though there hasn't been a partridge seen for nearly twenty years. You don't really need them for partridge shooting; you need old clothes and a flask of whisky. A sportsman who's a real sport will be satisfied with that.

Chapter 7: A First Look at Correcting the Run-on

Recognizing and Correcting Run-ons

Exercises 1, 2, and 3 (pp. 113–114)

Answers will vary depending on whether students choose simple, compound, or complex sentence structures.

Revising Run-ons

Exercise 1 (p. 115)

1. *Simple:* Intelligence tests for children are not always useful. They are a basic tool for measurement in most schools.

   Compound: Intelligence tests for children are not always useful, but they are a basic tool for measurement in most schools.

   Intelligence tests for children are not always useful; however, they are a basic tool for measurement in most schools.

   Complex: Although intelligence tests for children are not always useful, they are a basic tool for measurement in most schools.

2. *Simple:* Many people are opposed to gambling in all its forms. They will not even buy a lottery ticket.

   Compound: Many people are opposed to gambling in all its forms, and they will not even buy a lottery ticket.

   Many people are opposed to gambling in all its forms; furthermore, they will not even buy a lottery ticket.

   Complex: Since many people are opposed to gambling in all its forms, they will not even buy a lottery ticket.

3. *Simple:* Public transportation is the major problem facing many of our cities. Little is being done to change the situation.

   Compound: Public transportation is the major problem facing many of our cities, but little is being done to change the situation.

   Public transportation is the major problem facing many of our cities; however, little is being done to change the situation.

   Complex: Although public transportation is the major problem facing many of our cities, little is being done to change the situation.

4. *Simple:* Travel is a great luxury. One needs time and money.

   Compound: Travel is a great luxury, for one needs time and money.

   Travel is a great luxury; one needs time and money.

   Complex: Travel is a great luxury because one needs time and money.

5. *Simple:* The need for proper diet is important in any health program. All the junk food on the grocery shelves makes it hard to be consistent.

   Compound: The need for proper diet is important in any health program, yet all the junk food on the grocery shelves makes it hard to be consistent.

   The need for proper diet is important in any health program; however, all the junk food on the grocery shelves makes it hard to be consistent.

   Complex: Even though the need for proper diet is important in any health program, all the junk food on the grocery shelves makes it hard to be consistent.

Exercise 2 (p. 117)

1. *Simple:* The airline has begun its new route to the islands. Everyone is looking forward to flying there.

   Compound: The airline has begun its new route to the islands, so everyone is looking forward to flying there.

   The airline has begun its new route to the islands; consequently, everyone is looking forward to flying there.

   Complex: Ever since the airline began its new route to the islands, everyone has been looking forward to flying there.

2. *Simple:* The movie begins at nine o'clock. Let's have dinner before the show.

   Compound: The movie begins at nine o'clock, so let's have dinner before the show.

   The movie begins at nine o'clock; therefore, let's have dinner before the show.

   Complex: Since the movie begins at nine o'clock, let's have dinner before the show.

3. *Simple:* The studio audience screamed at the contestant. They wanted her to try for the big prize.

   Compound: The studio audience screamed at the contestant, for they wanted her to try for the big prize.

   The studio audience screamed at the contestant; they wanted her to try for the big prize.

   Complex: The studio audience screamed at the contestant because they wanted her to try for the big prize.

4. *Simple:* The baby covered his eyes. He thought he could disappear that way.

   Compound: The baby covered his eyes, for he thought he could disappear that way.

   The baby covered his eyes; he thought he could disappear that way.

Complex: The baby covered his eyes because he thought he could disappear that way.

5. *Simple:* The waitress smiled. She told us the specials of the day.

Compound: The waitress smiled, and she told us the specials of the day.

The waitress smiled; moreover, she told us the specials of the day.

Complex: The waitress smiled as she told us the specials of the day.

Chapter 8: Punctuating Sentences Correctly

The Eight Basic Uses of the Commas

Practice 1 (p. 122)

1. Problems with the water supply of the United States, Europe, Canada, and other parts of the world are growing.
2. Water is colourless, tasteless, odourless, and free of calories.
3. You will use on an average day 90 litres of water for flushing, 120 litres for bathing and washing clothes, and 95 litres for other uses.
4. It took 450 litres of water to create the eggs you ate for breakfast, 13 250 litres for the steak you might eat for dinner, and over 200 000 litres to produce the steel used to make your car.
5. By 1970, the English-Wabigoon river system that runs through Grassy Narrows, Ontario, had become polluted with mercury.

Practice 2 (p. 122)

1. The most overused bodies of water are our rivers, but they continue to serve us daily.
2. Canadian cities developed understandably next to rivers, and industries followed soon after in the same locations.
3. The people of the industrial age can try to clean the water they use, or they can watch pollution take over.
4. The Great Lakes are showing signs of renewal, yet the struggle against pollution there must continue.
5. Most people have not been educated about the dangerous state of our water supply, nor are all our members of Parliament fully aware of the problem.

Practice 3 (p. 123)

1. To many people from Canada, the plans to supply more water to the United States seem unnecessary.
2. However, people in the western United States know that they have no future without a good water supply.
3. In 1935, the Federal government initiated irrigation schemes on the Canadian prairies.
4. Of the total, 1.4 percent of Canadian farmland was irrigated by 1981.
5. Learning from the past, modern farmers are trying to co-operate with nature.

Practice 4 (p. 124)

1. Natural disasters, I believe, have not been historically significant.
2. They have, however, significantly affected the lives of many Canadians.
3. Canada's worst coal-mine disaster, at Hillcrest, Alberta, occurred on June 19, 1914.
4. In Springhill, Nova Scotia, furthermore, 424 persons were killed in the mines between 1881 and 1969.
5. Avalanches, storms, and floods, which are natural disasters, have also made their mark of the face of our country.

Practice 5 (p. 124)

1. Dear, your tea is ready now.
2. I wonder, Jason, if the game has been cancelled.
3. Dad, could I borrow five dollars?
4. I insist, sir, on speaking with the manager.
5. Margaret, is that you?

Practice 6 (p. 124)

1. 4,876,454
2. 87,602
3. 156,439,600
4. 187,000
5. 10,000,000,000,000

Practice 7 (p. 124)

1. "I won't," he insisted, "be a part of your scheme."
2. He mumbled, "I won't incriminate myself."
3. "I was told," the defendant explained, "to answer every question."
4. "This court," the judge announced, "will be adjourned."
5. "The jury," said Al Tarvin of the press, "was hand-picked."

Practice 8 (p. 125)

1. Kicking, the child was carried off to bed.
2. To John, Ben Wicks is the funniest cartoonist.
3. When you can, come and visit us.
4. Whoever that is, is going to be surprised.
5. Skin cancer seldom kills, doctors say.

Using the Comma Correctly

Exercise 1 (p. 125)

1. no commas
2. One breeding ground for these penguins, tiny Dassen Island, is northwest of Cape Town.
3. Today, fewer than 60 000 penguins can be found breeding on this island.
4. At one time, seabirds that stole the penguins' eggs were the only threat to the funny-looking birds.
5. Human egg collectors, not to mention animals that simply take the eggs, have constantly reduced the penguin population.
6. However, the worst threat to the penguins is oil pollution.
7. If a passing tanker spills oil, many penguins can die.
8. In 1971, an oil tanker, the *Wafra*, spilled thousands of litres of oil off the coast of Southern Africa.
(Note: Sometimes, in the case of a short introductory prepositional phrase or a very short appositive, commas are omitted.)
9. Every time there is an oil spill near this area, the number of healthy penguins declines.
10. The ideal situation, of course, is to make the oil tankers take a completely different route.

Exercise 2 (p. 125)

1. The Commonwealth Games were first held in Hamilton, Ontario, in 1930.
2. The first games, known as the British Empire Games, attracted 400 competitors from eleven countries.
3. By 1978, during the Commonwealth Games in Edmonton, nearly 1,500 (1500, 1 500) athletes from 41 countries competed.
4. Canada has been a leading supporter of these games, which are held every four years.
5. Memorable performances, feats by both Canadian and non-Canadian athletes, have become a benchmark of the Games.
6. In 1958, at Cardiff, Wales, ten world records were broken.
7. The "Miracle Mile" occurred in 1954 at Vancouver, when Roger Bannister of Great Britain defeated John Landy of Australia.
8. Elaine Tanner, furthermore, was the Games' outstanding swimmer in 1966.
9. In Edmonton, Canadian athletes won 45 gold, 31 silver, and 33 bronze medals in 1978.

10. Next to the Olympics, the Commonwealth Games are among the world's best international competitions.

Other Marks of Punctuation

Practice 1 (p. 127)

1. "The Hot House" is one of the short stories contained in Rosemary Sullivan's anthology *More Stories by Canadian Women.*
2. Nellie McClung said, "I'll never believe I'm dead until I see it in the papers."
3. no quotation marks
4. "Punk" is a particular form of rock music.
5. She read the article "Whiz Kids" in *The Review.*

Practice 2 (p. 127)

1. One of the best ways to remember a vacation is to take numerous photos; one of the best ways to recall the contents of a book is to take notes.
2. The problem of street crime must be solved; otherwise, the number of vigilantes will increase.
3. The committee was made up of Kevin Corey, a writer; Anita Lightburn, a professor; and T. P. O'Connor, a politician.
4. The bank president was very cordial; however, he would not approve the loan.
5. Robots are being used in the factories of Japan; eventually they will be common in this country as well.

Practice 3 (p. 128)

1. Three Canadian-born comedians have become well-known in the United States: John Candy, Dan Aykroyd, and Catherine O'Hara.
2. The official has one major flaw in his personality: greed.
3. no colons
4. The college offers four courses in English literature: Romantic Poetry, Shakespeare's Plays, The British Short Story, and The Modern Novel.
5. Arriving at 6:15 in the morning, Marlene brought me a sausage and cheese pizza, soda, and a litre of ice cream.

Practice 4 (p. 129)

1. Herbert Simon is—and I don't think this is an exaggeration—a genius.
2. George Eliot (her real name was Mary Evans) wrote Silas Marner.
3. You should—in fact I insist—see a doctor.

4. Unemployment brings with it a number of other problems (see the study by Brody, 1982)
5. Mass media (television, radio, movies, magazines, and newspapers) are able to transmit information over a wide range and to a large number of people.

Marks of Punctuation

Exercise 1 (p. 129)

1. To measure crime, sociologists have used three different techniques: official statistics, victimization surveys, and self-report studies.
2. "David" is one of the best-loved poems of Earle Birney.
3. The lake this summer has one major disadvantage for swimmers: seaweed.
4. Farley Mowat has written numerous books for adults; however, he also writes very popular books for children.
5. Tuberculosis (also known as consumption) has been nearly eliminated by medical science.
6. The Victorian Period (1837–1901) saw a rapid expansion in industry.
7. He promised me—I know he promised—that he would come to my graduation.
8. Do you know what the expression "déjà vu" means?
9. She wanted to go to the movies; he decided to stay home and see an old film on his new video cassette recorder.
10. She has the qualifications needed for the job: a teaching degree, a pleasant personality, two years' experience, and a love of children.

Exercise 2 (p. 129)

1. Many young people have two feelings about science and technolgy: awe and fear.
2. Mr. Doyle, the realtor; Mrs. White, the bank officer; and Scott Castle, the lawyer are the three people who will help us work out the real estate transaction.
3. The book was entitled *English Literature: The Victorian Age.*
4. "I decided to walk to school," she said, "because the bus fare has been raised again."
5. She brought a bathing suit, towel, sunglasses, and several books to the beach. (no colon after *brought*)
6. The conference—I believe it is scheduled for sometime in January—will focus on the development of a new curriculum.
7. The song "Don't Forget Me" comes from Glass Tiger's album *The Thin Red Line.*

8. The complex lab experiment has these two major problems: too many difficult calculations and too many variables.
9. The mutt—that is to say, my dog—is smarter than he looks.
10. Violent crime cannot be reduced unless the society supports efforts such as strengthening the family structure, educating the young, and recruiting top-notch police. (no colon after *such as*)

Exercise 3 (p. 130)

1. "Justa Juxta," a painting by Gordon Rayner, is one of the artist's abstract studies.
2. "Remember," the doctor told the patient, "the next time I see you I want to see an improvement in your condition."
3. The student's short story "Ten Steps to Nowhere" appeared in a collection entitled *The Best of Student Writing.*
4. The report stated specifically that the company must—if it wanted to grow—sell off at least 10 percent of its property.
5. The foreign countries she has visited are Mexico, Israel, and Morocco. (no colon after *are*)
6. My father enjoyed spending money; my mother was frugal.
7. These students made the high honour roll: David Hyatt, Julie Carlson, and Erica Lane.
8. The scientist showed the class a glass of H_2O (water) and asked them to identify the liquid.
9. He said that he would give us an extension on our term papers. (indirect speech, no quotation marks)
10. The work was tedious; nevertheless, the goal of finding the solution kept him motivated.

Chapter 9: Making Sentence Parts Work Together

Making Agreement within the Sentence

Practice (p. 131)

1. barks 2. wakes 3. become 4. deserve 5. throw

Practice (p. 133)

1. doesn't 2. were 3. doesn't 4. Were 5. doesn't

Exercise 1 (p. 133)

1. price, has 2. decision, requires 3. She, doesn't 4. elevator operator or security guard, sees 5. committee, agrees 6. Potato chips and soda, make up 7. One, is 8. racoons, were 9. assignments, were 10. Everyone, takes

Exercise 3 (p. 135)
Answers will vary.

Pronoun-Antecedent Agreement

Exercise 1 (p. 136)
1. The father mailed his son his high school yearbook.
2. No one wants his or her income reduced.
3. When a company fails to update its equipment, it often pays a price in the long run.
4. Women today have many more options open to them than ever before.
5. Everybody knows his or her own strengths best.
6. All of the workers anticipate their summer vacation.
7. If the campers want to eat quickly, they should help themselves.
8. This sort of bathing suit looks ridiculous on me.
9. The application says that you must pay a registration fee of $35.
10. The doctor said that those types of diseases are rare here.

Revising Sentences for Parallel Structure

Practice (p. 139)
1. dirty
2. sewing her own clothes
3. willingly explain material more than once

Exercise 1 (p. 139)
1. Winter in Edmonton is very windy and bitterly cold.
2. I would prefer fixing an old car to watching television.
3. George is a helpful neighbour, a loyal friend, and a dedicated father.
4. The apartment is crowded and dark.
5. The dancer is slender and graceful.
6. The nursery was cheerful and sunny.
7. My friend loves to play chess, to read science fiction, and to work out at the gym.
8. For homework today I must read a chapter in history, do five exercises for Spanish class, and work on my term paper for political science.
9. The painting reveals the artist's talent and imagination.
10. The cars race down the track, turn the corner at great speed, and then turn into the home stretch.

Exercise 2 (p. 140)
1. The dog had to choose between jumping over the fence or digging a hole underneath it.
2. She disliked going to the beach, hiking in the woods, and going on picnics.

3. As I looked down the city street, I could see the soft lights from restaurant windows, I could hear the mellow sounds of a night club band, and I could sense the carefree moods of people walking by.
4. The singers have been on several road tours, have recorded for two record companies, and have expressed a desire to make a movie someday.
5. They would rather order a pizza than eat their sister's cooking.
6. I explained to the teacher that my car had broken down, my books had been stolen, and my assignment pad had been left at home.
7. That night the prisoner was sick, discouraged, and lonely.
8. As the truck rumbled through the street, it suddenly lurched out of control, smashed into a parked car, and hit the storefront of my uncle's hardware store.
9. The teacher is patient, intelligent, and demanding.
10. He was determined to pass the math course, not only to get his three credits but also to gain a sense of achievement.

Misplaced and Dangling Modifiers

Exercise 1 (p. 142)
1. Wearing his tuxedo, Victor fed the dog.
2. While we were visiting Stanley Park aquarium, the dolphins entertained us.
3. Hoping to see the news, we had turned on the television set and were all ready by seven o'clock.
4. A woodpecker that had been considered extinct was found in Cuba.
5. After running over the hill, I noticed that the farm was visible in the valley below.
6. The truck, which was broken down on the highway, caused a traffic jam for kilometres.
7. I saw three spiders hanging from the ceiling in my bedroom.
8. After I wiped my glasses, the redbird flew away.
9. I listened to the neighbour's dog howling without a stop all evening.
10. After I had painted my room all afternoon, my cat demanded her dinner.

Chapter 10: Solving More Problems with Verbs

Correcting Unnecessary Shifts in Verb Tense

Exercise 1 (p. 145)
1. After I complete that writing course, I will take the required history course.

2. In the beginning of the movie, the action was slow; by the end, I was sitting on the edge of my seat.
3. The textbook gives the rules for writing a bibliography, but it doesn't explain how to do footnotes.
4. While working on her report in the library, my best friend lost her note cards and came to me for help.
5. The encyclopedia gave several pages of information about astronomy, but it didn't give anything about "black holes."
6. The invitation requested that Juan be at the ceremony and that he attend the banquet as well.
7. This is an exciting book, but it has too many characters.
8. The member of Parliament was doing just fine until along came a younger and more energetic politician with firm support from the middle class.
9. At the end of *Gulliver's Travels*, the main character rejects the company of people; he prefers the company of horses.
10. My sister arrives, late as usual, and complains that her dinner is cold.

Exercise 2 (p. 146)
Doctor Norman Bethune **grew** up in Gravenhurst, Ontario. He was educated in Toronto and **served** as a stretcher bearer in World War I. He contracted tuberculosis and thereafter **devoted** himself to helping other victims of the disease when he **practised** surgery in Montreal. He also **invented** or redesigned twelve medical and surgical instruments. Bethune travelled to Russia in 1935, joined the Communist Party, and **went** to Spain in 1936, where he organized the first mobile blood transfusion service during the Spanish Civil War. After returning to Canada, he shortly left for overseas again, this time to China, where he helped the Chinese Communists in their fight against Japan. "Spain and China," he **wrote**, "are part of the same battle." While there, he contracted an infection and died. Mao's essay "In Memory of Norman Bethune," prescribed reading during China's Cultural Revolution, urges all Communists to follow Bethune's example of selfless dedication to others. Bethune is the best known Canadian to the Chinese, and many Chinese visit his Canadian birthplace.

Using the Correct Sequence of Tenses

Exercise 1 (p. 148)
1. has stopped 2. would have 3. will buy 4. had never been 5. liked 6. will soon be 7. is 8. knew 9. would turn 10. had gone

Passive versus Active Verbs

Practice (p. 149)

1. The child dialled the wrong number by mistake.
2. My grandmother knitted the sweater very carefully.
3. The assistant took the attendance at the beginning of class.
4. The public did not know the facts of the case.
5. Somebody wore those purple platform shoes.

Solving Problems with Verbs

Exercise 1 (p. 150)

1. He ought not to drive so fast.
2. It is essential that Krista go to class tonight.
3. I wish I were a senior.
4. She sang for a huge crowd Saturday night.
5. I was shaken up by the accident *or* The accident shook me up.
6. The students studied the books.
7. My father asked me last night to help him build a deck.
8. I should have kept the promise I made.
9. I insist she keep her records on her side of the room.
10. The ship sank off the coast of Sable Island.

Exercise 2 (p. 151)

When the day arrived, my mother was jubilant. We **drove** to the synagogue. My aunt Sophie and her daughters **came** with us. Once in the temple, the women were not allowed to sit with the men. They had to go upstairs to their assigned places. I was **asked** to keep my hat on and was given a shawl to wear that I **had seen** before. I was **supposed** to watch for the rabbi to call me. My turn finally came. I was **led** to a table in the front. There I read from the Bible in Hebrew. I knew I **could have** read louder, but I was nervous. My mother had said that if I was good, she would be especially proud of me, so I **did** my best. Afterward, I was **taken** by my mother and other relatives to a fine kosher restaurant where we celebrated. I **received** a fine gold watch.

There is more than one way to correct the fragments and run-ons in the rest of the exercises in Part II. The following answers are possible corrections.

Chapter 11:   More Practice with Fragments and Run-ons

Exercise 1 (p. 152)

1. Toronto and Montreal, two of the largest cities in Canada, have very different cultures.

2. While Toronto, then known as York, was being laid out in the late 1700s, Montreal had a population of over 5000 and was a major fur-trading centre.
3. Now, in the twentieth century, Toronto is the dominant urban centre, while Montreal's population has been relatively stagnant.
4. C
5. Toronto is the capital of a rapidly industrializing province, while Montreal is a regional metropolis with Old World charm.
6. After Paris, Montreal is the largest French-speaking city in the world; Toronto's main language is English, with many European and Asian languages spoken.
7. Montreal is not only a key seaport in eastern North America but is also a rail centre.
8. The average citizen of Toronto is reasonably well-to-do; however, the cost of living has skyrocketed over the past few years.
9. Visitors to Toronto often comment on the safety and cleanliness of the city; clearly, there are few other North American cities with such civic pride.
10. Although Toronto may be more expensive than Montreal and Montreal may lack a strong economic base, they are two of the most accommodating cities in Canada.

Exercise 2 (p. 154)

1. Dinner in India is an experience that Western people find very strange, since things we take for granted are not always available there.
2. Whenever you eat an Indian meal, you are not given anything to drink, for it is not considered appropriate to drink a beverage with a meal.
3. Indian food is eaten with the right hand: you pick up a piece of bread or some rice and scoop up some food.
4. However, water for rinsing the fingers is given to you at the end of the meal.
5. Indian food is spicy, and there are many different pickles and relishes that are served with nearly every meal.
6. C
7. The habit of chewing betel leaves and betel nuts aids digestion and sweetens the breath.
8. Breakfast in India is unlike breakfast in Canada.
9. For breakfast, people in India eat dishes of rice and lentils; in addi-

tion, a special lentil soup is part of their first meal of the day.
10. Canadian tourists often try different kinds of food but always know that the best meal of all is a good juicy burger, all dressed.

Exercise 3 (p. 155)

1. Canada has a wide variety of distinctive and beautiful national historic parks and sites.
2. The flowers are in full bloom every spring in Grand Pré, site of an early Acadian settlement.
3. At Grand Pré, the Acadians were expelled by the British; this event was made famous in the poem "Evangeline."
4. C
5. Generals Wolfe and Montcalm decided the fate of Canada during the battle here in 1759.
6. Queenston Heights was the location of the decisive battle during the War of 1812.
7. Everyone on a weekend trip tries to climb Brock's Monument, named after the general who fell during the battle.
8. You can take a tour of Rocky Mountain House in Alberta, site of fur-trading posts dating from 1799.
9. Chilkoot Trail in northwestern British Columbia was the travel route during the Klondike gold rush.
10. Farther north at Dawson City, Yukon, is the actual site of the gold rush that made many fortunes.

Part II Review: Editing Sentences for Errors

Exercise 1 (p. 158)

1. Gypsies now are living in many countries of the world.
2. The international community of scientists agrees that these Gypsies originally came from India thousands of years ago.
3. After the original Gypsies left India, they went to Persia; there they divided into groups.
4. One branch of Gypsies went west to Europe, while the other group decided to go east.
5. C
6. C
7. Although the Gypsies needed the protection of the pope in Rome, they needed their independence even more.
8. In the year 1418, large bands of Gypsies passed through Hungary and Germany, where the emperor offered them his protection.
9. Between the fifteenth and eigh-

teenth centuries, every country of Europe had Gypsies; however, not every one of those countries enjoyed having them as guests.

10. Today, Gypsy families may be found from Canada to Chile, living much as their ancestors did thousands of years ago.

Exercise 3 (p. 161)

1. The laser beam, a miracle of modern science, already has many practical uses in today's world.

2. Laser beams are narrow, highly concentrated beams of light that burn brighter than the light of the sun.

3. Scientists have found many possible military uses for the laser, but they are hoping it can be converted into constructive channels.

4. C

5. The possibility of making a laser was first described in 1958, and two years later in California, the first laser beam was created.

6. Since they are so precise, laser beams are used in medicine to help make a specific diagnosis and to perform operations such as repairing delicate retinas and removing cancerous tumours.

7. In the area of communication, laser beams have the ability to carry thousands of telephone conversations at once, or to transmit all of the information in a twenty-volume encyclopedia in a fraction of a second.

8. Lasers are also used to help in the building of bridges and tunnels; they help make sure that both ends meet properly.

9. The word "laser" comes from the words "light amplification by stimulated emission of radiation."

10. The future uses of the laser seem endless, and it is up to us whether we want to use this invention for war or for peaceful purposes.

Exercise 5 (p. 163)

1. Porpoises, and their close relatives dolphins, are amazing animals.

2. Among their many tricks, they can play baseball and basketball, jump through hoops, ring bells, and raise flags.

3. Porpoises are able to use a kind of radar to find objects they cannot see.

4. The wonderful ability of porpoises to imitate human speech is a phenomenon scientists are studying closely.

5. A dolphin and a porpoise are often the same thing to many people.

6. Trained porpoises now do tricks for thousands of people who can observe them in zoos and marinelands across Canada.

7. Porpoises like to swim beside moving boats, because they are attracted to the sounds the boats make, and because they like to ride in the waves the boats make.

8. The first step in training a porpoise is to observe its natural behaviour.

9. Porpoises have always been helpful and friendly toward humans; indeed, stories of their good relationships with people go back thousands of years.

10. C

Part III: Mastering the Paragraph

Chapter 12: Working with the Topic Sentence

Standard Paragraph Form

Exercises 1 and 2 (p. 170)
Did you indent about an inch?
Does your paragraph have margins on each side of the page?
Did you begin each sentence with a capital letter?
Does each sentence end with end punctuation (a period, question mark, or an exclamation point)?

Finding the Topic Sentence of a Paragraph

Exercise 1 (p. 172)

1. We are the great "Let's junk it" society.

2. The airshaft was a horrible invention.

3. Anything can happen at a county agricultural fair.

4. This was one of the worst situations I had ever been in.

5. During those summer days, the sunporch was the centre of our lives.

Exercise 2 (p. 173)

1. Astrology is enjoying increasing popularity all across Canada.

2. The Canadian game of hockey was born during long northern winters uncluttered by things to do.

3. The brain is one of the most remarkable organs, a part of the body that we have only begun to investigate.

4. Visiting these houses was an expe-

rience that would always stay in our memory.

5. We should always be suspicious of offers that promise us something for little or no effort or money.

Distinguishing a Topic Sentence from a Title

Exercise 1 (p. 176)
1. title 2. title 3. topic sentence 4. title 5. topic sentence 6. title 7. title 8. topic sentence 9. title 10. topic sentence

Exercise 2 (p. 177)
1. topic sentence 2. title 3. topic sentence 4. title 5. topic sentence 6. topic sentence 7. title 8. topic sentence 9. title 10. topic sentence

Finding the Topic in the Topic Sentence

Exercise 1 (p. 178)
1. Remodelling an old house 2. College work 3. A well-made suit 4. Growing up near a museum 5. My favourite room in the house 6. A student who goes to school full time and also works part time 7. One of the disadvantages of skiing 8. Spanking 9. An attractive wardrobe 10. The freshman year of college

Exercise 2 (p. 178)
1. basement 2. Pierre Trudeau 3. an identical twin 4. rail transportation 5. the change that had come over my friend 6. current tax laws 7. *Reader's Digest* 8. streets 9. Canadian Tire 10. clipping coupons

Finding the Controlling Idea

Exercise 1 (p. 179)
1. T: vigorous exercise CI: reduces stress 2. T: St. John's and Corner Brook CI: differ 3. T: television violence CI: causes aggressive behaviour in children 4. T: athletic scholarships available to women CI: increasing 5. T: caffeine CI: adverse effects 6. T: Madame Benoit CI: amusing personality 7. T: training a parakeet to talk CI: takes great patience 8. T: babysitting for a family with four preschool children CI: difficult 9. T: hours between five and seven CI: most productive 10: T: foggy night CI: spooky

Exercise 2 (p. 180)
1. T: piano lessons CI: disaster 2. T: training of Japanese police CI: different 3. T: Olympic champion CI: characteristics 4. T: unethical financial dealings CI: negative impact 5. T: bicycle ride along the coast CI: breathtaking 6. T: grocery store CI: where people waste money 7. T: being an only child CI: not bad 8. T:

Rewarding children with candy or desserts CI: unfortunate habit 9. T: childhood hobby CI: often develops into promising career 10. T: writing of dictionary CI: incredible process

Choosing Controlling Ideas

Exercises 1, 2, and 3 (pp. 181–83)
Answers will vary.

Further Practice Writing the Topic Sentence

Exercises 1, 2, and 3 (pp. 184–85)
Answers will vary.

Chapter 13: Working with Supporting Details

Finding the Topic Sentence and Supporting Details

Practice (p. 188)

Answers will vary, but a possible answer is the following:

TS = Topic Sentence
SD = Supporting Detail

TS: Unlike solid rock, languages are remarkably adaptable, easily borrowing or coining new words as circumstances change. SD: The horse, unknown when the Spanish landed, soon took on a central role among the tribes, and words for the horse and its many uses were introduced. SD: One device was to borrow some form of the Spanish word *caballo*. Another was to invent a descriptive term. SD: Native people of eastern New York State used a word meaning "one rides its back"; in the western part, the word for horse means "it hauls out logs." Presumably these were the first uses of horses seen in the two areas. SD: Among the Kwakiutl of British Columbia, a steamboat was "fire on its back moving in the water." SD: To the Tsimshian of the same area, the word for rice was "looking like maggots."

Exercise 1 (p. 188)
1. TS. As the grayest, quietest, most culturally introverted major city in a gray, quiet, culturally introverted country, Ottawa is not a place where one expects to find architecture on the fringe. SD: But when the Canadian Museum of Civilization officially opened last week just across the river in the city of Hull, it took its place as one of the largest museums in the world and certainly one of the more curious—a wildly eccentric, million-square-foot [93 000 m²] limestone pile of curves and ellipses,

Antoni Gaudi crossed with late Frank Lloyd Wright, baroque quirkiness run amok. SD: Architect Douglas Cardinal's museum is more a fascinating curiosity than a masterwork. SD: But its flamboyance and seductive, Disneyesque natural history exhibits — life-size Indian homes downstairs, replica townscapes from the past 500 years upstairs — will surely make it the capital's biggest tourist attraction, it not Canada's.
2. TS: I cannot teach anyone to write fiction. SD: What I can do is to smooth the road for those who show natural talent as storytellers. SD: You must have the ability to write complete sentences in clear, straightforward standard English. SD: You need the imagination to create stories. SD: Passion, to love the characters you write about. SD: And you have to have stamina, to stick with it even when you don't feel like it.

Exercise 2 (p. 190)
1. TS: Norman Dyer hurried down Sherbrooke Street, collar turned against the snow. SD: "Superb!" he muttered, passing a basement gallery next to a French bookstore. SD: Bleached and tanned women in furs dashed from hotel lobbies into waiting cabs. SD: Even the neon clutter of the side streets and the honks of slithering taxis seemed remote tonight through the peaceful snow. SD: *Superb*, he thought again, waiting for a light and backing from a slushy curb: a word reserved for wines, cigars, and delicate sauces; he was feeling superb this evening. SD: After eighteen months in Montreal, he still found himself freshly impressed by everything he saw.
2. TS: "We're very insecure in this place, you know." SD: "You fly down here, you see a beautiful island, sun, coconut trees, beaches. SD: But I live here and I see a different reality, I see the university students parading Marx and Castro on the campus, I see more policemen with guns, I see people rioting downtown, I see my friends running away to Vancouver and Miami. SD: That's why I want you to put the money your company owes me in my Toronto bank account."

Distinguishing a Supporting Detail from a Restatement of the Main Idea

Exercise 1 (p. 193)
1. a. SD	b. R	c. SD	d. SD
2. a. SD	b. SD	c. R	d. SD
3. a. R	b. SD	c. SD	d. SD
4. a. SD	b. SD	c. R	d. SD
5. a. SD	b. SD	c. SD	d. R

Creating Supporting Details

Exercises 1 and 2 (pp. 196–97)
Answers will vary.

Chapter 14: Developing Paragraphs: Description

Selecting the Dominant Impression

Exercises 1, 2, and 3 (pp. 200–201)
Answers will vary.

Revising Vague Dominant Impressions

Exercises 1, 2, and 3 (pp. 202–203)
Answers will vary.

Recognizing Sensory Images

Practice (p. 204)
1. *hearing:* humming loudly *touch or taste:* milk, cream, cases of pop, and juice *sight:* large refrigerator case, various products in the case
2. *smell:* aroma of onion, caraway seed, and pumpernickel *sight:* baskets, fresh rolls and breads, counter
3. *taste, sight, smell:* cheese or smoked meat

Exercise 1 (p. 204)
Paragraph by Ian Adams
Sight: bottles of beer splintering against each other; wet, mangled cartons, bottles piling up on the conveyor; foreman running; four acres of machinery; conveyor belts
Sound: crunching smash, bell ringing, jangling vibrations, teeth-jarring rattle
Smell: stink of warm beer, sour sweat of my body

Exercise 2 (p. 205)
Paragraph by Heather Robertson
Sight: air frozen into little slivers of glass, light from the full moon reflected in the crystallized air, people scurrying, white clouds of breath, congealed breath like balloons in comic strips, tears running down cheeks
Sound: cars scream and groan
Touch: the cold freezes hands and feet to blocks of wood, it hurts to walk more than a few feet

Creating Sensory Images

Exercises 1, 2, and 3 (pp. 206–209)
Answers will vary.

Working for Coherence: Using Space Order

Exercise 1 (p. 211)
1. 3, 1, 5, 4, 2	4. 2, 3, 1, 4
2. 3, 5, 4, 1, 2	5. 4, 5, 1, 3, 2
3. 3, 5, 2, 1, 4	

Exercise 2 (p. 212)
Answers will vary.

Chapter 15: Developing Paragraphs: Narration

Using Narration to Make a Point

Exercises 1, 2, and 3 (pp. 225–26)
Answers will vary.

Working for Coherence: Using Details in Order of Time Sequence

Exercise 1 (p. 227)
1. 3, 1, 4, 2, 5   4. 2, 5, 1, 3, 6, 4
2. 5, 2, 3, 4, 1   5. 5, 4, 1, 6, 2, 3
3. 5, 1, 4, 3, 2

Exercise 2 (p. 228)
1. 1, 3, 2, 5, 4, 6, 7   4. 1, 5, 4, 2, 6, 3, 7
2. 1, 2, 6, 7, 3, 5, 4   5. 1, 3, 2, 7, 4, 5, 6
3. 1, 4, 5, 2, 3, 6, 7

Working with Transitions

Exercise 1 (p. 233)
First, Next, Finally

Exercise 2 (p. 233)
In the meantime, every second of every minute, suddenly, immediately, at first, in a short time, a few minutes later, Finally, So be it, then

Chapter 16: Developing Paragraphs: Process

Is the Process Complete?

Exercise 1 (p. 244)
1. No oven temperature is given for baking the popovers.
2. A first step might be to read any directions that are given on the machine itself. You are not told to press the "print" button when you are ready to print.
3. Don't forget to take out your original paper when you are finished.

Exercise 2 (p. 245)
1. Nothing is said about how or at what point you insert the air conditioner into the window.
2. Many steps are missing, including making the guest list, ordering and sending invitations, planning the rehearsal dinner if there is to be one, buying the wedding rings, making arrangements for a honeymoon, if there is to be one, as well as for flowers and the music at the ceremony.

Coherence in Process: Order in Logical Sequence

Exercise 1 (p. 246)
4, 8, 7, 10, 1, 3, 5, 9, 6, 2

Exercise 2 (p. 247)
3, 5, 4, 1, 7, 6, 2

Chapter 17: Developing Paragraphs: Comparison or Contrast

Evaluating the Two-Part Topic

Exercise 1 (p. 260)
Answers could vary depending on the purpose of the paragraph.
1. too broad 2. good 3. good 4. good 5. too broad 6. too broad 7. good 8. good 9. too broad 10. good

Working for Coherence: Recognizing the Two Approaches to Ordering Material

Exercise 1 (p. 264)
1. block; differences 2. block; differences 3. block; differences 4. point-by-point; similarities 5. point-by-point; similarities

Part IV: Structuring the College Essay

Chapter 20: Moving from the Paragraph to the Essay

How to Recognize the Thesis Statement

Practice (p. 308)
1. F   2. T   3. T   4. F

Exercise 1 (p. 309)
1. thesis 2. title 3. fact 4. thesis 5. title 6. fact 7. fact 8. title 9. fact 10. thesis

Exercise 2 (p. 309)
1. fact 2. thesis 3. fact 4. fact 5. title 6. fact 7. title 8. thesis 9. thesis 10. title

Finding Transitional Devices

Exercise 1 (p. 319)
    Like language and social organization, art is essential to man. As embellishment and as creation of objects beyond the requirements of the most basic needs of living, (art) has accompanied man since prehistoric times. Because of its almost unfailing consistency as an element of many societies, (art) may be the response to some biological or psychological need. (Indeed), it is one of the most constant forms of human behaviour.
    (However), use of the word (art) is not relevant when we describe African "art" because it is really a European term that at first grew out of Greek philosophy and was later reinforced by European culture. The use of other (terms) such as *exotic* (art), *primitive* (art), (art) *sauvage*, and so on, to delineate differences is just as misleading.

Most such (terms) are pejorative — implying that African art is on a lower cultural level. (Levels) of culture are irrelevant here, since African and European attitudes toward the creative act are so different. (Since) there is no term in our language to distinguish between the essential differences in thinking, it is best (then) to describe standards of African art.
    (African art) attracts because of its powerful emotional content and its beautiful abstract form. (Abstract) treatment of (form) describes most often — with bare essentials of line, shape, texture, and pattern — intense energy and sublime spirituality. Hundreds of distinct cultures and languages and many types of people have created over 1000 different styles that defy classification. Each art and craft (form) has its own history and its own aesthetic content.

Chapter 27: Writing under Pressure

Frequently Used Terms in Essay Questions

Exercise 1 (p. 382)
1. narration 2. comparison or contrast 3. discussion 4. definition 5. summary

Appendices

A: Parts of Speech

Exercise 1 (p. 392)
1.	verb	6.	adverb
2.	noun	7.	pronoun
3.	adjective	8.	preposition
4.	adverb	9.	noun
5.	adverb	10.	conjunction

Exercise 2 (p. 393)
Sentences will vary.

B: Solving Spelling Problems

Words Commonly Mispronounced

Exercise 1 (p. 396)
1.	separate	6.	quantity
2.	probably	7.	literature
3.	arctic	8.	hungry
4.	surprise	9.	handsome
5.	tragedy	10.	favourite

Exercise 2 (p. 397)
1.	library	6.	perform
2.	February	7.	laboratory
3.	government	8.	identical
4.	authentic	9.	promptly
5.	partner	10.	handkerchief

ie and *ei* Words

Exercise 1 (p. 398)
1. sleigh
2. believe
3. siege
4. veil
5. leisure
6. deceit
7. niece
8. weight
9. protein
10. ancient

Exercise 2 (p. 398)
1. foreign
2. reindeer
3. perceive
4. fiend
5. briefcase
6. achieve
7. mischief
8. relieve
9. height
10. yield

Forming the Plurals of Nouns

Practice 1 (p. 399)
turkeys, candies, plays, gypsies, deliveries

Practice 2 (p. 400)
banjos, stereos, torpedoes, studios, embargoes

Practice 3 (p. 400)
dishes, successes, flashes, boxes, peaches

Practice 4 (p. 400)
hoofs or hooves, scarfs or scarves, tariffs, chiefs, selves

Exercise 1 (p. 401)
1. puppies
2. mothers-in-law
3. teeth
4. cameos
5. phenomena
6. loaves
7. matches
8. mixes
9. enemies
10. bags

Exercise 2 (p. 401)
1. attorneys
2. watches
3. tangos
4. letters
5. libraries
6. echoes
7. glasses
8. deer
9. hypotheses
10. ratios

Doubling the Final Consonant

Practice (p. 403)
slip: yes, yes, slipping; *crack:* no, no, cracking; *broil:* no, no, broiling; *win:* yes, yes, winning; *control:* controlling; *fever:* feverish; *compel:* compelled; *differ:* difference; *design:* designer; *begin:* beginning

Exercise 1 (p. 404)
1. bitten
2. occurrence
3. wavering
4. preferred
5. preference
6. thinner
7. transferred
8. sailing
9. excellent
10. omitted

Exercise 2 (p. 404)
1. stopped
2. committee
3. committal
4. biggest
5. equipped
6. tapping
7. succeeding
8. hidden
9. listener
10. goddess

Words Ending in *-y*

Practice (p. 403)
funnier, business, varies, readying, accompanist, enjoyment

Exercise 1 (p. 405)
1. keys
2. loneliness
3. crying
4. cries
5. prayer
6. crayfish
7. monkeying
8. beautiful
9. theories
10. ceremonial

Exercise 2 (p. 406)
1. daycare
2. carrying
3. merciful
4. valleys
5. categorize
6. buried
7. burying
8. allies
9. chimneys
10. tried

One Word or Two?

Practice (p. 407)
already, already, all ready; all together, altogether, all together; all ways, all ways, always; anyone, anyone, any one; Every one, Everyone, Every one; may be, maybe, Maybe

Exercise 1 (p. 408)
1. bedroom
2. grandmother
3. already
4. all together
5. always
6. Everyone
7. maybe
8. cannot
9. nearby
10. Nevertheless

Exercise 2 (p. 409)
1. yourself
2. living room
3. dining room
4. anyone
5. bathroom
6. playroom
7. downstairs
8. No one
9. may be
10. roommate

C: Capitalization

Exercise 1 (p. 415)
1. Italian 2. Canadian Rockies 3. Bible 4. University of Alberta 5. Halloween 6. Bell Canada, Friday, Winnipeg, Manitoba 7. Cobalt 60, Canadian, Dr. Donald Green 8. Why 9. Canadian Auto Workers 10. West, A Prairie Home Companion

Exercise 2 (p. 415)
1. Tuesday 2. The Lord of the Rings, Christian 3. Thousand Islands International Bridge, St. Lawrence River 4. French 5. Far East 6. Kremlin, Soviet, Moscow 7. Dr. 8. Why 9. Graduate Record Examination, January 10. Confederation, Mesopelagia, Albertonia, Efisga, Canada

D: The Apostrophe

Exercise 1 (p. 418)
1. sun's, 2. dress's, 3. feet's, 4. Antony and Maria's 5. nobody's 6. his 7. 1700's or 1700s 8. That's 9. boys' 10. book's

Exercise 2 (p. 419)
1. ice's 2. geese's 3. Ann's and Chris's 4. someone's 5. hers 6. two's 7. can't 8. tree's 9. farmers' 10. brother-in-law's

E: Irregular Verbs

Exercise 1 (p. 423)
1. caught
2. crept
3. fled
4. burst
5. ridden
6. slid
7. rose
8. quit
9. frozen
10. wrung

Exercise 2 (p. 423)
1. given		6. felt
2. chosen		7. laid
3. thought		8. written
4. began		9. swung
5. brought		10. spoken

Index

To the owner of this book:

We are interested in your reaction to *The Canadian Writer's Workplace* by John Roberts, Sandra Scarry, and John Scarry.

1. What was your reason for using this book?

    _____ university course   _____ continuing education course

    _____ college course   _____ personal interest

                                          _____ other (specify)

2. In which school are you enrolled? _____

3. Approximately how much of the book did you use?

    ____ ¼   ____ ½   ____ ¾   ____ all

4. What is the best aspect of the book?

5. Have you any suggestions for improvement?

6. Is there anything that should be added?

Fold here

POSTAGE WILL BE PAID BY
 David Dimmell
  Publisher
College Editorial Department
**HOLT, RINEHART AND WINSTON
 OF CANADA, LIMITED**
55 HORNER AVENUE
TORONTO, ONTARIO
M8Z 9Z9

Tape shut